Autosegmental and
Metrical Phonology

Autosegmental and Metrical Phonology

John A. Goldsmith

Basil Blackwell

Copyright © John A. Goldsmith 1990

First published 1990
Reprinted 1990

Basil Blackwell Ltd
108 Cowley Road, Oxford OX4 1JF, UK

Basil Blackwell Inc.
3 Cambridge Center
Cambridge, Massachusetts 02142, USA

British Library Cataloguing in Publication Data
A CIP catalogue reference for this book is available from the British Library.

Library of Congress Cataloging in Publication Data
Goldsmith, John A., 1951–
    Autosegmental and metrical phonology / John A.
Goldsmith.
        p.   cm.
    Bibliography: p.
    Includes index.
    ISBN 0–631–13675–4 : ISBN 0–631–13676–2 (pbk.)
    1. Autosegmental theory (Linguistics)   2. Metrical phonology.
3. Lexical phonology.   4. Grammar, Comparative and general–
Phonology.   I. Title.
P217.7.G65   1989
414′ .6—dc20   89–1007
                                                                        CIP

Printed in Great Britain by TJ Press (Padstow) Ltd, Cornwall

Contents

Acknowledgements

The author and the publishers are grateful to The University of Chicago Press for permission to quote from Charles Hockett, *A Manual of Phonology*, *International Journal of American Linguistics*, 21, 1955, and 'Componential analysis of Sierra Popoluca', *International Journal of American Linguistics*, 13, 1947 © The University of Chicago Press and to Cambridge University Press for permission to reproduce a figure from George Clements, 'The geometry of phonological features', *Phonology Yearbook*, 2, 1985.

Introduction

I intend this book to serve several purposes. It is, first of all, an introduction to autosegmental and metrical phonology, designed to present the basic ideas of these geometrical models of phonological representation. The parties interested may be professional linguists who are involved in the subject, but have not had the opportunity to plunge into the ever expanding literature; they may be researchers in related fields such as cognitive psychology or artificial intelligence, for there is no doubt that such neighboring disciplines have much to say and much to learn in this area; last but not least, they may be students just beginning to gain some familiarity with how phonology and phonological theory work.

From readers, whichever group they may come from, I expect some familiarity with generative phonology, and how and why it is done. I might go so far as to say that I expect some sympathy with it as well; I will develop this point a little bit further below. In any event, the ideal reader will have spent a semester or so working through the substance of a rigorous textbook such as, for example, Kenstowicz and Kisseberth's (1979) *Generative Phonology*; for, while my own book will serve as an introduction to certain current theories of phonology, it is not an introduction to phonology itself.

Nor is it just an introductory textbook to current theories. I have attempted to bring together the central ideas of autosegmental, metrical, and lexical phonology to form a synthesis that is very much needed today. While much remains to be done, I believe that the proposals made here will contribute significantly to the problem. Central to this task is the development of the notion of autosegmental licensing, introduced in chapter 3. New suggestions are made concerning the relationship between syllable structure and autosegmental structure, and also between syllable structure and the metrical grid.

It is worth bearing in mind that the work on autosegmental and metrical phonology discussed in this book is a direct continuation of the traditional work of generative phonology that was codified in Chomsky and Halle's *Sound Pattern of English* (*SPE*) in 1968, and which defined to a large extent the nature of the questions that were central to phonological theory in the ten- to fifteen-year period beginning in 1965 (when generative phonology began to receive a widespread audience) and extending into the late 1970s, the era of what we may be permitted to call 'classical generative phonology'. Any number of phonological traditions that antedated generative phonology, both within the United States and without, have continued during this period (Anderson (1985) presents a recent perspective on these schools); other traditions have arisen during this same period which in larger measure reacted to perceived excesses in generative phonology, most notably natural phonology and natural generative phonology. Interested readers will find that the collection of papers in Dinnsen (1979) provides a sense of some of these divergent views that followed largely in the wake of the proposals of *SPE*.

Within this context, the autosegmental and metrical models of phonological representation may best be viewed as a continuation of the generative theories of the *SPE* period. This is not so much because they sustain the conclusions, or even because they maintain the questions, of the halcyon days of *SPE* phonology; for they do not. It is rather that the original justifications for the theoretical changes in the model of phonology that led to autosegmental phonology and metrical phonology were based on arguments that made, and still make, perfect sense within the very theoretical heart of generative phonology. No significant shift in theoretical goals or perspectives needs to be made to see why the autosegmental and metrical accounts are superior to the analyses offered by classical generative phonology.

It is for this reason that I said earlier that I will assume some sympathy with generative phonology on the part of the reader. There is good reason to believe that autosegmental and metrical phonology will be more successful than classical generative phonology in such areas as the link between phonetics and phonology, the decrease in the abstractness of underlying phonological representations, and the unfortunate degree of language-specific rule-ordering. To the extent that what were perceived as failures in these areas led some linguists away from the basic features of generative phonology, the present study may allow them to reconsider their views. Fundamentally, though, the theories of phonology that we will consider here share the characteristics that are familiar in generative phonology. We shall aim at producing explicit grammars, consisting of rules of various sorts, and underlying forms. The rules, applying sequentially and to some extent cyclically, produce an output, a surface representation, which serves as an input to a theory of phonetics.

I should mention what the generative grammarian says about the role of evidence and argumentation in phonology. If I had to summarize in just one statement the basic goal of the enterprise, it might be this: we attempt to formulate general models and principles of phonological analysis which can be successfully applied to a wide range of languages. Success may be hard to measure, but it consists largely in the ability the analysis grants us to see connections in various ways. First and foremost, a good analysis shows connections within the basic phonological facts. We hope to miss as few generalizations as possible in the data as we find it. Second, we expect our phonological theory and our analyses to be able to be connected to psychological theories, such as those of speech production, perception, and acquisition, and also to linguistic theories of syntax and morphology. Third, we expect our analyses to give us insight into the historical connections among languages and stages in the development of languages. All of these goals are important, though some are more difficult in practice to reach than others. To be sure, any hope that phonology has of making direct and successful contact with theories of psychology will be a give and take affair; where the two have results that appear to contradict each other, progress may not be easy in determining how the contradictions, apparent or real, can be overcome.

RELATION TO OTHER THEORIES

It is for the most part outside the scope of the present text to discuss the historical relationship of autosegmental and metrical phonology to other schools of phonological theory. The background of the workers currently involved in autosegmental and metrical phonology, as I have indicated, is with few exceptions classical generative phonology. Many observers, however, have noted clear connections and resemblances between the innovations made by autosegmental and metrical theories and certain of the insights of rather different schools, among which may be counted the prosodic analysis of Firth and the London school, the long (or simultaneous) component analysis of Zellig Harris and Charles Hockett, and tonal analyses of the sort proposed by Kenneth Pike. Certainly the important role that has been given to the syllable in recent theories is an acknowledgement on the part of generative phonologists of the importance of a notion that has been emphasized in most other phonological frameworks.

Hockett's classic *Manual of Phonology*, published in 1955, contains the following observations, which could with little change be used to introduce a discussion of autosegmental phonology; it comes after an introduction of the notion of feature:

It is obvious that whole utterances or texts could be transcribed as we have [done] . . ., with a considerable range of possible conventions of symbolization.

Such a transcription is comparable to the full score of a piece for orchestra, or even a piano piece written out on a grand staff; in contrast, our usual phonemic notation, consisting of an essentially linear sequence of symbols, with some diacritics, is comparable to a figured bass. There was a period in the history of music when the use of figured bass notation was quite adequate: performers were adept at 'realizing' a figured bass, at a keyboard instrument, in a way which might vary somewhat from one performance to another, but such that all variation fell within the range of what was 'non-distinctive' relative to the musical tradition of the time. This was true in large part because the total number of permitted simultaneous bundles of notes was relatively small, and the sequences in which they were permitted to follow each other were likewise highly restricted. For more complicated music a figured bass is not adequate. That we are able to use essentially linear transcriptions for speech is due to precisely the factors that rendered figured bass a reasonable and usable notation earlier in the history of music: the total variety of combinations of articulatory motion, and the sequences in which the various combinations occur, are in every language relatively limited and small in number.

The comparison of 'full score' componential transcription with a full orchestral score in music breaks down at one point, if we use for the former such componential analyses as those which have been presented above. In an orchestral score there is a line (a staff) for each instrument, and on it are placed the marks indicating at each moment what that instrument should be doing. Now the 'instruments,' in the case of speech, are certainly the various articulators in the mouth and the movable parts in the throat and at the back entrance to the nose. But we have not provided, in the 'full scores' given above, a separate 'staff' for each 'instrument' in this sense: rather, since in both Fox and Nootka oral articulators function almost exclusively one at a time, we have specified, along one single 'staff' of the 'score', which articulator is to function, and along other 'staves' what function it is to perform. (Hockett 1955: 155)

With hindsight, these analyses jump off the page and claim, with justice, historical precedence in the multilinear approach currently called autosegmental phonology. The same can be said of Bernard Bloch's work on phonemic analysis, as I have pointed out elsewhere (Goldsmith 1979). Hockett's (1947) analysis of Sierra Popoluca, which in turn engendered considerable discussion in the literature (e.g. Longacre 1952, Hamp 1954, Longacre 1955), is even more strikingly autosegmental, and grapples with the same problem that I deal with in the present book, the interaction of internal syllable structure and elements on separate autosegmental tiers (though, of course, Hockett used neither the term 'autosegmental' nor 'tier': he referred to Harrisian 'components' (Harris 1944, 1951)). The epigraph in chapter 1 below gives the reader a sense of the identity of Hockett's concerns and my own.

OUTLINE

As I noted at the beginning, this book is intended to serve the purposes of the near-neophyte as well as those of the professional linguist. I have chosen to introduce autosegmental phonology, in chapter 1, through the medium of tonal analyses. This choice on my part courts a certain danger: the danger that the reader, thinking somehow that tone systems are exotic and hard to tame, will transfer this trepidation to the theory being introduced.

Indeed, tonal systems are quite docile when approached from the correct theoretical perspective, as I hope to show, and can be used to shed a great deal of light on specific theoretical questions. My aim is to make the odd behavior of tonal systems seem natural, through the perspective of autosegmental representation. What was once odd, then, will seem odd no more, and this taming will eventually be transferred to thorny problems in more familiar territory. In chapter 2 we will look at problems of vowel length and geminate consonants from an autosegmental perspective, and encounter the notion of a *skeletal tier*. This in turn will solve not only phonological problems, but also morphological ones, such as the classic question of the treatment of vowels and consonants in Arabic.

In chapter 3 we turn to the treatment of the syllable, the hierachical unit that links vowels and consonants and provides organization to the skeletal tier of chapter 2. Here I introduce a novel notion, that of *autosegmental licensing*, which serves to link together autosegmental structure with the hierarchical structure of the syllable, crucially resting on underspecified lexical representations. Although it is new in this book, it is, I believe, the notion required for an understanding of how the important ideas explored in this book are interrelated – the notions of syllable structure, of syllable quantity, and of autosegmental association. Metrical theory, introduced in chapter 4, provides the key to how syllables are themselves organized in higher level prosodic units. Two notations, involving metrical trees and metrical grids, are currently used in the literature, and we will review the usefulness of each approach. These first four chapters provide a brief introduction to the basic concepts and principles of autosegmental and metrical phonology as it is being developed today.

In chapter 5 we turn to a different area, and discuss some of the central concepts of lexical phonology, which, though in some ways independent of the other work on phonological representations in this book, is important for understanding ongoing research. A number of at times intricate, and certainly interrelated, notions have entered the literature under the rubric of lexical phonology, and if one wants to be literate, a handle on these notions is crucial. Nonetheless, as I point out below, a good number of the substantive proposals made by lexical phonology seem to me to be only very rough approximations to the truth, and I offer the material in chapter 5 more for the conceptual clarifications that can arise out of a discussion of the issues than for the accuracy of solutions offered by lexical phonology. In addition, we will look at the treatment of English stress and vowel patterns, because the system has served as the testing ground for many theoretical proposals, and yet its complexity makes it extremely intimidating for the person who has not yet had the opportunity to go through the literature in fine detail.

In the final chapter, we consider the ways in which autosegmental phonology is currently leading phonologists to a much more articulated picture of the internal structure of the segment, which now seems to be no more atomic (i.e. indivisible) than the physicist's atom. I then turn to several theoretical issues in the treatment of phonological representations, explicating as clearly as possible what the concerns are and why they are important, and suggesting the direction in which my conception of phonological derivations is heading, towards a view which emphasizes the governing role of well-formedness conditions on word-level representations, and the ways in which these conditions, including syllable phonotactics, govern the application of phonological rules.

I do not think that this is always an easy book to read, but I have some hopes that it is clear. At some points, I have given fewer examples than I might have, in order to tighten up the theoretical statement, and to encourage readers to see how the theoretical ideas tie together neatly. To get the most out of reading this book, readers would do well to explore the notions discussed here in connection with additional data that they themselves are involved in.

I end with the pleasant task of thanking the various people who have helped me in the writing of this book. Several people have read various portions of this draft and made helpful comments, including Girmay Berhane, Nick Clements, Jan-Terje Faarlund, Judy Hochberg, Geoff Nathan, Cathie Ringen, Jerry Sadock, Ivan Sag, and Paul Smolensky. Other people have influenced the content of the book less directly, but significantly; lectures by, and informal discussions with, a number of linguists which I cannot directly cite in the text have certainly influenced my discussion, and I must cite in this regard Nick Clements, Bill Darden, Bruce Hayes, Larry Hyman, Alan Prince, Raj Singh, and Jean-Roger Vergnaud. I must acknowledge a special debt of gratitude to my wife, Jessie Pinkham, for her support in this never-ending process, and also to my patient editor at Blackwell, Philip Carpenter.

Finally, I would like to dedicate this book to the three people without whom this book certainly would never have been: my parents, without whom I certainly would not have been, and whose support made it possible for me to be a linguist; and Morris Halle, who as a teacher served as an inspiration, and without whom I am confident that there would be neither autosegmental nor metrical phonology today.

1

Autosegmental Representation

With the development of modern linguistics and the explicit formulation of the phonemic principle, this long-standing habit of visual
representation has taken the shape of an unstated *linearity assumption*: the distinctive sound-units or phonemes of a language are
building-blocks which occur in a row, never one on top of another
or overlapping. This assumption has been lifted in certain patent
cases: features of stress or tone, for example, which normally stretch
over more than a single vowel or consonant, have been called *nonlinear* or *suprasegmental* in contrast to the linear or segmental
vowels and consonants.... The point of view here assumed is,
essentially, simply that of removing the linearity assumption from
among our working principles.

'Componential analysis of Sierra Popoluca'
Charles Hockett (1947)

1.1 INTRODUCTION

Autosegmental representation differs from familiar generative and traditional phonemic representation in that it consists of two or more *tiers* of
segments. In the picture given to us by classical generative phonology –
and, indeed, most theories of phonology and phonological representation
– phonological representations consist of a string of segments. In
autosegmental representation, however, we posit two or more parallel
tiers of phonological segments. Each tier itself consists of a string of
segments, but the segments on each tier differ with regard to what
features are specified in them.

In the case of a tone language, for example, tones are represented on a
separate tier – the tonal tier – and on this tonal tier each segment is
specified for tone and for nothing else. The segments on the other, non-
tonal, tier are specified for all other features. This simple picture is

illustrated in (1). In (1a), the segments are not analyzed as features; in (1b), features are used to illustrate much the same representation.

(1)

(a) segmental	b	u	l	u	(b)	[+syll]	[−syll]	[+syll]
tonal		H		L		[+High]		[−High]

Each feature that plays a phonological role in a language will appear on exactly one tier; that is, features cannot appear on more than one tier. A tier can thus be defined by which features are found on it. The term *segment* unfortunately has a good deal of history to it that we do not want to carry over in every instance. The term was introduced into phonology in an era when it was taken for granted that the goal of phonological analysis was the slicing up into successive segments of the speech event. The resulting segments were units in time with a finite and identifiable length, and the phonologist could try to identify events that occurred during them or at the transition from one segment to another.

The term *segment* is still used in current phonological theory, but with a quite different meaning. The phonological analysis which we shall be engaged in is aimed primarily at providing a model of what a speaker or hearer knows. Our task is to determine how information about particular words is stored and manipulated in particular languages in such a way that something that we can refer to as an instance of *uttering* or of *perception* of a word can take place, an act that seems to the casual observer as being composed of a sequence of smaller events linearly arranged in time. What we shall find, as we proceed through this book, is that the image that we naively hold of such events being a sequence of simply ordered events is wrong. There is *something* right about it, of course, and alphabetic writing would not be as successful as it is if there were nothing right about it. But what we shall see is that the individual gestural components of articulation – the features of modern phonology – each have quite separate lives of their own, and an adequate theory of phonology will be one that recognizes this, and provides a way to understand the linkages between individual gestures of the tongue, lips, and so forth, and larger units of organization, such as the syllable.

Thus we will use the term *segment* in the way that it has come to be thought of in more recent parlance: as a term for an indivisible unit, ultimately a mental unit of organization.[1] Our first task is to see that these minimal units of organization cannot be thought of as strung together in a simple linear pattern. As our models of phonological representation become more articulate, and more complex, the term 'segment' becomes less and less appropriate, since there is no physical reality that is being segmented. We must drop those assumptions about what a segment is, and take it to be no more than the minimal unit of a phonological representation.

In addition to the segments on separate tiers, an autosegmental representation includes *association lines* between the segments on the tiers. We shall refer to a pair of tiers, along with the set of association lines that relates them, as a *chart*. From a purely phonetic point of view, the association lines represent simultaneity in time, or what we might call co-registration (though ours is not to be a purely phonetic point of view). It is necessary to include this information if there is to be a natural phonetic interpretation of autosegmental representations. Each tier represents a sequence of gestures (viewed from an articulatory point of view) or distinct acoustic transitions (viewed from an acoustic point of view). The tonal tier in (1), for example, represents the gestures that the larynx makes towards the tone of the word, and the non-tonal tier represents the gestures of the mouth. Unless we specify further, using association lines to indicate how the gestures of the larynx and the mouth match up, this two-tiered representation will not tell us which tone or tones are produced at the same time as each of the vowels are produced.

On the other hand, however, we must remember that while phonetic reality may motivate a phonological representation, it neither justifies nor ultimately explains it. Phonetic reality provides the stuff of which phonological theory provides the organization.

In (1), where there are the same number of vowels and tones, one might assume that the association would be one to one. Certainly on the most traditional of accounts, in which the sound stream is divided into successive vowels and consonants, that assumption would seem quite natural. The fact is, though, that there is no need for the number of tonal segments to match the number of vowels or syllables. In (2), we see a representation with two tones and three vowels. Here the Low tone is multiply associated; that is, two syllables are produced during the time that the Low tone is produced.

(2)
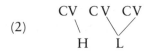

Conversely, two tones may be produced during the same period in which a single syllable is produced. This situation is represented as in (3). The linear ordering on the tonal tier shows explicitly that the High tone precedes the Low tone. By associating both tones with a single vowel, we indicate that the vowel is produced with a falling tone. The beginning of the vowel is simultaneous with the High tone; the end, with the Low tone.

$$(3) \qquad \begin{array}{c} \text{CV} \\ \diagup\diagdown \\ \text{H} \quad \text{L} \end{array}$$

There is a natural tendency to think of tone as being a feature of a vowel – as if vowels were more real or more substantial, somehow, than tones. Nothing in this formalism, or in the autosegmental perspective presented here, supports such a prejudice – for that is all it is – and part of becoming familiar with this approach to phonological representation includes becoming less attached to that conceptual metaphor.

We will study tone from an autosegmental point of view in this first chapter. There are several good reasons to begin the study of autosegmental phonology with a survey of how tone systems operate; the only reason not to do so is the fear that the reader will come to the study of tone with too much trepidation and a distinct sense of approaching the exotic. The fact is, though, that tonal systems are at present among the best understood of phonological systems, and once an autosegmental perspective is adopted, it is not hard to see that tonal systems do operate elegantly, like clockwork. In addition to this inherent interest, tonal systems are important for us to study because they are able to clarify theoretical questions that arise, and which might remain unanswered for some time, in the context of other prosodic systems.

We shall see that viewing tonal elements as segments on their own autosegmental tier – or being *autosegments*, as the convenient shorthand goes – allows us to state many phonological rules quite simply. In this chapter we shall look at examples from a number of different tone languages – several African languages, as well as a Mexican tone language, Mixtecan, which was described in one of the earliest thorough accounts of a tone system, an account which has remained a classic in the literature, Pike's *Tone Languages* (1948).

In later chapters we will also look at autosegmental systems in which other features are treated autosegmentally. The systems that are most reminiscent of tone systems are the vowel harmony and nasal harmony systems, which we will discuss in chapter 6.[2]

1.2 THE ASSOCIATION CONVENTION

Kikuyu is a major Bantu language spoken in central Kenya.[3] In each word in Kikuyu there are roughly – but only roughly – the same number of tones and vowels. The way in which tones and vowels are realized, however, is rather surprising.

Consider the data in (5), which consists of twelve verbs in one of the past tense forms. As shown in (4), each verb consists of a subject prefix, an optional object prefix, a root, and the tense suffix *irɛ*. From a tonal point of view, each of the first three of these components can fall into one of two classes, and in (5) we have given all of the twelve possible combinations. A Low tone is marked with a grave accent (`) and a High tone is marked with an acute accent (').

(4)	Subject Marker	⎛Object⎞ ⎝Marker⎠	Root	Tense Suffix
	to 'we'	mo 'him'	rɔr 'look at'	
	ma 'they'	ma 'them'	tom 'send'	irɛ

(5)		Subject 'to'	Subject 'ma'
	rɔr	tò rɔ̀r ìrɛ́	má rɔ́r ìrɛ́
		tò mò rɔ̀r ìrɛ́	má mó rɔ̀r ìrɛ́
		tò mà rɔ́r ìrɛ́	má má rɔ́r ìrɛ́
	tom	tò tòm írɛ́	má tóm írɛ́
		tò mò tòm írɛ́	má mó tòm írɛ́
		tò mà tóm írɛ́	má mà tóm írɛ́

If we take away the consonants and all of the vowels but leave the tone marked on each vowel, we find that (5) can be converted into the surface pattern of Low and High tones shown in (6). Two generalization jump out here. First, we see that the first two tones of each word are always the same: in the left-hand column, the first two vowels are both on a Low tone; in the right-hand column, the first two vowels are both on a High tone. Second, the final vowel in all twelve cases is High.

Furthermore, we see that in the top six cases – those involving the root *rɔr* – the penultimate vowel (the *i* of *irɛ*) is always Low in tone. In the

(6)	Tonal patterns									
	L	L	L	H		H	H	L	H	
	L	L	L	L	H	H	H	L	L	H
	L	L	H	L	H	H	H	H	L	H
	L	L	H	H		H	H	H	H	
	L	L	L	H	H	H	H	L	H	H
	L	L	H	H	H	H	H	H	H	H

lower six cases, involving the root *tom*, the *i* of *irε* is always High. That is, in both cases, the verb root controls the tone of the vowel that immediately follows it, but not its own tone. Finally, the tone of the vowel following the Object Marker *mo* is always Low; the tone of the vowel following the Object Marker *ma* is always High.

All of these generalizations observed in the tonal patterns will become comprehensible if we assume each morpheme to contribute a tone to the tone melody of the word as a whole, but without necessarily being *associated* to that morpheme. For example, let us analyze the morphemes in (4) with the underlying tones given in (7). However, these tones are

(7)

	to		ma		mo		ma		rɔr		tom		irε	
	L		H		L		H		L		H		H	

underlying unassociated, and remain so until the morphology has concatenated the morphemes to form a word, as in (8).

(8)
$$\begin{bmatrix} \text{to} & \text{ma} & \text{rɔr} & \text{irε} \\ \text{L} & \text{H} & \text{L} & \text{H} \end{bmatrix}$$

At this point, a rule applies that associates the first tone to the second syllable of the word. This rule is given in (9). It illustrates several notational conventions of autosegmental rules. A broken association line represents a structural change of a rule; the effect of the rule will be to add such an association line to the representation. The other material in this rule is the structural description of the rule, and serves to identify structures to which the rule can apply. (9) will associate the first tone of the word to the second syllable, and will convert (8) to (10).

(9)
$$\begin{bmatrix} C_0 & V & C_0 & V \\ T & & & \end{bmatrix}$$

(10)
$$\begin{bmatrix} \text{to} & \text{ma} & \text{rɔr} & \text{irε} \\ \text{L} & \text{H} & \text{L} & \text{H} \end{bmatrix}$$

At this point, an important device in autosegmental theory comes into play to associate the rest of the tones. The Association Convention has an effect on any representations that are not totally unassociated. (That is, it may affect a representation if it has at least one association line.) As presented here (11), the Association Convention adds association lines outward in a one-to-one fashion from the already present association line, associating from either tier only elements that are currently unassociated. The Association Convention will then convert (10) to (12).[4]

(11)   **Association Convention**
       When unassociated vowels and tones appear on the same side of an association line, they will be automatically associated in a one-to-one fashion, radiating outward from the association line.

(12)   to ma rɔr irɛ
           / / /
          L H L H

After the Association Convention has created the structure in (12), the first vowel is still toneless. When the verb is not preceded by another word, rule (13) will apply, to give us the correct and final form, given in (14).

(13)

(13) introduces another useful notation convention whereby a circle around a segment in a rule marks a segment which is not associated to another segment on the facing autosegmental tier (in this case, a vowel without a tone, or a tone without a vowel). Thus, (13) applies only to associate toneless initial vowels.

(14)   to ma rɔr irɛ
         \ / / //
         L H LH

1.3   MORE ON THE ASSOCIATION CONVENTION

As we have seen in the case of Kikuyu, the Association Convention allows for one-to-one association of elements. Another language-specific rule, (13), further associated certain other segments.

Other assumptions have been made in work on autosegmental phonology concerning automatic spreading – generally, assumptions that predict a good deal more automatic spreading without recourse to specific rules. For purposes of discussion here, I shall adopt the fairly weak position sketched so far – 'weak' in the sense that it attributes relatively little power to the general conventions of autosegmental phonology, and more to the rules of the individual grammars. This particular decision has been made primarily for ease of exposition, and a number of points will arise which suggest that a different, stronger position is preferable. We will return to this question in section 6.5 and propose a modification of this position.

The division of labor that was utilized between the Association Convention and language-specific rules suggests that other systems can be found where no further language-specific rules will associate the tones or vowels left unassociated by the Association Convention. In this case, vowels may be left toneless, and tones may be left vowelless. This is indeed the case, and one language where such things are to be found is Sukuma, a Bantu language of Tanzania (Goldsmith 1985a).

In Sukuma, a vowel may underlyingly be associated with a High tone, a Low tone, no tone at all, or the Low tone of a Low–High melody. (By *melody* I mean simply a sequence of tones that frequently come together in sequence, as a package.) These possibilities are shown schematically in (15). Cases (c) and (d) are by far the most common, for reasons involving the history of the language: case (c) evolved from Low-toned syllables, and case (d) from High-toned syllables, while (a) and (b) are largely found in borrowings.

(15) (a) CV (b) CV (c) CV (d) CV
          | | |
          H   L   L H

As we shall see, vowels and tones associate by means of the Association Convention, but that can leave either certain High tones or certain vowels unassociated. If a High tone remains unassociated, it is simply not realized phonetically. A vowel that is not associated with a tone is realized on a low pitch.

With this information in hand, let us turn to the ways in which simple infinitives are built up tonally in Sukuma. The infinitive is formed with the prefix *ku-*, an optional Object Marker, and a stem. The stem, in turn, consists of a *root* (generally of the form CVC), an optional set of suffixes (generally of the form VC), and a Final Vowel *-a*. All this is given schematically in (16), and will hold, in fact, for the other Bantu languages that we shall look at in the course of this book. From a tonal point of view, the root of an infinitive may have either no tone at all, or a Low–High tone melody; that is, it may be as in (15c) or (15d). These two cases are illustrated in (17) and (18). (19) gives the underlying forms for

(16)   Structure of the Sukuma verb

Subject Marker	Tense Marker	Object Marker	Root	Suffixes	Final Vowel
			.... stem		

the stems of (17), (18); the effect of the Association Convention is illustrated in (20), where the dotted line indicates the added association line. A later rule shifts the High tone in (20) one vowel further to the right.

(17)   Toneless infinitive

   ku gaagaan a   'to bustle around'

(18)   LH infinitive

   ku baabát a   'to grope one's way'

(19)   gaagan a   baabaat a
                          |
                          LH

(20)   gaagan a   baabaat a
                          | ┊
                          LH

A similar effect is found when we consider the tonal behavior of Object Markers. These too divide into two tonal groups. There are those, like *mu* 'him' in (21a), which are toneless, and those like *ba* 'them' in (21b), which have a LH melody. Combining these with the two types of infinitives in (19), we find four combinations, given in (21).

(21)   (a) ku mu lagal a   'to drop
                                           him'

   (b) ku ba lagal a   'to drop
          | ┊   them'
          L H

   (c) ku mu bon er a   'to see
          | ╱   for him'
          L H

   (d) ku ba bon er a   'to see
          | | ╱   for them'
          LHL H

The Association Convention predicts the associations given with broken lines in (21), and these are the correct (though not surface) results. The notable result is that of (21d), where a High tone remains unassociated because there is no unassociated vowel for it to associate with.

The forms derived by the Association Convention so far do not give the correct surface forms, however, because there is another general rule that plays a major role in the derivation of even the simplest of forms in Sukuma, a rule that shifts High tones one syllable to the right.

Rules of this sort are among the simplest rules encountered in autosegmental analyses, and our notation should reflect this simplicity. The conventions adopted so far allow us to express this simplicity. As we have seen, all material given in the formulation of a rule forms the structural description of the rule. Unbroken association lines indicate associations that already exist, while a dashed line in an autosegmental rule indicates part of the structural change. Similarly, an 'x' through an association line will indicate that the association line is to be deleted by the rule. (Some variants of an 'x' appear in the literature, such as a pair of short lines or a 'z' through the association line; cf. (54) below.) A simple circle around a segment, as we have seen, means that it is not associated to any segment on the facing tier.

These two notational conventions can be seen in the High tone shift rule given in (22). The unbroken line (which has, to be sure, an 'x'

(22)   High tone shift

$$V \quad C_0 \quad \textcircled{V}$$
$$\overset{\ast}{|} \; \cdots\cdots\cdots$$
$$H \cdots$$

through it, but is otherwise unbroken) indicates that the High tone is associated to the vowel on the left in the input. It would make no difference in the formulation of the rule if the H were written underneath the V on the right (as in 23a) or halfway between them (as in 23b); these rules are all completely indistinguishable. This rule will apply to the cases in (21b), (21c), and (21d), giving the surface forms in (24).

(23)   (a)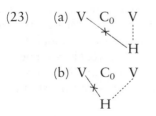

   (b)

(24)   (a) ku ba lagal a
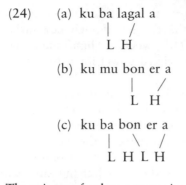

(b) ku mu bon er a

(c) ku ba bon er a

There is one further way to simplify the formulation of rule (22), High tone shift, which might occur to readers. As it is presently formulated, the rule adds an association line, and it also deletes an association line. In principle, it would certainly seem that there is nothing wrong in having a single rule perform both operations, but one might wonder whether there was not a connection between these two operations here. Indeed, there is: no High tone in Sukuma can be associated with more than one vowel, and it is true that the addition of the association line performed by this rule will have as a consequence the deletion of the previous association held by the tone.

The restriction in Sukuma limiting a tone to associating with only one vowel is, as we have already seen, not universal – far from it: it is a language-specific restriction, a setting of what is known in current parlance as a 'parameter'.[5]

The degree to which a language permits tones to be associated with more than one vowel (i.e., to spread, rather than to reassociate) seems to be a variable – a 'parameter' – across languages. It is entirely parallel in scope and status to the variation across languages regarding the number of tones that a vowel can associate with; this may vary from a minimum of zero, in some cases, to three in the most complex cases. I would suggest, therefore, that each language will specify a minimal and a maximal number of associations for vowels, and a minimal and a maximal number of associations for tones. A reasonably perspicuous notation for this notion will describe the minimum and the maximum as a pair of numbers (e.g. {0,1}), along with a label explaining which tier it refers to. For example, if vowels in a given language can associate with at most two tones, and if each vowel must associate with at least one tone, then we would indicate this as: *Vowel* {1,2}. In the case at hand, that of Sukuma, we wish to say that the restriction is *Tone* {0,1}: no tone may associate to more than one vowel. With this well-formedness condition available, we may now simplify the formulation of High tone shift (22), as in (25).

(25)   V   C$_0$ Ⓥ - *not assoc'd*
          | ⟋⟋⟋⟋⟋⟋   *before*
          H ⟋⟋⟋⟋

The restriction that we have just established represents a well-formedness condition on representations, and it is incumbent upon us to explain, therefore, what happens if the number of tones on a vowel should exceed the maximum, or not reach the minimum. I have already suggested what happens if, during the application of a rule, the maximum number of tones should be exceeded: the tone assigned by the rule is maintained, but the earlier tone is dissociated. We will look in greater detail below at what occurs if the minimum number of tones is not satisfied in a given representation. We shall assume, meanwhile, that the normal, unmarked situation in a language is $\{0,1\}$, i.e. for the minimum figure to be 0, and the maximum to be 1; departures from these parameters are set by the language in question. This specification is a matter of convenience, I hasten to point out, and nothing more.

Before leaving the general topic of the Association Convention, a few more comments are in order regarding the general pattern of tone to vowel associations found in tone languages. The term *Initial Association Rule* has been used to refer to the first rule that associates tones and vowels in the derivation, and it is useful to have such a term. In Kikuyu, the Initial Association Rule was given in (9). In the majority of tone languages, the Initial Association Rule associates the first vowel and the first tone, as in (26); the one-to-one association that follows from the Association Convention gives the pattern of one-to-one association from left to right. When there are more tones than vowels, one of two things can happen. If the language permits more than one tone per vowel, we can get a piling up of tones at the right-hand end of the word; if the language does not, then we are left with an extra tone that is associated with no vowel. The former case is illustrated by Supyire; the latter case is illustrated by Mixtecan. Each of these is discussed in the next section.

(26)   ⌈C$_0$ V
          | ⋮
          ⌊   T

There are other possibilities for the Initial Association Rule. Hausa appears to associate its tones from right to left, which is the result of the interaction of the Association Convention and an Initial Association Rule that associates the rightmost tone to the rightmost vowel (Newman 1986b). Thus, while (26) is the most common Initial Association Rule found, it is by no means universal.

1.4   FLOATING TONES

No discussion of tonal systems, nor any discussion of autosegmental phonology, could omit a discussion of floating tones. The theory predicts the existence of morphemes that exist on just one tier, a striking possibility that cannot be incorporated in other theories of phonological representation, and floating tones are an example of just this possibility.

Readers of the linguistic literature must beware, however. The term *floating tone* has been indiscriminately used with two rather different meanings. On the one hand, it has been taken to refer specifically to a morpheme that is underlyingly only tonal, that is, composed of segments only on a tonal tier. On the other hand, the term has also been used to refer to segments which, at a given moment in the derivation, are not associated with any vowel.

It should be clear that the two usages involve rather different, though related, senses. If a vowel should come to be deleted, then the tone associated with it may be said to become 'floating' in the second sense, though not in the first.

For an especially interesting case of a floating tone, we shall turn to Mixtecan – as I will call it, though there are many different tone systems of 'dialects' of Mixtecan to be found in the literature. The dialect described here is actually San Miguel El Grande Mixtecan.[6] The problem at hand involves a suffixal High tone which is underlyingly unassociated, but which associates rightward to the following word. Some words have this 'floating' High tone suffix; others do not. There is no synchronic basis for the explanation of this distinction. We must simply analyze the tonal patterns of words differently if they have a floating High tone. Words in general are bisyllabic, and since there are three tone levels in this language (High, Mid, and Low), we would expect, all other things being equal, that there would be nine tone classes of words (see (27)). All of these exist except for the last: there are no words with a Low–Low tone pattern, and thus we have eight surface tone patterns possible over the two syllables of a word.

(27)   High–High   Mid–High   Low–High
             sáná 'turkey'   kučí 'pig'   sùčí 'child'

             High–Mid   Mid–Mid   Low–Mid
             ñíʔi 'steam bath' beʔe 'house'   mìni 'puddle'

             High–Low   Mid–Low   *Low–Low
             báʔù 'coyote'   kutù 'nose'

But in addition to the tone pattern that a word can bear, five of the eight tone classes in (27) must be distinguished in another way, giving a total of thirteen tone classes. Words with any of the surface tone patterns in (28) may idiosyncratically have a High tone suffixed to them which is not realized when the word is pronounced in isolation, but which is realized when there is a following word for it to associate to. A pair of this sort is illustrated in (29).

(28)　　HH　　　　LH

　　　　HM　　MM

　　　　　　　ML

(29)　(a) k e e　'go away'　　(b) k e e　　　　'eat'
　　　　　| |　　　　　　　　　　| |
　　　　　M M　　　　　　　　　M M　H

Despite the fact that the floating High has no influence on its own word when pronounced in isolation, we have no problem in identifying the High tone, since it links onto a following vowel. In most cases this following vowel is the *immediately* following vowel; in other cases, there is some movement and shifting before the floating High actually associates with a vowel. A typical case is given in (30). There we see a word with a LH tone pattern (*sùčí*) change, and surface with a HH pattern, under the influence of the preceding verb, 'eat', whose underlying form is given in (29b). The verb contributes a (floating) High tone to the right, and this High then associates with the first vowel that it encounters, displacing the Low that was associated with the first vowel of the word *sùčí*. The disassociation of that Low tone is accomplished by the same principle that was referred to at the end of the last section, involving the maximum number of tones (here, one) that a vowel can associate with; a rule that adds a tone to a vowel in such a language will indirectly (but automatically) have the effect of removing the association of that vowel to an earlier tone. This dialect of Mixtecan has the property of requiring each vowel to have – maximally and minimally – exactly one tone. (Such a statement puts no requirement on how many vowels – zero, one, or more – a given tone must be associated with, however.)

By contrast, if the verb preceding the noun *sùčí* does not have a floating High tone (as with the verb in (29a), meaning 'to go away'), then *sùčí* will not change its tone, and will surface with its normal, underlying tone pattern, L H, as we see in (30b).

(30)   (a) sùčí 'child'   k e e   sùčí 'the child will eat'

$$\begin{array}{ccc} \text{s} & \text{ù} & \text{čí} \\ | & | & \\ \text{L} & \text{H} & \end{array}$$

$$\begin{array}{cccccc} \text{k} & \text{e} & \text{e} & & \text{s} & \text{ù} & \text{čí} \\ | & | & & \diagup & & | \\ \text{M} & \text{M} & \text{H} & & \text{L} & \text{H} \end{array}$$

(b)   k e e sùčí 'the child will go away'

$$\begin{array}{cccc} \text{k} & \text{e} & \text{e} & \text{sùčí} \\ | & | & | & | \\ \text{M} & \text{M} & \text{L} & \text{H} \end{array}$$

The full range of possible tone changes triggered by a floating High tone on the left is given in (32). This chart illustrates what appears to happen when a word with a given tone pattern is placed to the right of a word with a floating High tone. As the floating High tone associates, or (extending the metaphor) 'docks', onto the word to the right, we observe the tonal perturbations indicated in the chart. Unsurprisingly, words that begin in any event with a High tone do not appear to undergo a mutation, since the floating High, when it docks, will merely replace the old High with a new High, a move that has no audible effect. The rule that performs the docking is formulated in (31).

(31)

$$\begin{array}{ccc} \text{V} & \text{C}_0 & \text{V} \\ | & & \diagup \\ \text{T} & \textcircled{T} & \end{array}$$

(32)   When a word with the   it surfaces as:
               following basic pattern
               receives a floating High,

HH	HH
HM	HM
HL	HL
MH	MH; see text
MM	HM or MH; see text
ML	HL or MH; see text
LH	HH
LM	HM

The tone patterns in (32) are divided up by the first tone of the word: there are three patterns beginning with High, three beginning with Mid, and two beginning with Low. All words beginning with High or with Low will be directly accounted for by positing the association of a floating High to the first vowel of the word. When the word already begins with a High, there will be no audible change; when the word begins with a Low-toned vowel, the vowel picks up a High tone and loses the Low. The same generalization holds, indeed, for some of the words beginning with a Mid tone, but here the matter is not at all simple. Let us consider in order what happens to words with the tone pattern MM, ML, and MH.

(1) *MM* Words with a MM pattern fall under the same principle that we have just seen; their first vowel becomes High in tone, yielding a HM pattern. However, there is another possible form that MM words can take on in certain cases when they become the host to a floating High tone. To explain this and further complexities below, it will be useful to be able to have symbols for the vowels and consonants in order to express certain formulas. Let us call the first vowel of the word V_1, and the second V_2; the consonant preceding V_1 will be C_1 (which may be null), and the consonant between V_1 and V_2 will be C_2 (which may also be null). Thus the word is of the form $C_1 V_1 C_2 V_2$.

In several places in Mixtecan, we find that a special behavior is involved when words have a certain form, a form that we shall call 'monosyllabic' so that we have a simple name for these words (though we do not know, in point of fact, that they should technically be analyzed as having only a single syllable). This involves words of the form $C_1 V_1 V_2$, where V_1 and V_2 are phonologically identical (both 'a' or both 'e', etc.). 'Monosyllabic' words that are of the tone pattern MM have a special tonal behavior when they follow a floating High tone. After these MM words have become HM, they may optionally become HH, as illustrated in (33).

(33)   C a a   C a a   C a a
        | | →   / | →   //
        H M M   H M M   ᵒᵖᵗ· H M M

In order to understand better what is going on in (33), we must take two further steps. First, we recognize that a simpler analysis of MM words is available if we analyze them as containing a single Mid tone associated with two vowels; the deeper motivation for this involves a principle called the Obligatory Contour Principle (which we will discuss in section 6.4). In essence, the Obligatory Contour Principle says that we do not find two adjacent, identical autosegments unless they are separated by a word boundary. Second, we must anticipate a result that is the subject of the next chapter, involving the placement of vowels and consonants on a separate autosegmental tier, distinct from the tier to which tones associate; the latter we refer to as the *skeletal* tier. (Readers to whom this material is completely new may skip to the end of this section without loss of continuity, and return to it after reading chapter 2.) With this in mind, we may reformulate (33) as (34).

(34)

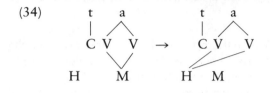

There appears to be a strong tendency for floating High tones that dock onto monosyllabic forms to spread over the entire word; we shall see another case of this in a moment.

(2) *ML*   The next case to consider is what happens to words with the tone pattern ML when a floating tone precedes them. ML words always change their tone when a floating High tone precedes, but just how they change depends on their internal structure. If the word is monosyllabic, in the sense defined above, *or* if V_1 is followed by a glottal stop, then the floating High simply attaches to the first vowel of the word, as in (35).

(35)   (a)

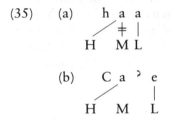

     (b)

((35b) is a hypothetical example, based on the reported regularities found in Mixtecan.) In (35) we do not take advantage of the theoretical points mentioned above, which we shall do in a moment. All other forms with the pattern ML shift the floating tone to the second vowel, as in (36), to which it then associates by rule (31). In either case, the effect of the raising High tone, floating rightward from the preceding word, is evident.

(36)

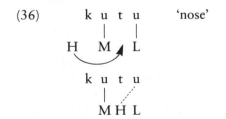

Parenthetically, when the floating High tone docks onto a monosyllabic form with a ML tone pattern, the word can become (at least in some cases) HH rather than HL, as illustrated in (37). This form is reported for the word *žuu* 'rock'. Interestingly, this word itself has a floating High tone, and it will normally contribute it to the following vowel through the effects of rule (31). However, when it has undergone the changes in (31), and is pronounced with a HH pattern, then the floating High to its right will no longer dock. This is predictable from the formulation of rule (31) given above, since it requires the floating High to be immediately preceded by an associated tone. In the case in (37), we see that a floating High preceded by another floating High will not undergo (31), and hence will not affect the tone of a following word.

(37)   ž u u   ž u u
          | | →   ╱ | →
      H   M L H   H   M L H

          ž u u
          ╱╱
      H   M L H

Formulating the rule that permutes the H as in (36), but not in the cases shown in (35), is possible if we use again the notion of the skeletal tier, the Obligatory Contour Principle, and if we make a special assumption regarding the phonological status of post-vocalic glottal stops in Meso-American languages: we shall assume that post-vocalic glottal stops are not true consonants, but rather play a role that is formally parallel to that of tones. (Their physical locus of articulation is, of course, identical.)[7] Thus, if the metathesis rule that properly applies in (36) is formulated as in (38), it will not be able to apply to forms in (35), as demonstrated in (39). What is crucial about the application of Floating H Metathesis is not the content of the C-positions (that is, the so-called 'onsets' of the syllables), which is why the material associated there is in

(38)   Floating H Metathesis

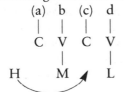

(39)   (a)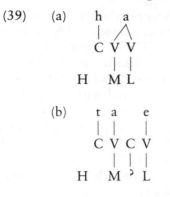

parentheses, but rather the content of the rest of the syllable and the material on the tonal tier.

(3) *MH*   Finally, we must briefly consider the fate of MH words preceded by a floating High tone. As the table in (32) indicates, these words undergo no tonal change. Although one could write a rule that deleted the floating High before words with the tone pattern MH, it would seem to be easiest to slightly generalize Floating H Metathesis (38), and allow it to metathesize a H over a following M when either a High or a Low follows. Under this analysis, when a floating High is followed by a MH word, the floating H will metathesize, and then dock onto the second vowel, inaudibly displacing the underlying High tone of the word.

One final point is worth making before leaving the subject of Mixtecan. The floating High tone that we have considered so far is part of the lexical entry of various nouns, verbs, and other segmentally realized forms. There is another floating High tone in the language, marking continuous or ongoing activity; it is prefixed to the verb, and has precisely the same effects as those found on the words considered so far. Thus, for example, the *kee* 'go away' takes on the form *kée* in the continuous – as we can clearly see now, this is the effect of a floating High tone prefix, which can undergo the effects of rule (31).

Before leaving the subject of floating tones, let us look briefly at another tonal system that contains a floating tone. Supyire, as described by Carlson (1985), displays a familiar pattern of tone to vowel association whereby the first tone will normally be associated with the first vowel (as by (26) above), and association then procedes to the right in a one-to-one fashion; if there is one more tone than there are vowels, then in many cases (perhaps in all cases; this point is not certain) the extra tone associates with the final vowel, yielding a contour tone on the final syllable. These points are illustrated in (40). The association of the extra

(40)   (a) mpi   'hare'

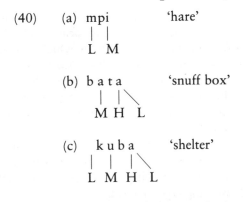

(b) b a t a   'snuff box'

(c) k u b a   'shelter'

tone we may take to be due to a rule that associates a floating Low.

The data in Carlson (1985) leave some uncertainty as to whether all other tones left floating on the right after the Association Convention has applied will associate to the last vowel. However, there are a number of nouns which have a lexically specified floating Low tone on their left-hand side, as shown in (41). Rather than modify our conception of the Initial Association Rule for such cases, it appears to be preferable to allow some means for certain lexically specified elements to be marked as *inert*, that is, as not participating in the autosegmental rules at a given stage in the derivation. The notion of an 'inert' element will be developed in greater detail in the next chapter, and can be seen to be a generalization of the notion of 'extrametricality,' discussed in chapter 4.

(41)   (a) v y ī   L   'cricket'
                |\
             L H L

(b)   n ɔ   'scorpion'
             |
       L   M

I will indicate that an element is marked inert by placing it in parentheses. Understood in this way, the underlying representation for the tone melodies in (41a,b) will be (L)HL and (L)M, respectively.

1.5 STABILITY

One of the fundamental aspects of autosegmental representation is the autonomy granted to the segments on each tier – the etymological source of the term 'autosegmental', in fact. This autonomy in turn leads us to expect that rules whose effect is to delete a segment located on one autosegmental tier will not affect an autosegment with which it was formerly associated. This effect is known as a *stability* effect, since it accounts for why an element such as a tone may display a stability – a resistance to deletion – even when the vowel it was associated with is deleted phonologically. Similarly, a tone can be deleted without its corresponding vowel undergoing deletion.

In a very large class of cases, when a tone is left unassociated by a phonological rule of vowel-deletion, the tone is reassociated with another vowel, which is the linguist's clue to the stability of the tone. A typical case is found in KiRundi, a Bantu language of Burundi.

In KiRundi, one of the central rules of the phrase-level phonology involves the deletion of the first of two vowels brought together across a word boundary. (Under certain conditions, the first vowel becomes a glide instead of being lost entirely.) This elision may occur, for example, between a subject noun and a following verb. The verb *bararima* 'they hoe' has a structure similar to that of the verb in the two Bantu languages we have seen, as given in (42). When an overt subject is placed in front of

(42)	ba	ra	rim	a
	Subject Marker	Focus Marker	root	Final Vowel

'they hoe'

this verb, as in (43), the subject noun will display its own inherent tonal pattern. The singular form of (42), however, begins with a vowel, as we see in (44), and elision occurs when a noun precedes the singular verb, as we see in (45). Thus, the first of two vowels that meet across a word boundary, as in (45), is lost; but if it bore a High tone, that tone is maintained on the remaining vowel. This stability is portrayed more graphically in (46).

(43)	aba-	goré	ba-ra-	rim-a
	prefix	woman	they-Focus	hoe

(44)	a	ra	rim	a
	Subject Marker	Focus Marker	root	Final Vowel

'(s)he hoes'

(45)   surface: umu-gor á-ra-rim-a

       from underlying: umugoré ararima

(46)   umu gor é ar ar i ma
      \\/ | / | | | |
      L   L   H   L   L   L

In Kirundi, vowel-initial words have no tone assigned by the word-level phonology to the first vowel of the word. (All word-initial vowels are inert in the sense discussed in the previous section; this property has also been called 'extratonality'.) Thus, when the High tone becomes floating by the deletion of the word-final vowel of *umugore*, the tone is automatically reassociated with the first vowel of *ararima* by the Association Convention. We thus see that the deletion of a vowel can leave unaffected the tone with which the vowel was associated. Similar effects can be found with nasalization and other autosegmentalized features.[8]

1.6   SPREADING RULES

A tone that is associated with a single vowel will, in certain languages, be spread, or doubled, to an adjacent vowel. For example, in Chichewa,[9] a Bantu language spoken in Malawi, a High tone on any vowel before the antepenultimate vowel will normally be doubled onto the following vowel. This rule is given in (47). For example, the first syllable of the stem of an infinitive is always assigned a High tone, and it will be doubled if the verb has four or more syllables, as we see in (48).

The rule in (47) uses the broken line notation that has already been discussed. However, there is another kind of spreading, or assimilation, that can occur in tonal or other autosegmental structures which spreads the association of a tone as far as possible in a given direction. This

(47) $V\ C_0\ V\ C_0\ V\ C_0\ V$
      | ⟋
      H

(48)   Chichewa infinitives
      ku yángana
      ku yángánitsa
      ku yángánitsitsa

means that the autosegment will be associated with all unassociated accessible segments on the opposite tier in one direction or the other, and so will be associated to all those unassociated segments to which it can link without crossing any association lines. The High tone in (49), for

(49)   C V$_1$ C V$_2$ C V$_3$ C V$_4$ C V$_5$ C V$_6$ C V$_7$
              | |
              H   L

example, would be able to spread rightward to V$_3$, V$_4$, and V$_5$, or leftward to V$_1$, but not to V$_6$ or V$_7$. This kind of spreading is indicated by an arrow in the autosegmental rule, pointing to the right for unbounded rightward spreading, or to the left for unbounded leftward spreading, or with two arrows for spreading in both directions, as shown in (50a,b,c), respectively.

(50)   (a) V   (b) V   (c) V
                |↗   ↖| ↖|↗
                T   T   T

Digo, a Bantu language of northeastern Tanzania, illustrates how unbounded spreading may operate in a tone language.[10] The surface tone pattern of Digo words is created by the interaction of several remarkable tone rules. The two most important rules we shall call *End Run* and *Rightward Spread.* The effect of the first of these is to reassociate the rightmost High tone of a Digo verb to the final vowel of the word, as in (51).

(51)   End Run (Digo)

         V X V]$_{word}$
         ⊬
         H

Underlyingly, there are no Low tones in Digo; vowels at that point either will be associated with a High tone, or else will simply unassociated. The structure of the verb in Digo is familiar, for it is virtually identical to that of the other Bantu verbs we have considered so far; see (52).

As we saw in Kikuyu, Subject Markers, Object Markers, and stems can be chosen from either of two tonal classes. Here the choice is between those that come with a High tone, and those that come without a tone.

A simple infinitive without a tone is pronounced with all low-toned syllables, as we see in (53a); a High toned infinitive has a High tone on

(52)   Structure of the Digo verb
    (a) Finite verb

Subject Marker	Tense Marker	(Object Marker)	Stem

    (b) Infinitive

ku   (Object Marker)   Stem

the final syllable. Two phrase-level rules apply to affect this final High if the word is phrase-final, turning it into a Rising–Falling pattern over the last two syllables; but I will leave these details out here, since they tend to obscure the immediate effects of the rules that interest us.

(53)   (a) Toneless infinitives

        ku rim a   'to cultivate'
        ku guz a   'to sell'
        ku ambir a   'to tell'
        ku vugir a   'to untie'
        ku vugir ir a   'to untie for someone'
        ku dezek a   'to spoil someone'
        ku gandamiz a 'to press, squeeze'

    (b) High tone infinitives

        ku reh á   'to bring'
        ku nen á   'to speak'
        ku aruk á   'to begin'
        ku puput á   'to beat'
        ku bombor á 'to demolish'
        ku gongome á 'to hammer'

The High tone on the final vowel of each of the verbs in (53b) is the result of End Run, which has shifted the High tone from the first vowel of the stem, as illustrated in (54). If an Object Marker with a High tone (which we may assume to be underlyingly associated) is placed in a toneless verb, we find the result shown in (55).

If two consecutive High tones are found in the underlying form, the one on the right is deleted, as in (56), where a High-toned object marker and a High-toned stem are found; the rule is given in (57). After the stem

(54)   ku puput á
        |
        H

(55)　　ku a ambir á　'to tell them'

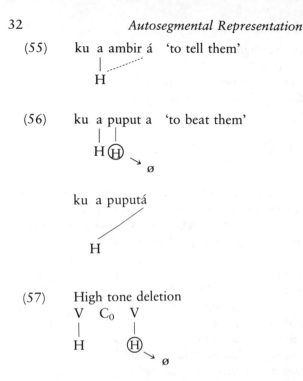

(56)　　ku a puput a　'to beat them'

ku a puputá

(57)　　High tone deletion

loses its High tone, the High tone from the Object Marker shifts by End Run to the Final Vowel. If, however, there are two non-adjacent High tones in the underlying structure, then both High tones will eventually surface. The one on the right will shift to the final vowel by End Run; the one on the left will undergo further changes, as we will see as we turn to some examples of finite verb forms.

The present tense form of the verb is built from the tense marker *-na-*, which is itself toneless. Some examples with a toneless verb are given in (58), where it can be seen that the third-person (singular and plural) Subject Markers contribute a High tone that shifts by End Run to the Final Vowel. When the present tense form of a High tone stem is formed, we find a pattern as in (59).

The derivation of the forms in (59) with only one tone are straightforward, and are given in (60). The derivation of the forms with third-

(58)　　Low tone stem *ku vugur a*　'to untie'
　　　　ni na vugur a　'I am untying'　　　　　　tu na vugur a
　　　　u na vugur a　'You are untying',　　　　mu na vugur a
　　　　　　　　　　　　　　etc.
　　　　a na vugur á　　　　　　　　　　　　　　ma na vugur á

(59)   High tone stem *ku puput á* 'to hit'
ni na puput á   tu na puput á
u na puput á   mu na puput á
a na púpút á   ma na púpút á

person subjects, however – *a na púpútá* and *ma na púpútá* – are not immediately obvious. The rules presented so far take us only as far as illustrated in (61).

(60) ni na puput a

          ‡
          H⎯⎯⎯⎯
                    End Run

(61)   a na puput a
           | ‡
           H   H

At this point, two rules come into the picture. The first is the rule of Rightward Spread which was mentioned above, as formulated in (62). This rule will apply to the second form in (61) , giving us the form in (63).

(62)   Rightward Spread

                    V
                    |↗
                    H

(63)   a na puput a
           |⁄⁄⁄ |
           H   H

Finally, a rule delinking a multiply linked High tone from the Subject Marker and the Tense Marker, as in (64), applies, giving us the final form, (65). Rule (64) will not apply to High tones that are singly linked. Digo has another characteristic that interacts with Rightward Spread-

(64)   High Delinking
         ⎰Subject Marker⎱   V
         ⎱Tense Marker ⎰   ⁄
                    ⤬ ⁄
                    H

(65)   a na puput a

$$H \quad\quad H$$

ing. At a certain point in the derivation, all voiced obstruents are assigned a Low tone. This is a rather common occurrence among African tone languages, where these Low-toned consonants are traditionally called 'depressor consonants', since they so frequently have the effect of lowering the tones of the vowels around them. The rule of Depressor Tone Assignment is ordered after End Run, but before Rightward Spread, giving us the ordered set of rules in (66).

(66)   **Rules:**   (57) High Tone Deletion
                      (51) End Run
                      (67) Depressor Tone Assignment
                      (62) Rightward Spread
                      (64) High Delinking

Depressor Tone Assignment (67) illustrates how a rule of insertion is formulated in the notation of autosegmental phonology, where the structural description and the structural change of a rule are not segregated. The element that is inserted is encircled, and the arrow pointing to it indicates that its addition is part of the structural change. In addition, as we have already seen, the broken association line means that the indicated line is added as part of the structural change. The specification 'C, +voice' is sufficient to restrict the rule to voiced consonants, on the assumption (which we take to be correct) that only the obstruents are marked in the lexicon for voicing; the sonorants and vowels, which are redundantly voiced, are lexically unspecified for voicing, and hence will not trigger (67).

(67)   Depressor Tone Assignment

$$\begin{bmatrix} C \\ +\text{voice} \end{bmatrix}$$

$$ⓁＬ↵$$

Depressor Tone Assignment applies after End Run, not blocking its effects; but the Low tones created by Depressor Tone Assignment do block the effects of High–Tone Spread. If a High-toned Subject Marker is joined to a High-toned stem, as in (68), the stem's High tone shifts by End Run to the Final Vowel. This shift is sketched in (68a), and the Subject Marker's tone spreads only as far as the Tense Marker, not being able to pass through the association line of the depressor consonant, as illustrated in (68b).

(68)   (a) a na babadur a   'he is forcing
            | something apart'
            H   H

        (b) a na babadur a
            |/ | | | /
            H L L L H

        (c) a na babadur a
            / | | | /
            H L L L H

The rule of High Delinking will first dissociate the High tone from the Subject Marker, since the High tone is multiply linked and thus satisfies the description of the rule. The rule cannot apply again to delink the High tone from the Tense Marker, since the High tone is no longer multiply linked. We thus arrive at the surface form, given in (68c).

If the depressor consonant is further to the right, spreading will go into the stem as far as that consonant, as illustrated in (69).

(69)   a na tabik a   'he is
        | | becoming
        H   H   distressed'

     a na tabik a
        | /   End Run
        H   H

     a na tabik a   Depressor
        | | /   Tone
        H   L H   Assignment

     a na tabik a
        |// | /   Rightward
        H   L H   Spread

     a na tabik a
        / | /
        H   L H

1.7 THE CONJUNCTIVITY CONDITION

Our final example of a Bantu tone system comes from KiHunde, a
language spoken in eastern Zaire.[11] Every morpheme in KiHunde
(except the verbal extensions) has either a Low tone or a High tone. No
single vowel can bear more than one tone, and although vowels can be
long or short underlyingly, on the surface the only vowel that can be long
is the vowel in the penultimate syllable of the phrase. It follows, then,
that only in penultimate position can a contour tone appear on the
surface, since contour tones are sequences of level tones. Although
KiHunde has an intricate tonal system, we will restrict ourselves to the
consideration of the interaction of three simple tone rules in this
language.

One of the rules operates at the phrase level, changing a sequence of
High–Low–High vowels to High–High–High, as in (70). This rule

(70)   Plateauing
        $V \; C_0 \; V \; C_0 \; V$
        $| \quad \neq \quad \diagdown \; |$
        $H \quad L \quad H$

applies whether the vowels concerned are in the same word or in separate
words. An example of the latter kind is given in (71), where we see the
normally Low prefix of the noun *mukátsi* 'woman' now appearing on a
High tone.

(71)   ni-na-témér-á   'I cut for someone'
        mu-kátsi   'woman'
        ni na témérá mú kátsi   'I cut for a woman'
        $| \;\; \not\!\!N \;\; \not\!\!N$
        $H \; LH \; L \; H$

Plateauing also applies when the vowels are all in the same word. In
the word *a-ní-mu-som-ér-a* 'I am reading for him' in (72), for example,
there is a High on the second vowel of the stem, and a High on the
Subject Marker. The High on the second vowel of the stem is placed there

(72)   ┌──── stem ────┐
        a   ni   mu   som   er   a
        Prefix Subj.   Obj. Root Suffix Final
               Mark.   Mark.   Vowel

morphologically as a way of identifying the present continuous tense. When we remove the Object Marker (which means here '[for] him/her'), then the tone on the root is raised to High by the effects of Plateauing, as in (73).

(73)   a ní sóm ér a   'I am reading [for someone].'

Plateauing is thus a late post-lexical rule whose effect is to create sequences of surface High tones. In principle, the rule might be written to change the features of the Low tone in the middle, rather than to reassociate the High tone on the right (or left) to the middle vowel. However, the theory of autosegmental phonology proposes that, when a phonological effect can be expressed by either feature-changing mechanisms or reassociative mechanisms, the latter are to be preferred. We would not expect to find a rule in a language where most of the effects could be described with a reassociation (as with (70)), but where some clear evidence indicated that the reassociation was not the mechanism actually chosen by the language. More generally, as we shall see below in chapters 5 and 6, we shall try to account for all assimilatory processes as reassociations. There is some reason, in addition, to believe that it is the High on the right that reassociates to the middle vowel position in (70), and not the High on the left that associates rightward.

The second rule that interests us also applies at the phrase level, and it has the effect of decreasing the number of consecutive High tones. The rule of Sandhi Lowering, given in (74), lowers a word-final High tone when the next vowel bears a High tone.[12] This rule applies across the

(74)   Sandhi Lowering

$$\begin{array}{ccc} \text{V} \ ]_{word} & \text{C}_0 & \text{V} \\ | & & | \\ \text{\textcircled{H}} & & \text{H} \\ & \searrow & \\ & \text{L} & \end{array}$$

boundary between a word and a following enclitic, as in (75a), or between two independent words, as in (75b). In (75a), the clitic object pronoun *kyo* has an underlying High tone that lowers the preceding High tone. In (75b), even that High tone is lowered by the following High tone on the (reduplicative) adverb *tsénétséene*.

There are cases where a floating High tone from the left-hand side of a word becomes associated with the word-final vowel of the preceding word. The word *mwewolo* 'yesterday', for example, always assigns a High tone to the final vowel of the preceeding word, as is illustrated in (76).

(75)   (a) ni- na-   tem- á   'I cut'
           Subj. Tense Root Final
                        Vowel
           ni-na-tem-a kyó   'I cut it'
                       it

       (b) ni-na-tem-a kyo tsénétséene   'I cut it quickly'

(76)   (a) ni- a-   som-ág-a   kitabo   'I read a book'
           Subj. Tense Root Suffixes book

       (b) ni- a-   som-ág-a kitabo mwewolo 'I read a book
                                       yesterday yesterday'

If the penultimate vowel of the word onto which the floating High tone attaches is itself associated with a High tone, we find the situation as in (77). The word *Yowáni* 'John' underlyingly has a High only on its middle syllable; the second High is the result of the following word. The structural description of Sandhi Lowering is not met, however, since the boundary mentioned in the rule does not fall between the vowels associated with the two High tones in question, and hence the rule does not apply. Here, therefore, we do find two consecutive High tones on the surface, produced by two words put in contact.

(77)   ni-a-someraga Yowání mwewolo   'I read for John
                        | \   yesterday'
                       H H
       I-read-for   John   yesterday

Sandhi Lowering and Plateauing may well be expected to interact. What would happen if a word ending in a High–Low–High sequence should be followed by a High-toned vowel? As (78) shows, the answer is that the Plateauing rule applies, and Sandhi Lowering fails to apply. Thus, Plateauing is itself ordered before Sandhi Lowering, giving the derived structure shown schematically in (79); Sandhi Lowering, furthermore, fails to apply to the form given there.

(78)   ni-na-mu-tém-ér-á kushe
       I-cut-for-him   well
       'I cut well for him'

       ni-na-tém-ér-á kyó muundu
       I-cut-for   it person
       'I cut it for someone'

(79)   V C_0 V C_0 V] C_0 V
     | ┼   \\.| |
     H   L   H   H

The reason that Sandhi Lowering fails to apply in (79) is of some interest. The structural description of the Sandhi Lowering requires that the tone to be affected be associated with a word-final vowel. As it happens, this requirement is, in one sense, met by the final High tone of the word on the left: the tone is associated with a word-final High. On the other hand, the final High is also associated with a non-final vowel. How should the associations indicated in the structural description of an autosegmental rule be interpreted? If an autosegment is multiply associated while a rule mentions only one of the lines in its strutural description, will the rule apply?

The correct answer depends on the nature of the rule, and in particular on whether or not the effect of the rule involves only association lines. If the rule changes or deletes the autosegment(s) in question, then the rule will not apply; the non-application of Sandhi Lowering is an example of this phenomenon. If the function of the rule is to add or delete an association line, then the rule will apply in any event.[13]

We will refer to this condition as the *Conjunctivity Condition* (80). In other words, if segment S has additional associations not mentioned in the rule, then it will not undergo any 'internal' effects, such as feature change or deletion. This principle will be important in the discussion of geminates in the next chapter.

(80)   **Conjunctivity Condition**
       If a rule R has the effect of modifying the feature specifications of a segment S, or deleting a segment S, and if the rule explicitly refers to a chart C (i.e., association lines linking two autosegmental tiers), then segment S will undergo the effects of the rule only if all of its association lines in C are explicitly mentioned in rule R.

1.8   CONTOUR TONES

The possibility of many-to-one associations between one tier and another opens up the possibility of treating rising and falling tones as sequences of level tones (High, Mid, Low, etc.) associated with a single vowel, as in

(81). This is a well established idea, to be sure, in the special areas of linguistics concerned with the treatment of tone languages, and the two-tiered representation that we have developed allows us to express this traditional notion simply and directly.

(81)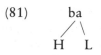

Rising and falling tones are generally referred to in the literature as *contour tones* or *dynamic tones*. In a language with High and Low tones, it is common to find falling and rising tones in addition, and among African tone languages it has been demonstrated in countless cases that these tonal patterns are best treated as sequences of High–Low and Low–High, respectively. In languages with more than two levels of tones, rising and falling tones can generally have their starting and ending points tonally identified with one of the level tones of the language.

In this section we shall look at just a few of the tonal intricacies of the Soyaltepec dialect of Mazatec, a Mexican language of the Otomanguean family, as described by E. Pike (1956). There are four tone levels in this language, which we shall call by number – '1, 2, 3, 4' – following Pike's notation and that of others working on Mexican languages. Tone 1 is the highest, tone 4 the lowest. Syllables can underlyingly have tones 1, 2, 3 or 4, or one of several contours which we shall call 2-1, 3-2, 4-2, and 2-4. The labels of these contour tones describe the tone perceived: a 2-1 tone is one that rises from the level of a 2-tone to that of a 1-tone. What we would like to convince ourselves of, however, is that these combinations of tones do indeed act phonologically as if they were concatenations of level tones, and even more, that they do so in ways consistent with an autosegmental analysis.

We will look at three characteristics that point in that direction. The first argument concerns contour tones that end in a 2-tone, on this analysis (in particular, contour tones 3-2 and 4-2), and it demonstrates that these tones do have, as their second half, a 2-tone. The argument involves a word-level rule that associates a 1-level tone to the vowel on the left when a 2-level tone is present, as in (82). As the formulation there notes, the 2-tone is simultaneously deleted. The effect of this rule is illustrated in (83).

When vowels with the contour tones 3-2 or 4-2 appear to the left of a 1-tone vowel, then the rule applies to them as well, spreading the 1 onto the vowel and deleting the 2-tone, as we see in (84). This is just what we expect, given the analysis of these contour tones into sequences of level tones; if the contour tones were viewed as different sorts of entities, this

(82)   Leftward High Spread

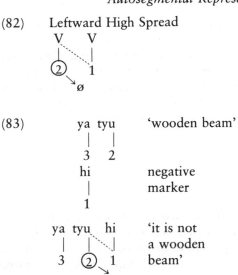

(83)   ya tyu   'wooden beam'
            | |
            3   2
            hi   negative
            | marker
            1

        ya tyu   hi   'it is not
        | | ̵͂ ̵| a wooden
        3   ② 1   beam'
              ↘ ø

would require a new interpretation. The significance of this kind of argument should not be underestimated. In principle – and this has been suggested for a number of natural languages – contour tones might have nothing to do with level tones, from a phonological point of view. It is

(84)   (a) Leftward High Spread applied to 3-2 words
                ni   su   'a dipper'
                | ∧
                3 3 2
                hi   negative
                |
                1
                ni su hi   'not a
                | ∧ | dipper'
                3 3②1
                      ↘ ø

        (b) Leftward High Spread applied to 4-2 words
                n če   'cooked corn'
                ∧ \
                4 2
                nče hi   'not cooked corn'
                ∧ |
                4 ② 1
                     ↘ ø

this kind of behavior with respect to rules of the language that is the criticial evidence in helping the linguist decide this issue.

A second argument in favor of treating contours as sequences concerns tones that end in a 1-tone – in particular, 2-1 and 3-1 contour tones. There is a rule which modifies the tone of words ending in a 1-tone when they follow words ending in a 1-tone. The modification consists of changing them into a 1-2 contour tone, as shown in (85). The effect of

(85)   ... V # ... V #

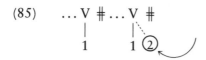

this rule is illustrated in (86a). When a word ends in a 2-1 contour or a 3-1 contour, then it also triggers the rule shown in (85), as we see in (86b) and (c). Again, this consistent pattern of behavior linking words that end with 1-tones and those ending in 2-1 and 3-1 contour tones demonstrates the analyzability of contour tones into level components.

Finally, there are cases in Soyaltepec Mazatec where we can virtually

(86)   (a) ho 'two'   thi cu   'he is saying'
              | | |
              1   1 1
           ho thi cu   'he is saying "two"'
           | | |\
           1 1 1 2

       (b) khi nti   'baby'
            | /\
            3 2 1
           ki te   'he danced'
           | |
           3 1
           khi nti   kite   'the baby danced'
            | /\ ||\
            3 2 1   31 2

       (c) nta   'well'
            /\
           3 1
           thi khye   'he is eating'
            | |
            1   1
           nta   thi khye   'he is eating well'
           /\ | |\
           3 1   1   1 2

see the contour tone take itself apart. A number of tonal reductions take place when a rising tone is followed by a 3-tone or a 4-tone, but among the most striking are those that take place when a 3-2 contour or a 4-2 contour is followed by a word with a 3-tone or a 4-tone. If these two are separated by a word-boundary, we observe the result shown in (87). This

(87) (a) 3-2 followed by 3-tone

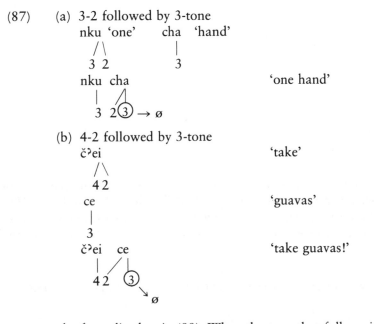

(b) 4-2 followed by 3-tone

process can be formalized as in (88). When the tone that follows is a 4-tone, then a similar process takes place, as we see in (89). In that case, the 2-tone also dissociates from its underlying vowel, but the 4-tone of the new host vowel remains associated. This is schematized in (90). These examples from Soyaltepec Mazatec illustrate the ways in which the tonological behavior of contour tones can best be understood by viewing them as a concatenation of level tones, with the autosegmental notation developed so far in this chapter.

(88)

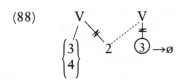

Much has been written about the question of whether rising and falling tones in Asian languages should be analyzed in similar terms, or whether they should instead be treated in some quite different way. It is

(89) 3-2 tone followed by 4-tone

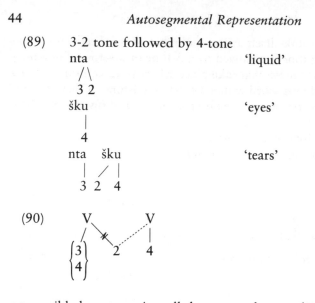

nta   'liquid'

šku   'eyes'

nta šku   'tears'

(90)

not possible here to review all the pros and cons of each approach, but interested readers may look at Yip (1980), Wright (1983), and Shih (1985) for a discussion of Fuzhou tone in which the decomposition of rising and falling tones into level tones is shown to be straightforwardly motivated.

1.9 TONE-BEARING UNITS AND RELATED NOTIONS

In our investigations so far in this chapter, tones have associated consistently with vowels – except in one case, that of Digo, where a rule associated a Low tone with each voiced obstruent. The strong tendency for tones to associate with vowels has been expressed here in two different ways. First, the Association Convention in quite general fashion specifies that tones universally will freely associate with vowels when both the tone and the vowel in question are unassociated. Second, all of our other rules of tonal association and reassociation have had the specific property of associating tones with vowels, rather than consonants. This is surely no accident. Furthermore, our rules have had endless streams of 'C_0's, indications of the irrelevance of the consonants in the formulation of the tonal rules (e.g., rule (31), (57), or (79)).

It is natural to expect a fuller account of these limitations on tone association. 'Limitations' of this sort can simplify rule formulation; if consonants are truly irrelevant to tonal association, either in general or in a particular language, then the constant reference to 'C_0' in our rules can be eliminated. Furthermore, when we consider types of autosegmental systems where features other than tones are involved, we shall see that consonants can well be the units to which other autosegments associate. The fact that vowels, then, are the 'tone-bearing units' in the systems presented in this chapter is a fact about tonal systems in particular, and not more generally about autosegmental phonology. How should this be stated, both in the general theory and in the grammars of the particular languages?

Any autosegmental representation must be composed of one or more pairs of autosegmental tiers between which association lines may be drawn. As we have observed, such a pair of tiers, with its association lines, is called a *chart*. In this chapter (except for the brief departure in section 1.4), the sole chart has consisted of the tier of tonal segments and the tier of vowels and consonants, plus the relevant association lines.

I shall suggest that defining which kinds of segments associate and which do not involves specifying on each of the two tiers of a chart those subsets of segments that are considered *Freely Associating Segments*.[14] Various terminology has been used in the literature for this basic concept; for example, in the chart consisting of the tier of tones and the tier of vowels and consonants, the Freely Associating Segments on the non-tonal tier are often referred to as the 'tone-bearing units'. By this is meant that these segments are affected by a generalized version of the Association Convention that refers not specifically to 'vowels' and 'tones', but generally to Freely Associating Segments. In its more general formulation, the Assocation Convention states, in part, that an association line will be added automatically to link two unassociated segments that are each members of the set of Freely Associating Segments within that chart. Furthermore, segments that are not freely associating would be ignored in the application of an autosegmental rule. If consonants were not freely associating in the chart in question, then they would not need to be mentioned in the structural description of a rule: their presence would simply be ignored.

In the simplest case, it is furthermore assumed that this specification can be accomplished in terms of the intrinsic feature assignments of each segment. Thus, in the case in hand, the Freely Associating Segments on one tier would be those marked [+syllabic], while on the tonal tier it would include all segments. This would be expressed formally, then, as {[+syllabic], ø}. These feature bundles specify for their respective tiers which segments are Freely Associating Segments; any segment meeting the requirement of its tier (respectively, [+syllabic] and ø) will fall into the category. The null symbol, ø, is, evidently, the null requirement, and any segment will trivially meet that requirement. Since we have assumed that features appear only on a single tier, we do not need to specify which set of features pertains to which tier: that question will never arise.

One immediate consequence of this approach is that the Freely Associating Segments on one tier cannot be individually marked for the *kind* of segments on the other tier in the chart that they will associate with, a point that will become more important in the next chapter as we consider the ways in which vowels and consonants associate with the skeletal tier, a concept alluded to in section 1.4 above. The precise relevance of this point may not be clear from the examples we have looked at so far, but an artificial example may clarify the point for present purposes. Extending the facts discussed in section 1.6 concerning depressor consonants, suppose we found a tone language in which it could be argued that the feature [±voice] for obstruents was autosegmentalized – i.e. that it appeared on an autosegmental tier separate from the consonants themselves – and furthermore that this tier of laryngeal specification was the same tier as the one on which the tones were found. We might then want to mark some of the autosegments on the laryngeal tier as being of the kind of laryngeal autosegment that associates with obstruents (these would be the autosegments that mark voice), and mark the others as the *kind* of autosegment that associates with vowels. For better or worse, this freedom would not be possible given the definition of Freely Associating Segment that we have just sketched, because whether or not an element on one tier freely associates with an element on the other tier is absolute – or, rather, is fixed for each chart once and for all within the language. The example may seem at this point contrived, but it is in fact less so than might be suspected.

In order to allow us a certain degree of freedom of analysis in future sections, we shall permit an extension of this first definition of Freely Associating Segment for a given chart. This extension will permit a matching of corresponding Freely Associating Segments, in the sense that was intuitively sketched in the preceding paragraph. If we wanted to allow High tones to freely associate with vowels ([+syllabic] elements), and Low tones with voiced obstruents, we would define the Freely Associating Elements of the chart as in (91).[15] The significance of this extended possibility will become clearer as we look at the relation of consonants and vowels to the skeletal tier in the next chapter.

(91)   {[+syllabic],[+High tone]; [+voice, −sonorant],[−High tone]}

1.10   SUMMARY OF FORMALISM

This chapter has introduced a number of new terms and concepts. The following remarks summarize the concepts we have looked at, and make explicit some points that were adumbrated earlier.

We have discussed the notions of *tiers*, *charts*, and *association lines*. Elements of the set of *Freely Associating Segments* in a chart are typically (but not in every single case) the segments that are linked by association lines. The *Association Convention* applies in a chart after at least one association line is present, and it applies only to pairs of unassociated segments. It may apply and reapply at any point during the derivation.

Language-particular rules may (1) add a single association line; (2) delete an association line; (3) add an unbounded number of association lines (i.e., the case of unbounded spreading); (4) change the features of a segment on a given tier; (5) delete a segment on a given tier; or (6) metathesize two segments on a given tier. Cases (4), (5), and (6) are cases maintained from classical generative (and, for that matter, non-generative) phonology; types (1), (2), and (3) are essentially autosegmental.

Association lines in a given representation may not cross, but no condition has been placed on rules that would block them from attempting to *create* situations in which association lines cross. The Association Convention and rules of unbounded spreading will not create line-crossing situations, since they are absolutely conditioned to affect only pairs of unassociated segments on tiers of a chart. If a rule is formulated to add a single association line, it can, in principle, cause a line-crossing situation. In this case, the same general principle holds as in the case where a line insertion rule gives rise to a situation where a segment exceeds its maximum number of associations: the line that the rule adds remains, but the line that formerly existed is taken to be the offending line, and is automatically erased.

The Initial Association Rule is typically one that associated the first Freely Associating Segment on each tier of a chart, but this is only a strong tendency, not a universal principle.

2
The Skeletal Tier

2.1 INTRODUCTION

In this chapter we will turn to what appears at first sight to be a set of phenomena quite different from the tonal patterns investigated in the previous chapter. We will begin by exploring some of the very special properties of long vowels and long consonants, odd entities whose precise characterization has eluded analysis along traditional lines. These long segments, we shall see, are best thought of neither as sequences of identical segments, nor as single segments specially marked with a feature of length. We will see, rather, that once again an autosegmental analysis with multiple association is the key to understanding the problem. Long vowels consist of a single vowel segment itself associated with two positions on a facing tier, as in (1a); long consonants are similarly analyzed as in (1b).

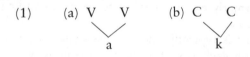

As the diagrams in (1) and (2) suggest, we will introduce in this chapter a new tier consisting of units that we will represent as C's and V's, and later, with syllable structure, more neutrally as undifferentiated X's. This tier has been called variously the *skeletal tier*, the *CV-tier*, and the *timing tier*, and we shall use these terms interchangeably, though we shall use principally the first of them.[1] The elements on the skeletal tier are often called *slots*, or *V-slots* and *C-slots*, since, as we shall see, they are the segments to which vowels and consonants must associate if they are to be realized. This tier will play a central role in the organization of the entire phonological structure, serving as the anchor points for elements on the various other tiers. Tones, for example, which we assumed in chapter 1 to associate directly to vowels, will rather be seen to associate to elements on the skeletal tier to which the vowels also associate.

Let us think for a moment about what it would mean for a vowel or a consonant to be doubly associated, as suggested in (1a) and (b). The fact that a single tonal autosegment can be multiply linked – that is, associated with more than one vowel – was an important step in our understanding of basic autosegmental phenomena, as we saw in the preceding chapter. We tacitly assumed there that vowels (to which we also assumed that the tones were associated) were basic and geometrically indivisible. If a tone should be spread over two vowels, then it would be, in effect, a 'long tone'; but the thought of calling a tone as in (2) a 'long tone' would never have occurred to us, since it seems self-evident that a tone spread over two vowels will extend longer in time than a tone associated with only one vowel.

(2)   CV   CV
              \   /
                T

But suppose that there were something – or rather, some tier – more basic than the vowels or consonants themselves; suppose that there were a tier to which vowels and consonants were associated, and on which only a very rudimentary set of features (perhaps just one, perhaps even none) were realized; suppose that the basic function of this tier, this skeletal tier, were to express the phonological length of units, and that when a vowel or consonant were linked to two of these basic skeletal units, we would have in our hands a long (or geminate) vowel or consonant. These suppositions together lead us to a rather different view of the nature of phonological quantity.

This will be our first goal, then: to show that each long vowel and consonant is associated with two units on the skeletal tier, as in (1a,b), and that all other segments – that is, 'normal', short, segments – are associated with just one unit on the skeletal tier. After an initial exploration of the value of this representation, we shall consider two properties of geminates that have received a certain amount of theoretical attention recently: their *integrity* and their *inalterability*. These terms refer, respectively, to the resistance displayed by the halves of geminates to being separated by rules of vowel epenthesis, and the resistance they display to phonological rules that might affect only half of them.[2] We shall then be in a position to address many of the questions that arise once a multi-tiered representation for length is admitted, and to explore the potential for deeper explanation of phonological phenomena.

If autosegmental representation allows for many-to-one associations, then geminate segments count as two-to-one associations in one direction. What kind of segments would be represented by one skeletal position associated with more than one segment on another tier, vocalic or consonantal? Certain kinds of diphthongs, we shall see, satisfy that description. Autosegmental representation also allows for morphemes to contribute segments on just one tier (as well as more than one tier). What would be the result of having a morpheme that had more elements on the skeletal tier than on the other tiers, or extra consonantal or vocalic segments that were underlying unmatched with skeletal positions? We shall address these questions in turn. Finally, we shall look at two cases where the structure of the material on the skeletal tier is itself determined independently of the segmental material. The languages involved are Sierra Miwok and Classical Arabic, and these two cases make crystal-clear the independent role played by the material on the skeletal tier.

First, however, we will sketch a simple model and see how it can be applied to shed light on a set of phonological processes in a language such as Luganda.

2.2   THE MODEL

We will now explore a representation in which one autosegmental tier is specified for the feature [±syllabic], where vowels are [+syllabic], and obstruents, liquids, nasals, and glides are [−syllabic]. This is the skeletal tier, and it is most convenient for us to allow each segment on that tier to be specified for the feature [syllabic] in one of three ways: positively specified, negatively specified, or not specified at all. We will represent these three kinds of positions with the symbols V, C, and X, respectively.[3] The other autosegmental tier will contain segments specified for the other features, and we shall adopt the terminological convention that any segments *not* on the skeletal tier may be called *autosegments*. In this case, these segments will be the consonants and the vowels of the words in question – they will define the quality, if not the quantity, of the consonants and vowels. Traditional terminology does not provide any suitable terminology for such a tier; we will call it, at the risk of possibly being a bit misleading, the *phonemic tier*. (It has also been called the *segmental tier* or *melodic tier*, but these are even more misleading, and I will not use them.) Let us turn to some facts from Luganda, and see how this model might be useful.

2.2.1   Luganda[4]

Luganda is a Bantu language spoken in Uganda (the names, in fact, are based on the same stem, -*ganda*). The language has both short and long vowels, and also short and long consonants (or single and geminate, as they are also described). There are five vowels (*i,e,a,o,u*), each with a short and a long version, and all contrast: see (3).

(3) Verb stems

lima	'cultivate'	liima	'spy'
wela	'refuse'	weela	'rest'
waba	'go astray'	waaba	'complain'
wola	'lend money'	woola	'scoop out'
tula	'become sharp'	tuula	'sit down'

Several systematic principles can be established governing the appearance of long vowels. One example can be illustrated by the data in (4) involving the class prefixes that are attached to all noun stems. Readers may be aware that in the Bantu languages every noun has a noun class prefix, usually the first or second morpheme of the noun, directly prefixed to the stem of the word. The Bantu languages vary somewhat in the number of classes that can be found in each, but Luganda is not too unusual in having twenty-one. Most stems owe a basic allegiance to a pair of classes, of which one class forms a singular noun and the other the corresponding plural. These pairs of noun classes include the classes that Bantuists have labeled 1 and 2, 3 and 4, 5 and 6, 7 and 8, and 9 and 10. Above 10, the class numbering is more complex; class 15, for example, is the prefix appearing on infinitives, and infinitives have no corresponding plural.

The class 1 prefix is *mu-*, as can be seen in (4); its plural, class 2, has the form *ba-*. When the stem to which the prefix is attached begins with a

(4)

mu kazi	'woman'	ba kazi	'women'
mu limi	'cultivator'	ba limi	'cultivators'
mu wala	'girl'	ba wala	'girls'

vowel, however, the vowel of the prefix *mu-* becomes a glide, the *a* of *ba-* deletes, and the following vowel lengthens:

(5)

mw aami	'chief'	b aami	'chiefs'
mw aana	'child'	b aana	'children'
mw eezi	'sweeper'	b eezi	'sweepers'
mw oogezi	'speaker'	b oogezi	'speakers'

This compensatory lengthening of the second vowel under loss of the full vowel value of the first is an important clue that an independent autosegmental tier is involved. While the long vowels in the plural column in (5) could conceivably be viewed as a total assimilation of the prefix vowel to the following vowel, no parallel interpretation is possible for the first column. Let us view each vowel as initially associated with a single V-element on the skeletal tier, as in (6). When two vowels are

(6)   (a) C V   V C V   (b) C V   V C V
             | | | | | | | | | |
             m u   e z i   b a   e z i

adjacent, the second associates with the V-slot of the first, and dissociates the vowel that was originally associated, as in (7).

(7)   (a) C V   V C V   (b) C V   V C V
             | ⟍ | | | | ⟍ | | |
             m u   e z i   b a   e z i

This double association is realized as length on the vowel, as we have seen; the rule that accomplishes this is given in (8). The vowel that has been left unassociated now is able to reassociate with the preceding C-slot if it is +high, but not if it is +low. (There are no mid vowels that

(8)   V   V
           ⧸ |
           α   β

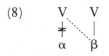

are in the appropriate position to see what would happen to them.) The reassociation is produced by the rule in (9), and the forms in (7) then become the forms in (10). The α and β refer to arbitrary segments. In (10b), the segment *a* is left unassociated. If it remains unassociated – as it in fact will – it will not be realized phonetically. The principle involved we may refer to as the *Linkage Condition*[5]: see (11). In (10a), we see that two segments, *m* and *u*, can associate with a single C-slot, giving us the sound represented orthographically as *mw*; conversely, the vowel *e* has

(9)   C
           ⌐ - - - - - -
           α ([+high])

(10)   (a) C V V C V   (b) C V V C V
             |⟍ | | | | | | |
             m u e z i   b a e z i

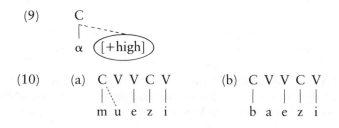

(11) **Linkage Condition**
A segment will not be phonetically realized if it is not linked to a
position in the skeletal tier.

associated with two skeletal positions. I should emphasize that the
association of the vowel to two slots on the skeletal tier is what is what is
responsible for the perceived length of the long vowel. *Moras* – that is,
the traditional unit of vowel length – correspond precisely in this case to
segments on the skeletal tier.

What is especially important about the process we have just looked at
in Luganda is the inherent connection between two changes, the lengthening of one vowel and the loss or desyllabification of the other. The
traditional term *compensatory lengthening* presents a mini-theory of this
connection. It suggests that vowel loss or desyllabification is fundamentally prior, and that the vowel lengthening is a consequence. In the formal
analysis suggested in rule (8), the chain of cause and effect is inverted.
Lengthening is taken to be basic, and to be the additional association of a
vowel to other V-slots than its original one. This reassociation leaves vowels
'stranded', in effect, and we observe either glide-formation or vowel-
deletion. We will return to this question of the direction of causality below
in chapter 6.

What is important here, however, is not which process of the two is
taken to be basic, but rather the fact that the connection between the two
processes has a firm basis in the formal model. At one level – that shown
in (6) – each segment is associated to a single skeletal slot; the particular
rules of the grammar then enter the picture and allow for reassociations
between the elements on each tier. In none of the cases seen so far are any
of the elements on the separate tiers changed in even a single feature: all
the observed changes are changes of association across tiers.

Let us look at a second process that induces lengthening in Luganda
vowels. The process is in fact an old one historically, and has been
reconstructed as a common historical inheritance from Proto-Bantu. A
vowel will always be long when it is followed by a nasal-obstruent
cluster, and this is true whether the segments should be members of the
same morpheme or come from distinct morphemes. Occurring clusters
are given in (12), and examples of long vowels before nasal clusters are
given in (13).

Nasal-obstruent clusters are the only significant clusters that exist in
Luganda. Abstracting away from the matter of glides created in the way
we have just seen, we can say that all words in Luganda can be divided
into underlying syllables of four types: (i) CV, (ii) CVV (always a long
vowel, not a sequence of two vowels, as we have seen), (iii) CVN (where

N stands for a nasal consonant), and (iv) CVC. In this last case, however, the consonant is not free to be anything; this kind of sequence never occurs word-finally, and the consonant must always be part of a geminate. In this respect it shares a property with the CVN sequence in (iii); this kind of syllable cannot appear word-finally, and the nasal is always homorganic to the following consonant. In short, the post-vocalic element never has an independent point of articulation. Either it is the second half of a long vowel, or it shares a point of articulation with the consonant that starts the next syllable. We will return to the question of how to characterize this system in detail in the next chapter, when we discuss autosegmental licensing.

(12)   Nasal clusters
        mp   nt   nc   nk
        mb   nd   nj   ng
        nf   ns
        nv   nz

(13)   ku siinza   'to worship'
        ku toonda   'to create'
        mu leenzi   'boy' (noun class 1)
        ku laba   'to see'
        kuu n daba   'to see me' (l > d after n)

A simple generalization emerges that links vowel length and nasal-obstruent clusters: only long vowels may precede nasal-obstruent clusters. Furthermore, when (and only when) a vowel precedes this cluster, the syllable division *on the surface* is between the long vowel and the nasal, rather than between the nasal and the following obstruent. The nasal-obstruent cluster thus behaves like the beginning of the subsequent syllable. If the nasal-obstruent cluster is not preceded by a vowel – that is, if it is phrase-initial – then the syllabification is different. The nasal becomes syllabic, and thus eligible to bear a tone. We shall return to the interaction of V-slots and tone-bearing characteristics below in chapter 3.

If we step back from this description of the facts for a moment and think about them from an autosegmental point of view, we see that once again a vowel-lengthening phenomenon is linked to another process, this time the creation of syllable-initial nasal-obstruent clusters. What could be more natural than to continue the same kind of analysis as was proposed above for glide-long vowel sequences?

We are thus led to the conclusion that a nasal segment is underlyingly accorded an associated position on the skeletal tier, just as we have seen other segments to be. We shall represent the skeletal position to which a nasal will underlyingly associate, and to which a vowel will reassociate, with the symbol X, indicating that it is unspecified for the feature [consonantal]. The last example in (13) will then be represented as in (14), underlyingly.[6] A reassociation entirely parallel to those that we looked at above now takes place, with the segment *n* reassociating to the following C-slot, making a complex segment *nl* (eventually becoming *nd*), and with the vowel of the prefix *ku* reassociating to the skeletal slot formerly occupied by the prefix *n*.

(14)
$$
\begin{array}{cccc}
\text{C V} & \text{X} & \text{C V C V} & \\
| \ \ | & | & | \ | \ | \ | & \\
\text{k u} & \text{n} & \text{l a b a} & \\
\text{inf.} & \text{1st} & \text{look-at} & \text{'to look at me'} \\
& \text{sg.} & &
\end{array}
$$

We shall write the lengthening rule as in (15), parallel to rule (8) above. This rule links the vowel with the X-position, making the vowel thereby a long vowel. Because the nasal is associated with an X-position, we know that it is syllable final rather than syllable-initial; that is, this formulation of the rule will not make the error of associating the vowel *b* with the C-position of a syllable-initial nasal.

(15)
$$
\begin{array}{cc}
\text{V} & \text{X} \\
\end{array}
$$
$$
\begin{array}{cc}
\alpha & [+\text{nasal}]
\end{array}
$$

Finally we must write a rule to reassociate the now floating nasal segment, a rule parallel to (9) above which associated the glides: rule (16). This rule creates a complex segment, a prenasalized stop, associated

(16)

$$
\begin{array}{cc}
& \text{C} \\
([+\text{nasal}]) & \alpha
\end{array}
$$

with one skeletal position. (17) is, then, the surface form resulting from the application of (15) and (16) to (14).

This treatment of lengthening suggests not only that a long vowel is a

(17)
$$
\begin{array}{cccc}
\text{C V} & \text{X} & \text{C V C V} \\
| \ | & & | \ | \ | \ | \\
\text{k u} & \text{n} & \text{d a b a}
\end{array}
$$

vowel doubly associated to skeletal positions, but that the nasal-consonant clusters of the type seen in (17) are phonologically parallel to contour tones, in the sense that on the skeletal tier they are associated to a single position, but on the tier containing the consonant and vowel autosegments they are composed of two segments. Thus, as it is with tones, so it is with consonants and vowels: associations can in principle be many to one, or one to many, across the various tiers. We will return to this point in section 2.2.4 below.

We have assumed up to now, without explicit discussion, that the underlying representations in Luganda contain material on both the skeletal tier and the phonemic tier, as well as the association lines joining them. One might wonder whether it is necessary to have both tiers underlyingly, or whether the underlying material on the skeletal tier might not be predictable, and therefore created by rule. Furthermore, one might wonder, irrespective of the answer to the preceding question, whether the association lines were not predictable (by the Association Convention, for example), and therefore unnecessary in the underlying representation.

It is not hard to show that some aspects of the skeleton in Luganda are not predictable, and therefore should appear in the underlying representations. In some contexts, whether a vowel is long or short is unpredictable, as we have seen in (3); similarly, geminates contrast with simple consonants after short vowels, as in (18). Thus, stems like -*liim*- ('spy') and -*bba*- ('steal') will contain at least the material shown in (19). These representations will later be found in larger structures, as in (20).

(18)   ku-yiga   'to learn'   ku-yigga   'to hunt'
           mu-go   'rim of a pot' mu-ggo   'stick'

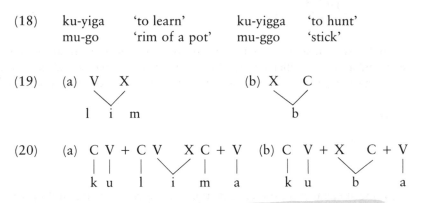

The elements on the skeletal tier with which the vowels and consonants will associate are predictable (except for the long vowels and consonants, which are lexicalized as in (19)); an element specified for a Point of Articulation is associated with a C-segment, and all others are associated with V-positions. This construction of the material on the skeleton takes place at word-level in Luganda, and is part and parcel of the syllabification process, an area that we will discuss at greater length in the next chapter.

The primary significance of the example that we have considered so far involves the use of the skeletal tier during the phonological derivation. The association between the skeletal tier and the phonemic tier has been largely one-to-one, with the only departures from this association either coming during the course of the derivation, owing to the effect of phonological rule, or, in the case of geminate consonants and basic long vowels, arising out of a lexical specification in which a single element on the phonemic tier is associated with two skeletal positions.

More strikingly autosegmental structures would naturally be expected now, involving representations that crucially contained segments that are unassociated, on either the skeletal or the phonemic tier. In the next two sections we will look at those two cases, before returning briefly to the case of multiple autosegmental association. We will then address the issue of compensatory lengthening, already touched on in this section, and after that will discuss some of the properties of geminate consonants and long vowels that have been noted in the literature, and consider to what extent these are reflections of their special autosegmental status – that is, how these properties follow from a two-to-one skeleton-to-melody association.

2.2.2 Floating skeletal positions and segments

In the discussion so far, we have seen that a phonological theory that incorporates the notion of positions on the skeletal tier contains a distinctive theory of quantity. This derives in large measure from the mismatch that can arise between autosegments and the positions on the skeletal tier, and the many-to-one association that can arise thereby.

In addition, it is possible to find cases in which a position on the skeletal tier remains unassociated (and is thus phonetically unrealized) but shows its presence by interacting with phonological rules sensitive to the organization of the skeletal tier.[7] We saw in Luganda, where the skeletal tier contains the phonological feature [±syllabic], that all extra underlying skeletal positions were underlyingly linked; these involved geminate consonants and long vowels. In French, on the other hand, so-called 'h-aspiré' words have the form given in (21).

Rules of French phonology that are sensitive to whether a word begins with a vowel or a consonant treat such words as if they began with a

(21)   C V C V C V   [ariko] *haricot* 'bean'
        | | | | | |
        a r i k o

consonant, though phonetically they begin with a vowel. For example, the masculine definite article *le* [lə] loses its vowel before a vowel, as in *l'éléphant* 'the elephant' (from *le éléphant*) but not before a consonant, as in *le garçon* 'the boy'. Before words like *haricot*, with the initial floating C-slot, the article keeps its vowel: *le haricot*, not *l'haricot*. Other phenomena support the consonant-initial character of h-aspiré words. There is a phonologically based rule that places the feminine form of certain adjectives and specifiers before vowel-initial masculine nouns. The adjectives *vieux* [vyø]/*vieille* [vyey] 'old (masc./fem.)', and *beau* [bo]/ *belle* [bɛl] 'beautiful' take the feminine form before vowel-initial mascu-line nouns, though the orthography distinguishes this 'induced' feminine, with the spelling *vieil* instead of *vieille* in the case of the first adjective (e.g. *un* (masc.) *vieil ami* (masc.)), and *bel* in the second case. H-aspiré forms do not trigger this gender shift, thus displaying the behavior of C-initial words (e.g., *un beau haricot* 'a beautiful bean'). (This description of the alternation is not the standard one, but the one that appears to be correct; a recent discussion can be found in Plank 1984.)

Two unrelated American Indian languages provide striking examples of this same use of empty word-initial skeletal C-positions. These examples are from Seri, a Hokan language of northwestern Mexico, and Onondaga, an Iroquoian language of North America.

In Seri, there are several stems that phonetically begin with a vowel but have an initial C-slot on the skeletal tier. This C-slot manifests its presence by its interference with the operation of several phonological rules, only some of which we will sketch here; more details can be found in the account on which this description is based, Marlett and Stemberger (1983).

Seri has an eight-vowel system, with four distinct vowel qualities, each appearing in a short and a long form, as in (22). In (23a), we see the distal prefix *yo-* on certain verbs stems. When a stem begins with a short, low vowel, as in (23b), the prefix *yo-* will normally trigger the deletion of the immediately following vowel, along with compensatory lengthening.

(22) i   ii
      e   o   a   ee   oo   aa

However, there are certain stems that do begin with a low vowel, but fail to trigger this rule; two examples are given in (23c).

If we write the rule operative in the deletion and compensatory lengthening as in (24), then its non-application to a form as in (23c) can be understood if we posit the structure given in (25). A stem with an unassociated C-slot will not trigger the rule in (24), since the C-slot will

(23)

(a) C-initial stems	(b) V-initial stems	(c) Empty C-slot
yo-meke	i-yoo-p	yo-amWx
from *meke*	from *ap*	from *amWx*
'be lukewarm'	'sew'	'be brilliant'
i-yo-pii	yoo-taX	i-yo-enx
from *pii*	from *ataX*	from *enx*
'taste'	'go'	'play stringed instrument'

(24)

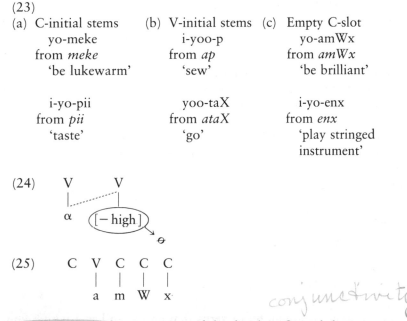

(25)

```
    C   V   C   C   C
    |   |   |   |   |
    a   m       W   x
```

conjunctivity

intervene between the V-position of the distal prefix and the V-position of the verb stem.

Another rule of Seri applies when two vowels *o* come into contact, converting them into a single, short *a*. This rule could be expressed as in (26) (though it also has an apparently syntactic condition on its application, which we ignore here). The rule deletes the second V-position and derounds the first vowel. (We may alternatively say that it deletes the first vowel instead of the second, or even that it leaves that vowel stranded; it makes no difference, for the vowel does not reassociate or reappear.) What is significant for our purposes is that there are two verbs in Seri that are apparent exceptions to (26) (*oł*, 'argue' and *oosx* 'sprinkle'), just as other stems are exceptions to (24). By reasoning similar to that above, we would suspect that they possess an empty C-slot at their beginning, as in (27). Viewed in this way, it is not surprising that such stems should fail to undergo rule (26), for once again the empty C-slot blocks the application of the rule, the form simply not meeting the structural

(26)

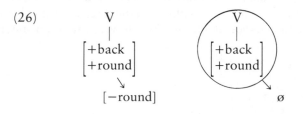

(27)
```
    C V - C V   V C C
    | |     \ /   | |
    y o      o   s x
```

description of (26), which requires two adjacent V-positions.

There is a third rule which applies when sequences of vowels arise after application of the two preceding rules. This rule will eliminate the vowel on the left in any such sequence of two vowels. As we have already seen, within the present framework it is not necessary to delete the vowel *per se*, but rather just the V-slot, since an autosegment not associated with any skeletal position will not be realized phonetically. The rule, then, is written as in (28).

(28)

Again, there is a handful of verbs that appear to begin with a vowel that do not trigger rule (28), as we see by the comparison in (29). The forms in the second column of (29) are again distal forms of the verb. The distal prefix, as we have seen, sometimes has the form *yo* and sometimes the form *iyo*. In (29a), the vowel of the prefix is lost; in (29b), the vowel of the prefix is maintained, just as if the stem began with a consonant.

(29)

	Stem		with /(i)yo/ prefixed
(a)	is	'be raw'	yis
	aaafk	'pound'	iyaaafk
(b)	ii	'feel'	iyoii
	isx	'grind'	iyoisx

Once again, the analysis available to us is of a stem with a floating C-position at the beginning, as in (30).

So far, all of these irregularities could have been handled by marking certain vowel-initial verb stems as exceptions to the three rules involved. However, other characteristics of the twenty-one verbs with an initial

(30)
```
    C V   V
       \ /
        i      'feel'
```

floating C-position support this analysis unambiguously. One such characteristic involves the rule of *i*-deletion.

A short *i* in an open syllable is deleted before a consonant, as indicated in (31). (We will discuss syllables in the next chapter; for now, the indications of syllables (σ) in (31) may be taken as an informal indication.) Thus, for example, when the prefix *si-* marking irrealis is added to the stem *-kaa* 'look for', the form *i-s-kaa* is derived (the initial *i* is not relevant to our point); similarly, the irrealis form *s-meke*, from the stem *meke* 'to be lukewarm', is derived from *si-meke*.

(31)

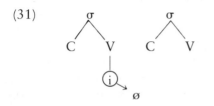

When the verb stem begins with a vowel, the rules of vowel deletion that we have already seen apply normally, and so, if the stem begins with a short low vowel (e.g. *-ap* 'sew'), that vowel is lost, and the *i* of *si* is lengthened (deriving *i-siip*). If the stem begins with any other vowel, then the vowel of the prefix is lost, as in *i-s-aafk*, from the stem *aafk* 'to pound', with an initial long *a:*.

However, the irrealis forms of the stems in which we have posited a floating C-position have a different surface realization for the irrealis prefix *si*. Here the short *i* of the prefix deletes, while the *s* geminates, as in (32).

(32)   C V́ C V C   (from the stem C V C)
        | | | | |
        s   a X   a X   'to be
                                                      hard'

Surface form: [ssaX]

Two things that happen here are of interest. First, the vowel *i* deletes, as if what followed were a consonant and not a vowel; this state of affairs points directly to the postulated C-position in these special stems. Second, in just these cases the *s* geminates; that is to say, it finds a second skeletal position to associate with. The position, of course, is the C-slot, and this may be derived by a rule as in (33). The association of this C-position leads to a formally natural account of the gemination associated with the otherwise exceptional class of vowel-initial stems; a rule-exception approach would offer no account of this coincidence. This

(33)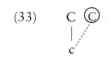

gemination occurs with all consonants that precede these verb stems. Furthermore, in five cases of prefix allomorphy, where the shape of a certain prefix is determined by whether the stem begins with a vowel or a consonant, the verb stems in question all behave as if they begin with a consonant. For example, the passive marker is *p* in front of verb-initial roots (e.g. *-p-esi* 'be defeated') and *aa*ʔ in front of consonant-initial stems (e.g. *aa*ʔ*-kani* 'be bitter'). The special verb stems in question act as if they begin with a consonant, as in *-aa*ʔ*-aX̌š* 'be hit', one of the stems for which we would postulate an initial floating C-position.

We find, then, that what appears to be irregularity in rule application in Seri is not a phonological irregularity at all, but rather an unusual match, or mismatch, between parts of the phonology that under more normal circumstances would be expected to be aligned. In this case the oddity is the mismatch between the material on the skeletal tier and the autosegmental consonantal and vocalic material available to associate with these positions. Viewed from a slightly more general perspective, we could say that the analysis offered here is parallel to an analysis of tone in which there are morphemes with a mismatch between the number of tones on one tier, and the number of tone-bearing elements that these tones have to associate with.

Another example of the same sort of phenomenon has been offered by Michelson (1985), involving stems in Onondaga that historically began with an *r*, but no longer do. All such *r*s have been lost synchronically in the language. Several indications confirm that there exists a class of stems that appear to begin with a vowel, but which on the skeletal tier begin with an unassociated C-slot. These stems are those that originally began with an *r*; an example is *ęhwętat* 'to make an opening', where the cedilla marks nasalization. We will refer to these as empty-C-stems.

The evidence that such stems should be analyzed as in (34) includes the

(34)   C V C C V C V C   ęhwętat 'make an opening'
        | | | | | | | |
        ę h w ę t a t

following points. First, the neuter agent prefix is *ka* when the stem begins with a consonant or the vowel *i*, but it is *w* when the stem begins with *e*, *ę*, or *a*. In front of empty-C-stems, the form chosen is *ka*, however, reflecting the presence of the C position on the skeletal tier. (Compare *te-w-ętaké* 'two days', with a regular stem beginning with *e*, to *te-ka-*

ęhwę́:tats 'it is making an opening', our empty-C-slot stem.)

Second, there is a prefix (the masculine plural agent prefix) which has the form *hati-* before a consonant-initial stem, and the form *hęn* before a vowel-initial stem. Before empty-C-stems, the *hati* alternant is used (e.g., *te-hati-yęhwę:tats* 'they are making an opening'; the *y* phonologically inserted).

Third, the sequence *a* + *i* normally coalesces to *ę*; for example, *ka* − *i*ʔtę:ʔ 'it's at home' surfaces as [kęʔtę:ʔ]. But if the *a* and the *i* are separated by an empty C-slot, this coalescence is blocked, as in [kaihwiyó] 'the good word'. Fourth, if a mid vowel (e,o,ǫ) is followed by another vowel across a morpheme boundary, the second vowel is normally deleted. (Thus we find [e-tę:ʔ] from underlying *ye-itę:ʔ*; the initial glide is also lost.) However, if the following stem is an empty-C-stem, this deletion is blocked; for example, *te-ye-ęhwętats* becomes [teyeęhwę:tats] 'she is making an opening', as expected.

Fifth, an apparent irregularity in a morphologically controlled epenthesis rule can be understood under this account. The vowel *a* (called a 'stem-joiner' by Iroquoianists) is inserted between a nominal root ending in a consonant and a verb root beginning with a consonant in the formation of a verb. This rule applies when the verb root is an empty-C-stem, as well. The verb meaning 'to be in', for example, deriving historically from the single segment **r*, consists today of a single C-slot; but this suffices to trigger the a-epenthesis, as in [kayaʔtáęnyǫʔ], from *ka-ya ʔt-C-ę-nǫ-ʔ* 'it has pictures in it', where C represents the empty-C-stem verb in question.

The lines of argumentation sketched so far involve cases where the presence of the C-slot either causes a rule to be triggered or blocks a rule from applying. In addition, just as we saw in Seri, there are additional reasons to support the postulation of an empty C-slot based on the naturalness of the reassociation of a segment to that empty C-slot. Two rules exist in Onondaga which reassociate a segment to an empty C-slot, and to only that. The first is a rule whose operation was briefly alluded to above, in the second argument mentioned. This is a rule that reassociates either an *i* or an *o* to a following empty C-slot; that reassociation creates what is transcribed as a *y* or *w*, phonetically, as illustrated in (35). In

(35)
```
    C V   C V C V     C V C C V C V C V
    | |   | | | | /   | | | | | | | |   surface:
    t e   h a t i     ę h w ę t a t s    [tehati-y-ęhwę:tats]
```

addition, there is a rule that associates a vowel leftward to an empty C-slot when the C-slot is immediately preceded by a consonant in the preceding syllable, giving a long vowel as illustrated in (36).

(36)
```
C V + C V C + C V C C V C V C V    [tewakę: hwętá:ti]
| |   | | |   \/  | | | | | | |    'I have made an
t e   w a k   ę  h w ę t a t i     opening'
```

There remains, thus, little doubt that these empty-C-stems must, indeed, be analyzed with an unassociated skeletal position underlyingly, specified as a consonantal element.

In light of our discussion so far, there is nothing in principle to rule out the possibility of an underlying representation with more segments on the phonemic tier than on the skeletal tier, the symmetric counterpart to the cases discussed in the previous section, illustrated in the hypothetical representation in (37). In our present state of knowledge, however, it appears that lexical *stems* of this sort do not exist, except when the skeletal tier forms a separate morpheme, a case that we shall look at in greater detail in section 2.3 below.

(37) C   V
```
     |   |
     b   a  l
```

I should emphasize precisely what it is of which no examples have been found: it is cases of stems (as opposed to affixes) in which there are elements on the phonemic tier to which there are no corresponding skeletal positions at the deepest level in which there may be found associations between the two tiers; furthermore, this gap is limited to languages where the skeletal tier of the stem is determined solely by the lexical entry of the stem, and not by additional grammatical or morpho-logical considerations. Thus, examples of the sort of mismatch sketched in (37) can be found in the case of suffixes,[8] and even in stems in the case of languages where the skeletal tier is determined independently of the choice of lexical stem (as we see in section 2.3 below).

If further investigation reveals this to be a true gap, as seems likely at this point, then an explanation for this would be called for. A formal explanation for the lack of underlying representations like (37) would look for an account of the difference between positions (or segments) on the skeletal tier and those on other (here, phonemic) tiers. The most striking difference is that, in the overwhelming percentage of cases, the elements found on the skeletal tier are derivable or predictable, given what we know the phonemic material to be. The converse, of course, is not true: knowing that the skeleton has the elements CVC on it does not tell us what is present on the phonemic tier.

In most cases, then, the skeletal tier material is predictable, and could be derived by rule from a single-tier lexical entry. This would mean that the underlying representation contained linear strings of consonants and vowels, and that the first constructive rule would be to assign a C-position on the skeleton to each consonant, and a V-position to each vowel. This is illustrated in (38). The only cases where this procedure would not obviously suffice would be (i) that of underlying geminate or long segments, which we have seen require two elements on the skeletal tier in their deepest representation, and (ii) that of representations with empty C-slots or V-slots.

(38) Splitting

$$
\begin{bmatrix} -\text{syllabic} \\ -\text{voice} \\ +\text{coronal} \\ +\text{anterior} \end{bmatrix}
\begin{bmatrix} +\text{syllabic} \\ +\text{voice} \\ -\text{high} \\ +\text{low} \end{bmatrix}
\rightarrow
[-\text{syllabic}] \quad [+\text{syllabic}]
$$
$$
\begin{array}{cc}
| & | \\
\begin{bmatrix} -\text{voice} \\ +\text{coronal} \\ +\text{anterior} \end{bmatrix} &
\begin{bmatrix} +\text{voice} \\ -\text{high} \\ +\text{low} \end{bmatrix}
\end{array}
$$

The second case, involving empty C- or V-slots, is a less serious objection, and its resolution paves the way for a possible response to the first objection. The linear underlying representations of the sort shown in (38) would contain the feature [±syllabic], as we see; a segment that was defined only for that feature would be a segment found in a fully linear representation representing only a place – eventually, after splitting – on the skeletal tier. If we permit underlying segments that are unspecified for all the features that will appear on the phonemic tier, then these segments will become, after the splitting procedure of (38), the floating skeletal positions that we require.

These elements could then be put to further use as a way of representing geminates (or long vowels). A lexically specified geminate, as in the artificial example *taddo* (of the sort we saw in Luganda, for example), could be represented as in (39) (where only some of the distinctive features have been included for simplicity's sake), which, after splitting, would become (40); C, of course, represents [−syllabic], as V does [+syllabic]. A later rule would associate the floating C to the phonemic material, producing the desired geminate. A similar procedure could represent long vowels.

(39)
$$
\begin{bmatrix} -\text{syllabic} \\ -\text{voice} \\ +\text{coronal} \\ -\text{sonorant} \end{bmatrix}
\begin{bmatrix} +\text{syllabic} \\ -\text{high} \\ +\text{low} \\ +\text{sonorant} \end{bmatrix}
[-\text{syllabic}]
\begin{bmatrix} -\text{syllabic} \\ +\text{voice} \\ +\text{coronal} \\ -\text{sonorant} \end{bmatrix}
\begin{bmatrix} +\text{syllabic} \\ -\text{high} \\ -\text{low} \\ +\text{sonorant} \end{bmatrix}
$$

(40)

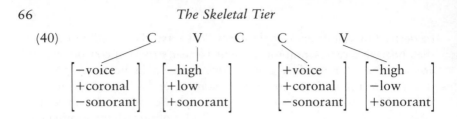

This discussion, it must be emphasized, presents a sketch of one approach to accounting for the apparent nonexistence of stems as in (37), and it must therefore appeal to a qualitative difference between the feature(s) that appear on the skeletal tier and those on the phonemic tier. In order for the explanation to work satisfactorily, we must provide an account for why the inverse of the barely specified elements of (39) could not exist, that is, segments specified for all features except the feature [syllabic] – a *t*, for example, specified for place of articulation, and manner, and voicing, but not for the feature [syllabic]. Such segments, if they could exist, would emerge at the end of the splitting procedure of (38) as segments on the phonemic tier but without a corresponding element on the skeletal tier. We are thus forced to look deeper for a difference between the characteristics of the elements on the skeletal tier and those on the phonemic tier. One such approach would say, for example, that *all* elements underlying the skeletal/phonemic tier splitting of (38) must be assigned (and thus associated with) a skeletal tier position; but this, alas, is no more than a disguised form of the conclusion that we are trying to reach.

For the moment, then, we must leave the question open, awaiting further studies and a deeper understanding of the way in which the skeletal tier is formed in those languages where it is phonologically predictable.

2.2.3   Multiple association

Just as the treatment of contour tones as the multiple attachment of level tones to single vowels is an important feature of the autosegmental analysis of tone systems, so too is the possibility of multiple associations of phonemic material to skeletal positions. We have already seen one example of this (the prenasalized stops derived by rule in Luganda, section 2.1), and in this section we shall consider several others.

It is important to emphasize that the multiple association that we are discussing here refers to a structure as in (41a), where two successive segments on a single tier are associated to a single position (or slot) on the skeletal tier; we are not discussing the kind of multiple association that might arise if elements on two distinct autosegmental tiers both associated with the same skeletal position, as in (41b). These two quite different types of structures have been called in the literature *contour* and *complex* structures, respectively (see e.g. Sagey 1986).

(41) (a)   x   (b)   A

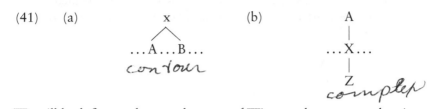

We will look first at the vowel system of Witoto, a language spoken in Peru, as described by Minor (1956). There are six basic vowels: *a, e, i, o, u,* and ə (transcribed as *î* by Minor; *e* and *o* are lax vowels, according to the author). However, what could be transcribed as sequences of vowels (identical or distinct) must be distinguished in terms of the length of the sequence. The sequence *ui*, for example, must be distinguished with respect to whether it is pronounced with the length of timing normally given to two moras, or to one. That is, just as many languages distinguish between a long and a short version of a single vowel (as in (42)), Witoto distinguishes a long and a short version of a sequence of vowels, a distinction that can be characterized in precisely the same way using the skeletal notation (43). Based on notions of syllable weight discussed in the next chapter, the two types of diphthongs represented in (43a,b) are called *heavy* and *light* diphthongs, respectively. For example, the final syllable – the sequence *ue* of *hipíkue* 'brook of the Caymita people' – has the phonetic value of two moras, while the final syllable of *əikue* 'I'm a man' has the phonetic value of one mora; they are otherwise identical. The former is represented as in (43a), and the latter as in (43b).

Since there are six basic vowels of Witoto, we would expect that there would be thirty-six possible diphthongs composed of two-vowel qualities, just as a tone language with three tones would be expected to have nine contour tones, all other things being equal, if two tones are permitted per vowel. In fact, of the thirty-six possible 'double' diphthongs in Witoto, thirty-two are attested (the missing sequences are *eu, ou, uə,* and

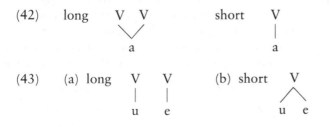

uo), a success rate at least as good as what is generally attested in the inventory of contour tones in a tone language.

There are, in addition, four sequences that are mono-moraic (as far as the skeleton is concerned) but are composed of three segments on the phonemic tier: these are described as *əaə, iaə, uai, aəi,* and are represented as in (44).

(44)

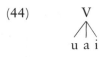

The treatment of multiple association to vowel positions is thus a straightforward one within the representational system that we are considering.[9] When we turn to the case of multiple association of consonantal material to skeletal position, a certain amount of care is necessary. In general, it is far more difficult to produce phonological reasons to think that what might be viewed as two consonantal segments only correspond to (or 'are associated with', as we would say now) a single skeletal position. Vowels offer greater opportunity in this respect, for the quantity of time devoted to their pronunciation is highly salient, both perceptually and with respect to phonological processes such as stress assignment.

The most striking cases where consonantal skeletal positions are doubly associated involve nasalization. We have already seen an example of this in Luganda, where all nasals followed by obstruents became linked to the following skeletal position, yielding pre-nasalized stops. We will look at another, similar situation in a moment.

The suggestion has been made on a number of occasions that affricates might best be treated in parallel fashion. After all, it has been pointed out, the affricate is inherently composed of sequential and even contradictory specifications: it begins as a stop and ends as a fricative. Why not use autosegmental notation to analyze the affricate as being, like a contour tone, a sequence of stop and fricative associated with a single skeletal position, as in (45)?

In principle, the suggestion is reasonable, and is correct, we may argue, in a few cases, but it is unlikely as a general analysis, in the light of what is presently known. Before discussing the problems that such an approach encounters, it is worthwhile trying to clarify whether there is indeed a problem to be solved by proposing the contour segment representation as

(45)

in (45). The observation that the feature that defines affricates ([delayed release]) is phonetically different from all other features is correct, but it hardly provides justification in itself for the analysis. Each feature is unique in some respect or other; that is in itself not a problem in need of theoretical resolution.

But the most striking difficulty for an analysis of affricates as in (45) is the same problem that traditional analyses of affricates as sequences of stop-plus-fricative have foundered on: affricates are often found in languages without fricatives (most dialects of Spanish, for example, have a voiceless alveopalatal affricate [č], but no fricative [š]). The treatment of contour tones as sequences of level tones is based virtually entirely on the knowledge we can get of the characteristic behavior of the component pieces of the contour tone, the level tones that compose it. If we could not identify the individual parts of the contour tone as existing units within the language, we would have little or no reason to propose a sequential analysis for the contour tones. (It may thus well be that some languages do have contour tones that are not decomposable into sequences of level tones; this case has been argued, for example by Newman (1986a), with regard to Grebo.)

One may look, then, for phonological evidence that rules treat affricates as stops when viewed from the left (so to speak), but as fricatives when viewed from the right. In general, this is not the case. Rood (1975) presents a clear case of a language (Wichita, a Caddoan language of North America) with a least three rules creating the palatal affricate *c* (i.e. *ts*): a sequence of *r* plus either *t* or *s* across morpheme boundary merges to *c*; a sequence of *t* plus either *s* or *r* across morpheme boundary creates *c*; and *t* followed by either the vowel *i* or any consonant, across a morpheme boundary, becomes *c*. Rood offers the suggestion that one can understand these rules (and the other rules that he explores) only against the background of, first, the impoverished segmental inventory of the language, and, second, a featural analysis in which the affricate *c* is marked as [+continuant], a feature specification it will then share with the true fricatives and the liquid *r*, and as [+interrupted], a feature specification that *c* will share with the true stops and with *r*. Rood's discussion leaves no room for viewing the affricate *c* in Witchita as a complex structure of the sort sketched in (45), and such cases seems to be typical. (Sagey 1986 presents two sets of evidence suggesting that affricates can form a natural class with fricatives to the exclusion of the stops in some cases, but the evidence there is far less than is needed to establish the case in general.)

There are cases that suggest that certain affricates are created auto-segmentally. These, however, require looking at more complex auto-segmental structures, those in which the feature structure is broken down into separate tiers for a large number of features. We will discuss this in more detail in chapter 6, but in the present context we may consider briefly a case in which an affricate is created in a form like that suggested in (45). This example is provided by Spanish, and involves its voiced stops, produced late in the phonology (see Lozano 1978; Goldsmith 1981a; Clements 1987). In Spanish, the voiced obstruents, written orthographically *b* or *v*, *d*, *g*, are unspecified for the feature [continuant], and the assignment of this feature proceeds in a way that is closely related to the pervasive process of point of articulation assimilation for nasals and laterals. As we shall see in more detail in chapter 6, the features used to specify the point of articulation of a consonant cluster together in a number of ways that indicate that they form the features of a distinct autosegmental tier, and we shall assume that the feature [continuant] too is on a separate tier at this point in the derivation.[10]

There is a late rule in Spanish affecting nasal consonants which makes them homorganic to the following consonant. (A similar rule makes an *l* homorganic to a following coronal consonant.) This process is best represented as a post-lexical autosegmental process which spreads the point of articulation autosegment leftward onto any preceding nasal consonant. (As Harris (1984) points out, the correct generalization is that a nasal in the rhyme of the syllable will receive its point of articulation from the element to its right; in the terms developed in the next chapter, we would say that a nasal in the rhyme does not license a point of articulation.) The rule for nasals is given in (46a), where the point of articulation (P of A) features are placed above the skeletal tier.

The voiced obstruents in Spanish, as mentioned above, are predictably stops or spirants, depending on the phonological context. In the case of structures created by rule (46a), the voiced obstruent is realized as a [−continuant], i.e. as a stop; thus, *un Beso* (where *B* represents a voiced bilabial unspecified for the feature [continuant]) is realized as [umbeso] *un beso* 'a kiss', with a bilabial stop. Put differently, if the consonant has participated in the rule of nasal point of articulation assimilation, it will 'become' a stop. Similarly, there is a rule of lateral assimilation in Spanish (Harris 1969: 18-20), assimilating an *l* to the point of articulation of a following dental, alveolar, or alveopalatal segment. When the *coronal* voiced obstruent (orthographically *d*) serves as the element that *l* assimilates to by this rule, it is realized as a stop, as in *el deðo* 'the finger', where the first *d* is a stop, following the *l* of the article. In all other cases but one, a voiced obstruent is realized as a [+continuant], i.e. as a fricative (e.g. [unaβaka] *una vaca* 'a cow', not *[unabaka]). The one other case to mention is phrase-initial position, where either form is possible, though the stop form is preferred (e.g. [bamanos] or [βamanos] *vamanos* 'let's go'). The important generalization seems to link together

(46)   (a)   [P of A]   [P of A]

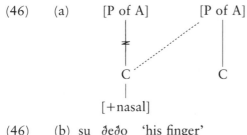

(46)   (b) su ðeðo   'his finger'
             el deðo   'the finger'
             un deðo   'a finger'
             su βeso   'her kiss'
             um beso   'a kiss'
             su ɣato   'her cat'
             uŋ gato   'a cat'

the application of two apparently quite different rules in a surprising way.

We now can write a rule as in (47), associating the autosegment [−continuant] from the assimilated sonorant to the following consonant.[11]

(47)   [P of A]

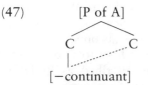

This discussion is all by way of introducing a case where affricates are best analyzed autosegmentally. In those southern South American dialects where there is an underlying alveopalatal fricative ž (corresponding to the orthographic *ll* and most *y*s, as the dialect of Buenos Aires), this segment is lexically marked as [+continuant]. When the process indicated in (47) applies to a ž – as with the sequence *nž*, which becomes a sequence of a nasal stop followed by an affricate [nǰ] – then we find a sequence of [−continuant] [+continuant] on the same segment, as in (48); thus, n + ž → ñ dž (e.g. *con llave* [kondžaβe]) 'with key'.

Now, it is worth emphasizing, first, that this analysis is not available for the truly underlying affricate in Spanish, the č, and, second, that in other cases arguments for the complex nature of affricates are hard to come by. Tonal systems often provide phonologically governed alternations between contour tones and level tones, creating and destroying contour tones by adding or deleting association lines. The parallel case to

(48)

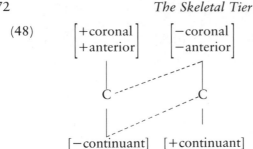

$$
\begin{bmatrix} +\text{coronal} \\ +\text{anterior} \end{bmatrix} \qquad \begin{bmatrix} -\text{coronal} \\ -\text{anterior} \end{bmatrix}
$$

C --------------------- C

[−continuant]   [+continuant]

expect here concerns alternations between stops and affricates, and alternations between fricatives and affricates.

The first, of course, is commonly found. Stops frequently alternate with affricates, but the conditions are based on articulatory structure; coronal stops frequently become affricates under the influence of a following vowel *i* or a yod (the glide *y*), for example. Stops do not typically simply become affricates when followed by a fricative. On the other hand, the second possibility – that of alternation between fricatives and affricates – is much rarer. One such case is found in Mayan,[12] where there is a phonological rule that changes (non-glottalized) affricates to their corresponding fricatives when they are immediately followed by a homorganic stop or affricate (e.g. *hač čičan* › *haš čičan* 'very little'). The fact that the right-hand condition treats stops and affricates as a natural class is not the interesting point, since the traditional analysis has always recognized that affricates are a subclass of stops (as opposed to being a subclass of fricatives). Rather, the question is how to understand the change that would in feature notation be described as '[+Delayed Release] becomes [−Delayed Release]'. If an affricate were described as in (45), then the change of *č+č* to *š+č* would be as indicated in (49):

(49)

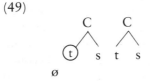

C   C

(t)   s   t   s

ø

But this formal representation gives no indication of the naturalness of the change; in fact, in this sequential representation of the affricate, the change in the affricate is taken to be on the left-hand side, while the crucial environment is on the right-hand side, quite the opposite of what would be expected. At this point, a reasonable conclusion is that affricates in an underlying inventory of segments are not analyzed autosegmentally, as in (45) or (49), while affricates that are introduced as a new type of 'segment' later in the derivation (in the post-lexical phonology; see chapter 5) are of that form.

2.2.4 *Compensatory lengthening*

We have already touched on the matter of 'compensatory lengthening'. The term refers generally to a process of lengthening a segment – most commonly a vowel, but not always – which is seen as a response to a prior process which removed or in some way shortened the segments previously present. One segment, we might say, makes up in length for what is lost to the utterance as a whole when another segment loses all or part of its own length.

This formulation leaves open whether compensatory lengthening is to be viewed as a historical process or as part of the synchronic grammar, and indeed, the term is used equally in the two cases. Our particular interest here is the nature of compensatory lengthening as a process in a synchronic grammar, a point where autosegmental representation is relevant.

There are two points to be made briefly in this section. The first is to clarify precisely what characteristics of autosegmental representation are helpful in understanding compensatory lengthening; the second involves the role that syllable structure plays in understanding compensatory lengthening.

If we allow ourselves a definition of compensatory lengthening (CL) that is defined strictly within an autosegmental framework, then we may say more directly that a process is an example of CL if it contains the material in (50), where X and Y are on the skeletal tier, and M is on a phonemic tier. In this representation, M and X are associated to each other, and Y is not associated to any element on M's tier. The process of CL associates M and Y, as the broken line suggests. At least one further condition must be met for this process to be an example of CL: Y must have been associated with an element on M's tier at an earlier stage of the derivation.

(50)   X   Y
        L_{----}
        M

Thus, for example, if a sonorant at the end of a syllable is deleted, and the preceding vowel is subsequently lengthened, we have a representation as in (51), which is a special case of (50), and hence of compensatory lengthening. The lengthening of the vowel in this case consists not of a feature change, but of the addition of an association line. It has been a characteristic of all of the autosegmental rules discussed in this book that they either delete an autosegment (in a few cases) or add association lines (or, in the odd case, delete an association line). It would not be wrong, in fact, to summarize the entire goal of autosegmental analysis as being the reduction of natural phonological processes to changes that can be expressed in the minimal autosegmental notation, a notation that includes at its core just deletion and reassociation. It is in this sense that compensatory lengthening should be understood as supporting the basic perspective of autosegmental phonology. In chapter 6 we shall also consider the extent to which the reassociation that actually constitutes the lengthening may be predicted by principles internal to autosegmental theory (a point that we will also touch on briefly in the discussion below in this chapter on Turkish).

The figure in (51) illustrates an important point with regard to the occurrence of compensatory lengthening: the element on the skeletal tier that is the recipient (so to speak) of the new association is virtually always in a particular position in its syllable, the coda. We have not

(51)

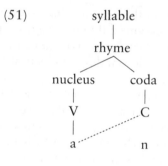

discussed the internal structure of the syllable so far, and that is the subject of the next chapter; nonetheless, a brief foray into this matter will be of use to us.

As we shall see in chapter 3, all utterances may be divided into sequences of syllables, and all syllables into an *onset*, consisting of an initial sequence of zero or more consonants, followed by a *rhyme*. The rhyme, in turn, is composed of a *nucleus*, containing the obligatory vowel of the syllable, plus the *coda*, a final section of the syllable that may contain either consonantal positions or positions that are also associated with vowel material on the phonemic tier. As this description suggests, the structuring that the syllable imposes is done on the skeletal tier; that is to say, the syllable is a statement of constituent structure imposed on the slots on the skeletal tier. Elements on the phonemic tiers (or tonal tiers, or any tier apart from the skeletal tier) may be said to be in the onset or the rhyme indirectly, for they may be associated with skeletal positions that are themselves in particular positions in the syllable.

We may now restate the generalization mentioned above regarding the relevance of syllable structure to compensatory lengthening: the target of reassociation – point Y in (50) – is in almost all cases in the coda of its syllable, rather than in the onset or nucleus. The following example from Turkish, based on Sezer (1985), illustrates this point.

It will suffice for our present purposes to assume that, when a single consonant appears between vowels, it is always syllabified as part of the onset of the syllable that contains the vowel on the right, rather than as part of the coda of the syllable containing the vowel on the left. Furthermore, if two consonants appear between a pair of vowels, the consonants belong to separate syllables: the first consonant forms the coda of the syllable to the left, while the second consonant forms the onset of the syllable to the right. Thus, the words *savmak* 'to get rid of' and *davul* 'drum' are syllabified as in (52).

(52)

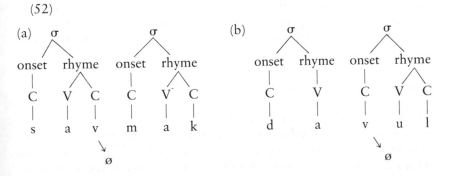

There is an optional rule of v-deletion which performs the deletion indicated in (52); the rule applies under complex conditions, and it creates the outputs shown in (53). Only in the case of (52a/53a), however, is there any compensatory lengthening – here, that of the

(53)

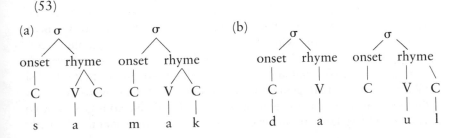

preceding vowel, which becomes long. The generalization involved is that an unattached skeletal position in the rhyme – and, in particular, in the coda – will reassociate to the closest available rhyme element, which here is the vowel on the left. An unattached skeletal position in the onset, however, remains unattached, and does not serve as the basis for any lengthening process.

The same generalization holds for the output of two other segment-deletion rules, optional rules that delete *h* and *y*. Sezer notes that 'in syllable-final position, *h* is deleted before a continuant or a nasal stop'. In all such cases, the *h* is in the syllable coda, and the immediately preceding vowel compensatorily lengthens (e.g., variation between [kahya] and [ka:ya] 'steward'; [sahte] and [sa:te] 'counterfeit'). When the *h* occurs as the onset of a syllable, it may be deleted after a vowel or a voiceless consonant, but here there is no compensatory lengthening (e.g. [sihirbaz] and [siirbaz] 'magician'; [tohum] and [toum] 'seed').

Again, *y* can drop in informal speech when it appears after a front vowel and when it is also followed by either a sonorant consonant or the vowel *i*. In the former case, it is part of a coda, and compensatory lengthening results from the deletion (cf. [seyret] vs. [se:ret] 'watch'); in the latter case, it is part of the next syllable's onset, and hence no compensatory lengthening occurs upon deletion (cf. [deyil] and [deil], but not *[de:il] 'is not').

2.2.5   The special behavior of geminates

There are several general characteristics of geminate consonants (and, to some extent, long vowels) that researchers in phonological theory have been investigating for some years, beginning in pre-autosegmental frameworks and continuing more recently within the skeletal theory that we are discussing here.[13] In this section we shall consider these special properties, and see some of the ways in which researchers have attempted to account for these characteristics within an autosegmental perspective.

(1)   The notion of 'syllable weight' is an important one in many languages, and we will discuss it in further detail in the next two chapters. Many languages draw a distinction between heavy and light syllables based on the number, and sometimes on the type, of segments within the syllable following its first vowel segment. A syllable such as [tek] has one segment following the vowel, and is thus often treated as a heavy syllable. Rules that are sensitive to syllable weight, or that establish syllable weight, treat geminate consonants as if they were two consonants. Thus, in a language in which a CVC syllable counts as a heavy syllable, and syllable boundaries occur between consonants when two

consonants appear together, we always find that, in a sequence like [bigga], the first syllable is treated as a heavy syllable. This is especially apparent in rules of accent placement. In this respect, geminate consonants act like sequences of consonants rather than, say, a single consonant marked [+long]. This generalization receives a natural explanation within an autosegmental–metrical theory of phonology, since metrical structure is built on the skeletal tier, and geminate consonants involve two positions on the skeletal tier. In languages with severe restrictions on syllable codas and onsets, the first of the skeletal slots of the geminate will close the syllable on its left, making that syllable metrically heavy. If a long consonant were a single segment, there would be no explanation for this general regularity.

(2) A second generalization that can be established is that geminate consonants frequently are allowed in positions where sequences of different consonants are not allowed. We have just seen an example of this in Luganda, and the same point could be made in languages as diverse as Italian and Japanese. A language may disallow sequences of distinct obstruents, but allow a geminate consonant. In this respect, geminate consonants do not seem to behave like sequences of consonants; somehow, it is as if their first half were *not* there. In a number of languages, we find that an obstruent must be associated with a syllable onset position; thus consonants will generally appear only in onset position, but may secondarily be associated with another position, one in the coda. This double association of a segment is, of course, a crucial use of autosegmental structure. We will discuss the nature of the syllable coda in more detail in section 3.4.

(3) A third generalization involves rules of epenthesis which insert a vowel in order to break up impermissible sequences. These rules generally fail to apply if their application would separate the halves of a geminate consonant. This characteristic has been said to reflect the *integrity* of geminate consonants, and suggests yet another way in which geminate consonants do not act like normal sequences of consonants.

For example, Frajzyngier (1980) discusses rules of epenthesis in Pero, a West Chadic language of Nigeria. Pero has a familiar five vowel system (*a, e, i, o, u*) with contrastive vowel length. Under several conditions, a short high vowel will be inserted to break up impermissible consonant sequences, and the roundness of the inserted vowel depends on the roundness of the following vowel (i.e., it is *u* if what follows is *o* or *u*, *i* otherwise), except in one case: if the epenthesized vowel is surrounded by palatal consonants and preceded by an *i*, it remains *i*. The restrictions in Pero on sequences of consonants involve two basic points. Except for nasal+palatal sequences (e.g, *nj*, as in Luganda), and geminate palatals *in the same morpheme*, palatal consonants may not be adjacent to another consonant. High vowel epenthesis will apply to repair any such contiguity, as when *ádd-jì* 'they always eat many' becomes [áddíjì]. Furthermore, sequences of three consonants will be broken up by an epenthesized high vowel as well, but whether the vowel is inserted in the position C_1–C_2C_3 or the position C_1C_2–C_3 depends on the phonological relationships among the three consonants. Owing to the application of various rules of assimilation, it will always be the case that one of the pairs C_1–C_2 and C_2-C_3 forms either a geminate cluster or a sequence of homorganic nasal+stop, but there will not be two such pairs in a single word. These pairs may not be separated by vowel epenthesis, and this restriction determines where the epenthesized vowel will appear. For example, *ádd-tù* 'eat many and come' has a vowel epenthesized after the geminate, becoming [áddúrù]; but when the two consonants of the stem are not geminate, the epenthetic vowel is inserted between them, as in *yekl-na* 'he mixed and came', which becomes [yéyɨllà], with the *n* assimilating to the preceding *l*. Thus, a geminate consonant displays a certain 'integrity', or a resistance to the insertion of a vowel that would break up its halves.

Similar phenomena have been noted in a wide range of languages. Guerssel (1978), for example, discussed precisely this problem in connection with a rule of schwa-insertion in the Ait Segrouchen dialect of Berber. Normally a schwa is inserted in the context C–CC, as in *t+bzəy* 'she is wet' [təbzəy], or *t+ffər* 'she hid' *[təffər]*. However, when the first two consonants of such a cluster form a geminate that has been created by a rule of assimilation, then the rule of schwa insertion fails to apply. Thus, *t+dlu* 'she covered' becomes [ddlu], and this form does not in turn undergo schwa insertion to become *[dədlu].

Again, in a similar vein, Bender (1968) reports that Marshallese, an Austronesian language of the Oceanic branch, has an epenthesis rule that inserts a rather fleeting vowel, somewhat shorter than an underlying vowel, when two consonants are adjacent. This epenthesis is not produced, however, if the two adjacent consonants are either identical or homorganic. There is one further statement, however: even two homorganic consonants will be separated by an epenthetic vowel if they appear word-initially. In the Eastern dialect, for example, the stem *lliw* 'angry', as in [yi-lliw] 'I am angry', surfaces with an epenthetic *i* as [liliw] when no prefixes are added to the stem. The behavior of Marshallese in this respect is extremely unusual.[14]

Several attempts have been made in the recent literature to provide a deeper understanding of the general behavior that has been sketched in these last few paragraphs. One explanation that has been offered for the integrity property is based on the idea that, in general, a rule will not apply if its effect is to create an association line that will cross an existing association line. (This idea itself seems to have a certain small number of counter-examples, but it certainly expresses a general tendency; in the case of rules that violate this generalization, the newly created association line is preserved, and the previously existing association line is deleted so as to avoid the illicit crossing of association lines.) If the phonemic tier contains the vowels and the consonants associated with the skeletal tier, then a rule that inserted both a V-position on the skeleton and a vocalic segment on the phonemic tier would create a line-crossing situation if it applied to break up a geminate, as in (54).

(54)

However, this account rests on the assumption that the epenthesis rule inserts a vowel segment as well as a V-position on the skeletial tier. The description given by Bender for Marshallese suggests that only a V-slot is inserted, and that the quality of the resultant vowel is produced by auto-segmental spreading from the neighboring vowels. Although the evidence is less clear in Pero, the spreading there of rounding from the vowel on the right suggests also that merely a skeletal V-slot is inserted by the epenthesis rule. Thus, this account of the integrity property depends on an assumption that is not at all certain — that epenthesis rules insert a particular vowel quality. At the very least, all other things being equal, this explanation suggests that, if an epenthesis rule did exist which only inserted a skeletal V-position, it could freely break up geminates, an unlikely result.

One might suppose that epenthesis rules that inserted vowel segments on the skeletal position might be able to apply to break up geminates, but then fail to be realized phonetically because they might never successfully be assigned a vowel on the phonemic tier. This approach, while interesting in principle, appears not to be tenable at this point, for two reasons. First, it suggests that, after epenthesis (in which a structure like (55) would be created), both C-positions on the skeletal tier would be expected to behave as if they were in syllable onset positions. (On this notion, see the discussion in the next chapter; this consequence was noted by G.N. Clements.)

Second, epenthesis rules will not infrequently place the epenthetic vowel in a different position if the 'normal' place for the epenthetic vowel

(55)

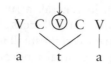

to go would be one that would break up a geminate. This is a character-istic that we observed above in Pero, for example. The hypothetical 'ghost' epenthesis sketched in (54) would fail to account for this, for on that account epenthesis can be successfully carried out from a deep, phonological point of view even in the case where it has the consequence of breaking up a geminate.

I will suggest a somewhat different view that will account for the bulk of these cases after discussing the notion of inalterability in the next paragraph.

(4)   A fourth generalization that has been noted is that rules that modify the segmental quality of consonants frequently fail to apply to geminates. This *inalterability*, as it has been called, of geminate consonants has been the subject of lively debate. We have already discussed above, in section 1.7, a principle that appears to be closely linked to the issue at hand, a principle we referred to there as the *Conjunctivity Condition*. (It has also been referred to in the literature as the 'Linkage Condition', a name which could lead to unfortunate confusion with principle (11) of the same name discussed earlier in this chapter.)

Readers will recall that the Conjunctivity Condition says that, if a rule deletes or modifies an autosegment A, then all relevant association lines associated with A must meet the structural description of the rule. Of course, if there are no association lines in the structural description of the rule — if the structural description of the rule operates entirely on one autosegmental tier — then this condition will put no restrictions on the application of the rule. If the rule only adds or deletes association lines, then the Conjunctivity Condition does not have any effect.

Current research suggests that this distinction correctly distinguishes between those phonological rules that do and those that do not apply to both single and geminate consonants. We may distinguish here between what have been called *true geminates* and *apparent geminates*. *True geminates* are multiply associated consonants, as in (56a); *apparent geminates* are those as in (56b). All of our observations concerning geminates apply to true geminates; apparent geminates will act like

(56)   (a) C   C   (b) C   C

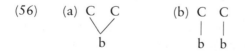

simple clusters. As far as is known, these two structures cannot be distinguished phonetically; the distinction is phonological. We will assume that all geminates that are internal to a single morpheme (*tautomorphemic geminates*) are true geminates, and that all geminates formed across a morpheme boundary are only apparent geminates, at least underlyingly. These assumptions involve an interpretation of the Obligatory Contour Principle, which we shall discuss in section 6.4.

One of the most striking and most widely noted examples in the literature that illustrates the different behavior of true and apparent geminates is found in Tigrinya, a Semitic language.[15] For reasons that we shall discuss below in section 2.3.2 (on Arabic, another Semitic language), we place vowels and consonants on separate autosegmental tiers. This point is not extremely important for the illustration at hand. In any event, in Tigrinya, true geminates are found in three cases: (i) within morphemes, as in the verbal root *fäkkärä* 'boast' (third-person masculine singular perfect), shown in (57a); (ii) in the case of geminates created by assimilation, as in (57b), since total assimilations must be created by the addition of an association line, as our theory tells us; or (iii) in the case of geminates created by morphemes whose suffixation produces a geminate, as in (57c), illustrating the result of attaching the third-person singular masculine suffix -*o* to a stem ending in a consonant.

In each of these cases, the geminate *k* fails to undergo a rule of spirantization (changing it to *x*), a rule that applies to both *k* and *q* when they are immediately preceded by a vowel. Examples where spirantization does apply are given in (58), where the symbol /q̣/ represents the spirantized *q*, and *x* the spirantized *k* (data from Schein 1981). In the

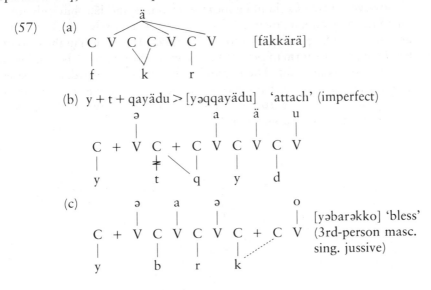

(57) (a)   C V C C V C V   [fäkkärä]

(b) y + t + qayädu > [yəqqayädu] 'attach' (imperfect)

(c)   [yəbarəkko] 'bless' (3rd-person masc. sing. jussive)

(58)   dəxäm   'weakness'
        mädämmäca   'buttocks'
        zäxti   'now'
        mäxdänti   'instrument for covering'
        suḏta   'silence'
        məbərax   'bless'
        ʔaxaləbti   'dogs'
        gäza + xa   'house-your'

three types of cases illustrated in (57), however, neither *k* nor *q*
undergoes spirantization. If spirantization is formalized as in (59), which
certainly seems reasonable, then the account needed to explain why
spirantization does not apply to the geminate cases will be found in the
Conjunctivity Condition. Spirantization fails to apply in (57) because the
rule of spirantization does more than add or delete association lines, and
in the case of a geminate consonant, only one of the skeletal positions to
which the *k* or *q* is associated is in the appropriate post-vocalic position.
Hence, spirantization will not apply to geminates.

(59) $\begin{bmatrix} -\text{sonorant} \\ -\text{anterior} \\ -\text{coronal} \end{bmatrix} \rightarrow [-\text{continuant}]$

         V   C

However, if two *k*s should appear next to one another, but only form
an apparent geminate, then the first *k* (being also post-vocalic) should –
and does – undergo spirantization in Tigrinya. This is seen in the second-
person masculine form of perfective and gerundive stems if they end with
the relevant consonant. For example, the form in (60) does undergo
spirantization, yielding [baräxka], since the stem-final *k* is in the appropriate position for spirantization, and the Conjunctivity Condition does
not block the rule's application.[16]

(60)   a   ä   a
              | | |
         C V C V C + C V   [baräxka] 'you blessed'
         | | | | | |
         b   r   k   k

2.3   MORPHOLOGICAL USES OF THE SKELETON

So far in this chapter, we have seen evidence that the skeletal tier is useful in the analysis of a number of phonological phenomena, such as compensatory lengthening, the behavior of geminate consonants, and certain kinds of apparent phonological irregularity. But we have not yet considered the relevance of the skeletal tier to morphology. In our discussion of the tonal autosegmental tier, we noted that there are morphemes that consist only of tones or only of non-tonal material. This was pointed out, for example, at the end of section 1.4, in the discussion of the continuous verbal marker in Mixtecan, where the morpheme consists entirely of a floating High tone. Elsewhere, it is easy to find phonological material in a tone language that has no tonal specification of its own, but inherits the tones that it eventually associates with from the context in which it is found. In both of these cases, the morphological material can be best understood as forming complete sequences on just one autosegmental tier. Thus, the phonological fragmentation of features onto separate tiers is matched by a morphological (or, if you will, functional) fragmentation in which the morphology is free to define morphemes on only one tier (although, in general, morphemes may consist of material on two (or more) tiers).

In this section, we will consider two cases where the morphology controls the structure of the skeleton. In the cases we have looked at so far, the structure of the skeleton has been projected from (i.e. determined by) the vowels and consonants that compose the constituent morphemes of the word. But since the skeletal tier is a tier, it may also be a morpheme of its own, and be composed by means other than purely phonological (i.e. predictable) ones.

2.3.1   *Sierra Miwok verb forms*

Let us consider certain alternations in skeletal structure found in verbs in Sierra Miwok, a Penutian language of California analyzed by Freeland (1951).[17] Verb stems can be divided into four types, of which we shall discuss here three. The division depends on the number of consonants in, and the syllable structure of, the underlying form, which is also the form used in the present tense (except for a reasonably small subclass of the Type III verbs, which undergo a modification in the present tense). Type I stems have the basic form CVCVVC (e.g. *kicaaw* 'to bleed'), where the second vowel is long; Type II, the basic form CVCCV (e.g., *celku*, 'to quit'); Type III, the form CVCCV, where the medial consonant is a geminate (e.g. *hamme* 'to bury'). In autosegmental terms, these three types will have skeletal structures as in (61). The association is predictably one-to-one everywhere except in Type I, where the second vowel is long, and Type III, where we find a geminate consonant.

(61)   Type I

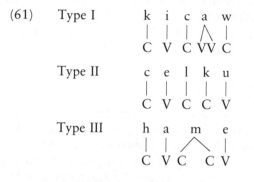

Verbs stems undergo considerable, and consistent, modification in various inflectional and derivational formations, and for each stem there are three modified forms that can be found in addition to the basic stem form; Freeland calls these derived forms the *second, third*, and *fourth stems*. In some cases these modifications can be viewed as being controlled by the immediately following suffix, while in others, they can be viewed as directly controlled grammatically. Some of the uses of these stem forms include the following: the basic stem form is used in the present, perfect, and volitional tenses; the second stem form is used with the future; the third stem form is used in the habituative; the fourth stem for is used as one of several infinitive-like forms. Bear in mind that the forms in (62) are not *words*, but *stems*, to which suffixes are added.

It may be instructive to consider how these stem modifications would be handled within a classical generative framework.[18] To do this, we must momentarily relinquish the understanding that geminates are treated autosegmentally, using the skeletal tier, to be sure. The alternations in each group would be broken down into a number of separate operations, with the underlying forms being the form appearing in the present tense. Let us consider how such an account would be likely to run.

The fact that there is a shortening of the vowel in the second stem form of Type I verbs is predictable from the more general fact that long vowels never occur in closed syllables word medially, or, as the segmental perspective might put it, in the environment – CC, where the two C's can represent either a cluster or a long consonant. This is an entirely general process in Sierra Miwok.

The second and third stems of Type II verbs would be formed by a metathesis rule, as in (63). The condition that the consonants be distinct

(62)

Gloss	Basic stem	Second stem	Third stem	Fourth stem
Type I				
bleed	kicaaw	kicaww	kiccaw	kicwa
jump	tuyaaŋ	tuyaŋŋ	tuyyaŋ	tuyŋa
take	patɨɨt	patɨtt	pattɨt	pattɨ
roll	huteel	hutell	huttel	hutle
Type II				
quit	celku	celukk	celluk	celku
go home	woʔlu	woʔull	woʔʔul	woʔlu
catch up				
with	nakpa	nakapp	nakkap	nakpa
spear	wimki	wimikk	wimmik	wimki
Type III				
bury	hamme	hameʔʔ	hammeʔ	hamʔe
dive	ʔuppi	ʔupiʔʔ	ʔuppiʔ	ʔupʔi
speak	liwwa	liwaʔʔ	liwwaʔ	liwʔa
sing	mɨlli	mɨliʔʔ	mɨlliʔ	mɨlʔi

(63)   Metathesis-A
$$C_i \quad C_j \quad V]_{\substack{\text{second,} \\ \text{third} \\ \text{stem}}} \rightarrow C_i \quad V \quad C_j$$

– that 'i ≠ j' – must be added to (63) so that the metathesis rule will not apply to Type III verbs. We will have to set up another metathesis rule to form the fourth stem form of Type I verbs, changing stems that end in VC into CV, but that cannot be the same rule as the metathesis rule in (63); this second metathesis is given in (64), and would have to be ordered much later, as we shall see.

(64)   Metathesis-B
$$V \quad C \quad]_{\substack{\text{fourth} \\ \text{stem}}} \rightarrow C \quad V$$

Gemination at the end of the second stem of all verbs would be analyzed as the result of a morphologically conditioned rule, as in (65). Another rule of gemination (66) will geminate the middle consonant of all three types in forming the third stem, unless it is already geminate, in which case nothing special happens.

Rules (63) and (65) apply in that order so that the metathesized

(65) Gemination-A

$C_i \rightarrow C_i \; C_i \; / \; —]_{\text{second stem}}$

(66) Gemination-B

$C_i \rightarrow C_i \; C_i / \; [\underset{\text{third stem}}{C} \; V - V$

consonant will be geminated (underlying *celku* > *celuk* (by metathesis) > [celukk] (by gemination)).

We might now postulate a rule to add a final glottal stop to any vowel-final stem in the second, third, or fourth stem, crucially ordered after metathesis (since its only function is to account for the final glottal stop in stems where metathesis could not put a consonant at the end of the stem in the past-tense form), and ordered before Gemination-A. This rule is given in (67). It will apply only to stems of Type III, since after metathesis Types I and II will have a stem-final consonant. (The reason

(67) Glottal Insertion

$\varnothing \rightarrow \text{ʔ} \; / \; V -]_{\text{second, third, fourth stem}}$

metathesis will not apply to Type III, readers will bear in mind, is that metathesis is restricted from splitting up geminate consonants, and although the geminate of Type III will indeed simplify to a short consonant in the past-tense stem form, this analysis must assume that such degemination has not yet occurred.) Glottal insertion presumably also provides the glottal stop that is metathesized by Metathesis-B (e.g. *hamme* > *hammeʔ* ... [hamʔe]).

Finally, we need to specify a rule to degeminate the geminate consonant of the Type III stems in the second and fourth stems. Should this rule apply before or after Metathesis-B? If we order Metathesis-B before gemination, we are forced to posit a strange intermediate stage in the derivation with an unlikely cluster of three consonants (that is, our example in the immediately preceding paragraph would pass through the stages *hamme* > *hammeʔ* > *hammʔe* [with a geminate followed by a glottal stop] > *hamʔe*). We could, on the other hand, order Metathesis-B after Degemination, leaving them both heavily morphologically specified; and so we shall leave it. Degemination is given in (68). This leaves us with the rules cited in (69).

(68) Degemination

$C_i \rightarrow \varnothing \; / \; C \; V \; C_i —]$

second, fourth stem

(69) (63) Metathesis-A (second, third, fourth)
      (67) Glottal Insertion (second, third, fourth)
      (65) Gemination-A (second)
      (66) Gemination-B (third)
      (68) Degemination (second, fourth)
      (64) Metathesis B-(fourth)

This analysis, with all its morphologically governed phonological rules, arbitrary rule ordering, and, frankly, its mind-boggling inelegance, ironically misses the most basic point of the formation of the past tense in Sierra Miwok. As we have informally noted, all the second stem forms are of the shape CVCVCC, with the last consonant a geminate, and the rules that we have hypothetically posited so far all endeavor to achieve that end without ever directly acknowledging it. Similarly, the fourth stem is of the form CVCCV, where the second and third consonants are *not* identical. That this truly is the goal of the Sierra Miwok morphology is driven home clearly by the way non-verbal nouns with more than three consonants are modified to match the template when they are used verbally. The stem for 'three', for example, is *tolookošu*; its 'basic' stem form, when used verbally, is *tolook*, and its fourth stem form is *tolko*. The *š* does not appear, because there is no room for it. The autosegmental account using the skeletal tier permits an account that directly expresses this. The lexical representation of verbs will look much like their 'basic stem' form. To form the second, third, and fourth stems, the skeletal strings in (72a, b, c) are used to replace the lexical skeletal tier of the verb stem. A consonant position which is the first half of what will be a geminate consonant is marked as 'inert' (recalling the discussion of floating tones in chapter 1) by enclosing it in parentheses. Such consonant positions are skipped by the Association Convention, and later are associated by rule to the following consonant. This is illustrated in (71).[19]

(70) (a) CVCVVC   (b) CVCCV   (c) CV(C)CV
          kicaw   celku   hame

As we approach the analysis of these data from the point of view of the model being developed in this chapter, we find that the problem divides into four parts: (i) the treatment of geminate consonants (and, less problematically, long vowels), and how they are marked on the skeleton; (ii) deciding how many distinct autosegmental tiers there are, and in particular whether vowels and consonants are found on distinct autosegmental tiers; (iii) establishing an appropriate definition of a Freely

(71)　　　C　V　(C)　C　V　　　　one-to-one association
　　　　　|　|　　　|　|　　　　(leaves (C) unassociated)
　　　　　h　a　　　m　e

　　　　　C　V　(C)　C　V
　　　　　|　|　　　\/　|　　　　association added by rule
　　　　　h　a　　　m　e

Geminate Formation:　　　Ⓒ　C
　　　　　　　　　　　　　　　　　\,|
　　　　　　　　　　　　　　　　　　c

(72)　　(a)　Second stem　CVCV(C)C
　　　　(b)　Third stem　　CV(C)CVC
　　　　(c)　Fourth stem　CVCCV

Associating Segment and making sure that the Association Convention established in chapter 1 works properly in this case; and (iv) accounting for the presence of the inserted glottal stops.

There are essentially two accounts that are possible within the theory established so far: one involves placing the consonants and vowels on separate tiers, while the other allows for a single phonemic tier in the sense that it has been developed so far in this chapter. In the first case, the vowel tier and the skeleton form a separate 'chart' in the sense defined in chapter 1, as do the consonant tier and the skeletal tier; we will therefore call this the 'two chart analysis'. The analysis that places vowels and consonants on the same tier establishes a single chart, and is thus a 'single-chart analysis'. Certain theoretical issues which we shall discuss in section 6.4 tend to force one analysis or the other, but both accounts are possible if we restrict ourselves to the data at hand from Sierra Miwok. It would therefore be instructive to see how the two approaches compare. As we shall see, the analysis that places vowels and consonants on different tiers seems to be preferable here for reasons that have to do both with establishing a straightforward account of the data and with maintaining a streamlined general theory. Nonetheless, it is only reasonable to say that the jury is still out on the final decision.

The basic idea that we want to work out is how to distribute the vowels and consonants to the appropriate positions on the skeletal structures as shown in (72). How does the Association Convention help in that task?

In the final section of chapter 1, we considered a more restricted and a less restricted procedure for defining Freely Associating Segments within a chart, i.e. within a pair of associating autosegmental tiers. Under the more restricted approach, each tier in a chart would have a subset of its members marked as Freely Associating Segments; these would be associated in a one-to-one fashion. If we adopt this stricter approach, it follows ineluctably that vowels and consonants must be placed on separate tiers, and that the correct representation of the words in (61) must be rather as in (73), in what we have called the two-chart analysis.

(73)   Type I

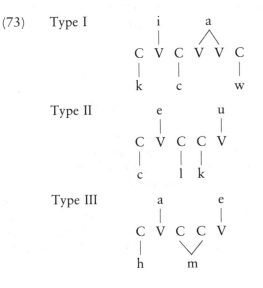

Each of these representations contains three tiers, and each contains two charts. One chart is the skeleton-consonant chart, where the Freely Associating Segments are the C-positions on the skeletal tier and everything on the consonantal tier (formally, $\{[-\text{syllabic}], \emptyset\}$, although we will be led to modify the use of the feature $[\pm\text{syllabic}]$ on the skeletal tier eventually). Similarly, the second chart is the skeleton-vowel chart, where the Freely Associating Segments are the V-positions on the skeleton and everything on the vowel tier.

The alternative single-chart approach requires that we make recourse to the extended and less restrictive definition of Freely Associating Segment proposed at the end of chapter 1. Under this conception, subsets of segments on a given autosegmental tier could be instructed (so to speak) as to which segments on the opposite tier of their chart they should view as Freely Associating Segments as far as they are concerned. Let us see how this conception would be worked out.

We have so far maintained the basic assumption that a given feature may appear on only one autosegmental tier. Let us relax this assumption momentarily with regard to the feature $[\pm\text{syllabic}]$, and allow it to appear on both the skeletal tier and the phonemic tier. The distinction being drawn on the phonemic tier concerns the inherent quality of the segments concerned; segments that are [+syllabic] have certain characteristics that [−syllabic] segments do not. The distinction being made on the skeletal tier concerns position − syntagmatic, structural position − in a syllable; what we have called V-positions are always positions in the rhyme of the syllable, for example. We cannot deal with this matter in its entirety until we treat the structure of the syllable in chapter 3, but these considerations are offered by way of making more plausible the use of what appears to be the same feature on two distinct tiers, the skeletal and the phonemic.

In this single-chart analysis, then, the Freely Associating Segments are:

$$\{[+\text{syllabic}],[+\text{syllabic}]; \ [-\text{syllabic}],[-\text{syllabic}]\}.$$

Let us consider how a basic stem such as *celku* and its second stem form *celukk* would be produced in the single chart approach. Assuming that the order of segments on the phonemic tier is *celku*, we start with the representations as in (74a) for the basic stem, and as in (74b) for the second stem form, where the morphology has replaced the lexical skeletal pattern by the pattern indicated in (72a), the morpheme of the second stem form. An initial rule associates the first consonant and the first C-position, as indicated by the broken line in (74). The Association Convention then scans from left to right, but we must specify (either

(74)   (a) Basic stem   C V C C V
                                 ⋮
                               c e l k u

         (b) Second-stem form   C V C V (C) C
                                  ⋮
                                c e l k u

universally or in a language-particular way) whether this means scanning the skeletal tier or the phonemic tier. Rather arbitrarily, let us suppose that the former choice is made; then the Association Convention will add association lines to (74a) and (b), converting them into the representations in (75).

We are finished with the derivation of (74a) and (75a); in (75b), however, with the assumption that it is the skeletal tier that is being scanned (this has also been called *skeleton-driven association*), the

(75)   (a) C V C C V   (b) C V C V (C) C
              | | | | | | | |
              c e l k u   c e l k u

(76)

unassociated V-position will be the next to be associated, as the Association Convention scans the material on the phonemic tier, looking for a Freely Associating Segment that is appropriate for the V-slot. This it finds with the *u* and (75b) is changed to (76). At this point, both the *k* and the final C-slots are still unassociated; on this single-chart analysis, the Association Convention is not (singlehandedly, at least) responsible for their eventual association. Rather, we must posit a metathesis rule as in (77), which will change (76) to (78a), for which the Association Convention will correctly give us the desired output, (78b). (We simplify here the treatment of the geminate C.) Readers will recall that the circle around the first *c* in (77) means that the segment is unassociated.

(77)   Metathesis

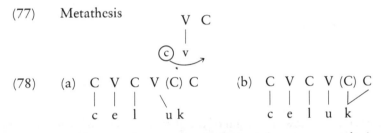

(78)   (a) C V C V (C) C   (b) C V C V (C) C
            | | | \ | | | | |/
            c e l   u k   c e l u k

In contrast, the two-chart approach derives the correct results in these cases without the troublesome metathesis rule. It is troublesome in that it is a rule whose function is clearly derived from the need to place the consonant in a position in which the Association Convention can operate on it, and it is furthermore a rule whose formal nature is quite different from the other rules we have looked at. Fortunately, then, it can be elegantly dispensed with on the two-chart approach. Instead of the forms given in (74) for the single-chart approach, we now have the forms in (79). The parentheses on the inert C still indicate, as above, that the C-position is ignored by the Association Convention, though it is later associated by the rule in (71). Now the one-to-one association provided

(79)   (a) Basic   (b) Second
           stem   stem form

                  e   u   e   u

           C V C C V   C V C V (C) C

           c   l k   c   l   k

by the Association Convention provides the associations given in (80a, b), and the geminate is then created by the rule in (71), converting (80b) to (80c). (80a) is the two chart representation of *celku*; (80c) is the representation of *celukk*, as desired. Since the two chart representation has the considerable advantage of eliminating the need for a metathesis rule, and also of allowing a more restrictive notion of Freely Associating Segment, we shall continue to use the two-chart representation from this point on in the discussion.[20]

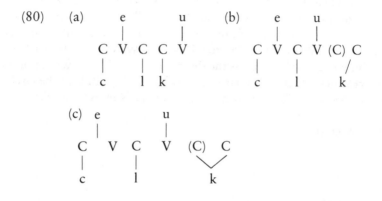

Let us consider now the origin of the glottal stops in (62). In two of the stems (*wo ʔlu* and *ʔuppi*), the glottal stop is truly a consonant that forms part of the stem, just like any other consonant. All of the other glottal stops play a very different role: they are there just to fill in skeletal positions that have no consonants assigned to them by the Association Convention. These all occur in the Type III stem, and differ from the Type II stem just in that they have two underlying consonants and not three. Thus, the second, third, and fourth stem forms of the first Type III stem ('bury') given in (62) are as in (81).

One-to-one association, plus geminate formation (71), gives us the representations in (82). Underneath each of them is indicated the correct surface form; we can see that all C-positions that are not yet associated receive what is called a *default* consonant, the glottal stop, by rule (83).

Let us return to the question of how geminate consonants should be represented, and justify the approach that we have used up to now. We are not raising the question as to whether geminates should be represented as single phonemic segments associated with two skeletal segments; that we take as established. The question is rather how a skeleton that exists independently in the grammar should be represented when part of the information found in the skeleton is that a pair of adjacent

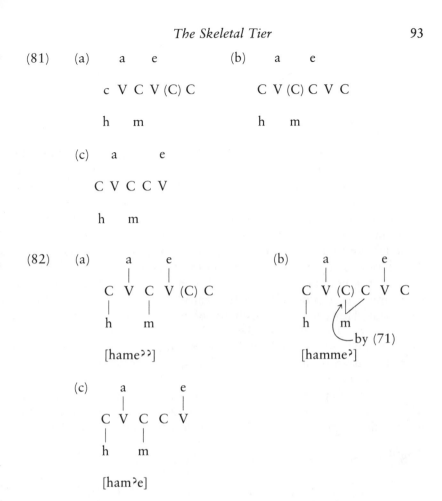

(83)   Default Glottal Stop Insertion

consonant positions should be understood as forming a geminate.

We will see another example of this morphological necessity in the next section when we look at the verb stem morphology of Classical Arabic. In Arabic as well, there is a two-chart representation with vowels and consonants on separate tiers. In the second conjugation we will find that the three consonants that form the underlying morpheme on the consonant tier distribute themselves over the four C-slots on the skeletal tier as in (84), always forming a geminate consonant in the middle of the stem.

(84)

The examples in (84) and (82b) illustrate the sense in which the treatment of geminates is primarily a problem for the operation of the Association Convention, and point to the fact that, while there are two skeletal positions actually present, we need to make the Association Convention see only one. In principle, we could do this in one of three ways: mark the first C-position as being formally invisible; mark the second C-position as invisible; or indicate somehow that the Association Convention is to treat the two C-positions as a single unit. This last solution has no straightforward implementation, since the Association Convention is a procedure so fundamentally based on a one-to-one alignment. However, the possibility of marking an element as being 'invisible' as far as the Association Convention is concerned – which amounts, after all, to simply indicating that it is not a Freely Associating Segment – is an open possibility, and it is, as we have already seen, the option that we shall choose.

Of the two C-positions that eventually become part of the geminate, which one should receive the special marking? Compare form (85a), which exists, with a form like (85b), which is not found in Sierra Miwok.

(85)   (a)   (b)

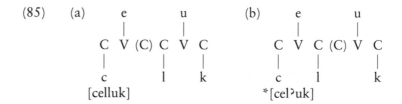

The important point for us to observe is that the example in (82c) shows us that, when there are two C-slots in a row, as in (85b), and the first, but not the second, is associated to a consonant, then the second remains unassociated until it gets a default glottal stop. Thus, the representation in (85b) cannot be the source of the geminate; it must be, as we have suggested already, the structure in (85a). That is, geminates must be analyzed as the result of skipping the first of two adjacent C-positions. It is a consonant with this marking that we have called an 'inert' consonant.

If we reflect further on this result, we find that other considerations lend credibility to the conclusion. Of the two skeletal positions held by the geminate, in virtually all cases the first is in the coda of one syllable and the second is in the onset of the next. It is common for consonants in syllable onsets to double leftward into preceding rhymes (as in, for example, Italian *raddoppiamento*), but less common for consonants to doubly associate to the right, from a coda into a rhyme.

We shall proceed with the assumption that the association to the coda position is accomplished by the rule in (71), although the discussion on compensatory lengthening in section 6.5 suggests that it may not be necessary to make the rule language-specific: it may be possible to derive this result from more general principles.

There are several ways to consider treating the long vowel derived in the basic form of Type I stems like *kicaaw* (cf. (70a)). The Association Convention will provide only part of the associations necessary, up to the point indicated in (86); again, observations on compensatory lengthening suggest that association to a floating rhyme position is automatic, but for now we will assume that a rule provides the final association needed to associate the third V position, a rule given in (87).

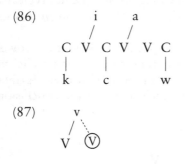

(86)

(87)

2.3.2   Arabic

From the lesser known case of Sierra Miwok, we turn now to the classic example of the use of the skeletal tier for morphological purposes, that of Classical Arabic. The first proposal for the skeleton as an autosegmental tier (McCarthy 1979a) was, in fact, embedded within an analysis of the consonantal and vocalic patterns of Arabic. We shall now look at this system, and see how the autosegmental skeletal tier allows a simple and direct statement of the patterns found in the Arabic verb system. We will consider one major theoretical issue that arises here, though the ultimate resolution of the question remains open. The question concerns whether morphological structure can directly influence the number of autosegmental tiers that exist in a given language, and whether the morphological status of an item is reflected by its position in the autosegmental structure of the word. The suggestion has been made, as we shall see, that each morpheme in Arabic appears on a separate tier. This suggestion, if correct, would have many consequences for our understanding of autosegmental representation, and we shall discuss some of them in this section.

It is convenient for our purposes to divide the Arabic verb into two components, consisting of the stem and the inflectional affixes marking agreement. The discussion that follows concerns the construction of the *stem*, then; and the formation of actual Arabic verbs requires the addition of further agreement markers and the application of later phonological rules, which we shall not consider here.

It is a well-known characteristic of the Arabic verb that it consists of three components that can each vary independently: the vocalic pattern, or 'vocalism'; the consonantal pattern, or 'consonantism'; and the organization of each of these into patterns of syllable structure. For example, the perfective active stem for the verb 'write' is *katab*, and the corresponding passive is *kutib*. The consonants together form a separate morpheme, each with roughly its own meaning, as morphemes typically will. Thus *fa ͨal* means 'to do', a perfective active form, and *fu ͨil* is its corresponding passive.

Knowing no more than these three forms, we might extract the vowel pattern as a separate tier, recognizing its autonomy as being parallel to the tone pattern of a tone language, as in (88). However, further observation within Arabic itself leads us ineluctably to the conclusion

(88)   a   u   i
                       /\   /   \
              k V t V b   k   V   t   V   b

that the consonants and the skeleton must form separate tiers. The choice of the patterns of C's and V's can be seen to be independent of consonantal morpheme (*ktb, f ͨl*). This modification of the syllable structure (or skeletal structure, more precisely) forms part of the derivational morphology of the language; verbal forms that are related by derivational morphology will be related as one skeletal pattern replaces another.

Within the classical account of the language, there are fifteen so-called 'conjugations' (with four more 'quadriliteral conjugations', which we may safely ignore for our purposes). These conjugations have nothing to do with the verbal conjugation types of the familiar Romance languages; they are, rather, formal categories which have strict formal phonological definitions and rough semantic definitions. The conjugations are essentially *patterns* of vowel and consonant positions. The actual vowel qualities are specified by the independent features of voice and aspect;

the actual consonant qualities are determined by the choice of lexical item. If there are fifteen conjugations for the verb in Arabic, by no means can every actual verb be found in each of these fifteen forms: rather, each verb can appear in a limited set of the conjugations. Nonetheless, the set of patterns available in the language as a whole can be seen to come down to the fifteen conjugations given in (89). There, the forms are given with the consonantal pattern *ktb*, and the simple vocalic pattern 'a' of the active perfective.

(89)

Conjugation	Stem
1	katab
2	kattab
3	kaatab
4	ʔaktab
5	takattab
6	takaatab
7	nkatab
8	ktatab
9	ktabab
10	staktab
11	ktaabab
12	ktawbab
13	ktawwab
14	ktanbab
15	ktanbay

Let us review these fifteen patterns informally. The first is the simplest, with no extra consonants involved, no gemination of the root consonants, and no long vowels. Conjugation 2 is distinguished by the gemination of the medial consonant, conjugation 3 by the lengthening of the first vowel. Conjugations 5 and 6 match 2 and 3 except for the addition of the prefix *ta+* (really *tV+*) in the former.

Conjugation 4 involves the initial consonant ʔ, and a different sequencing of the vowels and consonants than that seen so far. Conjugations 7 and 10 involve conjugation-specific consonants that appear on the first available consonant positions. Conjugation 8, as well as 12–15, involve the appearance of conjugation-specific consonants in a non-initial consonant position. Conjugations 9 and 11 involve multiple association of the final consonant across an intervening vowel.

One crucial assumption for this analysis of Arabic is that the consonants of the root and the vowels expressing voice-aspect appear on separate autosegmental tiers, and that these tiers are furthermore distinct

from the skeletal tier that is defined for each conjugation. In the discussion of Luganda, and of Seri, there was no reason to posit separate
tiers for vowels and consonants; in Sierra Miwok, the evidence is more
than suggestive, but less than definitive, on the matter. But there is a fact
about Arabic which makes it rather different from the other two cases,
for here the vocalism and the consonantism comprise separate and
distinct morphemes.

With the formal mechanisms at our disposal at this point, we may
specify ten of the fifteen conjugations in (89) easily: numbers 1–7 and 9–
11. These are defined by the skeleta given in (90). We may assume that
the conjugation-specific consonants are either associated underlyingly as

(90)   1. C V C V C
        2. C V (C) C V C
        3. C V V C V C
        4. C V C C V C
              |
              ʔ

        5. C V C V (C) C V C
              |
              ʔ

        6. C V C V V C V C
              |
              t
        7. C̓ C V C V C
           |
           n
        9. C C V C V C
       10. C C V C C V C
           | |
           s t
       11. C C V V C V C

displayed there, or else are treated morphologically as prefixes, and are
therefore prefixed to the consonants comprising the lexical root prior to
the association of the first consonant to the first consonantal position and
the effects of the Association Convention. The conjugations requiring
inert elements (conjugations 1, 2, 5, and 6) have those elements properly
in the coda; this creates geminate consonants and long vowels, as
discussed in the previous section.

We will be restricting our attention here to the treatment of the
consonantism, and the simplest way to do that is to consider just the
perfective active stems, which, outside of conjugation 1, exceptionlessly

have the vowel *a* everywhere. Within conjugation 1, there are a significant number of lexical exceptions to the statement that all the vowels are *a*, but, again, for our purposes we may restrict our attention to the case where all V-positions on the skeleton associate to a single vowel *a*. This association we may take to be accomplished by the rules in (91), applying to the chart consisting of the vocalic element *a* and the skeleton. The two rules perform the initial association and the spreading, respectively. The Freely Associating Segments on the skeleton are just the V-positions. (92) provides an illustration of the derivation of the fourth conjugation 4.

(91)   (a)
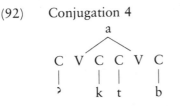
        (b) v
             | ↘
             V

(92)   Conjugation 4

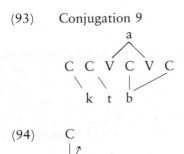

As (93) illustrates, if a C-position is left unassociated by the Association Convention, the final consonant spreads to it. This we may take to be the result of a consonant spreading rule (94), although an alternative account will be discussed in chapter 6.

Real, and new, questions arise when we turn to the treatment of conjugations in which there are conjugation-specific consonants that appear infixed among the lexical consonants, as in conjugation 8. The form given above (*ktatab*) does not make it clear that the second consonant of this conjugation is always a *t*; it is not, as this example

(93)   Conjugation 9

        a
       ⌢
C C V C V C
 \ \ | ⟋
  k t b

(94)   C
        | ↗
        c

might suggest, a conjugation in which the second consonant of the root appears twice. Thus, the consonantism *fˤl* appears as *ftaˤal*, and so on.

The basic problem, then, is how to deal simultaneously with the association of consonants to the skeleton when one or more of the consonants is morphologically conditioned by the choice of the conjugation (just as the choice of the conjugation also selects the precise skeletal shape). There are three ways in which this kind of distribution of consonants may be treated, and which of these we choose depends on the resolution of certain theoretical issues of much broader scope. Let us consider each in turn.

The first approach is to let the consonantism associate in the normal fashion, but to mark those C-position(s) that will host the conjugation-specific consonants as being *inert* (C). After association of the lexical consonantism, this will leave the inert C-positions unassociated; and morphologically controlled consonant insertion rules can then fill in the needed consonants. This approach would work as in (95) for conjugation 8.

(95)   Lexical shape of the skeleton: C (C) V C V C
        Underlying representation: C (C) V C V C

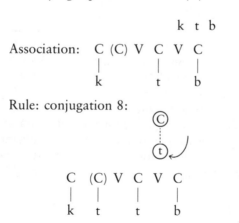

The analysis suggested here for conjugation 8 can easily be extended to the other problematic conjugations (12–15), though it may be worth pointing out that numbers 12 and 13 would differ not only in the precise formulation of the *w*-insertion rule, but also in the specification of inert elements in the underlying representation of the skeleton: Conjugation 12 would be of the form CCV(C)CVC, while 13 would be of the form CCV(C)(C)VC.

This approach has the disadvantage that it breaks up whatever is special about this sort of conjugation into two parts, the lexical entry for the skeleton, and a phonological insertion rule whose application is specially prepared by the inert element that we have put in the lexical entry for the skeleton. In addition, it has the effect of making the *t* that is inserted here unlike other morphemes in that it is derivationally inserted by what appears to be a phonological rule, albeit one with severe morphological conditioning.

The second approach requires a major relaxing of an important assumption that we have maintained so far, the principle that a single feature may appear on only one autosegmental tier. While it is true that we have considered relaxing this assumption slightly with regard to the feature distinguishing vowels and consonants, allowing it to be specified on more than one tier, this was, we suggested, a violation more of the letter than of the spirit of the assumption. The second approach to the Arabic consonantism drops the assumption entirely, and places the conjugation-specific material on the skeletal tier along with the C- and V-slots. This is illustrated for the conjugation 8 in (96). The fully specified elements on the skeleton would then be specified as not being members of the set of Freely Associating Segments.

(96)
$$
\begin{array}{ccccccc}
C & t & V & C & V & C \\
| & & & | & & | \\
k & & & t & & b
\end{array}
$$

The third approach to the problem was the one incorporated into the first autosegmental treatment of Arabic consonantism, and is like the previous account in one way, and unlike it in others. It has in common with the previous account that it allows phonological features to be specified on more than one tier. However, the third approach allows for consonants to be specified on more than one phonemic (non-skeletal) tier. In this case, this means putting the conjugation-specific *t* on one tier, and the root consonantism on a separate phonemic tier, as in (97). The vowel tier is left off the diagram; it would require a three-dimensional representation to express it clearly.

This arrangement, once again, saves us from the problem of line-crossing caused by the infixed consonant (*t*, here); we may assume that the two morphemes are as given in (97), with an underlying association

(97)
$$
\begin{array}{cccccc}
 & t \\
 & | \\
C & C & V & C & V & C \\
 \\
k & & t & & b
\end{array}
$$

line linking the two conjugation-specific elements, the skeletal string and the *t*. This third approach has been defended by appealing to a principle that we will discuss in chapter 6, a principle whose thrust is that, at a deep phonological level, separate morphemes must appear on separate tiers (the 'Morpheme Tier Hypothesis') (cf. McCarthy 1981).

In any event, of these three approaches, the first requires the least modification of the apparatus, and the last requires by far the most radical revision.

In summary, then, we have seen in this chapter a number of ways in which the development of the skeletal tier is a straightforward application of the ideas of autosegmental representation presented in the first chapter. The application of multi-tiered representation to this domain, however, opens up a number of new conceptions of the problems of vowel and consonant length, of metathesis, and of morphological control over syllable structure.

3
Syllable structure

The syllable has become something of a stepchild in linguistic description. While sooner or later everyone finds it convenient to use, no one does much about defining it. This is not a new situation: for many years phoneticians have been trying to find a phonetic basis for the syllable without reaching any very definite agreement. Opinion has ranged from those who denied its physical reality to those who have identified it physiologically with a chest pulse and acoustically with degrees of sonority. With the development of structuralist linguistics, the syllable has been carried over into phonemics. Here the emphasis has been laid on its relation to other features of linguistic structure, particularly tone, stress, quantity, and the like, which obviously were associated more directly with the syllable than with the individual phonemes.

'The Syllable in Linguistic Description'
Einar Haugen (1956a)

3.1 INTRODUCTION

From autosegmental structure we turn now to a traditional notion, that of the syllable, a notion which metrical phonology, the subject of chapter 4, is heavily dependent upon. While we can find antecedents to both metrical and autosegmental theories in the literature over the past several decades if we look hard enough, the same cannot be said about the syllable. The syllable is a unit of phonological description which has never ceased to be discussed at length in the phonological literature of this century. The classical theory of generative phonology in *The Sound Pattern of English* (Chomsky and Halle 1968), it is true, attempted to build a theory without any such notion, but phonologists both sympathetic and unsympathetic to that effort were quick to point out the inadequacies of the revision. Well-known discussions along these lines include Fudge (1969), Vennemann (1972), and Hooper (1972), remarks that came quickly after the publication of *The Sound Pattern of English*. To be sure, a clear and influential discussion of the syllable is found earlier in Hockett (1955), and Pike's discussions in various places were also influential; both Hockett's and Pike's work can be read today as virtually contemporary statements.[1] By the appearance of Kahn (1980), it was clear to even the most skeptical observers that the syllable could not be overlooked by phonological theory.

The rapid development of phonological theory over the past ten years has pointed out both the strengths and the weaknesses of the earlier work on syllable theory. Current developments in the field represent both continuity and rapid improvement in comparison with the antecedent work.

In the first section of this chapter, we shall review a number of traditional views on the nature of the syllable, and pose some of the questions that have traditionally been raised about the nature of the syllable and its interaction with other phonological processes. We will take a brief look at the two traditional views of the syllable, the sonority theory and the phrase-structure theory, and in section 3.4 we will introduce a different perspective on the formal problems of syllable analysis. We shall introduce a notion of *autosegmental licensing*, and interpret the syllable as a licensing structure, a structure whose function is to allow precisely one occurrence of autosegmental structure per prosodic unit. In section 3.5 we will explore the ways in which varying degrees of robustness of the coda – ability to license, in the terms we will develop – lead to different kinds of syllable and word structure. We will then look at the structure of Spanish and English syllables in some detail, a complicated area of study, and finally will close the chapter with a brief discussion of the role of the [±syllabic] contrast and the relation of syllable structure to prosodic phenomena such as stress and tone.

3.2   TRADITIONAL VIEWS ABOUT THE SYLLABLE

3.2.1   *Syllables as groupings*

Traditionally, there have been two views regarding the nature of the syllable. Both agree that the spoken utterance is divided up into units, or chunks of segments, but the first focuses on the alternating crescendo and diminuendo of speech, the oscillating rises and fall of energy. This view, which we may call the *sonority* view of the syllable, finds a clear statement in Bloomfield's *Language*:

In any succession of sounds, some strike the ear more forcibly than others: differences of *sonority* play a great part in the transition effects of vowels and vowel-like sounds. . . . In any succession of phonemes there will thus be an up-and-down of sonority. . . . Evidently some of the phonemes are more sonorous than the phonemes (or the silence) which immediately precede or follow. . . . Any such phoneme is a *crest of sonority* or a *syllabic*; the other phonemes are *non-syllabic*. . . . An utterance is said to have as many *syllables* (or *natural syllables*) as it has syllabics. The ups and downs of *syllabication* play an important part in the phonetic structure of all languages. (Bloomfield 1933: 120-1)

The second traditional view of the syllable is based not on the outer form of language, not on the measurable energy of a phonetic manifestation as in the first view, but rather on a more syntactic approach. This view is implicit in Harris (1951) and quite explicit in Haugen (1956a)[2] (quoted above), and it is that the syllable is a constituent definable in familiar phrase-structure terms, quite like the sentence. It is composed, we may say, of a certain number of slots, of syntagmatic positions, in which subsets of the phonological segments of the language may occur in well-formed utterances.

Thus Harris (1951: 151), for example, places the segments of Yokuts into two categories, labeling one 'C', the other 'V'; we have here the consonants and the vowels, of course. The Yokuts word, he suggests, can always be analyzed as a sequence of zero or more occurrences of the pattern CV, CVC, or what he indicates as CV., i.e. a long vowel; in sum, $(CV(\text{:}))_0$ CV (C) – since the word cannot end in a long vowel.

In reflecting on these two approaches, one oriented to the outer form of language, and the other to the inner form, it is important for us to home in on just what the precise characteristics are that we have come to expect in thinking about the notion of syllable. On the one hand, we expect to find certain *global* properties of syllable analysis; we expect that there will be some way to specify what a syllable is, so that we can then say that a larger unit – the word, or perhaps the utterance – consists of *n* instances of such syllables, with at worst an extra codicil or two to add. In short, on the global level, there should be an integral number of repetitions of the same local entity. The phrase-structure view of the syllable emphasizes this aspect. Haugen (1956a) cites the case of Sierra Nahuat (Key and Key 1953), in which the general structure of the syllable is (C)V(C) or CCV; once that statement is made, the statement of distribution of segments can be greatly simplified by observing that all segments except /p,k,w/ can appear in the coda, and onsets can contain any segments except /h,g./[3] Haugen (1956b) makes a similar point with respect to Kutenai in considerably greater detail.

On the other hand, we also expect some particular internal structure to the syllable; the sonority view expresses this more precisely. In order to see a bit more clearly what these expectations are, let us imagine two phonological situations that violate our expectations of how segments should put themselves together, and see how this derives from our implicit assumptions about syllable structure.

Let us imagine first an alternative world in which it is possible to identify an inventory of phonological segments in a language, and to divide the inventory up into two major groups. We do this, of course, in our own phonological world, and call these two groups 'vowels' and 'consonants'; in our world, however, elements from the two groups tend to alternate, unlike the situation to be described. In this first alternative language-world, words are divisible into an initial part and a final part; all segments in the initial part come from one group of segments, and all segments from the final part come from the other group. In such a system, nothing in any way comparable to the syllable would be found, for the word would have no repeating patterns of segment categories.

We cannot make up such an example using real sound segments, because the system would be wildly unpronounceable, but we can illustrate in the abstract what this kind of system would look like. Imagine a language with thirty-five basic elements that can be arranged to form words, subject to the following condition. The sounds (which we may represent with the graphic symbols A–Z and 1–9) are divided into two classes, and all well-formed words are composed of a sequence of one or more from one group (the 'letters') followed by one or more from the other group (the 'numerals'). HA16245 is thus well-formed, but H2D4T5 is not. Such a (non-natural) language[4] does divide its basic elements into two groups, but it does not form any repeating subgroup corresponding to our familiar notion of the syllable. We would not want to say that the word in this language has two syllables, the 'letter syllable' and the 'number syllable', because the two operate according to different principles, with different populations inside them. This example brings home clearly the sense in which the syllable arises because of the alternating, rhythmic character of sounds in the words that make up natural language.[5]

Consider a second example, which would be pronounceable, and yet is not what we would expect to find in any natural language. Imagine a language with a segmental inventory roughly like that of English, in which the segments could be divided into three groups: (i) a group we will call the obstruents, consisting of sounds represented by the symbols {ptk bdg cshfvj}; (ii) the vowels, represented by the symbols {a, e, i, o, u}, and (iii) the non-vocalic sonorants represented by the symbols {lr mn yw} – or O's, V's, and S's, respectively. In this second imaginary language, any sequence of segments is well-formed if adjacent segments do not come from the same set. Thinking of it in terms of a transition network, we could say that any path in (1) will be well-formed. Or we could put it in terms like (2). Strings like *bat, trip, slip, turpentine,*

(1)
$$
\begin{array}{c}
O \\
\substack{\uparrow\downarrow \quad \searrow} \\
V \rightleftarrows S
\end{array}
$$

(2)
$$
\ldots S \left\{ \begin{array}{c} V \\ O \end{array} \right\} \ldots
$$

$$
\ldots O \left\{ \begin{array}{c} S \\ V \end{array} \right\} \ldots
$$

$$
\ldots V \left\{ \begin{array}{c} S \\ O \end{array} \right\} \ldots
$$

pancake, or *candy* would be well-formed, but *napkin, radio, warm,* and *normal* would not be, and such oddities as *pmtmtapy* or *rbmtlk* would be fine. Furthermore, it would be hard to say quite where the syllables were in such a system. Whatever can be said about this language, it is a monstrosity as far as its caricature of the syllable is concerned. But if we believed that the natural ups and downs in sonority were the basis of syllable formation, we should not be surprised if we found such a language, one that I believe is impossible. If we take the phrase-structure view, such a system would have no natural description.[6]

Let us summarize, then. From a descriptive point of view, words (and thus utterances) should be factorable into sequences of syllables, which should have a specifiable internal structure that is roughly constant across the language. In general the syllables should not overlap; syllables thus may be said to partition words into a sequence of syllables.[7] That position cannot be quite held to; word-final positions quite often are the locus for additional statements, either tightening or loosening restrictions. Many languages (such as English) allow extra segmental material to appear at the end of a word that could not be syllabified according to the principles that appear to hold word-internally. This extra material at the end has been called a *termination*, an *appendix*, or has been said to be *extrasyllabic*. Conversely, there are languages where additional restrictions are put on what can appear word-finally. Lardil, for example, allows only apical consonants to appear word-finally, with no such restriction on what can appear syllable-finally inside a word.[8] Arabic, on the other hand, permits a supernumerary consonant word-finally. Similar subregularities can occur in word-initial positions, but this is a good deal less common. In a structure that is well-formed as far as syllable structure is concerned, one traditional view holds that each segment will belong to at least one syllable (on some views, *exactly* one syllable), except for those word-initial or word-final elements which the language has explicitly allowed to remain extrasyllabic.

This provision of extrasyllabicity for certain word-final (-initial) segments must be kept distinct from a different notion of extrasyllabicity that has been used, and which will arise again below. This notion derives from the possibility that consonants may fail to become syllabified during the syllabification procedure and thus be hanging in limbo, waiting for a syllable to come along for them; in that state of limbo we say that they are *extrasyllabic*. This latter notion, which we may call *contingent extrasyllabicity*, is an unstable situation, and we will distinguish it from the word-final status that languages may give to segments, which we shall call *licensed extrasyllabicity*, alluding to a more general notion. It has been suggested (by Selkirk, Prince, McCarthy, and others, following some general suggestions of Chomsky regarding grammatical structure) that all segments must be part of a higher-level organization, such as the syllable; each segment is licensed, on this view, by being a part of a larger unit, referring to the general condition as *prosodic licensing*. Clearly, such a notion can be seen to extend from segments all the way up through well-formed discourses. Word-final (-initial) segments that are permitted by licensed extrasyllabicity, then, are integrated into the large structure of the word by being part of the prosodic system not at the syllable level, but directly at the word-level.

3.2.2 Internal structure

Traditional work on the internal structure of the syllable has arrived at the hardly surprising conclusion that the syllable is a phonological constituent composed of zero or more consonants, followed by a vowel, and ending with a shorter string of zero or more consonants. The importance of these three spans has long been recognized, and various names have been given to these subparts of the syllable. We will refer to them as the *onset*, the *nucleus*, and the *coda*, respectively, as in (3), where the major constitutents of the syllable are indicated. The nucleus is often called the *peak*, in keeping with the more systematic terminology in Hockett (1955), who restricts the use of the term *nucleus* to the case where the *peak*, in his terms, is obligatory – which is, in our view, always the case. For Hockett, a *nucleus* is by definition an obligatory member of a unit such as the syllable, contrasting with a *satellite*, an optional element that is sister to the nucleus. As we see there, the nucleus and the coda form a unit together which is called the *rhyme* (also called the *core*).[9] In all languages we find restrictions on how many segments (and which ones) can appear in the three positions of the syllable; in many languages these restrictions are quite severe.

(3)

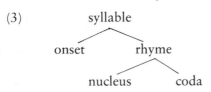

There have been suggestions made on a number of occasions[10] that the nucleus may be branching, in order to allow some or all long vowels or diphthongs to be fully contained with the nucleus. In general, these arguments are not very compelling. We will consider some of these possibilities in the course of this chapter, and find preferable alternatives in which the nucleus is a single, obligatory position. The coda, then, is all of the rhyme to the right of the single, obligatory, nucleus position.

Syllable structure is hierarchical structure organized on the skeletal tier, and on no other tiers. When we say that a vowel is in the nucleus, or a consonant in the onset, therefore, this should be understood as serving in the stead of a more cumbersome expression stating that the vowel is associated with a skeletal position in a nucleus position, or that the consonant is associated with a skeletal position in an onset position. Similarly, if we say that there is just one position in the nucleus, similarly, this does not rule out the possibility that more than one autosegment associates to it (see the discussion of Witoto in chapter 2, for example).

Two early studies involving reference to the syllable nucleus that invoke more than one position in the nucleus are Aschmann (1946) and the classic study of Pike and Pike (1947). In Totonaco, studied in Aschmann (1946), the post-vocalic glottal stop has a very special status differentiating it from any other post-vocalic consonant – so different, in fact, that there is no reason to think that there is a glottal stop that follows the vowel, rather than being a separate laryngeal (autosegmental) element that associates with the syllable nucleus, creating a 'laryngeal-ized' vowel, as Aschmann himself observes in a footnote. Several facts point in this direction. (i) Certain morphological processes add glottaliza-tion direct to the vowel, even in closed syllables; this would have to be treated as some kind of infixation process, an unappealing conclusion. (ii) Morpheme alternants that are otherwise selected by vowel-final stems are selected by laryngealized vowels. (iii) The appearance of laryngealiza-tion on the vowel does not affect the range of clusters that can appear in the coda. (iv) A phrase-level rule that lengthens vowels in open syllables also lengthens laryngealized vowels.

Pike and Pike (1947) also propose a complex nucleus for Mazateco, but the uniform amount of time attributed to this nucleus, independent of the multiple association of tones or vowels to that position, strongly suggests that what we are dealing with here is a single position on the skeleton, a nuclear position, to which up to three tones and three vowels can associate.

If the nucleus has just one position, the same cannot be said of the onset and the rhyme, for in many languages these positions can host several segments. There is considerable disagreement as to how to express the generalizations concerning what can appear in the onset positions, and in what order they must appear. One perspective that has considerable currency is that the inherent sonority of a segment, as Bloomfield referred to it above, can be used to predict the order of segments within the onset and within the coda. If vowels are more sonorous than non-vowels, and sonorants more sonorous than obstruents, and so forth, then it may be possible to posit a *Sonority Principle*, a principle in two mirror-image parts: (i) the segmental material in the onset of the syllable must be arranged in a linear order of increasing sonority from the beginning of the syllable to the nucleus of the syllable; and (ii) conversely, the segmental material in the rhyme of a syllable must be arranged in a linear order of decreasing sonority from the nuclear vowel of the syllable to the final segment of the syllable. This crescendo and diminuendo of sonority is heuristically presented in (4). Bloch and Trager offer a clear statement of this, echoing Bloomfield:

Sounds differ not only in quality but also in SONORITY. The sonority of a sound is determined primarily by the size of the resonance chamber through which the air stream flows. Thus, a low vowel is more plainly audible than a higher vowel uttered with the same force, and any vowel is more audible than a higher vowel uttered with the same force, and any vowel is more sonorous than any consonant. A sequence of sounds in a normal utterance is therefore characterized by successive peaks and valleys of sonority. The sounds which constitute the peaks of sonority are called SYLLABIC; and an utterance has as many SYLLABLES as it contains syllabic sounds. When a vowel is uttered alone or contiguous to one or more consonants, it is always syllabic. When two vowels are uttered without hiatus (a break or a pause between them), each may be the peak of a separate syllable or the two vowels may belong to the same syllable. The decisive factor is usually the distribution of the stress . . . whether each vowel is pronounced with a separate impulse of stress or whether a single impulse extends over both. (Bloch and Trager 1942: 22)

(4)   S   S   S

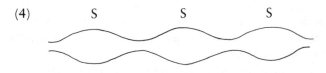

What, then, *is* sonority? Roughly speaking, it is a ranking on a scale that reflects the degree of openness of the vocal apparatus during production, or the relative amount of energy produced during the sound

– or perhaps it is a ranking that is motivated by, but distinct from, these notions. In any event, the sonority hierarchy is generally taken to be as in (5).

(5)   Sonority hierarchy

    vowels
        low vowels
        mid vowels
        high vowels
    glides
    liquids
    nasals
    obstruents
        fricatives
        affricates
        stops

It might be worthwhile to consider one or two examples of what the Sonority Principle permits or forbids. It clearly permits syllables like *plark* or *smant*, but disallows both *ltap* and *tapm*. Those do seem to be worthy and worthwhile predictions, but one major and one minor problem may occur to readers immediately. On the one hand, the Sonority Principle seems to be overly permissive in that it also allows syllables like *pnap* (since *p* is less sonorous than a nasal) and *taln*. On the other hand, it seems to treat /s/ wrongly both in the onset and in the rhyme, since *skin* or *tiks* are possible syllables in English, while /s/ is supposed to be more sonorous than the obstruent that in fact appears closer to the nucleus.

These problems are of rather different sorts. The first point derives from the fact that the Sonority Principle is intended as a necessary condition for basic syllabification, not a universal statement of syllables possible in any language. But it has also been suggested that the use of the sonority hierarchy should be sharpened. Rather than just requiring that sonority increase and decrease in a regular way in the onset and the rhyme, languages may further require that the differences in sonority between adjacent segments be greater than a certain amount. Hierarchies by themselves do not provide a notion of distance or degree of distance, and so efforts have been made to quantify sonority; for example, the one given in (6) is due to Selkirk (1982a).

With such a system, it would be possible to state precisely a requirement such as 'the difference in sonority of successive segments must be greater than 2'. While there is considerable skepticism that the ultimate

(6)   Sonority hierarchy

Sound	Sonority index
a	10
e, o	9
i, u	8
r	7
l	6
m, n	5
s	4
v, z, ð	3
f, θ	2
b, d, g	1
p, t, k	0.5

account of sonority is one based on an arithmetic system of this sort, there may be something right about an account that is sufficiently oriented to measuring sonority differences to be able to state unambiguously that liquids are halfway between obstruents and vowels. If this is correct, then we may characterize languages with respect to how much sonority difference they demand of successive segments.[11]

3.2.3   Links between syllable structure and segmental rules

Segmental phonological rules are frequently sensitive to syllable structure as well, in three ways. First, phonological rules can be conditioned to apply to a segment when the *structure* of the segment's syllable satisfies a condition. A typical instance of this kind of syllable sensitivity is the common rule laxing a vowel that is followed by a consonant in the same syllable. This phonological context is so common that a name has been given to syllables that contain a consonant in the coda; they are called *closed syllables* (in some traditions, *checked*), and all others are called *open syllables*. Québécois French has a rule of this sort: high vowels (/i/, /u/, and /ü/) are made lax in closed syllables. Thus, the masculine form of the adjective *petit* 'small' is [pti], with a tense vowel, while the feminine form *petite* is [ptɪt]. Second, a phonological rule may be conditioned to apply to a segment just in case that segment is in a specific location in the syllable. The most common kind of restriction of this sort involves processes that apply only to segments in the coda of a syllable, and not to segments in the onset. In German, for example, obstruents in the syllable coda become voiceless (*Freund* 'friend' [froynt], but *Freundin* 'friend', fem. [froyndən], etc.; see Venneman 1972). Harris (1983) notes several examples from divergent dialects of Spanish with rules affecting consonants in the coda; in Cibaeño Spanish, spoken in the Dominican Republic, the liquids *l, r* become glides when in the coda. Thus, *revolver* is realized as 'revo[i̯]ve[i̯]' (noting phonetically only the relevant segment), *carta* 'letter' as 'ca[i̯]ta', and *papel* 'paper' as 'pape[i̯]'. On the other hand, Lozano (1978) notes that in Buenos Aires Spanish the [i̯] glide undergoes a rule of fortition only in the syllable *onset*, becoming the voiced palatal fricative [ž], as illustrated in the singular/plural pair *le[i̯]/ le[ž]es* 'law/laws'.

A third way in which segmental rules are sensitive to syllable structure emerges when we consider rules of vowel epenthesis and deletion. Rules of epenthesis typically apply in phonological contexts which cannot be straightforwardly syllabified as they stand. On the other hand, rules of vowel deletion apply not infrequently just in case their output is consistent with the principles of syllabification of the language. The most common class of cases falling into this category is the class of rules deleting a vowel in a 'double open syllable' environment (VC – CV), a rule whose effect is to create CVC–CVC sequences; typically, such deletions will not apply to a vowel in a closed syllable if the resulting situation – a pair of consonants without a vowel – cannot be integrated into the neighboring syllables. A classic example of this is found in Tonkawa (Hoijer 1946, Kisseberth 1970, Phelps 1975), in which the second vowel will delete in such cases as /notoxo+oʔ/ yielding [notxoʔ], or /we+notoxo+oʔ/, yielding [wentoxoʔ]. However, /nes+kapa+oʔ/ surfaces as [neskapoʔ], not as *[neskpoʔ].

3.2.4 Links between syllable structure and prosodic structure

Prosodic rules involving tone and stress pay special attention to the syllable structure of a word. Languages frequently divide syllables into two types, which linguists metaphorically call *heavy* and *light* syllables (Newman 1972). Heavy syllables generally attract stress to them in ways that we shall explore in greater detail in the next chapter. Most commonly, languages define heavy syllables as those with two or more places in the rhyme, while light syllables are those with only one place – a short vowel – in the rhyme.

Just as accent systems commonly assign the placement of stress on the basis of syllable weight, which is itself defined solely in terms of the composition of the rhyme, so too we find that tone languages generally allow tones to freely associate only with positions in the rhyme of a syllable. It is true that we have seen depressor consonants in the onset associate with tones in Digo in chapter 1, but these tones were associated with the depressor consonants specifically because of their inherent feature specification. More generally, only segments in the rhyme of a syllable are associated by the Association Convention and rules of spreading. We will return to this issue in more detail in the last section of this chapter.

Returning to the notion of syllable weight, we have noted that by far the most important function associated with this notion concerns the placement of stress. The principles that assign stress may generally be divided into those that (i) place stress on a fixed syllable location in each word, typically the initial (Finnish), the final (French), or the penultimate syllable (Swahili); (ii) assign stress on the basis of morphological structure; (iii) assign stress on the basis of the internal make-up of the syllable, rather than on (or in addition to) the syllable's linear position in the word. (See chapter 4 on the notion of quantity-sensitivity.)

Languages do vary with respect to precisely which internal characteristics of a syllable make it more likely to receive stress, and those characteristics are the ones said to make a syllable 'heavy'. As we noted above, the most common characteristic chosen to define what constitutes a heavy syllable is the appearance of two positions in the rhyme. A long vowel, in this respect, counts as two positions; we can see from this that the tier that is relevant for this analysis is the skeletal tier, on the basis of the discussion in the previous chapter. Similarly, in the most common arrangement, a closed syllable, one ending in a vowel plus at least one consonant, equally counts as a heavy syllable. However, these are only tendencies; in many languages the primary distinction between heavy (i.e. stress-attracting) syllables and light syllables involves 'full' versus 'reduced' vowels. In the much-discussed case of Eastern Cheremis (see chapter 4), for example, stress is assigned to the last full vowel of the word. In the absence of a full vowel in the word, stress falls on the first syllable of the word. It has been suggested in the literature that full vowels in such languages should be analyzed as long vowels, with reduced vowels (described phonetically as schwa) treated as monomoraic vowels.

The strong prosodic parallel between long vowels and vowel–consonant sequences, then, suggests that the two skeletal positions associated with a long vowel are found in nucleus and coda position, as in (7).

Yup'ik, spoken in the United States and the Soviet Union, makes a quantity distinction in the establishment of the stress patterns assigned to words, but draws the weight distinctions in slightly different ways in two parts of its stress rule (Krauss 1985). *All* syllables with long vowels or diphthongs are stressed, and in addition, in Alaskan Yup'ik, an initial syllable is stressed if it is closed. Thus, an initial syllable is stressed if it is closed *or* has a long vowel or diphthong; otherwise, the second syllable is stressed.

(7)   syllable

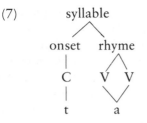

As a general rule, syllable weight distinctions are binary, and stress assignment needs to distinguish no further than between heavy and light syllables. Apparent exceptions to this are frequently just that: only apparently counter–examples. Stress assignment in Classical Arabic involves an important stress pattern, which we shall consider in the next chapter. Syllables are light if they are of the form CV; all CV: (i.e. with a long vowel) and CVC syllables are heavy. We noted earlier in this chapter, however, that in word-final position a *super-heavy* syllable may appear, which consists of what looks like a heavy syllable plus an extra consonant (i.e., CV:C or CVCC); e.g., *ḍárabt* 'beat' (first- and second-person singular), *hajjáat* 'pilgrimages'. These complex sequences are never permitted inside the word, where sequences of two consonants are permitted, with the first in the rhyme of one syllable and the second in the onset of the second. A closer look informs us that a deeper three-way distinction of syllable weight is not necessary. The super-heavy syllable can best be understood as the effect of a (language-specific) principle of licensed extrasyllabicity, according to which a single word-final consonant need not, and indeed must not, be assigned a position in the final syllable. This reinterpretation greatly simplifies our understanding of the stress system, and interprets word-final sequences of two consonants in much the same way as word-internal sequences of two consonants: in neither case do these sequences form exceptions to the general statement that consonant clusters are not permitted within a single syllable.

A small number of languages have been cited in the literature where there is a hierarchy of syllable weights, leading to a definition of syllable weight with more than two weight categories. For example, it is reported (Willett 1982) that in Southeastern Tepehuan, a Uto-Aztecan language, stress falls predictably on the first syllable of the stem, except that it will fall on the second syllable if the second syllable is heavier; i.e., stress falls on the heavier of the first two syllables and on the first if they are of the same weight. However, three degrees of heaviness must be established. Simple open (CV) syllables are the lightest, and syllables with long vowels or diphthongs (CVV) are the heaviest, but short closed syllables (CVC) are intermediate in weight. For example, we can see that long vowels are heavier than short closed syllables from an example such as *jiñcáam* 'my cheek', and heavier than open syllables from an example such as *vacóos* 'he went to sleep'. Short closed syllables, in turn, are seen to be heavier than open syllables from examples such as *comí-ñ* 'his back'. This kind of example, while rare, is not totally isolated. Such complex definitions of a scale of syllable weight appear to be limited to cases of non-recursive stress assignment (i.e. to stress principles that apply only to the first two or last two syllables of a word); but precisely why that should be true, if indeed it is, remains unclear.

A few languages have a three-way division that appears to be related to syllable weight. The best known case of this may be Estonian, in which syllables have traditionally been divided up into three categories of what we might call prosodic prominence, searching for a theory-neutral description: short, long, and overlong (also referred to as Q1, Q2, and Q3, respectively). CV syllables are short (Q1); CVC, CVV, and CVVC syllables are long (Q2). (Estonian distinguishes long and short vowels, though long vowels appear only in word-initial syllable.) Overlong syllables are described as having lengthened versions of the rhyme-final consonant (if there is one) and a lengthened version of the vowel *if* the vowel is long; a short vowel will not lengthen to long if it is found in an overlong syllable. Thus, Q1 syllables are of the form CV; Q2 are of the form CVV, CVC, or CVVC; and Q3 syllables are of the form CVV:, CVC:, or CVV:C:, where the colon indicates lengthening of the preceding element, vowel, or consonant. (It has been suggested (Tauli 1954) that, in the case of CVV:C: syllables, the lengthening that the colons indicate can be realized on either the vowel [CVV:C] or the consonant [CVVC:], or both [CVV:C:].) This suggests (Leben 1977) that there is a direct correspondence between the Q2 system of consonants and the Q3 system, which represents a lengthening of the rhyme of the Q2 syllable as a whole (though not to the extent of collapsing the intra-syllabic long/short distinction). Without entering further into the details, a strong case can be made that the contrast between the Q2 and Q3 system is distinct and orthogonal from that between the Q1 and Q2 system, and does not involve the internal structure of the rhyme. Thus, there is no single dimension of length in Estonian with three specifications.

3.3   SYLLABLE STRUCTURE ASSIGNMENT

Having talked a good deal about what syllables are and what syllable structure does, we can now ask how the structure gets there, for in *some* way syllable structure is dependent on the segmental content of the morphemes in an utterance. We assume that syllabification is a process that associates a linear string of segments with a syllable structure. What happens if more than one satisfactory match can be found between segments and syllable structure? On this last question, various principles have been offered, two of which will be discussed briefly in this chapter (the Maximal Onset Principle, and directionality of syllable structure creation).

More importantly, what happens if the segments of the underlying representation – the underlying forms that have been concatenated by the morphological component – cannot be parsed into successive permissible syllables? What if a string of three consonants is found in a language that does not permit such sequences? Consider the well-known example of Yokuts,[12] where the underlying form *logw-hin* in (8d) cannot be parsed into the acceptable CV(X) (i.e. CV, CVV, or CVC) syllables of Yokuts. (8) presents surface forms, with their underlying forms surrounded by slashes. An epenthetic vowel /i/ is therefore inserted to form the correct surface pattern [logiwhin]. How does this occur?

(8)   Yokuts
        Nonfuture   Dubitative

(a)	xat-hin	/xat-hin/	xat-al	/xat-al/
(b)	bok̓-hin	/bok̓-hin/	bok̓-ol	/bok̓-al/
(c)	dos-hin	/do:s-hin/	do:s-ol	/do:s-al/
(d)	logiw-hin	/logw-hin/	logw-ol	/logw-al/

Three kinds of proposals have received widespread attention in the literature, in large part in response to this last question, proposals that deal with building up syllable structure. Two of these proposals are 'vowel-driven', while one involves empty vowel positions (so-called 'degenerate syllables'). We shall refer to them as (i) the 'all nuclei first' approach; (ii) the linear scanning approach; and (iii) the total syllabification approach.

All proposals focus on the obligatory character of the syllable nucleus.[13] The first, the 'all nuclei first' approach, builds up nucleus (N), rhyme (R), and syllable (σ) structure from each syllabic element first, as in (9a), and then begins adjoining consonants in appropriate ways to these incipient syllables (see (9b)).[14]

We see at this point that the *w* in the first example is extrasyllabic in the sense of 'contingent extrasyllabicity' discussed just above. This special status is used to trigger a rule of epenthesis, given in (10); the notation C' has been used to indicate a contingently extrasyllabic

(9)   (a)

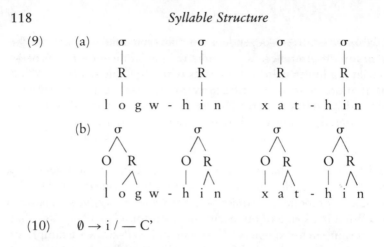

(b)

(10) $\emptyset \rightarrow i \, / \, — \, C'$

segment. The derivation in (9) then continues as in (11), with the *g* shifting from the coda of the first syllable to the onset of the new syllable; this effect is related to the Maximal Onset Principle, discussed below.

(11)   (a)

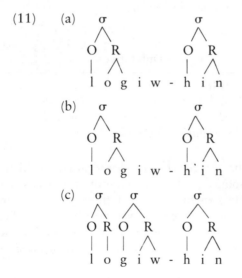

(b)

(c)

The second procedure scans linearly, either from left to right or right to left, depending on the language, constructing syllables in such a way as to build the largest syllables (i.e. the smallest number of syllables) consistent with the language's restrictions on possible syllables. In cases where there are too few vowels, wrongly placed, to provide syllables for all the consonants present, this procedure will yield the same result as the first one.

On either the first or the second proposal, there will be what we have called 'contingent extrasyllabic' consonants in the derivation of certain forms, as we have seen. In the third approach, the total syllabification approach, no such transient extrasyllabic elements are permitted; syllable structure is imposed equally on consonants and on vowels, and if no segmental material is available to fill an obligatory position (typically the vocalic nucleus of the syllable), then the structure is built anyway, with the nuclear position dominating no skeletal position. Here, directionality of syllabification is of utmost importance. This becomes clear when assigning syllable structure to the Yokuts example again, as in (12).[15]

(12)   Applying the CV(X) pattern of Yokuts
(a) Left to right

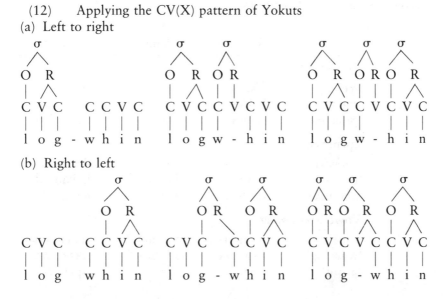

(b) Right to left

Clearly, quite different predictions about the resultant structure will be made depending on the direction chosen for application. The major advantage of the total syllabification approach is the naturalness with which it approaches the phenomenon of epenthesis, which can now be stated as a process that inserts a language-particular vowel into an empty vowel position that has already been established by the more general syllabification procedures; this approach to epenthesis then directly and unambiguously selects the right-to-left procedure in (12b). In (12b), the insertion of an *i* into the empty syllable nucleus gives us the correct surface form, *logiwhin;* a similar attempt applied to (12a) would give us the incorrect *logwihin.*[16]

The disadvantage of the total syllabification approach is the same as the advantage, for epenthesis is just one of a number of options that languages have for arriving at an acceptable assignment of surface syllable structure. Equally common procedures include cluster simplification, vowel shortening, and degemination, all of which would entail deletion of a syllable node on the total syllabification approach. For example, in Turkish (as cited by Clements and Keyser 1983:59), three processes are called into play to achieve well-formed CV(X) syllables when the morphology produces unacceptable sequences. In such cases, consonants will degeminate and vowels will shorten, and just in case these processes are unavailable as solutions (if, that is, the vowel is already short and there is no geminate to shorten), then epenthesis will apply, as we see in (13), where surface forms are given; readers can easily reconstruct the underlying forms.

(13)	Accusative	Nominative	Ablative
Degemination			
'feeling'	hiss+i	his	his+ten
'right'	hakk+ɨ	hak	hak+tan
'price increase'	zamm+ɨ	zam	zam+dan
Epenthesis			
'transfer'	devr+i	devir	devir+den
'bosom'	koyn+u	koyun	koyun+dan
'abdomen'	karn+ɨ	karɨn	karɨn+dan
Vowel shortening			
'time'	zama:n+ɨ	zaman	zaman+dan
'warning'	i:ka:z+ɨ	i:kaz	i:kaz+dan
'proof'	ispa:t+ɨ	ispat	ispat+tan

On the total syllabification approach, the underlying forms for representative examples of the nominative (suffixless) forms with syllable structure are those given in (14a), assuming again a right-to-left syllabification. On the other approaches, which allow for contingent extrasyllabicity, the underlying forms are those given in (14b).

As we have already suggested, the second example /devr/ has a natural account in the total syllabification approach, parallel to the Yokuts example above in all respects. But the first example, *his:*, does not at all do what might be expected; it does not become *hissi*. Instead, degemination occurs, giving a surface form *his*. We could, in a sense, say that degemination is preferred to epenthesis; we return to this point in a moment. In the third example, too, on the total syllabification approach, it is not patent why anything should happen to the representation in (14a)(iii); it is, after all, totally syllabified. On the second account, given

(14)

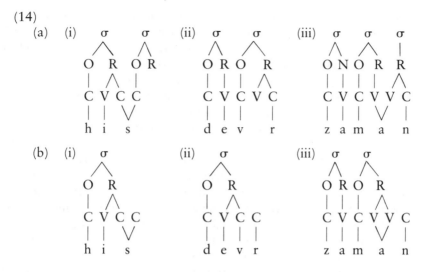

in (14b)(iii), we can identify an ill-formed character of the representation, the (contingently) extrasyllabic final C-position, just as in (14b)(i).

When all is said and done, we can identify two processes here: loss of a segment's second skeletal position (i.e. loss of its length), and insertion of an epenthetic vowel. The former is always preferred to the latter (in Turkish, as in most languages); this could be expressed in rule ordering, but it is a case of what we might call logical precedence rule ordering, rather than truly sequential ordering.[17]

When does syllabification occur? There is general agreement that syllabification is predictable, and thus need not be a property of underlying forms *per se*. Syllabification serves two kinds of purposes in the phonological derivation; we have already seen this in the discussion of epenthesis immediately above. Early syllabification can serve the purpose of exposing problems for the phonology, generally in the guise of unsyllabified (i.e. unsyllabifiable) material; these problems are then resolved by the various procedures we know as epenthesis, cluster simplification, and so on. But to make sense of that notion on a larger scale, we have to think of complete syllabification as a far stricter well-formedness condition that will hold true on a particular level in the grammar. That is, partial syllabification can be a problem only if there is some stage at which complete syllabification serves as a well-formedness condition on representations. What level is that?

The answer seems to be, in essence, that it is the level that defines the *word* in each given language. It is a surprisingly tricky business to establish what that domain is, and how to characterize it in a set of morphological and phonological rules. In the tradition of American structuralism, as in Nida (1949) or Bloch and Trager (1942), there is a notion of close and open juncture, which roughly corresponds to the SPE distinction between a + morpheme boundary and a # word boundary; see also Z. Harris (1951: 86-7). The phonological word might most simply be defined as a maximal string containing no open juncture. Harris (p. 130), for example, talks about the domain of sibilant harmony in Navaho as being the *word*, and defines that as the maximal stretch not containing a # word boundary. But for the most part, structuralists were comfortable only with distributional statements about phonemes that were dependent on the presence of a neighboring boundary segment. In the generative tradition, the concentration has been on the domain of rule application, and for the most part no single, clear notion has emerged as an appropriate characterization of the word in this tradition. (This may be changing; we return to this matter in chapter 5.)

In English, it is well known that this domain is smaller than what is orthographically taken to be the word; as has long been known, the normal prohibition against geminate consonants within words, for example, is apparently lifted in such forms as *unnatural* or *coolly* – which is to say, these forms do not display all the normal hallmarks of simple words of English. Many other general phonotactic statements can be made about the *word* in English, including (i) a prohibition that excludes a non-high vowel followed by a vowel (ruling out the schwa-vowel sequence found in *pap[ə] and mama*, for example, though this can be found in in a nonce-form such as *Indiana-ism* (on which, more below in chapter 5)), and (ii) the requirement that a single intervocalic consonant will syllabify with the vowel on the right (which does not happen across separate words, as we see in *take aim*, as well as in compounds such as *cat album*, where the *t* is clearly syllabified with the first syllable).

As we shall see in more detail in chapter 5, the suffixes of English have frequently been divided into two classes. For now, we may simply refer to them as the *stress-affecting* suffixes, such as *-ate, -ion, -ic, -al*, and *-ity*, and the *stress-neutral*, such as *-ness, -less, -ly*. In fact, the distinction is not so much between two groups of suffixes as between two *ways* in which suffixes can be attached to their bases. In the first case, the combined form of the base plus 'stress-affecting' suffix together forms a unit that acts with respect to many principles, especially stress, like an unanalyzed form, and thus will display internally (and especially in the neighborhood of the juncture between the base and the affix) modifications necessary to meet the conditions on being a word.

The combination of a base with a 'stress-neutral' suffix is not of this sort. Just how to treat the second kind of affixation, the kind found in *Indianaism* and *coolly*, is a question to which we will return in chapter 5, and it is not one on which there is current consensus. However, if we hold aside and in abeyance the treatment of stress-neutral affixation and compounding, then the level at which syllabification is obligatory will include *all* stress-affecting suffixes, and this will be at the final stage in the derivation at which only the *distinctive* features of phonology play a role. Thus, we may picture the phonological derivation as operating initially only with the distinctive features of the language, modifying and re-arranging the features and structures in such a way as to arrive at a proper syllabification of the string, at which point the word-level part of the derivation may successfully end. We shall refer to this as the *W-level*. It is the deepest level at which phonotactic conditions can be stated.[18]

In sum, then, we shall take syllabification to apply, throughout the derivation, to construct syllable structure in a minimal fashion (i.e. with the minimal number of syllables) to cover the maximum number of segments possible. A more general well-formedness condition is imposed on W-level that syllabification must be total (though we modify the notion 'total' in the next section).

3.4 LICENSING

We referred earlier to a notion of *prosodic licensing*, which required that all elements be a member of some syllable, or else be marked as contingently extrasyllabic. The conception that guided this condition was the view that language is a fully organized whole from the top down.

In this section I will suggest a different notion, that of *autosegmental licensing* (which I shall often just call *licensing*), which shares a certain general sense with the earlier notion of licensing, but is quite different in its specifics, and which sets much stronger conditions on possible structures. I will begin by sketching the basic idea, and then explain the motivation and some of the details behind the proposal.

The essence of the idea of autosegmental licensing is that there are prosodic units that are *licensers* – the syllable node as a primary licenser, and the coda node and certain word-final morphemes as secondary licensers. A licenser is endowed by the grammar of the language with the ability to license a set of phonological features – or, more precisely, autosegments, though at the moment the difference between the two can be ignored: however, although the *point of articulation* may consist of several features, it counts as one unit for the purposes of licensing for this reason. A given licenser can license no more than one occurrence of the autosegment in question. This unique licensing can be graphically represented in terms of a non-branching path that can be traced from the licenser to the autosegment (or feature) in question (see (15)). Finally, in line with the remarks above, all autosegmental material must be licensed at the level we called the W-level, the *word*-level. Elements not licensed at this level will not proceed to the post-lexical phonology, i.e. are deleted.

Imagine a simple case, a language that has only two distinctive vowel features (high and round) and one distinctive consonantal feature (point of articulation), and only CV syllable structure. The syllable node will always be a licenser for all of the distinctive features of the language, and we will mark licensers with the features that they license in braces. All autosegments would be licensed by being dominated by a position that is marked as a licenser for that feature. These features would then be licensed as in (15).

(15)

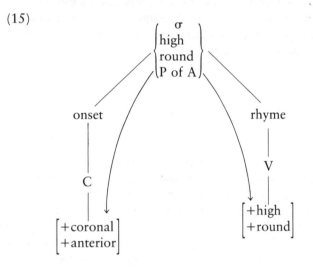

A language like the one above but which in addition permits the coda to be specified for the feature [nasal] (but not, e.g., the feature [point of articulation]) would appear as in (16), where some alphabetic symbols are used to replace more cumbersome features.[19]

The basic motivations for this analysis of syllable structure are as follows.

(1) If we focus simply on the phonologically *distinctive* features of a language, it has been noted on a number of occasions that there is a very strong tendency for each such feature to be specified no more than once within the combined domain of the onset and the nucleus. This observation – made for English by Fujimura and by Hirst, for example[20] – has generally been made with respect to the onset alone, but since there is

(16)

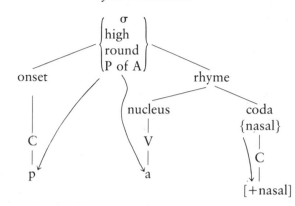

essentially no overlap between the distinctive features of the onset and those of the nucleus, the generalization can be extended. Thus, there is a maximum of one appearance of each distinctive feature over the onset–nucleus span; conversely, any feature that is distinctive in the language can appear in at least one position in the onset or nucleus. If the latter were not so, there would be a feature that could appear distinctively only in the coda; but that never occurs. Fujimura and Hirst have pointed out that significant simplification of the treatment of the onset can be achieved in this way in their treatments of English. A way of summarizing the point more generally is by noting that phonological systems have a tendency to limit to one occurrence per domain any distinctive feature under their control. For example, in the onset, there may be only one occurrence of the feature [+continuant]; hence an /s/ may never precede a fricative. Similarly, there may be only one occurrence of the feature [labial]; hence a /p/ or a /b/ may never precede the glide /w/.

(2) What is consistently unusual about the coda, in language after language, is that there are far fewer contrasts available in the coda, but, whatever contrasts are available there are a subset of the contrasts available in the first half of the syllable. Thus the coda is, as we have said, a secondary licenser: it has only a subset of the possibilities of contrast of the first part of the syllable. This notion has traditionally been called *weakening*, and is due, on our account, to the reduced licensing possibilities of the coda position. A particularly striking and important example of this is the case where the coda is incapable of licensing a point of articulation autosegment. In that case, nasals and obstruents that appear in the coda will either be homorganic to a following consonant – that is, they will share the point of articulation autosegment that is licensed by the following onset – or they will have a non-distinctive default point of articulation. We will look at such systems in more detail below; most

Bantu languages illustrate this point.[21] But more generally, we find codas in countless languages which do not have the privilege of bearing contrastive marking for voicing (German), or the feature [continuant] (modern Greek), and so forth.

(3) The third motivation for the notion of autosegmental licensing is the way in which syllable structure is linked to prosodic systems, both accentual and tonal. In both domains, the overriding generalization that needs to be accounted for is that the onset and the first element of the nucleus always count as a single unit, whether it is a matter of associating to tones or counting moras for stress. If there is a coda to the syllable in question, it may or may not count as a second unit. This follows directly from our account, as (17) illustrates for the tonal case. The two possibilities – whether the second mora gets a chance for its own tone – are the result of the parameter of whether the coda licenses a tone or not.

(17)

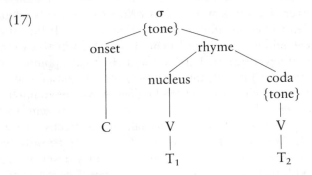

The same point holds, *mutatis mutandis*, for association to the bottom row of the metrical grid – which is to say, the same point holds for whether a syllable will be treated as being heavy from the point of view of metrical structure. In (17), above, regard T_1 and T_2 as elements on the bottom row of the metrical grid (see section 4.6); licensing conditions determine whether one such association is permitted or two. We have thereby derived one of the most striking generalizations known about syllable structure: in a language that has a quantity system, the onset plus the first mora of the syllable count for one unit as far as stress is concerned, and the rest of the rhyme will count for the second unit. The irrelevance of onset structure for syllable quantity follows precisely from our notion of autosegmental licensing, in that the syllable whole, as a licenser, acts for the onset and the nucleus, while the coda acts as a secondary licenser, free as such to license association to a second grid position.[22]

Summarizing, then, we take the syllable node to be the main licenser of the syllable. Logically associated with the syllable node is the set of all of the distinctive features of the language. For a segment bearing that feature to associate with a point on the skeletal tier, it must be possible to trace a unique, non-branching, path up and down from the top licensing node to that skeletal point. When the syllables of a language have a coda position – which is in most, though not all, languages – the coda is a *secondary licenser*, that is to say, a node that also serves as the point of origin of a licensing path down to the skeleton. The language will assign a subset – typically, a small subset – of the features of the language to the coda position, thus allowing only a small set of possible contrasts in the coda.

Two other types of association will always be licensed by the syllable, and will be licensed in a language-particular way by the coda. These are (i) association to tone; and (ii) association to the bottom (mora) row of the metrical grid. If the coda of a language licenses association to tone, then the syllable will give the appearance of associating to one tone when it is light, and to two when it is heavy. Similarly, treating association to the metrical grid (the formal counterpart of moras as far as the stress system of the language is concerned, and the subject of the next chapter) allows us to see why the onset plus the first element of the rhyme 'counts as' – i.e. associates with – one mora, while the presence of additional material in the rhyme may or may not count as a second metrical beat, or mora, in a way that is language-dependent.[23]

In addition to the coda as a secondary licenser, many languages permit another kind of secondary licensing at word-boundary, which is what we have called 'licensed extrasyllabicity'. The licenser in such cases is an element that we shall refer to as 'Ω', and the features that it licences are the features that may appear in word-final *terminations* (to use Fudge's term) or *appendices*. In English, as we shall see, this is limited to the features [continuant] and [voice]. In Arabic, on the other hand, any word-final consonant[24] can appear as a licensed extrasyllabic element. What is most surprising about this appendix to the Arabic word is that the Ω-licenser licenses association to the metrical grid as well. This has as a consequence that the appendix of the Arabic word counts as a mora, and contributes to determining the stress placement of an Arabic word. Arabic quite generally is a quantity-sensitive language, which is to say that the coda also licenses association to metrical positions. Put another way, the coda and the Ω-position in Arabic are both secondary licensers licensing the same subset of features of the language. We will return to the matter of Arabic in the next chapter, when we deal with stress placement.

We shall see below, in our discussion of English final -*th*, that word-final morphemes can also be secondary licensers.

3.5 RHYME RESTRICTIONS, POINT OF ARTICULATION, AND MAXIMAL ONSET

If we focus on the internal structure of the rhyme, we can establish a useful classification of recurring possible rhyme types.[25] As (18) suggests, some particular restrictions on syllables and their segments are straightforward and quite common. It is common, for example, to find a

(18)   Table of possible coda contrasts

Type of syllable	Example
(a) $CV_i(V_j)$	Diphthongs and contrastive vowel length: Hawaiian
(b) CV[X, no P of A]	A nasal or obstruent permitted in the coda if it is homorganic with the following consonant or otherwise predictable P of A: Selayarese, Luganda, Irula, Axininca Campa
(c) CV[X, sonorant]	Like (b), but also glides and liquids allowed in rhyme: standard Hausa
(d) CVX	Coda can have anything the onset can

restriction prohibiting consonants from the coda entirely; such languages are said to be strict 'CV' languages. Languages like Fijian, Hawaiian, and other Polynesian languages, for example, permit no consonant in the coda; furthermore, only one consonant can appear in the onset (19a) (Pukui and Elbert 1971). Another common pattern is as is found in Hausa (Bargery 1934), where syllables are of the form CVC, but the syllable-final consonant can only be a glide, a liquid, a nasal homorganic with the onset, or an *s*, as described in (19b). In still other languages another common pattern is found, the final one on the list, in which only a single segment – either vowel or consonant – may appear in the coda, as in Yokuts. (This is sometimes referred to as a language with 'CVX' syllables.) The situation may be straightforward and simple, with all possible consonants appearing in the coda. Alternatively, there may be restrictions; Alabaman, for example, does not permit /b, c, ɬ, or w/ in its coda (Rand 1968).

If the most striking gross restrictions on possible syllable types involve specifying the number of segments from the two major classes, consonant and vowel, in each of the major constituents of the syllable, then the next most important set of restrictions arises out of the distribution of point of

(19) (a) Hawaiian

kai	'ocean'	mala	'ache'
kae	'to refuse'	ma:la	'garden'
ʔelemakule	'old man'		

(b) Hausa

gulbi	'river'		
sarne	'pagan'	(< Arabic *azne*)	
murful	'hearth'	ɓauna	'buffalo'
muraafuu	'hearths'	ɓakanee	'buffalos'
auduga	'cotton'	bambanta	'to differ from'

articulation specification. Let us consider how this might be so.

All languages allow for there to be a contrastive point of articulation specified in the onset of the syllable. This is realized superficially in the contrast allowed, for example, between such simple syllables as *pa*, *ta*, and *ka*. Some languages permit a second, *contrastive*, point of articulation to be expressed, but this will be expressed in the coda. English is such a language, and it thus allows a contrast between such syllables as *pip*, *pit*, and *pick* [pik]. Very few languages allow two contrastive points of articulation either within the onset or within the coda.[26] Thus, in English, for example, the onset structure allows up to three segments in a cluster, as in *strap*. Only the point of articulation of the middle consonant is contrastive, though; there is a contrast between *strap*, *scrap*, and *sprat*, but no contrast in point of articulation (or anything else) with regard to the fricative preceding the stop, or the point of articulation of the liquid following the stop; liquids rarely or never have distinctive points of articulation. Thus, there is one and only one contrastive point of articulation in the onset in English.

The same holds true for the rhyme; whatever lengthy material may be added to the coda of the English syllable, its point of articulation is predictably alveolar.[27] Such a specification is non-distinctive, and within the context of a framework such as lexical phonology (see chapter 5) it will not appear until the post-lexical phonology. At the stage in analysis at which contrastive and only contrastive phonological material is specified, a maximum of one point of articulation may be specified in the onset and the coda of the syllable.

A familiar pattern of restrictions on point of articulation is found in languages in which the coda can contain a liquid or nasal preceding an obstruent, but in which the nasal, if it is there, must be homorganic to the final consonant. English represents a subset of such a system, i.e. a system with further restrictions. This pattern, it should be clear, fits in precisely with the generalization noted above: while the coda may be specified for one distinctive point of articulation, it may not be specified for two distinctive points of articulation. If there is an obstruent ending the syllable, it will be the site of association of that point of articulation, and the preceding nasal will receive its point of articulation specification only by sharing, as in (20a); (20b) is not allowed.

(20)   (a)

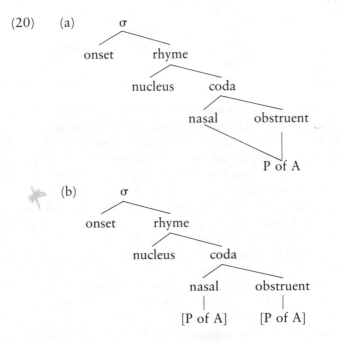

These characteristics, and others like them to which we return in a moment, would to our usual way of thinking be treated as properties of the syllable; we would list them as characteristics of what can appear in the syllable. However, a quite different perspective opens up from the point of view of autosegmental licensing, allowing us to turn the matter on its head – at least from the traditional point of view – and regard the restriction not so much as a restriction on syllables (though to some extent it is that) as rather a restriction on the point of articulation autosegments.

When the onset and the coda are both licensed to receive distinctive points of articulation, we find the kind of systems mentioned so far, as in English. When the onset, but not the coda, can license point of articulation, we find a situation in which, by definition, the coda cannot support a contrastive point of articulation. The coda will then be restricted either to those segments that are not contrastively defined by a point of articulation (such as a vowel, a glide, or a liquid), or to adopting a point of articulation parasitically from the following onset (the case of a geminate consonant or the first half of a homorganic nasal cluster (*mb*, *nd*, etc.)), sharing it via a double autosegmental association, or to inserting a default consonant, again with no contrastive point of articulation. This is an extremely common situation, and we will look at another example, that of Selayarese, in a moment. Licensing of the point of articulation allows us to see nasal-stop clusters in English codas in much the same terms as we do in the set of languages that require that the final consonant of their coda be homorganic with a following consonant. The difference in the two cases is whether the coda can license one or no points of articulation, respectively.

Let us consider an example of a language in which the coda is not a licenser of point of articulation. An excellent example of a language of this sort is Selayarese, an Austronesian language spoken in Indonesia, as described, and in part as analyzed, by Mithun and Basri (1986). The segmental inventory is given in (21).

(21)

	Labial	Dental/ alveolar		Palatal	Velar	Glottal
p	b	t	d	j	k g	ʔ
	mb		nd	ñj	ŋg	h
	m		n	ñ	ŋ	
		s				
		l	r			
i	u					
e	o					
	a					

Onsets in Selayarese have a maximum of one consonant; vowel length is not contrastive, and, underlyingly, syllables are of three basic sorts, which we may call short, nasal, and checked, bearing in mind that these are just temporary terms used for description. Stressed syllables must be heavy, so if stress falls on a CV syllable, the vowel lengthens (with one exception, involving epenthetic vowels, which we will return to below); otherwise, open syllables have a light rhyme. Nasal syllables end in a single, nasal consonant, which is homorganic to the following consonant in the next syllable's onset. If that consonant is *l*, then the nasal segment totally assimilates, becoming *l*. If the nasal syllable is phrase-final, then the point of articulation of the nasal segment is velar (and the nasal is thus an angma); see (22).

The third type of syllable, the checked syllable, is the most volatile type. Mithun and Basri analyze it as a syllable closed by a glottal stop,

(22) pekaŋ   'hook'   pekampekaŋ   'hook-like object'
      bambaŋ   'hot'   bambambambaŋ   'sort of hot'
      maŋŋaŋ   'tired'   maŋŋammaŋŋaŋ   'sort of tired'

      tunruŋ   'hit'   tunruntunruŋ   'hit lightly'
      soroŋ   'push'   soronsoroŋ   'drawer'
      dodoŋ   'sick'   dodondodoŋ   'sort of sick'
      nunruŋ   'hit'   nunrunnunruŋ   'hit lightly (intrans.)'
      roŋgaŋ   'loose'   roŋganroŋgaŋ   'rather loose'

      jaŋaŋ   'chicken'   jaŋañjanaŋ   'bird'
      keloŋ   'sing'   keloŋkeloŋ   'sort of sing'
      gintaŋ   'chili'   gintaŋgintaŋ   'chili-like object'
      hukkuŋ   'punish'   hukkuŋhukkuŋ   'punish lightly'

      lamuŋ   'grow'   lamullamuŋ   'plantation'
      luŋaŋ   'pillow'   luŋalluŋaŋ   'small pillow'

but note that such glottal stops 'undergo pervasive assimilation', and note furthermore that the glottal stop is the only segment inserted by a purely phonological rule. We will analyze it as an empty coda position.

In determining how to analyze checked syllables, we must look at two types of information: distributional information, and alternations undergone by morphemes that end in checked syllables. We find that syllable-final glottal stops never occur when the next syllable begins with a voiceless consonant. As Mithun and Basri observe, this serves as the basis for a rule geminating voiceless consonants, in leftward fashion, when a checked syllable precedes. (See (24a), essentially their rule, reformulated in (24b).) Otherwise, all closed syllables in other positions are closed by a glottal stop, both before voiced consonants, and phrase-finally. These possibilities are illustrated in (23).

We may now begin to generalize about underlying syllables in Selayarese. The coda is optional, but if it appears underlyingly, the only specification it may have is nasal; it may also be totally unspecified. All other information – in particular, the information regarding point of articulation – is filled in by a later rule. These will include either the autosegmental gemination rule in (24), the rule that makes otherwise unspecified nasal consonants into velars and otherwise unspecified non-nasal consonants into glottal stops, or certain other processes discussed in Mithun and Basri. Thus, the coda licenses only the feature [nasal] – nothing else. This illustrates a clear example of a language of type (b) described in (18) above.

Selayarese has several other interesting rules and processes, including a vowel-lengthening process that lengthens vowels in stressed open

(23)   Prefix /ta²/, i.e.

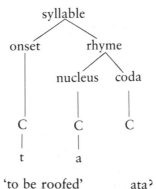

ta²ata²	'to be roofed'	ata²	'roof'
ta²enteŋ	'to be erected'	enteŋ	'stand'
ta²inuŋ	'to be drunk (liq.)'	inuŋ	'drink'
tappela²	'get lost'		
tattuda	'bump against'		
takkaluppa	'faint'		
tassambaŋ	'stumble, trip'		
ta²bessolo	'slip'		
ta²do²do²	'be sleepy'		
ta²jai	'be sewn'		
ta²garaŋ	'get stained'		
ta²muri	'smile'		
ta²no²noso	'be shaken (liquid)'		
ta²lesaŋ	'be removed'		

(24)   (a) C   C   (b) Ⓒ   C
              ╪- - - -╯   ╲- - - -╯
              ²   [−voice]   [−voice]

syllables, in line with the generalization that we return to in section 3.9
below, that stressed syllables should be heavy. A syllable that is already
closed is heavy, and so a stressed syllable (indicated with underlining)
that appears in an open syllable is lengthened: see (25).

The requirement that a stressed syllable be heavy means that a second

(25)   sa:sa   'cut (grass)'
         sassa   'wash'
         ²a:pa   'what?'
         ²appa²   'four'
         ke:ke   'dig'
         kekke²   'to tear'

rhyme element should be present, and it is not surprising that this element is not nasalized (since something would have to introduce that nasalization). But it is not predictable that what should associate with the second rhyme position in the derived long rhyme of a stressed syllable should be the vowel, rather than, say, the following consonant. In fact, the facts are a bit more complex. Stress is normally on the penultimate syllable, but in certain cases it may appear to be on the antepenult. This arises because an underlying form may end in the consonants *s, l,* or *r,* i.e. in a consonant that has no contrastive point of articulation. The word then undergoes an epenthesis rule, which inserts an empty vowel position, eventually surfacing as a copy of the preceding vowel. Forms with these epenthetic vowels are thus very clearly marked by special stress, i.e. on the antepenult rather than the penult. This is illustrated in (26). This epenthetic vowel can also be distinguished from a true underlying vowel in that it will not appear when the form has a suffix such as *-aŋ* 'comparative'; cf. (27).

(26)	Underlying	Derived	Gloss
	katal	katala	'itch'
	sambal	sambala	'vegetable dish'
	no'nos	no'noso	'shake liquid'

(27)	Underlying	Derived	Gloss
	lohe	lohe	'many'
	lohe-aŋ	loheaŋ	'more'
	lamber	lambere	'long'
	lamber-aŋ	lamberaŋ	'longer'

Finally, we note that epenthetic vowels, when stressed, do not lengthen: rather, the following consonant becomes geminate. See (28), where (a) illustrates the case of an epenthetic vowel, and (b) illustrates the normal case of an underlyingly trisyllabic form. The (a) form is a good illustration of the way a stress rule (here, penultimate stress) can apply within the base word (*sahala*), before epenthesis, and in the outer word. Epenthesis of the final *a* clearly *precedes* stress on the outer cycle, i.e. the whole word, since it is the epenthetic vowel that is stressed; however, the epenthetical vowel is equally clearly not available at the point when stress is assigned to the simple word *sahal*.

Our account of these data, in the light of licensing theory, is straightforward, though somewhat complex in the light of the number of different systems that interact. The coda of a word-internal syllable can license no more than the feature [nasal]; liquids and *s* cannot appear in

(28)　　　　Underlying　　　Surface　　　　Gloss

(a)　sahal　　　　sahala　　　　'profit'
　　　sahal+ku　　sahalakku　　'my profit'

(b)　sahala　　　　sahala　　　　'sea cucumber'
　　　sahala+ku　　sahala:ku　　'my sea cucumber'

this position. Thus, a word-final secondary licenser, which, like codas, does not license point of articulation, must be established for the language that licenses only the features [liquid], [lateral], and [continuant] – an appendix Ω to the word. At the W-level, such appendices are linked by rule to an empty position on the skeleton ((30b), appendix conversion). Thus there are two sources of empty skeletal slots created during the word-level derivation. One such element is inserted into a light stressed syllable, and the other is created by the appendix conversion rule. In both cases, a rule of vowel spreading applies to the right.

(29)　　Bisyllabic　　　　　　　　　　　Trisyllabic

　　　　/sahal/　'profit'　　　　　　　　/sahala/　'sea cucumber'

(a)　Underlying representation

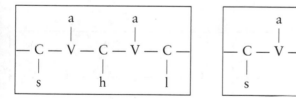

(b)　Syllabification

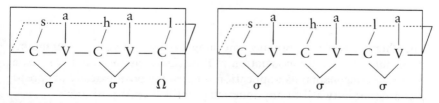

Ω = appendix

(c) Stress

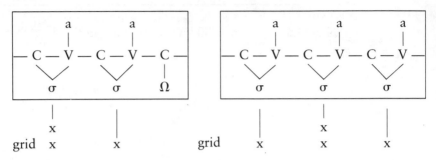

(d) Mora addition, appendix-conversion

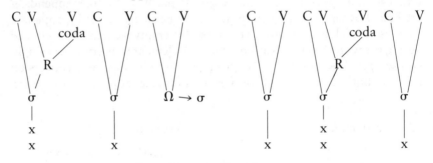

(e) Vowel-spreading

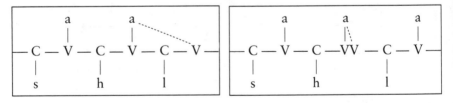

Epenthetic vowels do not become long because there is a minimum/maximum of (1, 2) for association.[28] Rule (24b) will then apply to create geminate consonants; its application is extended post-lexically to spread a consonant leftward to any remaining unfilled coda position.[29]

Axininca Campa, an Arawakan language of Peru (Payne 1981) has

(30)   (a) Vowel-spreading

(b) Appendix-conversion

long and short vowels, but allows only word-medial syllables to be closed, and then only by a nasal which is homorganic to the following (syllable-initial) consonant, as in (31). Thus, no element of the rhyme has an independently marked point of articulation, and the only nonvocalic feature licensed in the rhyme is the feature [nasal].

(31)	antari	'large (animate)'
	impoke	'he will come'
	saŋko	'sugar cane'
	tagaŋȼhi	'to burn'
	sagaari	'fox'

Let us now turn briefly to another point regarding the asymmetry of onset and coda. Important ambiguities can arise in the syllabification procedure when one or more consonants appear between vowels in a language that permits consonants to appear in the coda. VCV sequences are almost always resolved in favor of a syllabification that puts the consonant in the onset of the syllable to the right: (32a) rather than (32b). It appears as if it were more important to the syllable to have an onset than to have a coda; this has been called the *Maximal Onset Principle.*

In terms of licensing, a coda element is licensed by a secondary licenser, while an onset element is licensed by the primary licenser, the syllable. A syllabification algorithm that constructs well-formed licensing structures with the minimum number of licensers will (i) construct the fewest possible syllables consistent with the phonological string, a well established result; and (ii) syllabify an intervocalic segment in an onset rather than a coda, since the latter would require establishing one more licensing unit. That is, a structure as in (32a) has two licensers, the two primary licensers, while that in (32b) has three – two syllables and a coda. Put another way, the principle that syllabification is established by means of the fewest possible number of licensers has, as one of its consequences, the Maximal Onset Principle.

(32)   (a)

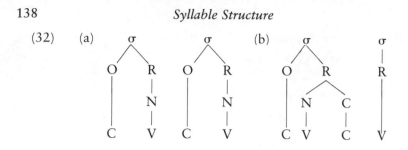

One case has been studied in the literature in which a single intervocalic consonant in underlying form is consistentiy syllabified with the preceding consonant, that of Scots Gaelic.[30] However, there is evidence that the consonant that follows the vowel in Scots Gaelic is licensed by the syllable, the primary licenser, while the consonant that precedes the consonant (in, say, a VCCV cluster, as in *L'endal* 'to follow') is licensed by a secondary licenser. To put the matter in a way that seems paradoxical, we may say that in Scots Gaelic the coda precedes the nucleus of the syllable, and the onset follows it; but what we mean in saying that is that the primary licenser licenses material to the right. The theory, of course, permits such a thing, and predicts that if either position has no restrictions on which position can accept segments with contrastive points of articulation, it will be the position licensed by the primary licenser, which in this case is the post-vocalic segment (see (27a)). Since the secondary licenser does not license point of articulation, the language turns out to be the mirror image of Hausa, sketched above.

Bosch (1988) argues that this is so, on the basis of her reanalysis of the epenthesis rule proposed in Clements (1986). She argues that, under the relevant conditions, epenthesis can be said to apply just in case a structure is unsyllabifiable, if we say that a consonant in the *pre-vocalic* coda cannot license a point of articulation; in order for it to associate with a point of articulation, it must autosegmentally share it with an element on the left. Thus, *eg-Liš* 'church' or *oibre* 'works' is possible, since the sonorant has no distinctive point of articulation, as is *baL't'iŋ* 'villages', since, though the *t'* is specified for a point of articulation, it shares it with the preceding liquid which is in a position to license it. However, a sequence like *urpel* 'tail' or *Alba* 'Scotland' contains a labial specification in a (prevocalic) 'coda' position, i.e. one dominated by a secondary licenser, unable to license a point of articulation. Thus, the structures are not well-formed, and epenthesis applies, giving us the respective surface forms [urùpəl] and [aLàbə].

Thus, the generalization that onsets are strictly preferred over codas, when we are dealing with a single intervocalic consonant, appears to be a theoretically well motivated principle, and also a well documented generalization. In the cases where there are several consonants intervoca-lically, language-particular principles must be appealed to in order to determine the correct syllabification.

3.6. EXAMPLES

3.6.1 *Spanish*

Logically, one might expect that descriptions of the syllable might include statements like 'the syllable in this language may include up to four segments'. In fact, however, while similar statements have been proposed for the major constituents of languages (for the onset and the rhyme, in particular), such statements are not generally proposed for the syllable as a whole. Let us look at Harris's (1983) analysis of Spanish, which includes a clear statement of length restrictions on the rhyme.

Harris argues that the rhyme in Spanish may have up to three segments, as it does in *cl[aus]tro, cl[ien]te, cr[uel]dad, tr[iun]fo;* it may not have four, as it would in the (five-segment) impossible syllable **m[uers]to.* He further shows that *s*, which may end a syllable following a vowel (V), glide (G), liquid (L), nasal (N), or obstruent (O), may not follow a sequence of three segments in the rhyme, even when that sequence is otherwise permissible. This is accounted for if the rhyme in Spanish cannot contain more than three segments. Harris presents the array of forms given in (33), indicating with an asterisk the systematically impossible forms. Twenty-six of the (thirty-three) asterisks derive directly from the limitation on the number of elements in the rhyme.

If Spanish allows a maximum of three elements in the rhyme, even more common are languages that permit a maximum of two elements; we have already seen Yokuts as an example of such a language. On the other side, the onset side, it is common to find languages that permit only one consonant in the onset. Yokuts is, again, an example of such a language.

But to say that the syllable of a given language permits a certain number of segments in its onset, or in its rhyme, is not to say that any combination of vowels or consonants can appear in any order in such a position — far from it, in two respects. Within both the onset and the coda, there are severe co-occurrence restrictions on the consonants that may appear there.

Let us turn now to the analysis of English, which has proven to be an extremely difficult task over the years.

(33)

	Medial	Final		Medial	Final
(a)			**(b)**		
1. V	pa-ta	tapa	Vs	pas-ta	res
2. VG	au-tor	lei	VGs	claus-tro	seis
3. VL	sal-ta	mar	VLs	pers-picaz	vals
4. VN	com-pra	sartén	VNs	mons-truo	Mayans
5. VO	seg-mento	red	VOs	abs-tracto	Félix
6. VGL	*	*	VGLs	*	*
7. VGN	*	*	VGNs	*	*
8. VGO	*	*	VGOs	*	*
(c)			**(d)**		
1. GV	nue-vo	apio	GVs	fies-ta	ꭗpues
2. GVG	*	buei	GVGs	*	*
3. GVL	fuer-te	fiel	GVLs	*	*
4. GVN	siem-pre	Juan	GVNs	*	*
5. GVO	diag-nosis	Goliat	GVOs	*	*
6. GVGL	*	*	GVGLs	*	*
7. GVGN	*	*	GVGNs	*	*
8. GVGO	*	*	GVGOs	*	*

3.6.2 English

Simply counting the number of elements allowed, as we have said, is not enough for English. We may not have two obstruent stops in the onset (*ptim*, *tpim*), or two nasals (*mnick*), or two fricatives, except, possibly, for *sf* and *sv* (*fsack*); many other combinations are impossible, too. Not only are various combinations ruled out, but those that are allowed are typically allowed in only one particular order. Thus we have in the English onset *sn* but not *ns*, *sl* but not *ls*, and so forth.

We shall assume that there are twenty-one consonantal segments at the W-level in English, and that there are seven features used to identify these segments. The most striking distinction – that of point of articulation – we shall not analyze into separate distinctive features, but shall rather treat as a single dimension, a matter that we will deal with in more detail in chapter 6. The other features each have only one value, the marked value, specified at this level. Thus, for example, voiceless obstruents (*p*, *t*, *k*, *s*, etc.) are unmarked for voicing, as are voiced sonorants (*m*, *n*, *l*, etc.). The liquids are unmarked for point of articulation, since their point of articulation is fully predictable. Coronals and nasals may be left unmarked for point of articulation, in which case they will receive their point of articulation either by assimilation from a neighboring element or by default; the default value is *coronal*. Thus a surface *t*, for example, will be the reflex of a segment totally unspecified underlyingly; an *s* is specified as [+continuant], an *n* is specified as [+nasal], an *m* as [+nasal] and labial, etc.; cf. (34).

(34) Segment	P of A	Voice	Affr.	Contin.	Nasal	Liquid	Lateral
p	labial						
t	(cor.)						
k	velar						
b	labial	+					
d	(cor.)	+					
g	velar	+					
č			+				
ǰ		+	+				
f	labial			+			
θ	dental			+			
s	(alveol.)			+			
š	pal.-alv.			+			
h	laryng.			+			
v	labial	+		+			
ð	dental	+		+			
z	(alveol.)	+		+			
ž	pal.-alv.	+		+			
m	labial				+		
n	(cor.)				+		
l						+	+
r						+	

Two explicit and structured accounts of this in the literature may be found in Fudge (1969) and Selkirk (1982a). They conceive essentially of setting up a set of slots – or, rather, a phrase-structure, a set of immediate constituents – into which segments may be placed. If necessary, a restriction can be put at the top of such a slot, indicating that it is 'for consonants only', or 'for obstruents only'; but having said that, any segment fitting that description can then appear there, unless some other filter or negative statement should rule it out. There are no especially natural ways of expressing constraints across sister (or 'cousin') nodes in the syllable tree, but both Fudge and Selkirk augment their accounts with a number of additional statements concerning the collocational, or co-occurrence, privileges of the segments in the syllable.[31] Fudge's proposal posits essentially the structure in (35), which generates a large number of sequences of segments along with an accompanying structure. These sequences must then satisfy certain additional positive conditions, and must fail to be ruled out by certain negative conditions, or filters.

(35)

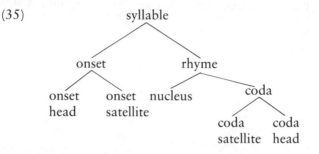

In (35), I have used the term 'head' to refer to a position that is locally obligatory, in the sense that, if there is just one segment in the onset, it must be in the onset head, and if there is just one segment in the coda, it must be in the coda head.

Fudge proposes that all non-vowel segments in English (36a) can appear in the onset head position, and the sonorants other than y can appear in the onset satellite position (36b).

(36)   (a)

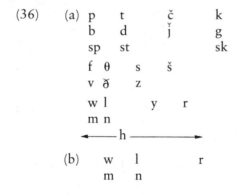

This account of English onsets is much too permissive, to be sure, and so to this Fudge adds several conditions. If there is an element in the onset satellite – if the onset is branching, we might say – then the first element must be either a stop, an s+stop, or a voiceless fricative. In this case, however, it may not be alveopalatal (i.e. *č*, *ǰ*, or *š*). This accounts for data of the sort shown in (37a). Second, if the element in the onset satellite is a nasal, then the head element must be an *s* (37b). Third, a labial consonant in the onset head cannot be followed by a *w* (37c); and fourth, a coronal onset head cannot be followed by an *l* (37d).

(37)   (a) stop, spark, skunk; but *chlap, *jwell
          (b) snark; but not *pnark, *bnark, *fnark
          (c) *pwark
          (d) *tlark

One attractive alternative to this treatment of the onset mentioned by Fudge is that given in (38), in which *s* is given a separate syntactic position, allowing the nasals to be removed from the onset satellite position, and removing the second restriction mentioned above. That restriction will, however, be replaced by a related restriction prohibiting *s* from preceding a fricative, *y* or *h*.

(38)

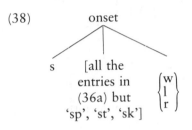

Fudge suggests that this analysis is suspicious because it gives such a privileged position in the onset to *s*, requiring a full 'slot' or statement in the phrase-structure account of the onset. It seems that the crucial point is that underlyingly the *s* in a structure such as (38) is unspecified for both point of articulation and voicing, and that it is specified as nothing else than its feature [continuant]. Its point of articulation – predictably alveolar in this position, unless an *r* follows (e.g. *shrimp*), in which case it is predictably alveopalatal – is specified by a late (post-lexical) rule; the restriction that it cannot have a point of articulation is connected with the more general fact that the onset and the coda in English syllables may each license no more than one contrastive point of articulation. As (39a) illustrates, the only feature of *s* that needs to be licensed in a *sC* is the [+continuant] feature. That the *s* cannot precede a fricative follows, again, from licensing, since two [−continuant] elements cannot be simultaneously licensed,[32] as illustrated in (39b); the path from the licensing syllable node cannot branch. As this example illustrates, the notion of licensing can serve as a kind of bookkeeping for the prosodic unit (here, the first part of the syllable), making sure that its various allowed features show up just once in its domain.

    With regard to the restriction against /pw/ and /bw/ clusters, we may follow a number of linguists[33] and analyze both labial consonants and round consonants (both w and rounded consonants such as k^w) as being [+labial]. The restriction noted above (37c) against such clusters as *pw*

(39)   (a)

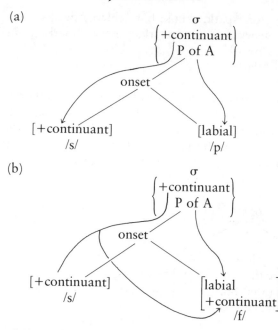

(b)

or *bw* then follows from the fact that only one position in the onset is licensed for the feature [labial].

Any account of English syllable structure will need to posit a number of additional linear restrictions on co-occurrence, as we have noted. Let us explore a little further the ways in which the notion of licensing can be used, or extended, to help clarify how such additional statements might best be stated.

Consider the following fact about English tautosyllabic clusters, one that holds across both onsets and codas: an s, specified just as [+continuant], cannot co-occur with a voiced consonant (i.e. one specified as [+voice]):[34] *sb, *sd, as well as *sj, *sv, both in onset and coda. Similarly, in the coda we do not find a sequence of voiced obstruent plus s (or z), except for in the word *adze*. How do we express this generalization? There are voiced continuants, after all, so we cannot say that the features [continuant] and [voice] cannot appear in the same licensing unit. Just as we have thought of licensing as a way for the syllable to organize its distinctive phonological information by means of non-branching paths of licensing, we may say that syllable licensing places restrictions on just how such paths may overlap. In this case, the restriction is that, if the feature [continuant] and the feature [voice] are both licensed by the same licenser, the paths must be common; i.e., the same segment (or syllable position) must contain both features. We will state this as in (40). From the point of view of the syllable as an organization device used for production, and more importantly, for perception, such principles of organization make a great deal of sense (see Fujimara, in press). From a perceptual point of view, they allow the feature-detecters to base their decision over a relatively large phonetic span – the whole onset plus nucleus, or the whole coda – and help in a decisive fashion to fix the phonological, or segmental, position to which that information should be assigned. In the case at hand, the feature [continuant] and the feature [voice] can be detected independently over the larger spans just mentioned, and the constraint in (40) will directly help determine how the span should be interpreted in a segmental representation.

(40)   Onset, coda

$$\left\{ \begin{array}{l} +\text{continuant} \\ \ +\text{voice} \end{array} \right\}$$

The oddest onset restriction in English is the one that restricts alveopalatals from appearing in a cluster (e.g. (37a)). This restriction does not hold in word-final codas, where we find *inch, bulge, barge,* and *flange,* for example. We will state this as in (41).

(41)   Onset

$$\left\{ \begin{array}{l} +\text{affricate} \\ \ \text{feature} \end{array} \right\}$$

In sum, then, so far we have the phrase structure rules of (42a); a linear precedence statement in (42b) that requires that continuants be initial in their onset; and feature statements (40) and (41). The analysis of the rhyme is considerably more problematic. Like the onset head, the coda head can be filled by almost any of the English non-vowels except /h/. Fudge suggests that both the short vowels and the long vowels and diphthongs in (43) appear squarely in the nucleus position, a point to which we return in a moment.

(42)   (a) Syllable → onset + rhyme
            Onset   → x x x
        (b) [+continuant] > x

(43)   (a) short vowels: I, ε, æ, Λ, U, o
        (b) long vowels: iy, ey, ai, ow, uw, yuw, a:
        (c) diphthongs: au, oi

As we noted at the beginning of this section, it is important to bear in mind that the greatest complexity of consonant clusters in codas appears word-finally. Here we find such sequences as those of *Pabst*, *next* [kst], *ask*, *asp*, *lax* [laks], *flint*, and so on. Word-internal syllable structure is much more restricted in its possibilities, and a range of treatments has been offered in the literature. On the one hand, we have accounts as in, e.g., Myers (1987), which describe word-internal syllables as being of the form $C_oV(X)$, allowing either a long vowel or a short vowel plus a single consonant – illustrated by the first two syllables of *Ticonderoga* – but *no consonant clusters in rhymes of syllables that are not word-final*, and *no coda consonants in rhymes of syllables with long vowels when non-final.* At the other extreme, and more commonly, we have analyses such as Selkirk (1982a), according to which only inflection material counts as a special word-final appendix, so that by inference any other word-final syllable is a possible word-internal syllable. This latter position surely allows for too much; words like *selfmic* or *taptligee*, though composed of sequences of possible (uninflected) monosyllables, do not strike us as likely or possible English words. The much stronger position that Myers sketches must deal with such familiar cases as *mountain*, which certainly appear to have a first syllable with a long vowel followed by an *n*.[35] The question is particularly thorny when considering rhymes with long vowels, and in the absence of a clear consensus regarding the facts, we must regrettably leave the matter unresolved. We may, however, fruitfully explore briefly the nature of codas involving short vowels.

As we noted above, non-final rhymes typically do not have consonant clusters in their coda. Thus we may find such CVC syllables in English as appear in words like *monadnock*, *Winnetka*, *synapsis*, *opthalmic*, *conduct*, or *after*; but longer coda clusters in general are not found internally, nor are such clusters found after a long vowel. Word-finally, however, longer clusters and sequences are found (*next*, *probe*); but the possibilities are not so simple that we can describe them as whatever-is-found-word-internally-plus-something-else.

Restricting our attention initially to sequences involving obstruents, we find that, if the obstruent is voiced, no cluster is possible, as we noted before (cf. (40)). If it is voiceless, an *s* may precede or follow (*ask*, *asp*, *axe*) and a *t* may follow (*apt*, *act*).

We shall follow Fudge in ascribing a special status to word-final consonants, the word-final appendix licensing that we have discussed. Fudge, for his part, suggests an appendix constituent that may contain a coronal stop, a fricative, or a cluster of the two – i.e. *t*, *d*, *s*, *z*, *θ*, or *st* – where, in addition, voicing is non-distinctive; that is, the *s*, *z*, *t*, and *d* appear only adjacent to segments of the same voicing, and *θ* and *st*, quite evidently, do not stand in a contrastive opposition to their voiced counterparts here. In short, in this position a stop or fricative may appear; but (holding aside the matter of θ for a moment) no distinctive feature other than [continuant] may appear. That is, there is no distinctive point of articulation, voicing, or even order, of these elements. So far, the strategy of what we have done is this: in word-internal syllables, any single consonant can appear in the coda, but word-finally, obstruent clusters may appear. When that happens, the consonant that has the greater range of distributional possibilities is the one on the left; therefore, we attribute the possibility of the second consonant to a word-final appendix position.[36]

We are thus led to a clarification of the notion of word-final termination that we touched on in the exposition of the notion of licensing above. Earlier accounts have focused on cases like that of Arabic, where any word-final consonant is extrasyllabic. However, if we take extra-syllabicity to be a *kind* of autosegmental licensing, then we would expect to find different degrees of 'thoroughness' with regard to which segments could be extrasyllabic in a language. In English, only coronals are. That is to say, only elements that are not specified for point of articulation, or, putting it more properly, only the features [voice] and [continuant], are extrasyllabic in English: only a segment specified for those features, and no more, will be part of the regular word-final appendix in English.

This leaves unaccounted for, however, the matter of the contrast between θ and s, as in *fifth* and *cliffs*. This terminal θ (that is, one that appears after an obstruent) appears in *fifth, si[ks]th, (eighth), twelfth, hundredth, thousandth, length, strength, depth, width*, and *breadth*, and in no other words in the English language.[37] Clearly there is a generalization here, of which the weakest possible is that the *-th* is a separate morpheme. We may state the connection between the otherwise exceptional distinctive point of articulation and the presence of a distinct morpheme by saying that the dental point of articulation is licensed word-finally by the suffixal morpheme itself, rather than by canonical syllable-internal structure or by the regular word-final extrasyllabicity (see (44)).[38]

Within the coda itself, Selkirk suggests that there are two positions available for obstruents, as in (35) above, with the restriction that the second element be [+coronal]; she reserves the appendix for what she calls an 'inflectional element', i.e. separate inflectional morphemes. Fudge, on the other hand, puts no such morphological restriction on what can appear in the appendix, allowing him to say that the only obstruent clusters that appear in the rhyme are *sk, sp*, and, by symmetry, *st*. Thus, on Fudge's account, a word like *next* [nekst] has only a *k* in the coda; the *st* is in the appendix. For Selkirk, the *k* is in the first coda position, and the *st* cluster together is in the second coda position (see (45)).

(44)   Depth

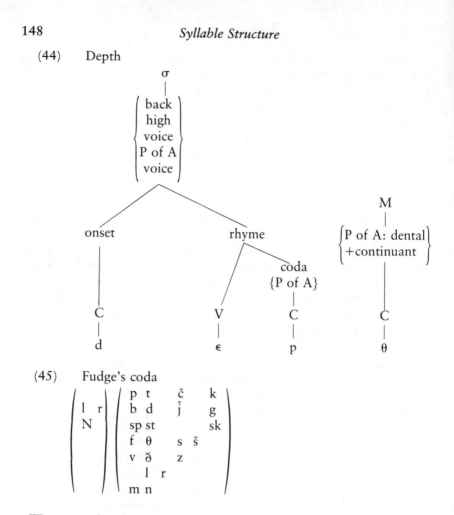

(45)   Fudge's coda

$$
\left(
\left|
\begin{matrix} l & r \\ & \\ N & \end{matrix}
\right|
\left(
\begin{matrix}
p & t & č & k \\
b & d & ǰ & g \\
sp & st & & sk \\
f & θ & s & š \\
v & ð & z & \\
& l & r & \\
m & n & &
\end{matrix}
\right)
\right)
$$

We suggest that the correct position takes a bit from Fudge's analysis and a bit from Selkirk's. There is a single word-final appendix, which permits (or licenses) only the distinctive feature [continuant], giving rise, then, to the segments *s*, *t*, with voicing filled in by rule. There are two obstruent positions in the coda itself, of which the first can only be filled by *s*. We may note, furthermore, that when an *sC* cluster is present, a following *s* is always part of a separate morpheme; while *ask* and *aks* 'axe' are both possible, or *tax* and *task*, a word like *masks* (or *masx*?) cannot exist as a monomorphemic form. In short, only one continuant is permitted, or licensed, by the syllable coda; any additional continuants are licensed in their capacity as separate morphemes (see (46), for example). We take this complementarity to show that the pre-consonantal *s* of *ask* and the post-consonantal *s* of *axe* are the same kind of thing, so to speak. This may seem rather obvious – both are *s*'s, after all – but rather a lot of

(46)
  Sixths [sɪksθs]

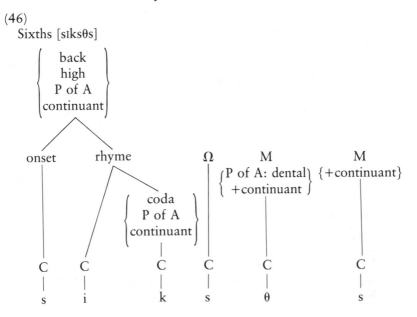

consideration has been given to the possibility, as we saw, that *s* + stop sequences are in fact single segments, as far as syllable structure is concerned.

So far we have looked only at obstruent clusters in the coda, but other clusters are possible. A nasal in the coda satellite is always homorganic to the following element in the coda head, and it may be followed only by an obstruent (stop or fricative): cf. *hemp, mint, mink, fringe, inch, prince, lymph, lens,* etc., though there are certain other restrictions on voiced fricatives that are not alveolar (i.e. restrictions against words like **lemv* or **lenthe*). Thus, for example, while *v* can appear in a coda, it cannot co-occur with another segment.[39] The generalization may be stated as in (47), where the notation, as before, says that, if the features [point of articulation], [voice], [continuant], and another — any other — are simultaneously licensed by the coda, they must be on the same segment; i.e. the coda cannot then branch. Similarly, *l* in the coda satellite can be followed only by an obstruent or a nasal (cf. (48a), from Selkirk 1982a), while *r* in the coda satellite can be followed by any single

(47)   Coda
$$\left\{\begin{array}{c} \text{P of A} \\ \text{voice} \\ \text{continuant} \\ \text{feature} \end{array}\right\}$$

segment other than ð, and can be followed by *st* as well (48b).

The examples of rhymes we have considered so far all involve short vowel nuclei, however. When we consider long vowel nuclei, the situation becomes more complex. Long vowels of all sorts are permitted before any single consonant that may appear in the coda (*tribe, rage, fire,* etc.). The fact that these consonants need not be alveolar demonstrates that they cannot be viewed simply as belonging to the word-final appendices considered earlier for word-final obstruent clusters. If anything is special in the word-final syllable *tr[ay]b*, it is the second mora of the nucleus, since in non-word-final position such a vowel have to be short.

(48) (a) Sonorant+[+voice]

	Alveolar	Labial	Velar	Dental	Alveopal.		Nasal
n	land		(bang)		lunge		
r	lard	orb	(Kharg)		purge	warm	barn
l	bald	bulb			bulge	elm	(kiln?)

(b) Sonorant+[−voice]

					Affric.	Fricative	
	Alveolar	Labial	Velar	Dental	alveopal.	Alveolar	Labial
n	lint	lamp	ink	month	hunch	prince	(Bamf)
r	heart	harp	lark	hearth	arch	purse	wharf
l	hilt	help	elk	health	gulch	pulse	elf

Summarizing, then, in word-final syllable position we find two possible positions above and beyond what is possible word-internally: a final position, the appendix, which is specifiable only for the feature [continuant], and a post-nuclear position, which may entertain only *s* (as in *ask, asp*) and sonorants: post-vocalic glides (*tr[ay]b, f[ey]l*), liquids (*b[ul]b*), and nasals (*hemp*). This is summarized in (49).

3.7   THE ± SYLLABIC CONTRAST

The introduction of syllable structure into our phonological representation gives rise naturally to the question of whether *syllabicity* should be thought of as a structural property, that of being in the syllable nucleus,

(49)

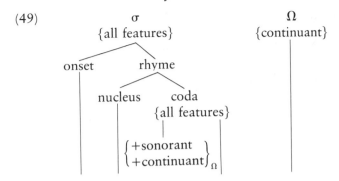

Ω = word-finally only

rather than as an inherent property of skeletal positions (or of auto-segments on other tiers). Syllable structure allows a graphic means of defining what it is to be a vowel, since there is essentially an identity between something's being a vowel and its being the nucleus of a syllable.[40]

This possibility suggests two revisions of our scheme as developed so far. The first involves the elimination of the feature [syllabic] from the skeletal tier, a modification that brings the skeletal tier down to bare bones, letting it consist of segments that are specified for no features at all. This modification, which has been investigated at some length,[41] has been variously called the 'X-tier theory' (contrasting with the CV theory, since the units on the skeletal tier are all interchangeable and identical) and the 'timing unit' or 'timing tier' theory.

The attractive aspect of this account, which eliminates all features specific to the skeletal tier (which would hardly be called a 'CV' tier anymore), is its apparent success in removing redundancy, the overlap in function between syllable position and whether a position is a C or a V. One might even then be tempted to go so far as to say that all elements on the skeletal tier are totally predictable, both in quantity – here, projecting a skeletal element as we did, by splitting, in chapter 2 – and syllabic quality, the result of what kind of node in the syllable tree comes to dominate the skeletal position. On this view, *pit* might go through the three stages in (50), where neither *i* nor any other segment is specified for a feature [syllabic].

The second, closely related, point that arises involves the treatment of the contrast between vowels and glides. There are a number of languages in which the distinction between glides and high vowels is phonologically predictable, and it has long been a question within phonological theory as to how this predictability can be naturally accounted for. Bloomfield (1933: 122) calls this 'natural' syllabification; Pike warns us that

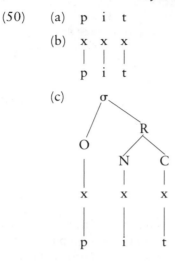

(50)   (a)   p   i   t

(b)   x   x   x
       | | |
       p   i   t

(c)

intertwined with this problem is another: the possible necessity for a phoneme of syllabicity. . . . Instead of using separate consonant and vowel symbols for /y/ and /i/, for example, the same symbol *i* could be used for both, with a syllabic marker under it every time it is the peak of a syllable – not occasionally only, and not replaced by a stress mark on stressed syllables only. (Pike 1952: 619)

Can we say that there is natural syllabification in some languages – a single phonological entity, an element on a separate autosegmental tier, that is sometimes transcribable as a [y] (if it is in onset or coda position) and sometimes as an [i] (if it is in nuclear position)?[42] In general, the answer is surely yes, but there are many accounts in the literature that contain segments that *must* be non-syllabic glides (they never syllabify as vowels) or, conversely, *must* be vowels (they do not desyllabify as glides). In such cases, we must indicate the type of segment that is in question, and we may be able to indicate which part of the syllable the segment in question 'wants' to associate with.

Guerssel (1986) reports an interesting asymmetry between vowels and glides in his discussion of Berber. There are two phonological segments that will surface either as vowels ([i], [u]) or as glides ([y],[w]), depending on the phonological context; cf. (51). The glides will appear when adjacent to vowels. We can confidently say that these are glides that become syllabified: not the reverse, however, because there are syllabic *us* and *is* that never appear as glides, such as the demonstrative suffix *u* and the first person singular object clitic *i*: cf. (52). In fact, there are minimal pairs such as /wd̩i/ 'fall' and /ud̩i/ 'fold'. When the glide /y/ seen above is attached to the vowel-initial stem, the result is unambiguous (53a); when it is attached to a glide-initial stem, one glide or the other must become the nucleus of the syllable, but either possibility is allowed (53b).

(51)   (a) i/y 3rd-person singular marker

        i-ru   'he cried'

        y-ari   'he writes'

        aha y-ru   'that he cried'

    (b) u/w construct state marker

        u-mazan   'messenger'

        w-ansa   'place'

        arra w-mazan 'messenger's kids'

(52)   aryaz   'man'

        aryaz-u   'this man'

        arba   'boy'

        arba-y-u 'this boy'

        tessim-i 'she raised me'

        tenna-y-i 'she told me'

(53)   (a) ur y-udi   'he did not fold'

    (b) /ur y-wḍi/ > [ur yuḍi] or [ur iwḍi] 'he did not fall'

Even more striking are minimal pairs like /wci/ 'give' and /ucy/ 'wake up', where each root has one glide and one vowel. In the forms in (54) they are homophonous, but in (55) they show a distinct range of possible forms. What makes the underlying vowel /i/ distinct from the glide /y/ is not its inherent content – at least, not as far as features are concerned – but rather its underlying specification that it be associated with a syllable nucleus. A true vowel, so to speak, is inherently marked as being in a syllable nucleus; what we call a glide lets its syllabic position be determined passively, by context.

(54)   (a) ur uci-x   'I did not give'

    (b) ur uci-x   'I did not wake up'

(55)   (a)   ur y-uci wma   'my brother did not give' /wci/

      or ur i-wci wma

      but *ur y-ucy uma

             *ur i-wcy uma

    (b)   ur y-uci wma   'my brother did not wake up' /ucy/

      or ur y-ucy uma

      but *ur i-wci wma

             *ur i-wcy uma

Guerssel suggests that the range of possible variants can best be understood as being the result of syllabification at the phrase-level being free to
iterate either from right to left or from left to right. The underlying form
for (55a) is given in (56); the two possible surface forms are given in
(57a,b). The principles of syllabification are to form a CV(C) syllable,
with onsets obligatory; word-medial empty onsets (i.e. in intervocalic
position) are, according to Guerssel, filled with a default *y*.

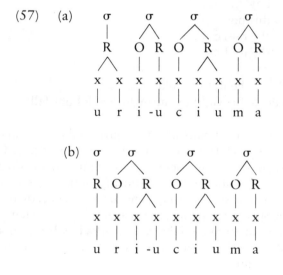

It remains at this point an open question as to how best this distinction
should be drawn – whether this apparently local property ('local' in the
sense that the syllabicity of the true high vowels is a property of the
segments themselves, not of some larger unit) should be represented
underlyingly as structure, or in terms of features. The approach developed
in this chapter suggests that the most natural way to express the situation
in Berber is to incorporate a segmental feature [syllabic], and specify that
the true high vowels are (non-redundantly) [+syllabic]. In order for this
feature to be licensed, they will have to appear in a position, the syllable
nucleus, that licenses this feature.

3.8   RULES TRIGGERED BY IMPROPER SYLLABIFICATION

The requirement that all phonological material be syllabified at W-level provides considerable motivation for rules to effect changes in the segmental composition of the string between the output of the morphology and the W-level. We have seen examples of this in the case of Yokuts and Turkish; virtually all languages illustrate some aspect or other of this process.

English, too, can provide a simple illustration of this. Certain roots contain consonant sequences that are syllabifiable only when a vowel-initial suffix is added. Thus, *damnation* is clearly analyzed morphologically as *damn* plus *ation*, but the root *damn* is phonetically [dam] when it appears in isolation, or even before a word beginning with a vowel. A few other roots with the sequence *mn* display the same behavior in English, such as *hymn* [hɪm], which shows its second consonant in *hymnal*, with the suffix *-al* (there is no suffix *-nal* in English), or *autumn* (cf. *autumnal*).

If syllabification occurs after the suffixation of the relevant vowel-initial suffixes, then at that point we can say that all unsyllabified nasal sonorants are deleted. In the terminology mentioned above, proper syllabification is a strict well-formedness condition on the W-level. Suffixes (and other morphological processes, like compounding) differ with regard to whether they demand that their base – that which they affix to – be a well-formed W-level structure. Compounding takes well-formed W-level structures as input; the *-al* suffix does not.[43]

English has other strategies available at this point, however; not *all* segments unsyllabified at this point are deleted. Liquids are syllabified instead. For example, the word *meter* is underlyingly /me:tr/, with no vowel between the /t/ and the /r/; in this respect it differs from *metal*, whose underlying form is just /metal/. This difference can be seen in the adjective forms derived by adding the suffix *-al*. In the one case *metric* is derived; in the other, *metallic*.

Having thus concluded that *meter* is underlyingly /me:tr/, we observe that the root may appear as a word. Its last two segments violate the sonority hierarchy, and the final /r/ remains unsyllabified. Instead of deleting, like the final /n/ of *damn*, the /r/ becomes a syllabic /r/ on the surface.

As we have noted, a number of languages have been cited in the literature in which the onset may have no more than one member and the rhyme is limited to having no more than two skeletal positions, leaving only the possibility of a long vowel or a closed syllable with a short vowel; Yokuts, as mentioned above, is such a CVX language. When the morphology places morphemes together, the resulting string may in principle violate this syllabification pattern in one of three ways: (i) a cluster of three distinct consonants may be created; (ii) a long vowel may be followed by two consonants; or (iii) a geminate consonant may be adjacent to another consonant. None of these situations can be reduced to syllables with no more than two elements in the rhyme and no more than a single element in the onset.

There seems to be a strong tendency for this impasse to be settled differently in the three cases; epenthesis of a vowel is the most common solution for the first case (though deletion of one of the consonants is another possibility), and the choice must be made as to whether the consonant will go after the first or after the second of the three consonants in the cluster. In the second and third cases, however, it is more common for the long vowel or consonant to lose one of its skeletal positions and become short.

Ter Mors (1988), basing her work in part on Broadbent (1964), points out that in Sierra Miwok contrastive length in both the vowels and consonants is expressed if and only if it is possible to do so without violating the CVX syllable structure.[44] True clusters of distinct consonants, however, which are not syllabifiable within the CVX pattern, trigger an epenthsis of ɨ; see (58). A long vowel, as in the stem *hika:h* 'deer', will shorten before two consonants, as we see in the alternation in (59). There the ɨ is epenthetic, triggered by the unsyllabifiable sequence /hj/ at the end of the word; this created third syllable allows the length of the vowel to surface.

(58)   (a) underlying: wɨks + j + ni + ʔ

(b) syllabification

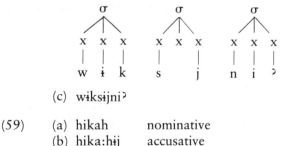

(c) wɨksɨjniʔ

(59)   (a) hikah   nominative
          (b) hika:hɨj   accusative

The processes that a language develops in order to properly syllabify the segments that compose its morphemes comprise a large part of its phonology. We shall return in chapter 6 to further considerations of the mode of rule application that is involved in such situations.

3.9 SYLLABLE-BASED RULES INVOLVING QUANTITY

We suggested in section 3.2 above that many languages assign stress on the basis of the weight of the syllables in a given word. Weight, in turn, is intimately linked to the notion of quantity, the number of positions in the rhyme of the syllable. A common direction of cause and effect is the one just mentioned, in which a weight contrast in the syllables found in underlying form (or some representation close to underlying form) is used in the determination of stress. But the other direction of causality is possible as well: quantity can be the effect of stress, as we saw in Selayarese. Stress can be placed either on the basis of underlying quantity or in some other way, but once the stressed position(s) have been determined, this can in turn influence the surface quantity of the syllables of the word. We have not yet covered the representation of stress in metrical notation, but nonetheless we can express this notion as in (60).

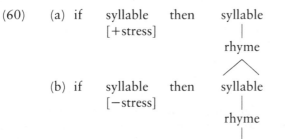

(60) (a) if syllable then syllable
           [+stress] |
                               rhyme

      (b) if syllable then syllable
           [−stress] |
                               rhyme
                                 |

These formulas truly abuse our notation! They are halfway between being statements of what we find on the surface as a tendency – 'when the syllable is stressed, it tends to have a long rhyme' – and familiar phonological rules that can be called upon to make a change. They fail in that second function in that they do not inform us what change to make in a syllable if it is stressed; a real, well-thought out rule would explain that, perhaps as in (61).

We shall come back to this point below, but for now we may simply emphasize that it is important for us to develop not only a formal

(61)   σ   σ
        [+stress]   [+stress]
           | → |
        rhyme   rhyme
         /\   /\
        x   ø   x   x

synchronic account of the data in given languages, but also some way of expressing clear generalizations that may not be generalizations across rules *per se* but which rather, like the generalizations of (60a,b), sit at a higher level.

One of the earlier arguments in the generative literature for the importance of the syllable is based on this recurring pattern (Vennemann 1972).[45] A vowel in a non-final stressed syllable in Icelandic regularly lengthens when followed by a single consonant (*kátlar* 'kettles', vs *ké:til:* 'kettle'); this could (and, we know now, should) be understood as a lengthening of vowels in all stressed open syllables. In the terms of our present discussion, this involves a requirement that stressed syllables be bimoraic, and if the syllable is open, having no consonant in the rhyme to make it inherently heavy, then the vowel must lengthen to arrive at the same result.

The syllable was especially relevant, Vennemann argued, because the notion of a 'word-medial open syllable' would not simply reduce to the statement that a stressed vowel followed by a single consonant would lengthen (i.e., $V \rightarrow$ [+long] $/ - CV$). If a stressed vowel was followed by a consonant cluster of the sort that could begin a syllable (p, t, k, or s, followed by r, j, or v), then it too would lengthen (e.g. *ti:tra* 'shiver'). Therefore, we may conclude, direct reference to syllable structure is necessary.

Anderson (1984) extends this point, developing the material within the current model. He proposes, in particular, that Icelandic, like Swedish and Norwegian, has a syllable rhyme that is divided into a nucleus and a coda. All syllables may have a coda, but the nucleus will be bimoraic – composed of two skeletal positions – if the the syllable is stressed, and monomoraic if the syllable is unstressed. There is a heterodox element to Anderson's assumption about syllable structure here, because he furthermore suggests that, when a vowel is followed by two consonants, C_1 and C_2, then, even if C_2 is in the onset of the following syllable, C_1 will move into the nucleus of the syllable along with the vowel, as in (62).

(62)   Anderson's account of Icelandic, Swedish, Norwegian

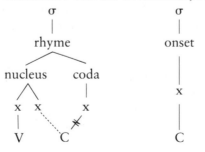

Thus, all VC rhymes are in the nucleus of the syllable, on Anderson's analysis, except word-finally, in which case the consonant remains in the rhyme, but outside the nucleus. Given such a seating arrangement for the nucleus and the rhyme, Anderson arrives at the simple principle of mora-counting for the nucleus mentioned above, but none for the rhyme *per se*: the *nucleus* is branching if and only if the syllable is stressed.

This seems unlikely to us for two reasons. First, the reshuffling in (62) is not a generally well motivated practice, and it seems in general unlikely that we will find instances of segment reassociation that are not due to the inherent ill-formedness of the initial association (as opposed to being triggered by a contextual factor, as is the case in (62), i.e. the following consonant). Second, the coda is being used, after rule (62) applies, as a way of ignoring (i.e., not counting for mora purposes) *a single consonant which may occur word-finally, one that we would rather ignore*. Otherwise, consonants following the vowel get pressed into the nucleus! This is precisely the kind extrasyllabic appendix that we have seen in other cases, including the account of English above.[46] Anderson's point may then be stated that stressed syllables have bimoraic rhymes, and unstressed syllables have monomoraic rhymes – even if these should include one of the short diphthongs of Icelandic, two vocalic elements associated with a single skeletal position.

A second mora of the Icelandic syllable (or nucleus, on Anderson's account) which is created by rule (and thus is not in an already closed syllable) is always associated with the vocalic material of the nucleus, giving us long vowels in such stressed syllables. Thus, along with rule (61), we will have a rule (63) that reassociates a vowel to an extra mora.

(63)   X $\textcircled{X}$

          |

          v

Anderson suggests that in Norwegian and Swedish, however, if a nucleus gets a second mora by rule – because the syllable is stressed, and there is not a long vowel or a vowel plus consonant already in the nucleus – the extra mora will be assigned differently. It is, instead, the following consonant that will geminate – typically, the consonant from the following onset, as in *tycka* 'to think' [tykka]. (This is surely reminiscent of Selayarese, again!) Anderson assumes, in line with the largest part of the Scandanavian tradition, that there is a vowel length contrast, but that there are no underlying long consonants.

A consonant that geminates, however, may be word-final in a word that ends in a short vowel and a single consonant. In Anderson's analysis, this is a consonant that appears in the syllable 'margin' (or coda), not the nucleus; on our reinterpretation, this consonant is extrasyllabic, in the termination of the word. Such a consonant will also geminate, as with all words written orthographically with a double consonant (e.g. *mann, venn*, etc.)

In addition to (63), then, we would also have a rule that (as Anderson notes) would have precedence over (63), and that would geminate a consonant, when possible, to fill the extra mora created by rule (61).

(61), recall, was a rule intended to make explicit a change necessary to express the intuition that lay behind (60a). But (60b) is also relevant, because underlying long vowels in Norwegian and Swedish shorten in unstressed syllables. We must invert (61), therefore, and add a rule as in (64). On Anderson's account, the mora that is deleted in such unstressed

(64)   σ   σ
        [−stress]   [−stress]
            | → |
         rhyme   rhyme
          /\ |
         x   ∅   x

positions is in the nucleus, and by construction unstressed syllables would not have a mora associated with a consonant. By eliminating the notion of nucleus, as we have suggested doing, we make it impossible to write the shortening rule as in (64); minimally, we would have to write it as in (65).

(65)   σ
        [−stress]
            |
         rhyme
          /\

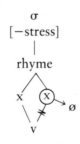

There is a larger generalization that none of the formalisms so far have captured, though. We will have to wait for a later section to discuss it thoroughly (section 6.5, on automatic spreading), but we can see the basic point already. The representations we are currently using provide us with two rhyme positions – two moras – for certain syllables that we call heavy. Metrical representation allows us to represent a stressed position as one with two (or more) grid marks assigned to it. The tendency roughed out in (60) – that metrical prominence and syllable weight tend to be in harmony – can be stated as a general measure against which to judge the relative well-formedness of W-level structures. This much is universal; what is language-particular is the degree to which languages have rules that operate in order to improve the stress/syllable weight harmony.

A similar example of the not uncommon phenomenon that we have been considering is found in Chimalapa Zoque (Mexico, Mixe-Zoque) (Knudson 1975). Stress is assigned straightforwardly in this language, along the following lines. If the ultimate syllable is a monosyllabic stem, it receives primary stress, but otherwise primary stress falls on the penultimate syllable. If the word has three or more syllables, the initial syllable is also stressed, though not with a primary stress.

A stressed syllable is always heavy, as in (67a) or (67b). If it is closed, then that suffices to satisfy the heaviness condition, as in the first column in (66), from Knudson. If it is open, then the vowel will be lengthened, as in the second column.

(66)   Vowel lengthening in Zoque

Gloss	Incompletive (-pa)	Imperative
bend	kítpa	kí:tɨ ʔ
kick	képpa	ké:pa ʔ
dig	táhpa	tá:hɨ ʔ
scold	kóspa	kó:sa ʔ
leave	pì:cɨ́mpa	pì:cɨ́:mɨ ʔ
pass	kɨ̀:túkpa	kɨ̀:tú:lɨ ʔ

(67)   (a)   [+stress]   (b)   [+stress]
                            syllable   syllable
                               | |
                            rhyme   rhyme
                             /\   /\
                            V   X   V   X
                            |__/ | |
                             v   v   c

Zoque presents other features of interest to autosegmental theory, because the glottal stop acts quite differently from the other consonants. The most striking fact is that a stressed syllable closed by a glottal stop, and preceding another syllable with a filled onset position, as in (68), does not act like the other closed syllables: the presence of the glottal stop in the rhyme of the syllable does not satisfy the conditions of the language, and the vowel in fact lengthens, parallel to the case of the stressed syllables in the second column of (66). I have placed the glottal stop on a separate tier, for there are various pieces of evidence that that is the correct structure. For example, in the case at hand, the vowel segment reassociates to the second rhyme position, as indicated by the broken line in (68). This gives rise to a coda position doubly associated, to a vowel and to a glottal stop. The glottal stop, being shorter in duration than the vowel, is outlasted by the vowel, and the total effect of the rhyme is perceived as a vowel that is interrupted by the glottal stop, or, if one prefers, rearticulated after the glottal stop. These facts are illustrated in (69).

(68)

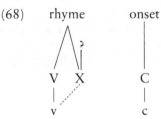

(69)

Gloss	Incompletive	Imperative
climb	kíʔmpa	kíʔimɨʔ
ask for	céʔkpa	céʔekaʔ
disembowel	pɨ́ʔcpa	pɨ́ʔicɨʔ
find	páʔtpa	páʔatɨʔ
swallow	wúʔkpa	wúʔukɨʔ
pull out	cóʔppa	cóʔopaʔ
wash clothes	nɨ̀ʔicéʔepa	nɨ̀ʔicéʔaʔ

KiHunde, a Bantu language that we looked at in chapter 1, presents an interesting example of a language where late (phrase-level) phonological rules have a heavy influence on surface syllable types. Syllables in KiHunde, as in most Bantu languages, may be closed only by a nasal; vowel length is underlyingly contrastive as well. Both syllables with long vowels and syllables closed by nasals have two tone-bearing positions – two moras – and this is a crucial piece of information in making sense of the tonal system of the language. The underlying vowel length contrast is neutralized on the surface, however, in favor of short vowels in *every* position except the phrase-penultimate position, where the length contrast is maintained.[47] It is reasonable to interpret this as the result of a prosodic prominence assigned to the phrase-penultimate position, along with a phrase-level process reducing all other syllables to monomoraic status, as by (65).

In our discussion of the tonal system of KiHunde in chapter 1, we noted several rules that apply at the phrase level in KiHunde phonology, applying freely across word-boundary.[48] These rules operate on structures that do not contain long vowels outside of the phrase-penultimate position; the length of any vowel outside of that position has been lost, so to speak, by the time that such phrase-level rules come round to apply. There is a series of earlier rules, however, that apply strictly within words, and that apply to a deeper level of representation at which syllables may have one or two moras. Looking ahead to chapter 5, we call this the 'lexical phonology'. Without an understanding of the inter-relation of these two systems, the language would be totally incomprehensible; with such an understanding, most of its workings become straightforward.

For example, in chapter 1, we noted a verb in the present continuous tense: I have indicated the stem of this verb in (70) in brackets.[49] In the

(70)   a ni mu [som er a]   'I am reading for him'
            | | |
            H   L   H

present continuous, a tonal melody LH is assigned to the beginning of a stem which has a low-toned radical, giving us straightforwardly the form in (70). When the radical – the first syllable of the stem – has a long vowel, or two moras for whatever reason, both tones of the LH melody will associate with that first syllable, giving rise to a syllable with a rising tone. On the surface, such rising tones can appear only on the penultimate syllable, and rising tones are simplified elsewhere by the rules in (71). Thus, a present continuous based on a verb like *i-wonshira* 'to sleep' will have the most unusual tone pattern derived in (72).

Why is it that this tone pattern – *a-ní-wónshira* – is so highly unusual

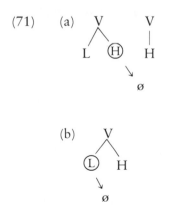

(72) (a) a ni [won shi ra] 'I am sleeping'

            | [| |

          H   LH

(b) a ni [won shi ra]

           | | by (71b)

         H   H

in KiHunde? We saw in chapter 1 that the rule of plateauing creates the appearance of several High tones in a row, but it does this by spreading. High tones that abut across a word boundary, we saw, undergo a rule of Sandhi Lowering, which lowers the High tone on the left. There is a rule of the earlier lexical phonology which also, quite ruthlessly, gets rid of all sequences of High tones on successive syllables (or mora, if you prefer). This rule, given in (73), operates differently from the otherwise similar rule that applies at the phrase level, for (73) leaves untouched the High

(73) Meeussen's Rule

V C_0 V

| |

H   Ⓗ

        ↘

         ø

tone on the left. A High toned verb in the present continuous does not receive the Low–High melody, like the Low toned verbs mentioned above; it rather receives a High tone – its own lexical tone – on its stem. But this High tone is deleted by Meeussen's Rule (73) when a High tone immediately precedes. (74) illustrates this with a High toned verb, *i-témera* 'to cut for someone'.

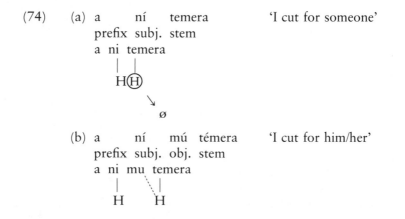

(74) (a) a   ní   temera   'I cut for someone'
prefix subj. stem
a ni temera

          | |

       HⒽ

          ↘

           ø

(b) a   ní   mú   témera   'I cut for him/her'
prefix subj. obj. stem
a ni mu temera

          | \ |

        H   H

And *that* is why the surface form *aníwónshira* in (72b) is so strange! One would think that KiHunde had done everything in its power to prevent two High tones in a row from surfacing; for two High tones juxtaposed early on, in the lexical phonology, will be simplified by Meeussen's Rule, and two High tones juxtaposed across a word-boundary will be simplified by the rule we looked at in chapter 1. But in addition to the apparent sequence of High tones created by the plateauing rule, we find two odd cases of High tones on adjacent syllables –the case investigated in some detail in chapter 1, and the other the case created by the disappearance of Rising tone contours that were allowed in the deep phonology, but were ruled out by the superficial prohibition against long vowels on the surface outside of penultimate position.

The various Yup'ik dialects (spoken in Alaska, Canada, and the Soviet Union) have complex interactions of stress assignment and quantity assignment (see Krauss 1985). The study of the dialect variations, and their placement in the evolution of the more complex eastern dialects, reveals a number of independent, but related, principles at work. There is an underlying contrast of long and short vowels, a contrast that is the basis for the heavy/light syllable distinction in the language. Syllables can be either open or closed, as well, but a closed syllable with a short vowel does not behave like a heavy syllable in Yup'ik (which means essentially that it does not act as 'stress-attracting'; this is discussed again in section 4.2).

All heavy syllables are stressed, and in most dialects any sequence of two or more light syllables will give rise to a rhythmic pattern of stress on alternate syllables, as in example (14) in chapter 4, though we are presently not concerned with the precise rules that assign stress. What we are interested in are the modifications that occur when an open syllable appears in a stressed position.

Now, a distinction must be made between two kinds of vowels in Yup'ik, where there are two *kinds* of vowels: the so-called full vowels (*a*, *i*, *u*), and the reduced vowel, orthographically rendered as *e* (phonetically and phonologically schwa). Bearing this in mind, we may observe that Yup'ik has a rule that lengthens any short *full* vowel in an open syllabale that is stressed. But the reduced vowel is inherently incapable of being lengthened, as (75c) illustrates. In (75) I represent stress with underlining.

In Central Siberian Yup'ik, the stressed schwa syllable is simply immune from lengthening. In Central Alaskan Yup'ik, however, something else intervenes in order to allow a second mora to appear on the stressed open syllables: the following consonant is geminated.[50] Thus the form in (75c) form becomes [a tǝp pik].

The natural way to express these related systems is to posit for both a rule that ensures two skeletal positions to all stressed syllables, as in (61)

(75) (a) /qa ya ni/   'his own kayak'
              qa <u>ya</u> ni   alternating stress, from the left
              [qa <u>ya:</u> ni]

      (b) /qa ya pix ka ni/ 'his own future authentic kayak'
              qa <u>ya</u> pix <u>ka</u> ni
              [qu <u>ya:</u> pix <u>ka:</u> ni]

      (c) /a tə pik/   'real name'
              a <u>tə</u> pik
              a <u>tə</u> pik   no lengthening of ə; see text

above for the Scandanavian languages. (76) will lengthen a long vowel in such a position. A syllable that has a short vowel, but is closed by a consonant, does not get an extra mora; thus, as far as these principles are concerned, although a VC rhyme does not make a syllable stressed, it does go so far as to make the rhyme be considered bimoraic as far as inherent quantity is concerned.

(76)   rhyme

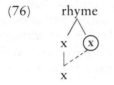

We will consider the suggestion below (section 6.3) that the schwa is a skeletal position with no vocalic features associated to it; hence a schwa would not satisfy the structural description of (76), and the extra skeletal position would be left unassociated in Siberian Yup'ik, and thus unpronounceable. In Central Alaskan Yup'ik, an additional rule, (77), is added.

(77)   onset

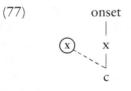

3.10 SYLLABLE-BASED PROSODIC RULES INVOLVING TONE

There is an intimate relation between syllable structure and such prosodic behavior as is found in tonal and accentual systems. The whole of the next chapter is devoted to the treatment of accentual systems, and a good deal of that involves the particulars of the difference in accentual behavior of heavy and light syllables; this is the traditional domain of metrical phonology. Other than a few brief remarks, then, we will concentrate here not on stress but on the relation between tone and syllable structure.

As we have already noted, both tone and stress systems come in what have been called *quantity-insensitive* and *quantity-sensitive* forms. A quantity-insensitive tone language will allow the same number of tones (often just one) per syllable regardless of the internal make up of the syllable. A quantity-sensitive system will allow one tone to a light syllable – typically of the form CV – and two tones to a syllable with more material in the coda (perhaps limiting the tone-bearing codas to those that have a sonorant, as in Lithuanian (Kenstowicz 1970)). Most Bantu languages are quantity-sensitive, allowing two tones on a long syllable and only one on a light syllable. For example, in Kirundi we find examples as in (78a), but not as in (78b) (Sabimana 1986).

(78)   (a) u mu gore 'woman'   i-bi-goori 'maize'
               | | | |/
               L H   H L

        (b) *u mu gore
               | /\
               LHL

Clements (1984), on the other hand, argues that the primary rules of tone association in Kikuyu assign one tone per syllable, regardless of weight, though the system does maintain what can be interpreted as vestiges of an earlier stage at which heavy syllables displayed different associative behavior.

These general characteristics of tonal association can be best understood from the point of view of licensed association. Since tone is a distinctive feature in a tone language, by definition, the syllable is always a licenser for that feature. Thus the onset-plus-nucleus will always be able to license one, and exactly one, tone. In a quantity-insensitive system, there is no more that need be said about tonal licensing. In a quantity-sensitive tonal system, as in Kirundi, the coda is also a licenser for tone, and thus a second tone can associate with a coda in such systems.[51]

According to the picture that has emerged from this study of the syllable, the syllable is a linguistic construct tightly linked to the notion of possible word in each natural language, though not, strictly speaking, reducible to it. The syllable at this word-level is an organization of distinctive feature information in smaller constituents, and in this organizational task the syllable is aided by secondary licensers at the beginning and end of words. In addition, we have focused on the ways in which the coda, acting as a secondary licenser, behaves as a 'minisyllable', with a limited degree of ability to license distinctive features.

This situation holds at the phonological word-level, but not at more superficial phonetic representations, where the pattern that emerges is more like the Bloomfieldian conception of alternating rising and falling sonority. Many, but by no means all, of the properties of the more phonetic representation are transferred to the deeper, more 'information-oriented', word-level. In the next chapter, we turn to the rhythmic patterns of stress found above the syllable within the word – the rhythm of metrical systems.

4

Metrical Structure

4.1 INTRODUCTION

In this chapter we turn to the theory of *metrical phonology*. The development of metrical theory in the last few years has been on the basis of two distinct formalisms, one using metrical trees, as in (1a), the other involving metrical grids, as in (1b). The two perspectives are relatively similar, to be sure; in fact, the two formalisms were originally developed in the same paper.[1] The metrical tree involves the establishment of constituent structure similar in character to that of syntactic representations, based on lowest-level constituents that are 'rhyme-projections', i.e. syllables without the onset material. Throughout the first five sections of this chapter, as we use σ in arboreal metrical structures, we shall draw only those branches from the σ that dominate material in the rhyme of the syllable (e.g. (1a), where 'F' stands for 'foot'). The grid representation, in (1b), represents horizontally the basic beats of the utterance, and vertically the strength assigned to that beat in the rhythm of the word or phrase – the more x's over a beat, the more prosodically prominent it is taken to be.

The order of exposition in this chapter will be based largely on the

(1)   (a)   Metrical tree

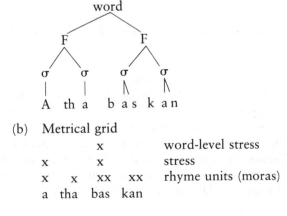

(b)   Metrical grid

		x		word-level stress
x		x		stress
x	x	xx	xx	rhyme units (moras)
a	tha	bas	kan	

actual historical development in the literature, a development that put the original emphasis on the theory of metrical trees, and only later produced an articulated theory of metrical grids that came to rival the theory of metrical trees. The parallels between tonal and grid association discussed at the end of the last chapter seem to me to point strongly in the direction of a grid-based theory, and we shall return to this below.

What the two versions of metrical theory share in common is the idea (i) that the study of stress is different in kind from the study of other phonological characteristics; (ii) that it is fundamentally a study of the relative prominence of syllables and higher-level units, such as the foot; (iii) that the most important characteristics determining stress patterns are *rhythm* (i.e. alternating prominence) and *sensitivity to inherent syllable (or rhyme) weight*; and (iv) that stress representations are hierarchical. The precise formal way in which the hierarchical nature of stress is expressed differs in the two approaches, but both share the goal of expressing the hierarchical relationship found among syllable rhymes, secondary stress patterns, primary word patterns, and ultimately phrase-level prominences.

Both approaches to metrical theory have explored and utilized the notion of *extrametricality* as well. As a first approximation, we may understand extrametricality to be a marking on a unit (a mora or a syllable, in the most common cases), making it invisible as far as the rules are concerned that build metrical structure. Rhythmic prosodic structures will often have a touch of syncopation at the edges of words, where the expected alternating beat may be missed; that phenomenon at the periphery of the word is accounted for by means of the formalism of extrametricality. When we look at the metrical grid below, we will see that the notion applies, more strictly, to grid positions rather than to segments or segmental constituents, as in the arboreal approach.

4.2   METRICAL TREES: BOUNDED FOOT STRUCTURES

As we have noted, the original insights of metrical phonology were expressed within an *arboreal* framework, i.e. one using trees. In this model, the part of phonological material that is relevant to stress is taken to be only the rhyme, as a way of expressing formally the observation that the content of the rhyme is relevant for stress assignment, while the onset is not. These rhymes are then organized into simple constituents. In the original form of metrical notation, each constituent had at most two daughters, and each was labeled with a rhythmic weak (w)/Strong (s) labeling of the daughter nodes. The idea is a simple one, which allows a direct representation of a number of traditional notions, and also permits an elegant formulation of principles of stress assignment in many languages. The organization into rhythmic constituents is done in several steps.

First, syllable rhymes are organized into constituents called *feet*; feet in turn are organized into constituents that make up the phonological word. An example of this is given in (2).

(2)

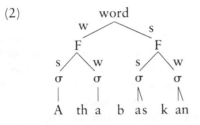

When we look at the stress systems of languages around the world, we find that we can divide them very roughly into those with a tendency towards rhythmic repetition of stress on alternating syllables, and those with no such tendency – where, rather, stressed syllables can be *any* distance away from one another. Into this latter group would fall, naturally enough, those languages with only one stress per word, independent of the length of the word.

This observation is expressed in metrical theory in terms of the assignment of metrical feet to a word. We begin by postulating that the sequence of rhymes of a word must be analyzed into stress feet in such a way that every rhyme is part of some stress foot, in much the same way that every segment must be syllabified or licensed, and that every word in a sentence must be part of some higher-level syntactic constituent, excepting the odd stray syllables which are adjoined to the larger word structure. When the feet are constructed, we specify whether they are *left-headed* or *right-headed*.[2] In the former case, the leftmost rhyme of the foot is stressed; in the latter, the rightmost rhyme of the foot is stressed. 'To be stressed' means nothing more or less, formally speaking, than to be in the head-position of a metrical foot, and so any non-head rhymes in a metrical foot will be unstressed. Let us call this *Rule Parameter 1* in the definition of a metrical rule: the structure created is either (i) left-headed or (ii) right-headed.

We will focus, for the rest of this section, on feet that are no longer than two syllables in length – what are called *bounded* feet. These may, of course, be either left-headed or right-headed.

We must specify if these feet are to be constructed rightward from the beginning of the word, or leftward from the end of the word. This *directionality of rule application* – which can be either left-to-right or right-to-left – is our *Rule Parameter 2* in the specification of a metrical rule. This is necessary because, in applying a rule of alternating stress (i.e. bounded, binary foot construction), if a word has an odd number of syllables to be gathered into binary feet, then there will certainly be one syllable left over. Given the requirement that feet be established for all syllables, this will mean that we will be forced to create a 'degenerate' foot at the end of such a word (see below).[3]

Two notations are currently in use to express the fact that a syllable rhyme is in the 'head' or 'dominant' position of a foot, i.e. in the position that receives the foot's stress. The original way requires that only binary-branching structure be used, and marks the head (or stressed) constituent with an 's' (for 'strong'), and the other constituent with a 'w' (for 'weak'). This is illustrated in (3), where the σ's, as before, indicate syllables, and F stands for 'foot'. Feet with only one syllable do not need to have their single position labeled as in (3c). These solitary feet are referred to as 'degenerate feet'. We will refer to this notation as the *s/w (metrical) notation*. The left-headed type is sometimes referred to by its traditional name in poetics: a *trochaic foot*, or *trochee*. The right-headed type is similarly called an *iambic foot*, or *iamb*.

(3)   (a)   (b)   (c)
         Left-headed foot   Right-headed foot   Degenerate foot

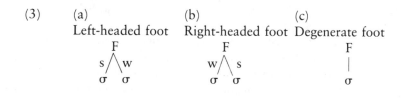

An alternative notation (reminiscent of a notation used in dependency phonology (Durand 1986) and that developed in Lerdahl and Jackendoff 1983) distinguishes the left-headed and right-headed cases by placing the node representing the foot constituent geometrically above the head, i.e. on the rhyme that is stressed. We shall refer to this as *head-marked (metrical) notation*; (4) would be the translation of (3) into this alternative notation.

(4)   (a)   (b)   (c)
         Left-headed foot   Right-headed foot   Degenerate foot

              F   F   F
              ⟍   ⟋ |
             σ σ   σ σ   σ

Head-marked notation offers a number of practical advantages, and we shall make considerable use of it. There is an asymmetry in this notation not present in the s/w notation; what *was* the strong position is still marked as something special, being now the element directly under the 'mother node' of the metrical constituent; however, the weak positions are not explicitly marked, and the way is left open for feet to contain more than one non-head position. This would mean that metrical constituents could directly contain *any* number of syllables, a proposition that the s/w notation was designed explicitly to rule out.

Parameters 1 and 2 create four simple systems for assigning binary feet across a word, as in (5). The syllables that bear stress are marked with a circumflex underneath. This is not normally a part of metrical notation; I have included it just to help readers interpret the metrical notation at this stage.

(5) (a) Left-headed binary feet, erected from left to right

     F   F   F   F   F   F   F

σ σ σ σ σ σ σ   σ σ σ σ σ σ

  (b) Left-headed binary feet, erected from right to left

     F F   F   F   F   F   F

σ σ σ σ σ σ σ   σ σ σ σ σ σ

  (c) Right-headed binary feet, erected from left to right

     F   F   F F   F   F   F

σ σ σ σ σ σ σ   σ σ σ σ σ σ

  (d) Right-headed binary feet, erected from right to left

     F   F   F   F   F   F   F

σ σ σ σ σ σ σ   σ σ σ σ σ σ

Let us look at a concrete case of such a system. MalakMalak, a language spoken in Western Arnihem, Australia (Birk 1976), illustrates the assignment of left-headed binary feet from right to left, as in (5b). Words with four to eight syllables and words of two syllables manifest the alternating stress pattern clearly, as we see in (6a–f). Words of three syllables may either show the expected pattern, as in (6g), a stress pattern that gives the word an emphatic force, or, more normally, will display the stress pattern shown in (6h). Primary stress, not indicated here, is on the first stressed syllable.

The description presented so far of MalakMalak leaves open two related points. First, we must determine how the non-emphatic stress pattern of the trisyllabic form is to be generated. Second, we must say

(6)

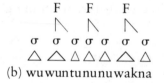

F   F   F   F
∧   ∧   ∧   ∧
σ σ σ σ σ σ σ σ
△ △ △ △ △ △ △ △

(a) nuŋ ku řun tu wö rö wak ka   'You (pl.) would have given them meat' (8 syllables)

F   F   F
∧   ∧   ∧
σ σ σ σ σ σ σ
△ △ △ △ △ △ △

(b) wu wun tu nu nu wak na   'He would have given you (sg.) meat' (7 syllables)

F   F   F
∧   ∧   ∧
σ σ σ σ σ σ
△ △ △ △ △ △

(c) nön kö rö nö yun ka   'You (pl.) will lie down' (6 syllables)

F   F
∧   ∧
σ σ σ σ σ
△ △ △ △ △

(d) ařkiniyaŋka   'We are all going to stand' (5 syllables)

F   F
∧   ∧
σ σ σ σ
△ △ △ △

(e) munankařa   'beautiful' (4 syllables)

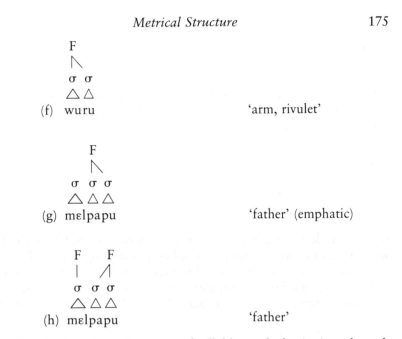

(f) wuru   'arm, rivulet'

(g) mɛlpapu   'father' (emphatic)

(h) mɛlpapu   'father'

something further about the status of syllables at the beginning of words having odd numbers of syllables. In (6b), (6d), and (6g), they are not assigned a foot, and thus are not stressed, but I have indicated already that such stray feet are indeed countenanced by the theory.

The answers to these two questions are related. Metrical theory guarantees that all syllables will, at least initially, be organized into feet, unless they are specially exempted from this by means of extrametricality, and feet will be of the *maximum* size permitted by the language and the word in question. When two binary feet have been erected on a five-syllable word like the one in (6d), the remaining initial syllable is in fact assigned a foot, giving us the representation in (7).

(7)

$$
\begin{array}{ccccc}
\text{F} & \text{F} & & \text{F} & \\
| & \wedge & & \wedge & \\
\sigma & \sigma & \sigma & \sigma & \sigma \\
\triangle & \triangle & \triangle & \triangle & \triangle \\
\text{ař} & \text{ki} & \text{ni} & \text{yaŋ} & \text{ka}
\end{array}
$$

Since this stress on the initial syllable is not present on the surface, we must posit a rule that *deletes* such non-branching feet. The simplest formulation would be that in (8), which we will revise in a moment. The single line descending from the foot node indicates that there is exactly one daughter node under F, and F is thus non-branching. The rule says that such a foot is deleted. (Such stray syllables are, by convention, assigned to the nearest foot at word level.)

(8) 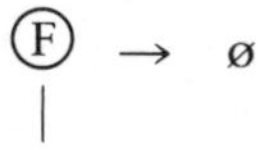   Ⓕ → ø
         |

However, we see that this rule does not apply to trisyllabic forms
(except under emphasis, a form that we shall not deal with directly). We
modify (8), therefore, to (9). (9) says that when two feet (i.e. four

(9) 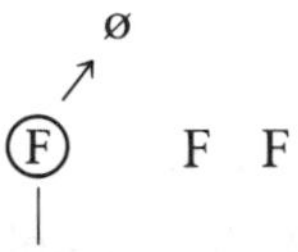   ø
             ↗
         Ⓕ   F F
         |

syllables) follow a non-branching foot, that foot is deleted. In a trisyllabic
word, only one foot follows the initial non-branching foot, as illustrated
in (10). In that case, the initial non-branching foot is not deleted, and the
labeling is reversed on the remaining foot to avoid a 'stress-clash', i.e. a
sequence of two successive stressed syllables. This rule is given in (11).

(10) 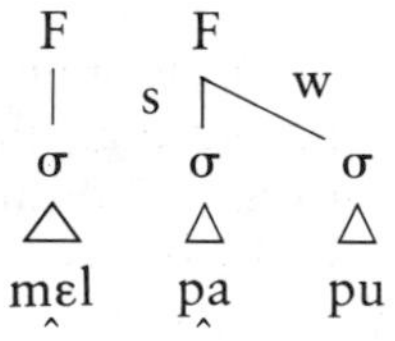   F   F
           | s ╱╲ w
           σ   σ   σ
           △   △   △
          mel   pa   pu

(11) 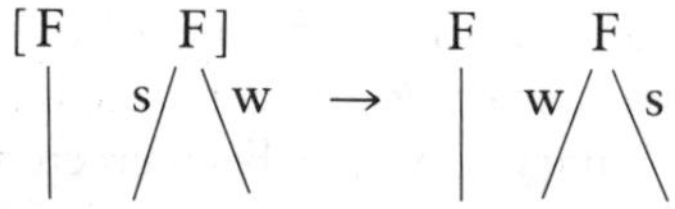   [F   F]   F   F
        | s╱ ╲w   → | w╱ ╲s

Careful readers may begin to see here a problem with a strictly
'arboreal' theory of metrical structure. The notion of *stress-clash* is an
important and pervasive one, referring to a general and widespread
tendency for languages to avoid representations in which adjacent
syllables are stressed. Rule (11) clearly is intended to avoid the clash
situation described in (10), just as (9) has the effect of avoiding a stress-
clash. But the notation fails to reveal that the degenerate status of the first
foot (which is, after all, what the rule is formally looking for) creates a
stress-clash only because the *non*-degenerate feet are trochaic (strong–
weak); that is, what is most relevant is a local condition of the terminal
elements (here, the syllables). Furthermore, the reason that a stress shift is
possible in trisyllabic words but not, for example, in five-syllable words
is very likely due to the fact that, if strong/weak labeling of the second
and third syllables *were* reversed in a five-syllable word, as by (11), it

would reduce the clash between the first and second syllable, but it would also establish a clash between the third and fourth (see (12)). In such cases, the stress-clash can only be avoided (at least if we are restricted to one step in the repair) by deleting the initial foot, and that is what rule (9) does.

The notion of stress-clash is crucial, and these limitations of the arboreal metrical notation have been perceived as setting the stage for the replacement of metrical trees by a metrical grid, which we will turn to in section 4.6. The stress-clash is another structural condition that defines well-formed W-level representations, and we see here in MalakMalak's alternative strategies for clash avoidance a situation paralleling the ways we saw in the last chapter in which languages seek to maximally syllabify their segments. In Turkish, for example, we saw that long segments would be shortened if that shortening produced a sequence that could be directly syllabified; if it was not adequate, then an epenthetic vowel would be inserted. Just so here: if reversal of strong/weak labeling will avoid the clash, it is effected. If not, deletion of a degenerate foot is undertaken.

(12)

$$
\begin{array}{cccc}
F & F\ F & F \\
| & \diagdown & \diagdown \\
\sigma & \sigma\ \sigma\ \sigma & \sigma\ \sigma \\
\triangle & \triangle\ \triangle\ \triangle & \triangle\ \triangle \\
\end{array}
$$
wu wuntu nu nu wak na

clash!

4.3 QUANTITY-SENSITIVE BOUNDED FEET

In most stress systems, the internal structure of the syllable is highly significant in determining how stress feet are established – that is, where stress will fall. As we have noted, it is frequently found that languages establish a binary distinction involving the *weight* of a syllable, dividing syllables into heavy and light syllables. The principles of stress foot establishment will need to have access to sylllable weight if they are to place stress feet correctly in these systems, known as *quantity-sensitive* systems.

One approach that has been taken within the framework of metrical phonology is to focus on the question of whether or not the rhyme constituent of the syllable is geometrically branching, defining a heavy syllable as one with a branching rhyme and a light syllable as one without a branching rhyme. If, furthermore, we take foot structure of the sort just outlined in the preceding section as structure built not on syllables (as we would expect) but on rhymes, we can integrate the geometry of the rhyme with the geometry of feet. Typically, heavy syllables demand to be stressed in quantity-sensitive systems, which means that they must appear in head ('strong') position.

Alternatively, we may put the matter negatively, and say that the weak position of a foot cannot dominate a heavy rhyme; or, paraphrasing in yet a third way, we can say that *weak nodes do not dominate branching nodes*. This weak-nodes-don't-branch principle of metrical theory produced some of the more interesting early results, although, as we shall see below, this was almost certainly an illusory formal result. In any event, such a principle would allow a structure as in (13a), but not as in (13b), in a language, for example, where bounded, left-headed feet were found.

(13)

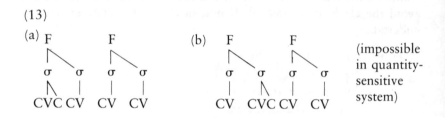

It should be clear that, if we depend heavily on such a principle, it is all the more important that metrical structure be built on rhyme projections, not on the syllable itself, since the syllable will almost always be branching, if it has both an onset and a rhyme.

Not all languages *are* quantity-sensitive; not all languages let the internal structure of the syllable interfere with the construction of foot-level prosodic structure. We could imagine that the way to specify whether the language is quantity-sensitive or not is to specify whether it respects the weak-nodes-don't-branch principle. Early metrical theory's method for expressing whether or not a language is quantity-sensitive in this way was different, in fact. In order to maintain that principle for another purpose, even in quantity-insensitive systems (we will see what that purpose was in a moment), Hayes suggested using instead a different notion to segregate the quantity-sensitive from the quantity-insensitive systems. He suggested that all languages will impose the weak-nodes-don't-branch principle on the *foot*-structures that they create, but that languages may differ with respect to whether they extend the domain of this prohibition down into the rhyme structure that the foot-tree is geometrically sitting upon. In the quantity-sensitive systems, the structures to which the foot-defining principles extended included the rhyme structures; in quantity-insensitive ones, the prohibition would stop at the rhyme node itself, would not look inside, and therefore would not be aware if, perchance, a branching rhyme were to fall in a weak metrical position. This, then, is our Parameter 3: *Quantity-sensitivity*: limitations on well-formed metrical structure include (do not include) the highest level of internal structure of the rhyme.

Among languages with quantity-sensitive bounded feet, we find those in which stress falls on alternating syllables when the syllables are all light, but in which a heavy syllable may not be skipped over, but must rather be stressed. Among the languages with this system is Yup'ik, a language we have already discussed.

There are many intricate complexities in the prosodic systems of the Yup'ik dialects discussed in Krauss (1985), but we may limit ourselves to some of the simplest processes of accentuation, which come out clearly in Central Siberian Yup'ik. Here we find just the sort of situation mentioned above: heavy syllables are stressed, and if we scan the remaining, light, syllables from left to right, we can group them into pairs of syllables to form iambic feet, as in (14). However, one must bear in mind in this case that heavy syllables are defined as syllables with long vowels; closed syllables with short vowels are *not* heavy syllables. (See, for example, the second syllable of (14a).) In addition, the final syllable is never stressed; or, as we shall say, it is *extrametrical*. The digraphs *ng*, *gh*, *ll* represent single sounds. Examples are divided into syllables for ease of reading. Stressed syllables are underlined. The derivation of form (14e) is given in (15).

To repeat, this treatment of quantity-sensitive foot construction involves a direct linking of the structure of rhymes to the stress pattern of the word, and as such it is, or was, the single most significant result of the

(14)

(a)	aang qagh <u>lla</u>gh llang <u>yug</u> tuq	'he wants to make a big ball'
(b)	ang <u>yagh</u> llagh <u>llang</u> yug tuq	'he wants to make a big boat'
(c)	qa <u>ya</u> ni	'his own kayak'
(d)	qa <u>yaa</u> ni	'in his (another's) kayak'
(e)	sa <u>gu</u> <u>yaa</u> ni	'in his (another's) drum'
(f)	qa <u>ya</u> pig <u>ka</u> ni	'his own future authentic kayak'
(g)	qa <u>ya</u> pig <u>kaa</u> ni	'in his (another's) future authentic kayak'
(h)	a <u>te</u> pik	'real name'
(i)	ang <u>yagh</u> lla ka	'my big boat'
(j)	ang <u>yagh</u> lla kaa	'it is his big boat'

(15)   (i) sa gu yaa (ni)   final syllable is extrametrical

            (ii) sá͞ gu yaa (ni)   one iambic foot is constructed

           (iii) sá͞ gu yaa (ni)   a second foot is constructed

metrical theory that crucially depends on *trees*, the arboreal theory. It provides a tight theoretical link between the internal geometry of the syllable and the well attested fact that heavy syllables attract stress. However, some reasons for skepticism regarding its ultimate correctness have already crept into the discussion unannounced: in Yup'ik, closed syllables with short vowels do not count as heavy syllables, even though one would certainly think their rhymes were branching. As noted in the last section of chapter 3, this tight fit is probably illusory, and we shall return to this question, and consider a looser connection between syllable weight and metrical prominence, in connection with the metrical grid below.[4]

4.4   UNBOUNDED FEET

We noted above that early arboreal metrical theory placed a restriction on metrical trees that branching could be only binary, permitting structures as in (16a) or (b), but not (c). This restriction could be said to follow naturally from the formal restriction that all lines must be

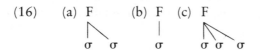

(16)   (a) F   (b) F   (c) F

               σ   σ   σ   σ σ σ

labeled either w or s. But not all feet are in actual fact restricted to a length of two syllables; if the strong syllable of each foot is stressed, we must certainly leave room within the theory for stress systems in which the stresses are much further apart than two syllables. In some systems, they can be an unbounded distance apart. How do we represent this, if arboreal theory disallows (16c)?

One arboreal account suggests that what is available here is branching rhyme structure, as in (17a) or (17b), for unbounded left-headed and right-headed feet, respectively. We noted above that there would be occasion to invoke the weak-nodes-don't-branch principle even in a quantity-insensitive system; this is the occasion. We can invoke it now to

(17)   (a)   foot   (b)   foot

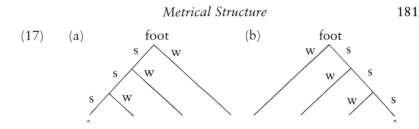

guarantee that all unbounded feet will be as in either (17a) or (17b), but never as in, say, (18a) or (18b). To put the matter slightly differently, and more generally, there may be reason to allow feet that are indefinitely long, but there is no need to allow various kinds of foot-internal geometrical structure, for contrasts of this sort are not found.

(18)   (a)   foot   (b)   foot

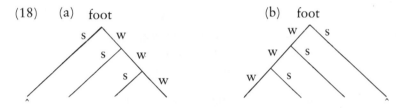

This will be our *Parameter 4* for the establishment of foot structure: a foot node may (may not) dominate another foot node. If it may, then the recursive structure in (17) is allowed, and unbounded feet will appear in the language; if not, then only binary branching feet of the sort we have seen before will appear.

In allowing for larger feet, we actually mean to do more than simply permitting them; we wish to *require* these larger feet. We wish to emphasize that the size of the foot that a language establishes for its words will be the largest size possible, subject to the constraints imposed more generally by the grammar. This has been referred to as the *maximality condition*, and we shall take it generally to hold. In scanning a string of syllables in order to establish appropriate foot (i.e. stress) structure, the language will establish the largest feet consistent with the segments that it finds and the constraints inherent in the language itself.

This is not an arbitrary stipulation, to be sure; it reflects a general tendency that we have encountered before. In the area of syllable structure, we always find the fewest number of syllables established consistent with the underlying segmentation and the permitted syllables of the language. This is especially striking in the case of a language that epenthesizes vowels when there are too many consonants in the underlying representation for well-formed syllabification to proceed. The principle that is always operative is this: in the derivation that mediates the underlying representation and the word-level form, we create as few structures as are consistent with the requirements for a well-formed surface form. As we noted briefly in chapter 3, one such requirement for a well-formed surface form is that which comes under the rubric of *prosodic licensing*: all syllables must be prosodically licensed, by being structured in a foot or by being marked as extrametrical. In section 6.5 we will return to this general characteristic of phonological rules – the minimal characteristic of applying as few times as possible in order to satisfy both underlying and surface constraints; or, to put it slightly differently, to require that underlying and surface forms be as similar as possible, again subject to the respective well-formedness conditions, or tactics.

Let us summarize the parameters we have established so far for the construction of feet:

Parameter 1: Left/right-headed feet
Parameter 2: Left-to-right/right-to-left application
Parameter 3: Quantity-sensitive/-insensitive
Parameter 4: Bounded/unbounded feet

The discussion above regarding how to formalize unbounded feet provided one account, using nested foot structure as in (17). An alternative which has been adopted in more recent work utilizing head-marked notation approaches the matter more directly, and simply distinguishes two kinds of metrical structures: (i) those whose maximal branching is binary, and (ii) those without any limitation on the maximal number of nodes that can be dominated. We shall forgo the more cumbersome notation in (17) in favor of allowing directly for multiply branching foot structures. With this head-marked notation, which we shall henceforth adopt, (17a,b) would be replaced by (19a,b). (19a) would mark a language with word-initial stress only, such as Latvian, (19b) a language with word-final stress, such as French (cf. (20)).[5]

(19) (a) F   (b)   F

(20) (a) átsvabinaasimies   'we shall liberate ourselves'
      (b) [otosɛgmãtál]   'autosegmental'

Now, a system in which left-headed, unbounded, quantity-sensitive feet are constructed will stress all heavy syllables, plus the first syllable – all other things being equal. The mirror-image system, with right-headed, unbounded, quantity-sensitive feet, would lead to the stressing of all heavy syllables plus the last syllable. One language for which this last-stress system has been described is Western Greenlandic (Eskimo), a language related to Yup'ik.

The two types of quantity-sensitive unbounded foot systems described above (left-/right-headed) agree in that they both make heavy syllables stressed. Yet there is an inherent phonetic prominence that might be difficult to distinguish from stress 'itself' (whatever that is, a difficult phonetic point!) in a system that assigns stress exactly to syllables that are inherently prominent. In fact, there are very few reported cases of languages in this group. Although Greenlandic has been cited in the literature (e.g. Hayes 1980 and Prince 1983) as possessing a stress system in which heavy syllables and the final syllable are stressed, this is not an easy point to establish, according to the analyses cited in Rischel (1974). It is not self-evident how the stress reported on the final syllable is to be properly distinguished from the high tone that is placed on one of the final three syllables of the word. (In the simplest case, a high tone appears on both the ultimate and the antepenultimate.) The prominence perceived and reported on the preceding syllables may or may not be something in addition to the inherent quality of a heavy syllable.

To establish the existence of a prosodic prominence that we would want to call stress in a system where it is typically the heavy syllables that are prosodically prominent, it would appear that we would like best to find either heavy syllables that are not stressed (so that by contrast we would know when we had encountered a stressed heavy syllable) or light syllables that are stressed. While Western Greenlandic does satisfy the latter requirement in that final syllables are often said to be stressed, as Rischel emphasizes, that perception may in this case result from a confusion with an intonational phenomenon.

We will return shortly to other systems which are best analyzed as having quantity-sensitive unbounded feet, but in which the evidence does *not* include phonetic evidence of secondary stresses on each heavy syllable. However, in order to discuss such cases, we must first turn to the matter of word-level, primary stress.

4.5   WORD-LEVEL STRUCTURE

In addition to talking about stressed syllables, we need a way of expressing the notion of *primary stress* in a word. A primary stressed vowel is always a stressed vowel, of course; what we need to express is the prominence of one of the stress feet with respect to the other stress feet of the word. We will extend the notations used so far to represent relative prominence of stress feet. In the s/w notation, we will represent primary stress as a foot which is itself dominated by a branch labeled 'S', as in (21a). Using the head-marked notation, we represent the same word as in (21b).

(21)   (a)

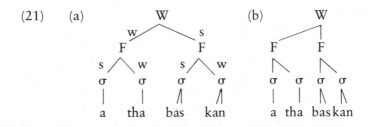

This approach suggests a plausible and appealing hierarchy of levels, in which rhyme-level metrical structure organizes segments, foot-level metrical structure organizes rhymes, and word-level metrical structure organizes feet. This strict hierarchy has not been respected in all the work on metrical structure, as we shall see. It has been suggested, for example, that in certain cases the rules that organize syllables into feet may fail to apply (in particular, if their structural requirement fails to be met by the rhymes composing the word), and in that case the word-level rules may apply directly to the syllable-level metrical structure without an intervening foot-level structure. We will return to this issue shortly.

The system described so far appears to assume that the principle(s) of a language that establish the primary, or word-level, stress always select a syllable that has already, on other grounds, been assigned secondary stress (i.e. head-position in a foot). While this is frequently the case – English works this way, for example – it is not always true, and languages that violate this orderly bottom-to-top sequence are more easily dealt with using the formalism of the metrical grid (section 4.6 below).

The rule (or rules) that establishes metrical structure at this second level – ranking the relative prominence of feet within the word – is a separate rule from that which establishes the structure of the feet, and in principle would be specified in the same way as the rule that creates foot-level structure, i.e. by specifying a value on each of the four parameters. In practice, however, only the first parameter really matters in establishing word-level structure.[6] If there are no bounded feet at the word level, directionality does not matter, and there is nothing corresponding to syllable weight to be concerned about at this level, either. In short, in systems in which the estabishment of foot structure logically precedes that of word-level structure, the word-level primary stress is chosen from the first or the last foot of the word, corresponding to left-headed and right-headed word-level tree structure, respectively.

We may, then, add a fifth parameter, and use our established parameters to define word-level metrical rules as well: *Parameter 5:* The structure is at word (foot) level.

In most languages, what is called *primary*, or *word-level*, stress is the assignment of a special tonal (or intonational) melody to the syllable in question, in addition to the stress effects perceived on the other secondarily stressed syllables. In such languages, including English, there is in this way a natural distinction between a primary stress and a secondary stress.

Certain languages, however, have been described as having only a single word-level stress which can be analyzed coherently only if we assume that this single stress is the result not of one foot being assigned to the whole word, but rather of several feet being assigned, along with a regular word-level structure. In this case, however, the non-primary stresses are not phonetically realized. To account for such systems, we must postulate a parameter − not for a rule, now, but rather for a language as a whole − which we will call *suppression of non-primary stress*. In a more complete account of a stress system, this would no doubt not be a single parameter, but rather an extreme point along a continuum, for the phonetic effects corresponding to secondary stress − the effects assigned to a syllable in head-of-foot position − vary quite a bit from language to language. In the case at hand, we consider a language that has no phonetic means for expressing assignment of secondary stress: the phonetic effects are only indirect, in that the secondary stress system is used in order to determine location of primary stress.[7]

Let us consider now a kind of quantity-sensitive system, where typically the stressed syllable is a heavy syllable; the only case where a word's stressed syllable is not heavy is where the word consists of only light syllables. But in this kind of system, unlike what we have seen in a case such as Yup'ik, there is only one syllable stressed per word, allowing us to assign a clear constrast between stressed and unstressed heavy syllables.

Consider the following descriptions that have been proposed equally for the pronunciation of forms of Classical Arabic, as in (22a), or of Eastern Cheremis (22b) (from Hayes 1980), an Altaic language of the Soviet Union (cf. Kiparsky 1973, Ingemann and Sebeok 1961). In these cases, the principle that governs the assignment of word stress is that the last heavy syllable is stressed, and if there is no heavy syllable then the first syllable is stressed. (Readers should recall that the final consonant in Arabic is extrasyllabic, and plays a role in the assignment of stress; see the discussion below, as well.[8])

(22) (a) kitaabun, manaadiilu, yušaariku, mamlakatun
kataba, balaḥatun
(b) šiičaam, šlaapaažəm, püugəlmə, kiidəštəžə, tələzən

Such a system can be directly accounted for in the following way. First of all, unbounded, quantity-sensitive, left-headed feet are established. A right-headed word-level structure is created, and the secondary-stresses are suppressed. This is represented in (23). In this way, the disjunctive expression of the stress principles – 'do this if there are one or more

(23) Eastern Cheremis, Classical Arabic

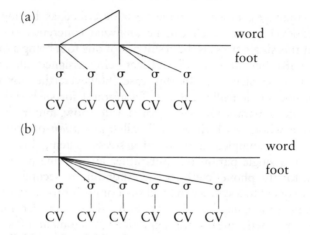

heavy syllables, do that otherwise' – is eliminated in the metrical approach, which sees the two cases as fundamentally unified in the principle of the assignment of a maximal quantity-sensitive foot. Similarly, this metrical analysis can unify the statement of a stress system in which the first heavy syllable is stressed, or, in the absence of any heavy syllables, the last syllable is stressed. This is the result of establishing unbounded right-headed feet, and a left-headed word-level structure. Mnemonically, we can say that the system we have established so far captures neatly stress systems that place 'stress on the last heavy syllable, or else the first syllable', and also systems that place 'stress on the first heavy syllable, or else the last syllable'.

One case that has been reported in the theoretical literature on stress which is the mirror-image of the system in (23) is that of Komi Jazva, a Permic language of the Finno-Ugric family, briefly cited in Kiparsky (1973), drawing on Itkonen (1966). As we have noted, such a system can be straightforwardly handled by means of metrical principles that establish right-headed quantity-sensitive feet, with a left-headed word-level structure, as in (24).

(24)   Komi Jazva type of system: first heavy syllable, or last syllable

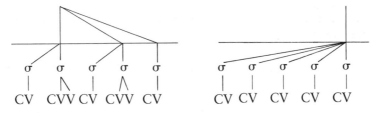

However, there are many stress systems are problematic in light of the
analyses given so far, and Odden (1979) argues that the following kind of
system is rather more common than either the Eastern Cheremis or the
Komi Jazva type. The literature reports that there are systems where
stress will fall on the last heavy syllable, or, if there are none, on the *last*
syllable. (Hayes 1980 cites Aguacatec Mayan (McArthur and McArthur
1956) as such a language.) This is the opposite of what we found in the
Eastern Cheremis case, to be sure. Conversely, there are systems where
stress will fall on the first heavy syllable, and, failing that, on the *first*
syllable; see (25). There are examples of this sort from Khalkha
Mongolian;[9] and Odden points out that Lake Miwok (Callaghan 1965),
Lhasa Tibetan and Lushootseed also display the same pattern.

Again, this is the opposite of what would be expected in light of what
has been said so far. If stress falls on the *last* heavy syllable in a word,
then it follows immediately that the language must erect left-headed
unbounded feet, since the word-level structure can pick out only the first
or last foot, and a right-headed foot-system will always stress the last
syllable. We would expect such a left-headed tree to arise covering the
entire word if there were no heavy syllables in a word. The pattern of
'stress the last heavy syllable, otherwise the last syllable' is therefore
unexpected, but not uncommonly found.

Let us express schematically the stress pattern reported for these two
additional kinds of systems as in (26) and (27).[10] These representations –

(25)   Khalkha Mongolian (from Odden 1979, citing Poppe 1951)
       daaga   'Filly'
       tailwar   'commentary'
       utaa   'smoke'
       noxoi   'dog'
       xutagaar   'knife (instr.)'
       daagaar   'filly (instr.)'
       xooloi   'throat'
       dalaigaar   'sea (instr.)'
       xada   'cliffs'
       axan   'older brother'

especially the (b) parts – are hardly self-explanatory. It is not clear, in particular, whether the left-headed structure in (26b) and the right-headed structure in (27b) should be conceived of as a foot- or a word-level constituent.

(26)   First heavy syllable, or else first syllable (Khalkha Mongolian)

(a)   (b)

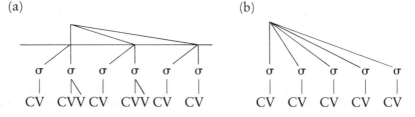

(27)   Last heavy syllable, or else last syllable (Aguacatec Mayan)

(a)   (b)

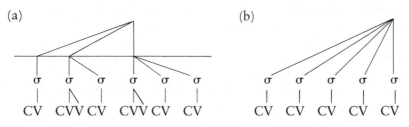

Within arboreal metrical theory, there are two approaches to this problem that have been explored. Both involve the notion of a foot with an *obligatorily branching* node in head (strong) position. The first, in addition, involves allowing for the possibility of word-level metrical structure with no foot-level metrical structure in the case of words with no heavy syllables. The second approach avoids that, but instead proposes two foot-assignment rules, one for each of the two cases, which is to say, one foot assignment rule for the words with one or more heavy syllables, and another rule for words with no heavy syllables. Let us consider these possibilities in turn.

To account for a system as in (26), if the foot-construction algorithm (that is, the mechanism that constructs foot-level metrical structure) is instructed to build an unbounded left-headed foot with the stipulation that its head *must* dominate a heavy syllable (this stipulation would have to be institutionalized as another parameter in our rule formulation, that of 'obligatory branchingness'), then there will continue to be no problem in establishing appropriate feet in cases like (27a), and a language like Aguacatec will look much like Eastern Cheremis (23a). However, the algorithm will simply fail to apply to a case where there are no branching rhymes, which is precisely the point of requiring that the head of the foot be branching.

At this point, we may attempt to capitalize on the fact that we know independently that, in a system like Aguacatec, the *word-level* metrical structure assigns greatest prominence to the rightmost foot, and hence is right-headed. If no rule establishes foot-level metrical structure, then the word-level metrical feet can just take the rhyme-nodes as their terminal elements, building structure as in (28).

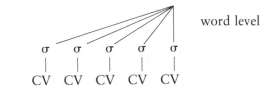

This approach has been discussed at length in the literature, but another, and simpler, possibility within the arboreal metrical framework seems more direct. We are considering, recall, a language that contains a rule that builds left-headed feet where the head *must* be a heavy syllable, and in which the last heavy syllable is stressed (i.e. (27)). In a word with only light syllables, the system will establish no foot structure. It would seem equally reasonable, rather than to call upon the word-level rule now, to simply add a second foot-assigning rule to the grammar of the language to deal with this case. We have seen that languages that stress the last heavy syllable can go two ways with respect to how they treat words with no heavy syllables: either they stress the first syllable (Cheremis, (22b), (23)), or they stress the last syllable (Aguacatec, (27)). In the former case, we posit an additional *unbounded* quantity-insensitive *left*-dominant foot-assigning rule, or else leave our system unchanged; in the latter, we could posit an unbounded quantity-insensitive *right*-dominant foot-assigning rule. In order to see that the rule systems will work correctly, we need to convince ourselves of two things: that languages may in fact contain more than one foot-assigning rule, and that the quantity-sensitive rule will have priority in applying ('will be ordered first') on principled grounds. Let us consider these in order.

The proposition that languages can contain more than one foot-establishing rule is uncontroversial. For example, according to Lynch (1978), stress is assigned in Lenakel to verbs and adjectives on the penultimate syllable – analyzing the word from the right-hand end – and also to odd-numbered syllables counting from the beginning (i.e. left-hand end) of the word. This pattern can be seen in such forms as /tɪnagamařolgeygey/ 'you (pl.) will be liking it' and /nɪmamařolgeygey/ 'you (pl.) were liking it'.

Second, the fact that the quantity-sensitive foot-construction rule should have priority in applying over quantity-insensitive rule follows from the Elsewhere Condition (see also section 5.1.2), a principle that gives priority in application to the more specific rule when we are faced with two rules competing to apply to a form, where by 'more specific' we mean the rule that will apply only to a proper subset of the forms to which the other rule could apply. Thus, the idea that the stress assigned by the second, quantity-insensitive, rule is a 'default' rule, picking up the pieces left over by the quantity-sensitive rule, is recognized by the theory.

An especially interesting class of metrical systems was recognized early on in the metrical literature (McCarthy 1979; Halle and Vergnaud 1978; see also Prince 1983; Goldsmith 1987b), in which only one stress or accent is observed per word, but where the notion of a span of even-numbered syllables plays a crucial role. The effect of one stressed syllable per word (traditionally called *culminative accent*) is, again, the phenomenon we have referred to as 'suppression of secondary stress', but the presence of domains consisting of stretches of even-numbered strings of syllables indicates that bounded feet have been constructed. Haas (1977) discusses Creek, a Muskogean language presently spoken in Oklahoma and Florida, a language in which both tonal and accentual structures are found. In a word with no inherently accented syllables, the tonal accent is placed on the last even-numbered light syllable counting from a heavy syllable, if there is one, or else from the beginning of the word, as in (29). If the ultima is heavy, tonal accent may or may not fall on it; additional complications apparently arise here. (29d) gives an example of one of these words, over which quantity-sensitive right-headed feet have been constructed from left to right. Degenerate feet (on the right end) are deleted, and a right-headed word-level tree is then constructed.

4.6   METRICAL GRIDS[11]

The metrical grid is another formal means of representing stress, and it may appear at first sight rather different from the metrical trees we have been using. Simply put, the metrical grid is a set of three layers (or perhaps more, if more levels of stress appear motivated; cf. n. 6) that run parallel to the string of syllables that make up the word. The lowest layer contains a series of 'x's, one for each mora in the string. This row would best be called the *mora row*, or Row 0, but it is frequently called the *syllable row*. The next layer up, the layer that represents simple, or secondary, stress, contains an x only above those syllables that are

(29)   (a) All syllables light
ifa̲   'dog'
ifo̲ci   'puppy'
amifo̲ci   'my puppy'
hici̲ta   'one to see one'
ahi̲cita   'one to look after one'
imahi̲cita   'one to look after for someone'
isimahi̲cita   'one to sight at one'
itiwanayi̲pita   'to tie each other'

(b) All syllables light except the penultimate
ca̲:lo   'trout', 'bass'
so̲kca   'sack'
poco̲swa   'axe'
fami̲:ca   'canteloupe', 'perfume'
ałakko̲ycka   'appreciation'

(c) Heavy syllable followed by string of light syllables
akto̲pa   'bridge'
wa:ko̲ci   'calf'
hokta̲ki   'women'
iŋkosapi̲ta   'one to implore'
alpato̲ci   'baby alligator'
yakapho̲yita   'two to walk'

(d)

stressed, and in effect marks the head of feet; we will call this the *foot
row*, or Row 1. Finally, on the top layer, the *word row*, or Row 2, an x
appears only above that syllable that receives the main stress of the word,
as illustrated in (30). Additional layers can be added if degrees of phrase-
level prominence should be described.[12] The height of the columns, as we
see, represents the degree of stress prominence placed on each syllable.

(30)   x   Row 2 (word)
             x   x   Row 1 (foot)
             x   x   x   x   Row 0 (mora/syllable)
            ge ne ra tion

This notation differs from the metrical tree notation that we have developed so far in at least two ways. First, there is no notion of metrical constituency involved so far in these metrical grids.[13] The second syllable of (30) is no more associated with the first than with the third syllable, though there is certainly no reason why grid marks on a given row could not be grouped into constituents with a bit more formalism (see e.g. Halle 1987, Halle and Vergnaud 1988). Second, the notation is better able to capture a notion of stress-clash, of the sort we referred to above in looking at MalakMalak.

The term *stress clash* refers primarily to a situation in which adjacent vowels are stressed, as in (31). Stress systems do frequently construct restrictions either to prevent such situations from arising or to eliminate them where they occur. In addition, the term has been used to describe

(31)   x x   Row 1
           x x x   x   Row 0
           cv cv cv   cv

situations where primary stresses are on successive stressed vowels, even when these stressed vowels are not literally adjacent. This view suggests that, just as stressed vowels somehow prefer to be surrounded by unstressed vowels, so too primary stressed vowels would prefer to have only secondarily-stressed vowels as their nearest stressed neighbors – a condition on vanity, so to speak.

The definition of clash in a metrical grid can be made slightly more perspicuous if we put an o on top of any x that has not got an x on top of it. Thus (30) would be as in (32a); (31) as in (32b).

(32) (a)   o   x   Row 2   (b)   o   x   x   o   Row 1
           x o x o   Row 1   x   x   x   x   Row 0
           x x x x   Row 0   CV CV CV CV
           ge ne ra tion

We can define a clash easily, then, as the occurrence of two successive x's without an o in between. The clash appears on the second layer in (32b), and a clash would also arise on the third layer in (33), for the same reason.

(33)   x   x   o   o   Row 2
           o x o   x   o   x   o   x   Row 1
           x x x   x   x   x   x   x   Row 0
           CV CV CV # CV CV CV CV CV

In a moment we will turn to how rules are written to establish metrical grids. Before doing that, it might be useful to point out that the differences between metrical trees and grids, once established, are in *some* respects more apparent than real. Any metrical tree written with the head-marked notation that we have adopted can be turned into a metrical grid just by keeping the nodes of the tree (and replacing them with the grid mark x) and dropping the connecting lines; see (34).

(34)

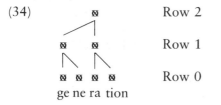

Row 2

Row 1

Row 0

ge ne ra tion

Trees cannot be reconstructed in a unique way from grids, as we have described them, because the grids do not indicate whether an x on a given level which is not sitting under another x should be construed as forming a constituent with a higher-level x to its left or its right. But the notations become even closer if we allow bracketing on grid marks to be indicated, as has been suggested.

Another way of viewing the difference between the perspectives of arboreal and grid theory is this: arboreal theory takes itself to be an account of hierarchical structure of the phonological material itself, or of the skeletal tier, where the head/non-head distinction of syntax is matched by the strong/weak distinction. Grid theory, for its part, takes the metrical grid to be an autonomous structure, with certain internal principles (such as those defining and controlling clash) that are distinct from those of segmental phonology, whose terminal (or bottom row) elements are autosegmentally linked to syllable positions via the principles of autosegmental licensing discussed in the preceding chapter. On this latter view, which I believe to be correct, more complete phonological structures look like (36), or like (29) of chapter 3 above, in the discussion of Selayarese, with a grid constructed autonomously from the skeleton, but associated to it subject to licensing conditions of syllable structure.

There are three basic rules of grid construction. One is called the *End Rule*, which places a grid mark on the extreme left or extreme right of whatever domain it is specified for. These instructions may be abbreviated as ER (Initial) and ER (Final). In a simple case, for example, if the End Rule operates at the foot level, applying at the left end, it will stress the first syllable of the word. But to specify that the rule is adding grid marks at the foot level (and not the word level), we must specify more than just

ER(Initial) or ER(Final): we must specify the grid level as well. Thus, the correct statement of the End Rule will include two specifications: (i) Initial or Final; and (ii) a grid level, typically Foot or Word. The case mentioned earlier in this paragraph would then be 'ER(Initial, Foot)'.

When the End Rule applies at the word level, its effect is to place a grid mark on top of the leftmost (or rightmost) grid mark on the foot level, not the absolutely leftmost (or rightmost) syllable. Each grid level acts, we might say, as a *projection* for the next higher level to act upon.[14]

The example in (7) above from MalakMalak would be expressed as in (35), and the primary word stress, which falls on the first stressed syllable, would be assigned by the rule ER(Initial, Word).

(35)   x   Row 2
          x   x   Row 1
      x x x   x   Row 0
    ař ki ni yaŋ ka

An important notion that interacts frequently with the application of the End Rule is that of *extrametricality*. An element on the metrical grid can be marked as extrametrical if it is at either the extreme left or the extreme right end of its level. Thus, in the most frequent case, the lowest-level grid mark of a word-final (or word-initial) syllable is marked as extrametrical, which is indicated by putting it in parentheses. The result of this is that further rules which may attempt to place higher-level structure (e.g. foot-level markings) will be blind to the existence of that grid mark, and hence of that syllable.

Watjarri, a language of Australia (Douglas 1981), can be simply described with these notions. The final syllable is extrametrical, a condition that appears to be the rule rather than the exception in languages of the world (cf. Ito 1988). At the foot level, both ER(Initial) and ER(Final) apply, giving stress to the first and penultimate syllables. At the word level, ER(Initial) applies, making the first syllable the recipient of the highest, word-level stress, leaving the penultimate with a secondary stress; see (36).

The second central rule of the grid is the rule of *Perfect Grid*, which corresponds to the process of establishment of bounded feet across the word in arboreal metrical representations. Perfect Grid, as Prince has formulated it, is a rule that moves across a word (we must specify whether that scanning is from left to right, or from right to left), assigning grid marks to every other grid mark on the immediately lower row. We will furthermore allow ourselves the freedom to specify whether Perfect Grid should assign grid marks to the odd-numbered positions in its direction of scan or to even-numbered positions. The former is called

(36)   Prosodic structure: kuṭayarapula

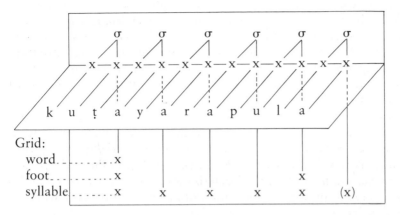

peak first assignment, since it assigns a grid mark to the first position, third position, and so on, while the latter is called *trough first*, since it does not assign a grid mark to the first, but waits till the second. If Perfect Grid applies at the foot level, and scans from left to right, assigning grid marks to the odd numbered syllables, it will assign stress to the first, third, fifth, etc., syllables of a word, as in (37).

(37)   x   x   x   x   x   Row 1
          x x x x x x x x x   Row 0
          CV CV CV CV CV CV CV CV CV

The application of Perfect Grid in (37) was formulated to apply (i) at foot level; (ii) from left to right; and (iii) on odd-numbered positions ('peak-first'). We could let Perfect Grid apply again, changing only the first setting, allowing it to apply at the next grid level up, (but still left-to-right and peak-first), giving us the represenation in (38).

(38)   x   x   x   Row 2
          x   x   x   x   x   Row 1
          x x x x x x x x x   Row 0
          CV CV CV CV CV CV CV CV CV

Perfect Grid is a rule whose inherent function is clearly to create sequences of stressed–unstressed units. In the direction in which it is scanning, it has this property built right into it. However, if it is scanning from left to right, for example, it may find itself in a position to apply in such a way as to stress a syllable that is immediately followed by a stressed syllable (if, for example, ER(Final) has already applied on the same grid row; quantity-sensitive rules may lead to parallel cases, as we shall see). Normally, Perfect Grid will not apply in such a case to create a stress-clash; it is, as it were, so dedicated to establishing a perfect grid that it keeps its eyes open to what is ahead of it as it scans. In certain languages, though, while it is less common, the rule that introduces alternating stress *will* create a stress-clash as it proceeds in its proper direction. If this is the case, we say that the rule of Perfect Grid is allowed 'Forward Clash Override'.

The third important grid rule arises in the analysis of quantity-sensitive systems. We have seen that in arboreal metrical treatments, what distinguishes heavy syllables is their characteristic *inability* to be placed in the weak position of a foot. There being no feet in the grid, we may well expect a rather different characterization, and in fact what we find is a more direct expression of the notion of inherent prominence with less formal gadgetry.

The lowest row of the grid, we said above, is a row of grid marks where each mark corresponds to a mora. If Perfect Grid is assigning a grid mark on the second row to alternate marks on the first row, then it will always assign a grid mark to one of the moras of a heavy syllable. Strikingly, some systems that otherwise avoid stress-clashes (Tulatulabal and Estonian, as Prince 1983 notes) will allow a stress on the first syllable following a stress heavy syllable, suggesting that the correct analysis is as in (39).

(39)   x   x   Row 1
           x   xx   x   x   Row 0
           CV CVV CV CV

A rule that assigns a row 1 grid mark (i.e. stress) to the second of the two grid marks of a single heavy syllable automatically has its effect 'corrected' by shifting that stress to the first, since the first mora of a heavy syllable is always more sonorous and more prominent than the second. We will refer to this as *weak mora stress correction*. Diagrammatically, (40a) is automatically and immediately corrected to (40b). We will see an example of this in Arabic below.

(40)   (a)   x   (b)   x
                  x x   x x
                  C V V   C V V

This correction for the effects of Perfect Grid is one way in which heavy syllables are guaranteed to receive stress; but there are languages, we have seen, that are quantity-sensitive – that is, assign stress to their heavy syllables – without having an alternating stress pattern, and thus without the rule of Perfect Grid. Within grid theory, this effect is achieved directly, by a rule called simply *Quantity-Sensitivity (QS)*. QS will apply to create a grid mark, or series of grid marks, on the foot row over any heavy syllable.[15]

The system that a language uses to establish a metrical grid, then, consists in essence of a small set of rules built out of the four principles that we have seen: (i) rules that mark peripheral elements as extrametrical; (ii) the End Rule; (iii) Perfect Grid; and (iv) Quantity-sensitivity. Complex systems can arise in which several ordered rules from this set must be established, although in most cases, remarkably enough, a quite small set of rules from this set suffices to establish the metrical grid for the whole language.

As a example of how metrical grids could be used in slightly more complex situations, let us consider how the stress patterns of (i) Classical Arabic, (ii) Damascene Arabic, and (iii) Cairene Arabic would be treated using the grid.[16] All three dialects share a number of basic properties concerning syllable structure. In general, no clusters of more than two consonants occur word-internally, but word-finally a CC cluster is permitted. In addition, a CVVC syllable is not permitted word-internally, but is permitted word-finally. These two special word-final possibilities are traditionally known as *super-heavy* syllables. As noted in the preceding chapter, they are the result of a secondary word-final licenser providing licensed extrasyllabicity. These extrasyllabic elements, however, play a regular role in the stress assignment in all three dialects. The precise nature of the stress assignment for words with final long vowels contains, unfortunately, some unclear points.[17] The remaining generalizations are as follows.

Classical Arabic
1 A final superheavy syllable is stressed.
2 Otherwise, the rightmost heavy syllable (that is *not* in final position) is stressed.
3 If there are no heavy syllables, then the first syllable is stressed.

Damascene Arabic
1 A final super-heavy syllable is stressed; a final CVV syllable is stressed.
2 Otherwise, if the penultimate is heavy, it is stressed.
3 Otherwise, the antepenultimate is stressed.

Cairene Arabic
1   A final heavy or super-heavy syllable is stressed.
2   Otherwise, if the penultimate is heavy, it is stressed.
3   Otherwise, count from the rightmost heavy syllable (if there is one) or
    (otherwise) from the beginning of the word; stress the penultimate or
    the antepenultimate, depending on which is in an odd-numbered
    syllable.

As we have already mentioned, one of the striking facts about Arabic is
the special metrical character of the extrasyllabic final consonant that
'creates' the super-heavy syllables. McCarthy (1979 and elsewhere)
suggests a structure as in (41a) for them, with a Chomsky-adjunction;
Selkirk (1981) suggests (also citing Aoun 1979) that the proper analysis
takes the extra consonant as a kind of 'degenerate syllable', i.e. a syllable
with a missing nuclear position (41b). Our own account is that the
extrasyllabic consonant is licensed by a word-final secondary licenser
that, like a syllable, licenses association to the grid. This captures Selkirk
and Aoun's intuition as well, for the secondary licensers are limited
generalizations of the least restricted licenser, the syllable.

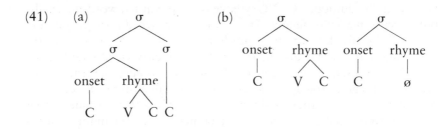

We will establish skeleton-to-grid associations straightforwardly as in
(42). 'C' in these diagrams indicates 'coda'; 'R', 'rhyme'. The final mora
(i.e. the final element on Row 0) is extrametrical. However, extrametricality cannot apply to the second mora of a long vowel: it can only affect
(i) an entire light (CV) syllable, or (ii) the secondarily licensed final C of a
super-heavy syllable. The reason for this is clear, and involves what
Prince (1980) has referred to as the *Syllable Integrity Principle*: the
notion that prosodic constituent structure cannot violate syllable structure, a possibility that arises concretely within grid theory. In the
examples given in (43-5), be sure to note the effects of weak mora stress
correction. These segment-to-grid associations are intended to hold,
mutatis mutandis, across the three dialects. How, now, do the dialects
differ?

(42) kitaab
katabt
banaa
katabti
ʕaalamu
maktaba
šajara

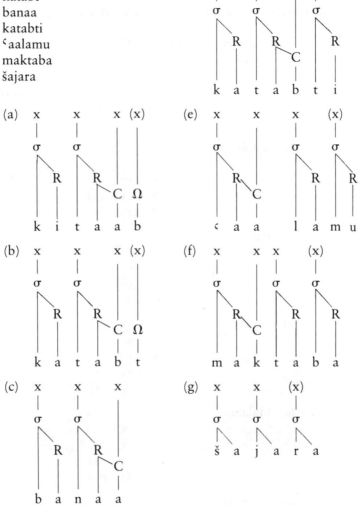

Cairene and Damascene both fairly clearly show evidence that the rule of Perfect Grid applies, as Prince (1983) is at pains to demonstrate, with Cairene spreading its Perfect Grid from left to right, peak first, guaranteed to place a grid mark on either the penultimate or the antepenultimate, and to place one on the final syllable of a CVV word. As we noted above, a grid mark that is placed on the second mora of a heavy syllable is automatically replaced on the first syllable (weak mora stress correction). After Perfect Grid has done its work, the End Rule (Final, Word) applies, assigning word-level stress to the rightmost stress assigned by

Perfect Grid. This is illustrated in the Cairene forms in (43a)–(f) and (j), (k). In (43g)–(i), the Cairene pronunciation of some longer forms from Classical Arabic are given, following the same principles.

(43)   Cairene (Perfect Grid L → R))
         (a) kitaab

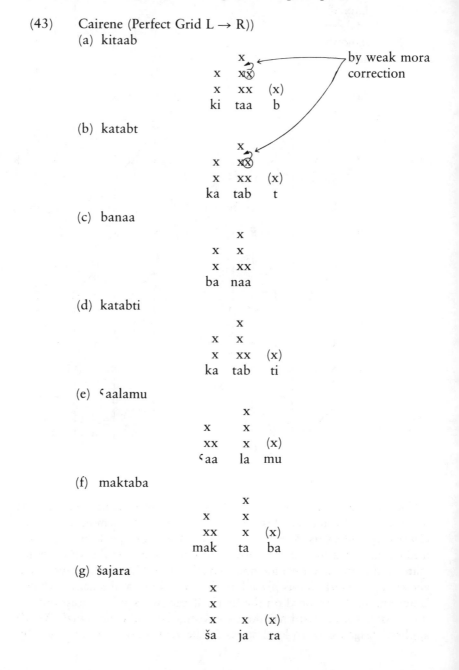

         (b) katabt

         (c) banaa

         (d) katabti

         (e) ʕaalamu

         (f) maktaba

         (g) šajara

(h) šajaratun

```
                        x
        x               x
        x       x       x       x       (x)
        ša      ja      ra      tu      n
```

(i) šajaratuhu

```
                        x
        x               x
        x       x       x       x       (x)
        ša      ja      ra      tu      hu
```

(j) muxtalifa

```
                x
        x       x
        xx      x       x       (x)
        mux     ta      li      fa
```

(k) martaba

```
                x
        x       x
        xx      x       (x)
        mar     ta      ba
```

In Damascene, by applying from right to left, in a trough-first manner, Perfect Grid is certain to land a grid mark no further in than the antepenultimate, and that only when the final syllable is extrametrical and the penultimate is light (e.g., *dárasu*). The details are sketched in (44), using examples from McCarthy (1980). In several cases, again, a grid mark assigned by Perfect Grid is shifted to the nucleus of its syllable (weak mora correction). The End Rule, again, applies at the word-level, stressing the rightmost foot level mark, though in most of these cases, there is only one element on that row.

(44)   Damascene

```
                x                                       x
                x⊗                                      x
        x       xx      x       (x)             x       x       (x)
        (a) ma  daa     re      s           (c) ka      ta      b


                x                                       x
                x                                       x⊗
        x       xx      (x)                     xx      x       (x)
        (b) ka  tab     ti                  (d) kaa     ta      b
```

```
        x                              x
        x                      x       x
        x    x   (x)           xx  xx  (x)
(e)    da   ra   su     (h)   saa ruu   k
```

```
       x                                   x
       x⊗                          x       x
       xx   x   (x)            x    xx  xx
(f)   mad  ra   se     (i)    da   ras  tuu
```

```
        x
        x
        x   xx  (x)
(g)    da  ras   t
```

Finally, in Classical Arabic, there is no evidence of Perfect Grid appying at all, and yet heavy syllables clearly play a crucial role. The Rule Quantity-sensitivity is operative here, then, instead of Perfect Grid, together with the End Rule (Initial, Foot). These two rules will place foot-level grid marks, and the word-level rule of End Rule (Final, Word) will select the rightmost one of this set to be the word-level stress: (45a)–(d) illustrate the effects.[18]

(45)　　Classical Arabic

```
(a)                              x
                         x       x
                         xx  x   xx  (x)
                        kaa  ti  baa   t
```

```
(b)                              x
                             x   x
                         x   xx  x   (x)
                        ya  šaa  ri   ku
```

```
(c)                      x
                         x
                         xx  x   x   x  (x)
                        mam  la  ka  tu   n
```

```
(d)                      x
                         x
                         x   x  (x)
                        ka  ta  ba
```

4.7   FURTHER DISCUSSION OF EXTRAMETRICALITY

We have touched several times on the notion of extrametricality, most notably in the discussion of Arabic stress placement. In this final section, we shall discuss some further aspects of this notion – how it fits into analyses proposed within metrical theory, and in particular how it might best be used in the analysis of the stress system of English, a system studied in great detail by a number of students of phonological theory.

It is worth pointing out that in a number of informal discussions of extrasyllabicity and extrametricality in the literature, it has been suggested that the two notions are parallel in some sense. This is not a very illuminating analogy, in my view. The extrasyllabic consonants we looked at in Arabic are fully integrated into the prosodic structure through a secondary licenser, and if they are extrametrical, it is only by the same principles that in other cases make perfectly normal CV syllables extrametrical. The two notions are quite different, as (42) illustrates.

The primary function and justification of the notion of extrametricality is its ability to show, simply and directly, ways in which forms need to be adjusted or modified in order for our simple inventory of rules in metrical theory to work correctly. I have intentionally put the matter tendentiously and provocatively, of course; put that way, it sounds like a matter of trying to sell a procrustean bed to a weary, and likely wary, buyer. But we are always in the position of wondering, when faced with non-trivial data from a language, how to come up with a straightforward statement of a generalization. We are accustomed to thinking about how to modify and complicate the *rules* in a minimal sort of way to fit the data; that is the familiar procedure in classical generative phonology. Nothing prevents us, however, from thinking about the process slightly differently, and asking whether there are not principles – sometimes general, sometimes specific – that modify or prepare the representation for the effect of the phonological rule. The best result would be that we would come up with a limited set of ways in which representations could be doctored and a seriously limited class of metrical rules could be made available to the theory. That is the goal of metrical theory, and the purpose of employing the notion of extrametricality, and the strategy has been quite successful.

Let us consider the case that Hayes (1980, 1982) makes for extrametricality in English. Chomsky and Halle (1968) begin *The Sound Pattern of English*, after some opening remarks, with the statement (p. 69) that verbs assign stress[19] to final syllables with long vowels or a final cluster of two consonants, and to penultimate syllables otherwise. They give the well-known list in (46) illustrating these three categories of stress placement. Nouns, however, assign stress regularly to the penultimate syllable if it is heavy, or else to the antepenultimate, if the penultimate is light: cf. (47). Chomsky and Halle proceed to point out that primary

(46)

I	II	III
astonish	maintain	collapse
edit	erase	torment
consider	carouse	exhaust
imagine	appear	elect
interpret	cajole	convince
promise	surmise	usurp
embarrass	decide	observe
elicit	devote	cavort
determine	achieve	lament
cancel	careen	adapt

(47)

I	II	III
America	aroma	veranda
cinema	balalaika	agenda
asparagus	hiatus	consensus
metropolis	horizon	synopsis
javelin	thrombosis	amalgam
venison	corona	utensil
asterisk	arena	asbestos
arsenal	Minnesota	phlogiston
labyrinth	angina	appendix
analysis	factotum	placenta

adjectives (as in (48a)), those not formed by affixation, follow the same stress pattern as in (46), while those formed with an adjective-forming suffix, as in (48b), follow the pattern in (47).

(48) (a) solid   supreme   absurd
         frantic   sincere   corrupt
      ✓ handsome   secure   immense
      (b) personal   anecdotal   dialectal
         maximal   adjectival   incidental
      И vigilant   complaisant   repugnant

Hayes (1980, 1982) has suggested two ways in which the notion of extrametricality can be used to directly make Chomsky and Halle's generalizations.[20] First, he suggests that projecting the forms in (46) and (47) onto a metrical grid, and marking the final syllable of nouns as extrametrical, will allow us to state the main English stress rule in simple metrical terms. A quantity-sensitive, bounded foot construction procedure, operating from the right edge, will then place stress on the penultimate if it is heavy, and on the antepenultimate otherwise. Various modifications of the forms of the rules that we have looked at in this chapter have been suggested, but Hayes's main point is one that I would like to incorporate, however it is formalized: the placement of stress on the syllable of the penultimate mora can be thought of as Perfect Grid applying its way leftward in a trough-first fashion, or as left-headed quantity-sensitive bounded trees. English, however, builds only *one* such quantity-sensitive foot structure when it initially builds a word. The argumentation here is moderately complex, and we will not delve into it. A notation that is frequently used expresses the generalization that the final syllable of a noun is extrametrical as illustrated in (49). A similar rule will mark all adjective-forming suffixes as extrametrical, except for *-ic*, which normally forms words that follow the stress pattern of *primary* adjectives, i.e., with penultimate stress.

$$(49) \qquad \sigma \to (\sigma) \: / \: — \:]_{noun}$$

The notation in (49) makes better sense within the arboreal approach than the grid approach that we have discussed so far. After all, metrical trees are established directly on top of rhyme structures, and to mark a syllable as extrametrical is simply to say that a foot will not be constructed on top of it, as in *melanin* (50a). The stray extrametrical syllable will later be adjoined to the foot by a rule known as 'stray syllable adjunction', as indicated by the broken line, placing the syllable in its neighboring foot. In certain versions of grid theory, the bottom row of the grid strictly marks syllables, even in quantity-sensitive languages like English; and in such a theoretical perspective, too, it is a little more straightforward to express the generalization in (49). This is done by marking the grid position of the final syllable as extrametrical, creating a representation as in (50b).

(50)   (a) word   (b)   x
            | x
          foot   x   x   (x)
                                                | | |
          σ   σ   (σ)   σ   σ   (σ)
          △   △   △   △   △   △
          mɛ   la   nɪn   mɛ   la   nɪn

The very real advantage to Hayes's suggestion regarding the treatment of nouns is that the principle that places stress on the penultimate or antepenultimate is an extremely common one, frequently called the *Latin Stress Rule*, though we have seen its effects elsewhere, in Damascene Arabic, and similar stress constructions can be found around the world. What is crucial is that the final syllable here plays no role, and extrasyllabicity is a way of expressing that inertness.

Looking at the verb patterns in (46), and the similar non-derived adjectives, Hayes suggests, following Chomsky and Halle, that there is a quantity-sensitive pattern here as well, sensitive to the number of consonants in the rhyme. However, the usual pattern of 'heavy syllable = branching rhyme' does not work here; following Chomsky and Halle's suggestion, we would have to say that it takes two consonants (or one long vowel) to make a heavy syllable. This looks like a super-heavy Arabic syllable; Hayes suggests that we can reduce this situation to the familiar one, which arboreal grid theory is equipped to handle, by making the final *consonant* in *all* English words extrametrical (though it makes a difference only in the case of verbs and adjectives). What looks like two final consonants on a word is perceived by the phonological system as only one; what looks like one consonant, to close the syllable, is not visible to the metrical system, and such a syllable is therefore treated as if it were open. This would produce an arboreal structure as shown in (51).

(51)

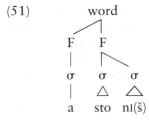

The framework developed in this book raises questions about such an analysis. To make clear why this is so, we will review the basic principles of our approach, and see what we can do to approach the empirical generalizations that are at hand. Looking ahead, our licensing-oriented approach predicts that there will be a close relationship between the way that segmental material is licensed, on the one hand, and its metrical properties, on the other. Our account of the complexities of the English word-final syllable, summarized in (49) of chapter 3 and repeated as (53) below, should be lined up with the complexities of the definition of syllable weight of the word-final position in English.

Returning to our picture of the interaction of syllables and the grid, I

have indicated that all segments must be licensed, and word-final segments have the option of being licensed either by the regular syllabification principles of the codas of the language, or, if there is one, by a word-
final appendix (or else by a morpheme-specific licenser, a minor possibility which we will overlook here). Metrical structure is not built directly
on rhyme structures, or on syllable structures, but rather on the bottom
row of the metrical grid. But the question must be settled as to which
licensers (and thus, in effect, which phonological material) associate with
a separate grid position. In a language with codas *and* word-final
appendices, four possibilities exist, in principle. Syllables always associate to grid positions, but (i) codas may or may not, and (ii) appendices
may or may not. Whether codas associate to grid positions is precisely
what is traditionally called quantity-sensitivity, as we have noted. The
second is a separate, and independent, matter. We thus arrive at the
possibilities sketched in (52). But in addition, we must determine whether
the final grid position is extrametrical, thus leaving us with eight possibilities (or six, if (52d) is impossible, as seems likely), since each of the
systems in (52) can appear either with or without final extrametricality.

   It becomes our task, therefore, to see what the present theory has to
say about English accent, especially when merged with the specific

(52)   Ranges of mora-sensitivity in the metrical system

        (a) Totally quantity-insensitive: neither coda nor appendix
            licenses grid association

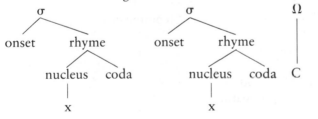

        (b) Totally quantity-sensitive: codas and appendices both
            license grid association

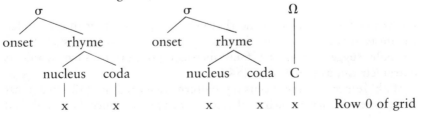

(c) Codas license grid association, but the appendix does not

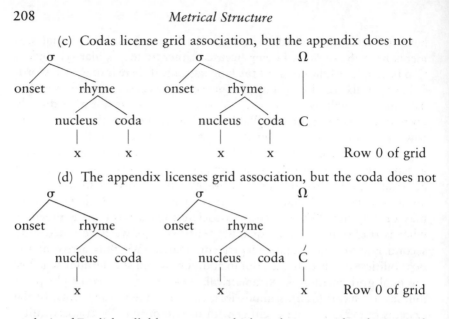

(d) The appendix licenses grid association, but the coda does not

analysis of English syllable structure which we have considered, repeated here as (53). Let us focus our discussion on the behavior of the stress patterns of English nouns. It is clear that words ending with two short open syllables allow a common pattern of antepenultimate stress, as in words like *Canada*, *America*, or, perhaps, *Kennedy*. If the primary

(53)

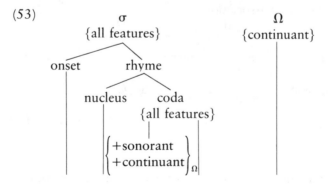

Ω = word-finally only

pattern of English stress is the rhythmic pattern inherent in a bounded (quantity-sensitive) system, then antepenultimate stress in such forms strongly suggests that the final metrical position in such words is extrametrical, as sketched in (54).

With respect to the licensing patterns sketched in (52), we must determine whether English is of type (b) or type (c), since the fact is well

(54)   x
         x
         x   x   (x)
         | | |
         σ   σ   σ
         △   △   △
         C a   n a   d a

established that English is quantity-sensitive. Furthermore, we must ask
how the extrametricality of the final grid element (as in (54)) operates
when the final syllable is heavy, i.e. is associated with more than one Row
0 grid position. The answer to the latter question depends on the former,
since logically we need to know how word-final segmental material
licenses grid positions before we can see whether these positions are
capable of being marked extrametrical.

The key to the answer lies in several proposals and generalizations
made in Ross (1972), who notes that there are two quite large exceptions
to the statement that the final syllable of a noun will not be stressed: first,
if the syllable contains a long vowel or diphthong, as in (55), that syllable
will bear a stress; second, and perhaps even more interesting, the
segmental composition of the final consonant is highly relevant in
determining whether a final syllable ending in a short vowel plus
consonant will behave like a heavy (bimoraic) syllable or not. Ross
argues that the generalization of (56) emerges from a consideration of a
wide range of cases. These points are illustrated in (57) (from Ross
1972).

(55)   Noun, final long vowel or diphthong

         hurricane   anecdote
         dynamite   magistrate
         artichoke

(56)   (a) A (word-final) syllable that ends in **two** consonants will
              attract stress (i.e. be heavy) – unless it consists of the
              following clusters:

              $n \begin{Bmatrix} t \\ s \end{Bmatrix}$ $r \begin{Bmatrix} t \\ d \\ n \end{Bmatrix}$ t s   s t

              Such syllables may, or may not, be stressed; they must be
              lexically marked.

         (b) A (word-final) syllable that ends in a short vowel plus
              one consonant will be stressed if it ends in 'one of the

sounds {p, b, f, v, š, ž, k, g}' (p. 250). If the final syllable ends with a coronal consonant or a sonorant, then whether the syllable receives stress or not must be lexically marked.

(57) (a) Words ending in clusters not listed in (56a)

parallax	cataclysm	asterisk
anthrax	Heffalump	insect
transept	Ozark	cobalt
Kennebunk	Podunk	cataract

(b) Words ending in clusters listed in (56a):

| | Final σ unstressed | |
Final σ stressed	Antepenult. stressed	Penult. stressed
sycophant	elephant	opponent
event	covenant	lieutenant
pederast	Everest	Massachusetts
Kibbutz	Horowitz	resistance
romance	inheritance	comfort
davenport		culvert
Mozart		

(c) Words ending in a short vowel, plus a single consonant from Ross's list in (56b), with final stress

handicap	Bandersnatch	Mamaroneck
lollypop	tomahawk	Carnap
shamrock	Beelzebub	shishkabob
shindig	Ahab	fisticuff
Jackendoff	balderdash	Wabash
Yugoslav		

(d) Words ending in short vowel plus sonorant

| | Final σ unstressed | |
Final σ stressed	Antepenult. stressed	Penult. stressed
Abraham	modicum	amalgam
diadem	marjoram	decorum
wagwam	strategem	harem
caravan	Saracen	Waukegan
Marathon	cinnamon	Wisconsin
ikon	garrison	Byron

samovar	integer	October
metaphor	vinegar	semester
alcohol	capitol	utensil
daffodil	funeral	apparel

(e) Words ending in a short vowel plus single alveolar obstruent

| | Final σ unstressed | |
Final σ stressed	Antepenult. stressed	Penult. stressed
Endicott	Connecticut	Narragansett
baccarat	Lilliput	Pawtucket
Ichabod	pyramid	Mohammed
katydid	invalid	bicuspid
sassafrass	syllabus	meniscus
albatross	rhinoceros	papyrus
Alcatraz		Fernandez
topaz		

This suggests the following analysis, linking the syllable structure for the word-final syllable in (53) with Ross' generalizations in (56).

1 Segmental material licensed in word-final position only – the strictly word-final position for /s/, /t/, and the post-vocalic position for sonorants and /s/ – do not associate with grid positions. Thus, English is of type (52c), where codas license grid association but appendices do not, and all word-final special licensing arrangements count as appendices, even if not strictly word-final in location.[21]
2 Word-final consonants with non-alveolar point of articulation cannot be in appendix position, though, as argued in chapter 3. They must therefore be licensed in the coda, and must associate with a Row 0 grid position, forming a heavy syllable.
3 Because there are two appendix positions in the word-final English syllable (post-vocalic, and absolute word-final), it is possible to have clusters that are not moraic, i.e. are not associated to the grid, as illustrated in (58). Of the seven clusters listed by Ross, our account predicts *nt*, *ns*, *rt*, and *st*; two others, *rn* and *rd*, can be accommodated by letting Ω license the features [voice] and [nasal]. The status of the *ts* cluster remains unclear (cf. Ross 1972: 248, fn. 15).

As Ross points out, there is a wide range of cases in English where the account presented so far would predict stress on the final syllable but

(58)

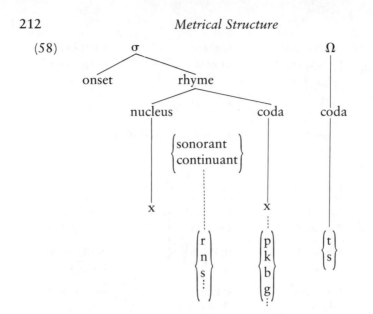

where none is present, owing to the presence of a stress on a penultimate short vowel in open syllable. This case is exemplified by the normal pronunciation of the word *Arab* [ǽrəb]. Ross proposes a rule destressing a short vowel when immediately preceded by a stressed lax vowel in an open syllable. Drawing on unpublished work by James Fidelholtz, Ross contrasts this pronunciation of *Arab* with the non-standard, but possible, [éyræ̀b], with stress on both syllables; here, the stress on the second syllable is constructed by the principles described above, and then is *not* deleted by the rule operative in the pronuciation [ærəb]. Other examples that work like *Arab* are given in (59).

(59)   scallop   bishop   Eric
         cherub   sheriff   relish

Summarizing our account of English nominal stress, we characterize English as a language with the syllable structure illustrated in (53), with word-final appendix material that does *not* associate with a grid position, though coda material otherwise will.[22] The final element on the metrical grid is extrametrical. (We have seen this motivated, at least, in words of three or more syllables.) This extrametricality is not permitted to apply in such a way as to violate the Syllable Integrity Principle discussed above, which is to say, it will not mark a mora (Row 0) position as extrametrical when it is the coda of a closed syllable.

Hayes's other principle use of extrametricality involves the behavior of secondary adjectives, as in (48b). As we observed above, Hayes proposes marking all adjective-forming suffixes as extrametrical, a direct and elegant means for expressing the empirical generalization proposed in Chomsky and Halle (1968). Ross (1972) argues, however – convincingly, in my opinion – that the basic principles of stress assignment to nouns and adjectives are in fact the same, once the character of the particular word-final consonants is adequately taken into account. In fact, arguing that analysis into base-plus-adjective-forming suffixation is responsible for the stress pattern in (48b) leads to quite implausible morphological structures being assigned to polysyllabic English adjectives. Ross goes into this point in some detail, but we will review the matter briefly. Consider, for example, the large number of English adjectives that end in -*ent*. While some are arguably derived by suffixation (*depend/dependent*, *exist/existent*), the case for suffixation for others is weak (as in (60a)), or nonexistent (60b).

(60)   (a) competent (from *compete?*)
                confident (from *confide?*)
                provident (from *provide?*)
    (b) evident
             exuberant
             impudent
             flamboyant
             delinquent
             affluent
             belligerent
             intelligent

In sum, while there may remain a number of issues to be argued in greater detail, a strong case can be made, in my opinion, for the superiority of an account of English stress that uses extrametricality, as proposed by Hayes, on the metrical grid, but not in a way sensitive to morphological category. Furthermore, syllable structure and its attendant licensing potential is the connection between the segmental composition of a word and its projection on the metrical grid.

It is fitting to close this chapter with a discussion of what has been called the *Peripherality Condition* (Harris 1983), which states that all extrametrical units are 'peripheral', that is, they appear at the left-hand or right-hand side of the grid. If the stress in question is assigned at word level, then extrametrical elements would have to be word-final or word-initial; if it is assigned at phrase-level, then the elements would be phrase-initial or phrase-final. This condition on what may be extrametrical places heavy restrictions on our use of the notion, which is, in a sense, both good and bad for the theory. It is good in that the range of systems that can be described by the theory remains theoretically well behaved and comprehensible; it is bad, perhaps, if serious counter-examples arise.

The Peripherality Condition expresses a generalization that holds over a goodly range of cases in which extrametricality might persuasively be proposed, and cases have been proposed in which extrametricality marking seems to fall away from a morpheme as soon as it is no longer peripheral, as would be predicted. Harris (1983), for example, suggests that a stem-final rhyme in Spanish nouns and adjectives may irregularly and lexically be marked extrametrical, precisely because it is stem-final; he argues that the peripherality requirement is satisfied by this requirement. Words in Spanish are normally stressed on the penultimate syllable, as illustrated in (61a), but this general principle yields to the more exceptional antepenultimate forms as in (61b) when the stem-final syllable is extrametrical, on Harris's account. (In addition, other words have stress on their final syllable.)

(61)   (a) lágo   'lake'
             estructúra   'structure'
             vecíno   'neighbor'
             b[wé]no   'good' (masc.)
         (b) ling[wístika]   'linguistics'
             aristócrata   'aristocrat'
             múltiplo   'multiple' (n.)
             número   'number'

Harris (1983) notes furthermore that, when suffixes are added to such stems as in (61b) in such a fashion that the extrametrical syllable is no longer peripheral in the stem, it becomes susceptible to being stressed, as illustrated in (62). In (62b), the suffix that is added is itself extrametrical, a condition that makes it possible to show that the preceding syllable can now bear stress.

Harris considers a wide range of alternatives, and argues his case in detail; interested reader are encouraged to refer to Harris (1983). The example given here illustrates dynamically what appears to hold more generally: extrametricality markings strongly tend to be peripheral (though one might observe that the sense in which the extrametrical syllables in Spanish are peripheral – peripheral in the stem, not the word – bends our expectations of what counts as peripheral). The following case, from Paamese, illustrates what a language would look like if lexical extrametricality marking on a syllable were permitted to occur in a non-peripheral position.

(62)   (a) déspota 'despot'

```
                x
        x      (x)      x
        |       |       |
[[  d   e   s   p   o   t   ]   a   ]
   stem                          word
```

(b) despót-ic-o 'despotic'

```
                x
        x       x  (x)        x
        |       |   |         |
[[  d   e   s   p   o   t   i   c   ]   o   ]
   stem                                  word
```

(c) despot-ísm-o 'despotism'

```
                    x
        x       x   x           x
        |       |   |           |
[[  d   e   s   p   o   t   i   s   m   ]   o   ]
   stem                                     word
```

Crowley (1982) reports that in Paamese, an Oceanic (Austronesian) language, stress normally falls on the antepenultimate vowel when there are three or more vowels in the word, as in (63). There are several conditions under which stress fails to fall on the antepenultimate vowel.

(63)   visókono   'morning'
       manekólii   'darkness'
       vasíie   'all'

Most of these are phonological, and Crowley presents only a limited set of materials to judge the precise form of the rules involved. It appears that high vowels that are adjacent to non-high vowels become phonological glides, syllable structure permitting, and are not counted in the metrical structure as vowels, a not uncommon phenomenon. If the high-vowel-turned-glide is preceded by another vowel, that preceding syllable receives the stress, as in (64a); otherwise, stress falls on the following vowel, as in (64b).

(64)   (a) úriovu   'end wall of house'
           votéitasi   'seabed'
       (b) iáli   'they will walk'
           luáli   'you two walk'

What is remarkable about Paamese, however, is that certain vowels must be diacritically (i.e. arbitrarily) marked as being unstressable. Thus, Crowley analyzes a word such as *tahósi*, with penultimate stress, as having an unstressable vowel in the first syllable, forcing stress to fall on the penultimate. If the antepenultimate is unstressable in a longer word (and there are quite a few words of this sort), stress will fall on the pre-antepenultimate, as in *mólatine* 'man', or *táripenge* 'lazy'. When suffixes are added to words, stress continues to fall on the antepenultimate vowel of the entire word, as we see in (65a); that the same kind of stress shift appears in the forms with 'unstressable' antepenultimate vowels (cf. (65b)) supports the notion that stress is assigned in these forms as with other words. This set of facts suggests that antepenultimate vowels can be marked extrametrical in Paamese, violating the Peripherality Condition.

(65)   (a) ínau   'I'
            ináu-lii   'oh, me'
            inau-lií-risi   'oh, me again'

       (b) mólatine   'man'
            molatíne-se   'only the man'

In this chapter, we have seen some of the basic motivations for, and techniques of, metrical phonology, and have seen how they interact with the analysis of syllable structure. Many important issues have been ignored, or just barely touched upon, including phrase-level stress and intonation, the effect on segmental phonology of the establishment of the foot as a unit of constituent structure, and the effect of metrical structure on other prosodic systems, such as tone and vowel harmony. Some of these will be dealt with, albeit briefly, in the following chapters; others must, unfortunately, be left for readers to pursue in the literature.[23]

5

Lexical Phonology

5.1 INTRODUCTION

I suggested in the introductory chapter that the theories of autosegmental and metrical phonology are a direct outgrowth of the generative research program developed in *The Sound Pattern of English* (Chomsky and Halle 1968). Another theoretical development of this classical generative enterprise which has been influential in the last several years also deserves our attention: *lexical phonology*.

In the late 1970s and early 1980s, a number of theoretical proposals concerning the relationship between what in pregenerative years would have been called *morphophonemic* rules and *purely phonological* rules were synthesized into a framework called lexical phonology.[1] Some of these proposals are independent of the theories of phonological representation that we have been discussing in this book, but the approaches – lexical phonology on the one hand, and autosegmental and metrical phonology on the other – have had considerable influence on each other in the last few years. Of these interactions, perhaps the most active and fruitful has been that between *underspecification* theory within lexical phonology and the most recent work on autosegmental representation.

Lexical phonology can be divided into two distinct, but related, theories, a theory of phonology and a theory of morphology. We will begin with a discussion of the theory of phonology, focusing on the issues of the Strict Cycle Condition, the Elsewhere Condition, structure preservation, and underspecification theory. Since so much of the literature on the subject assumes a knowledge of English morphology, I present a brief overview of the principles of English stress and segmental phonology that bears on the morphological questions. Then we will look at the motivation for the various divisions of English morphology that have been made, focusing on Kiparsky's conception of the organization of English morphology as outlined in Kiparsky (1982a), and some modifications made more recently. Finally, we shall consider the knotty problem of cyclic derivations, focusing our attention on English, and concluding that the word-based morphology of English establishes a relationship of an interesting sort between the morphological structure and the phonological structure.[2]

5.1.1   The theory of lexical phonology

Lexical phonology begins with a division of phonology into a *lexical component* and a *post-lexical* component. (These sectors have also been called 'cyclic' and 'post-cyclic,' but the infelicitousness of the latter terms has become apparent more recently, since the lexical phonology may, on most views, contain non-cyclic parts as well.) The post-lexical component has also been called the *phrasal phonology*.

The post-lexical phonology involves two major sorts of rule applications: (i) those operating crucially across word-boundaries or making crucial use of phrasal or syntactic structure, and (ii) those that fill in, specify, or refer to non-distinctive features – the 'sub-phonemic' rules, we might say. For example, the principles discussed in chapter 2 that govern the appearance of the stops and spirants in Spanish have both of these properties: they specify a difference that is not contrastive in Spanish, and they do so on the basis of a phonological (or phonetic) principle that is not sensitive to whether the context material is in the same word or a different word. Thus, we find the stop version of *b*, *d*, or *g* when a homorganic non-continuant sonorant precedes, whether it is in the same word or the preceding word.

The class of lexical rules is also composed of two subtypes. Lexical rules involve, first, those phonological adjustments that are fundamentally occasioned, or triggered, by the juxtaposition of morphemes, such as the velar softening of /k/ in *electri/k/* when the suffix /-ity/ is added, forming *elektri[s]ity*; cf. (1). We may also include here the shortening that occurs to the stem vowel of strong verbs when the past-tense suffix is added (e.g. *plead/pled*, *feed/fed*, *feel/felt*, perhaps *say/said*).[3] Second, there are those lexical phonological rules that perform the modifications in the segmental structure required when the underlying form fails to satisfy the phonotactic conditions that make a string a well-formed word, such as the condition that the segments all be assigned to well-formed syllables.[4] In this second group we may include all the types of epenthesis rules discussed in chapter 3 above, such as in Turkish or Selayarese.

(1)   Velar softening
        k → s/ — i

Lexical rules, as their name suggests, apply within the lexicon, and hence before all post-lexical rules and without reference to any phonological material in neighboring words (see (3) below). The representations in the lexicon are described using only the *distinctive*, or *contrastive*, features of the language, and hence lexical phonological rules can make reference only to the distinctive features of the language, and to none of its redundant or predictable phonological features, such as the aspiration of stops in English. Similarly, since vowels in English, as in most languages, are non-contrastively voiced, vowels are not marked for voicing in the lexical phonology. It then follows that voicing cannot spread in an assimilatory way from vowels to neighboring segments in the lexical phonology, as has been suggested in various places in accounts that have been offered for post-vocalic voicing of consonants. The principles that lie behind this general move will be discussed further below under the rubric of the 'eliminate redundant features' principle of underspecification theory; we will refer to this as the *first principle of underspecification theory*.

A feature that is simply predictable within a language is barred from the lexical phonology by what we may call *feature filters*, as in (2). In principle, these filters could take in more than a single segment. A post-lexical rule will fill in such predictable features (here, voicing).[5]

(2)   Conditions on the feature *voice*
       feature filter: no voice specification with sonorants
       $*\begin{bmatrix} \alpha\text{voice} \\ +\text{sonorant} \end{bmatrix}$

Features may also be left unspecified underlyingly in another way, and for another reason, only to find the feature specification filled in during the course of the lexical derivation. That is, it may be possible to rule out *underlying* specification of certain features in certain positions, though not by filters of the sort in (2), which are in effect throughout the lexical derivation. Certain kinds of underlying specification may be, and should be, filled in by the effects of lexical phonological rule. Thus a lexical phonological rule, which will typically act across morpheme boundary for reasons we turn to in just a moment, will also have the function of filling in a value of certain unspecified features. Thus in Zoque, for example,[6] there is a rule that voices non-continuant obstruents after nasals (see (4a)). To express the *naturalness* of finding voiced non-continuants after nasals, we can leave the voicing underlyingly unspecified in such an obstruent, getting a free ride on (4a) to do the work of filling in the voicing specification. In fact, this gets at the heart of an important conception: changes that accompany the juxtaposition of morphemes created by the morphology (so to speak) are normally in the direction of what is somehow felt to be a simpler structure even as far as monomorphemic forms are concerned. However, this result would not

(3)	Model of lexical phonology

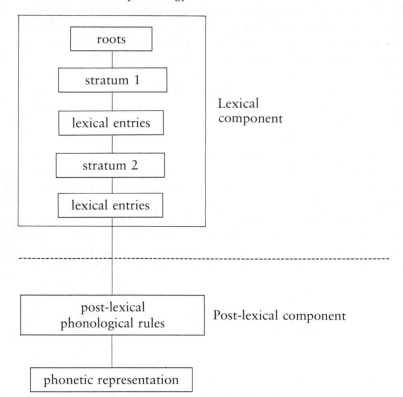

force the post-nasal consonant to be underlyingly unmarked for the feature [voice], something that we might actually want to do.

There is a good deal more to say about this, but in any event, the situation I have just described represents one current point of view regarding underspecification within lexical phonology, and we will return to the matter in section 5.1.5 below.[7] In the meantime, we will use the phrase *the second principle of underspecification theory* to refer to the view that features should be left unspecified if a lexical phonological rule would be capable of filling them in.

Consider the case of the tense vowels in English, which typically (and most clearly in the case of mid vowels) have an offglide. The presence of the *y*-glide in [ey], or the *w*-glide in [ow], is obligatory, and in no way contrasts within English with its absence; there is no tense [e] or [o] without the glide. Because no contrast is possible, the presence or absence is not phonologically distinctive (or contrastive), and hence it is not part of the lexical phonology. The rule or generalization responsible for the

(4)   (a) Voicing after a nasal

$$\left[\begin{array}{c} -\text{sonorant} \\ -\text{continuant} \end{array}\right] \rightarrow [+\text{voice}] \: / \: [+\text{nasal}] \: -$$

(b) Examples from Zoque (cf. (66), ch. 3) (Wonderly 1951: 120)

min 'come' + pa → minba 'he comes'

nʌm 'say' + pa → nʌmba 'he says'

pʌn 'man' + čʌki figure → pʌnǰʌki 'figure of a man'

presence of these offglides is thus a part of the post-lexical phonology, and it follows that no such diphthongs can be created (or found, for that matter) within the lexical phonology.

The notion that only contrastive features play a role in the lexical phonology, and that feature combinations that are not permissible underlyingly continue to be illegal throughout the lexical phonology, may suggest – quite correctly – that the output of the lexical phonology, the last stage at which these generalizations are in force, is roughly comparable to the phonemic level of traditional structuralism. This is in several ways a useful parallelism to bear in mind, though in at least one major respect the structuralist conception fails to match up: the lexical phonological representation is very much *word-bound*. It cannot, in principle or in practice, include in its domain of generalization any material outside the word. Thus, as rules of morphophonemics in pregenerative structuralist phonology could assign a given underlying morphophoneme to any of several distinct phonemes, but not to any particular allophone, so too lexical phonological rules can have as their output an element that satisfies the constraints of the lexical phonology, even though in its actual phonetic form it may have to undergo some post-lexical rules that modify it in further ways.[8]

5.1.2   The Elsewhere Condition

Work on lexical phonology, following Kiparsky (1982a,b), has put to considerable use a general principle which he has called the *Elsewhere Condition* (cf. Kiparsky 1973).[9] The Elsewhere Condition states, in informal terms, that, when two principles of operation are in conflict at a certain point in the derivation, then the one whose domain of operation is more restricted has priority of action. For example, given the statement that all obstruents are voiceless in a given language, and the statement that all affricates are voiced, the latter will have priority over the former in the case of a particular alveopalatal affricate. Even though the affricate is indeed an obstruent, the effect or application of the first principle is overridden by the second, more specific, statement, since it concerns only affricates. Thus the more general statement must content itself with applying only 'elsewhere' – elsewhere from where more specific statements hold sway.

In some cases, the two principles that may come into conflict in this way – a conflict that the Elsewhere Condition serves to resolve – may be simply rules of the language. Typical cases of this sort are pairs (or sets) of mutual bleeding rules. For example, Lardil (see Hale 1973) has a rule deleting a vowel after another vowel (e.g. *wanka* + *uɽ* becomes *wankaɽ*), and a rule inserting *w* between *i* and *u* (e.g., *keɳṭi-uɽ* becomes *keɳṭiwuɽ*). The latter rule applies in a more specific environment, and hence takes precedence over the former, more general, rule.[10]

Kiparsky (1982a,b) suggests that lexical entries can enter into an Elsewhere relationship with phonological rules. This means that when there is a conflict between what is specified in a given lexical entry and what a rule wants to do to that lexical entry, then the more specific of the two will win out, and the more general will cede. Clearly, suggests Kiparsky, the lexical entry is the more specific of the two. That may sound, at first blush, like saying that no phonological rule ever gets to apply to anything, but that is not so. It is true that the rule of velar softening in (1) will not be able to apply to a word like *king*, by this reasoning; but that is just the effect that Kiparsky is trying to derive – the effect that lexical rules will not undo segment combinations inside of morphemes. Velar softening will not be blocked from applying to cases where the *k* and the *i* are in separate morphemes, as in *elektrik-ity*, since, according to Kiparsky, *elektrik-ity* is not, in the relevant sense, a lexical entry. *elektrik* is a lexical entry, yes; we might say that the suffix *-ity* is a lexical entry (though in Kiparsky (1982a), he chooses not to say that); it may even be the case that the combined production *elektri[s]ity* is a lexical entry; but *elektrik-ity* is not, never has been, and never will be a lexical entry. Hence even augmenting the Elsewhere Condition to the point where lexical entries can block the effects of lexical phonological rules will nonetheless leave those phonological rules free to apply across morpheme boundaries (or, for that matter, any time the form has been crucially modified with respect to what its underlying, or lexical, form was).

Lexical phonological rules, then, will not be able to win in a conflict with a specification in a lexical entry, but nothing will bar them from applying to *fill in* a feature specification that was left unspecified for one reason or another. If the lexical entry is silent with respect to the feature specification of a given segment, then the lexical rule can apply even strictly within a morpheme, for the Elsewhere Condition is not going to block it from doing so – nothing will block it. Hence lexical rules should have the property of being able to change feature specifications when they apply across morpheme boundaries, but they may fill in feature specifications of segments left unspecified even within single morphemes; for example, the voicing of a stop after a nasal in the same morpheme in Zoque can be filled in by the rule in (4a). These points are often summarized in the following way: lexical rules are feature-changing in derived environments, but have only a filling-in function in non-derived environments. The first part of that statement is also known as the *Strict Cycle Condition*. The name is a bit cryptic, but it alludes to a conception of these facts as resulting from a principle that a rule must apply to phonological material at the first chance – the first cycle – or else for ever hold its peace, and must never return to that earlier cycle to have an effect. We will return to the notion of the cycle below, in our discussion of strata.

Kiparsky proposes, then, that lexical rules and lexical entries enter into an 'Elsewhere relationship' during the lexical phonology – more specifically, within each stratum of the lexical phonology. The Elsewhere Condition would be dropped, he suggests, as a principle relating the final lexical entries with the post-lexical rules. Thus a post-lexical rule would be just as capable of *changing* a feature it found while trying to apply strictly within a word or morpheme as it would be to make a change across a word or morpheme boundary.

5.1.3 Structure preservation

The notion of *structure preservation* is an important one within lexical phonology. It is based on the idea that there are constraints on possible underlying segments in the inventory of a given language, and constraints on possible autosegmental associations, and that the same constraints that apply to underlying representations hold throughout the derivation during the lexical phonology (and that these constraints are then dropped during the post-lexical phonology).

The particular conception of structure preservation presented in Kiparsky (1985) is one whereby rules whose output would otherwise violate a constraint on permitted phonological structures in the lexicon are prevented from applying. If there were a constraint against voiced labials in a language as in (5), for example, with voicing on a separate tier, then a voicing assimilation rule as in (6) would be blocked from applying to a sequence *p-d*, for example.

(5) $*\begin{bmatrix} +\text{anterior} \\ -\text{coronal} \\ +\text{voice} \end{bmatrix}$

(6)   [−son]   [−son]
              ͭ ͭ ͭ ͭ ͭ ͭ ͭ ͭ ͭ ͭ |
                    [+voice]

We may refer to this interpretation of structure preservation as *change-inhibiting* structure preservation, in the sense that, by including this principle in our grammar, we will insure that fewer featural changes, or changes of autosegmental structure, will occur than would have been the case without it. Any rule that would create a violation will be blocked from applying. This is not the only possible interpretation of the basic notion of structure preservation in the lexical phonology, and we will briefly explore some alternatives below, whereby rules that create changes must ensure that additional changes be made so as to guarantee, as far as is possible, that representations respect the various positive and negative conditions placed on them within the lexical phonology.

It is, in fact, difficult to provide clear examples of the change-inhibiting interpretation of structure preservation, in part because it becomes more important than ever to justify the precise formulation of the phonological rule(s) involved. To illustrate this, we will look in some detail at a case study that has been offered in support of change-inhibiting structure preservation, and suggest that alternative views of the data are preferable, views that leave no work for this version of structure preservation. The point is an important one, bearing directly on the question as to precisely how rules apply.

Kiparsky (1985) presents the following analysis of Catalan in detail, based on work by Mascaró (1976).[11] He would like to show that a *lexical* rule of nasal assimilation is responsible for the homorganicity of nasal+consonant sequences, such as *bi*[nt]ε 'twenty', where both consonants are coronal. However, the [n] there is not just coronal: it is also dental, a non-distinctive feature of all Catalan *t*s, which the *n* has taken on derivatively, because nasals are thoroughly homorganic with a following consonant in Catalan. Liquids, on the other hand, are alveolar but again, not distinctively so. Thus, a phonetic contrast between alveolar coronals and dental coronals exists, but not distinctively or contrastively. Since the dentality of *t* is not distinctive, Kiparsky suggests, that feature could not have been assigned by the *lexical* assimilation rule: the feature that distinguishes dentals from alveolars is not yet permitted in the lexical phonology, since it is not distinctive. There must be two stages of nasal assimilation in our derivation. One assimilation rule is arguably lexical, on Kiparsky's view, because it applies before a word-level rule that deletes certain word-final consonants in clusters; this sequence of rules, applying in a feeding order, creates the forms shown in (7).

(7)   (a) /bint/   [bin]   *vint*   'twenty'
        (b) /bɛnk/   [bɛŋ]   *venc*   'I sell'
        (c) /kamp/   [kam]   *camp*   'field'

The fact that the [n] in (7a) is alveolar rather than dental is a crucial aspect of Kiparsky's discussion. The word-final *t* has been deleted at word-level, leaving behind a nasal that has been specified for *part* of its point of articulation, the part that is distinctive within the Catalan lexicon. The nasal in *bint* is thus coronal and non-high; it is distinct from *m* and *ñ*, not to mention from *ŋ*. But it is not yet specified as to whether it is dental or alveolar. This is not specified until the post-lexical default rules have a chance to apply. They assign coronal obstruent stops to a dental point of articulation, an assignment shared with a preceding nasal; but a coronal nasal (other than /ñ/) that is not part of a complex segment is always alveolar.

So far, while this is an interesting treatment, it is an argument for underspecification, not for (change-inhibiting) structure preservation. No rule has failed to apply because its output violated a lexical constraint. This is the next, and for our current purposes, crucial, part of the argument.

Kiparsky proposes that the rule of nasal assimilation in Catalan is as in (8).[12] In these structures, as on several occasions before, we have put the point-of-articulation features on a separate tier, and as before, we note that we will return to this matter in chapter 6. Rule (8), a lexical rule, is

(8)   nasal   [nasal]
                           |
        skeleton   C_ _ _ _ _ _ C
                         ‾ ‾ ‾ ‾ ‾ ‾ ‾ ‾ ‾|
        P of A   [α P of A]

intended to account for the obligatory homorganicity of nasal-consonant sequences. Kiparsky explains that he understands his formalism *not* to apply in case the skeletal position on the left is already associated to any features or autosegments that are incompatible with the change (by disagreeing, for example), a matter that becomes crucial in the post-lexical functioning of this rule, as we shall see.

One significant problem to focus on, however, is that (8) does not function to rule out lexical sequences of non-homorganic nasal+consonant sequences, since they would be unaffected by the rule.[13] To the contrary, Catalan nasals simply cannot bear a distinctive point of articulation underlyingly when preceding a consonant word-internally. What we *really* need is two things: a restriction against assigning an underlying point of articulation to a nasal that precedes a consonant,[14] and a rule spreading point of articulation to just such nasals. We will return to this reanalysis in a moment.

Kiparsky suggests that there is a lexical restriction on the point of articulation that can associate with a nasal, disallowing any velar nasal ŋ that is not in a nasal-consonant cluster, i.e. that is not immediately followed by *k* or *g*. He proposes the formula given in (9). This is the place

(9)　　* [−back]
　　　　　┿
　　　　[+high]
　　　　　|
　　　　[+nasal]
　　　　　|
　　　　　C　　in an unlinked matrix

where (change-inhibiting) structure preservation as such comes into the picture. The rule of nasal assimilation (8) will be tested to see whether its application may be blocked – to see if its output violates the condition in (9). In some cases, rule (8) applies at the phrase level (see (10) below); in other cases, involving *ñ* and *m*, it does not. The question arises as to whether preservation of the structure in (9) is the reason for its non-application in this latter class of cases.

But is (9), indeed, a proper statement of a structural property that must be maintained in the lexical phonology? Is it the proper way to indicate that ŋ can appear only when followed by a velar consonant? I will suggest a more appropriate alternative below, but it is fair to note that there has been little serious effort, in either the generative tradition or any other, to develop a theory of natural phonological constraints on representations. If Stanley (1967), for example, offers certain formal ways of representing dependencies, it can hardly be said that an effort was made in the formulation to provide a means to represent commonly found constraints in an especially simple and direct fashion. In this book, we have attempted to take some steps toward providing such a formulation, with the {minimum,maximum} specifications of autosegmental association discussed in chapter 1, and, more importantly, the concept of autosegmental licensing.

We shall suggest that the important structural properties maintained in the Catalan representations derive from licensing properties of the Catalan syllable. If this is correct, and if we are correct in taking these licensing conditions to be phonotactics of the word-level representation, then we do not have here a case of a condition that must hold pervasively throughout a derivation, serving as the basis for the inhibition of a rule's application. These syllable phonotactics will, instead, hold at the word level, and will only indirectly influence what is likely to arise as an underlying form.

We may briefly review the structure given in (9) that Kiparsky suggests is preserved through the derivation. He indicates that the filter should block structures in which there is no [−back] autosegment associated with a [+high] nasal consonant. It is the second principle of underspecification, the one eliminating the unmarked value of a distinctive feature from underlying representations, that necessitates this backwards statement, i.e. prevents a positive statement that such [+high] nasal consonants must be [+back], i.e. velar. Put another way, the second principle of underspecification prevents us from saying directly that velar nasals must be in a doubly linked matrix, which is what Kiparksy suggests is the crucial factor. We return to a licensing approach to the matter below.[15]

In any event, Kiparsky proposes two lexical rules: (8), an assimilation rule, and (9), a filter.

There is now the phrase-level nasal assimilation process to explore. The facts, briefly, are these, following Kiparksy (1985: 95): an *m* hardly assimilates – it assimilates only to a following *f* (10a); an *n* assimilates to any following point of articulation (10b); *ñ* does not assimilate at all, nor does ŋ.

(10)   (a)   assimilation of *m*
               so[m] amics   'we are friends'
               so[ɱ] feliços   'we are happy'
               so[m] dos   'we are two'
    (b)   assimilation of /n/
               so[n] amics   'they are friends'
               so[m] pocs   'they are few'
               so[ɱ] feliços   'they are happy'
               so[ŋ] grans   'they are big'

Now, not all conceivable combinations of points of articulation of a nasal and a consonant can arise across a word boundary. The data available suggest that the generalization is that only the *n* – the nasal literally unmarked for point of articulation, thoughout the lexical phonology[16] – assimilates with respect to the contrastive points of articulation, as Kiparsky argues. The only other post-lexical assimilation is 'subphonemic', i.e. not involving the lexically contrastive features of the language (the difference between a labial and a labio-dental, in this case).

However, the analysis employing change-inhibiting structure preservation achieves this end only indirectly. Kiparsky assumes (and I agree with

him here as well) that rule (8) applies in both the lexical and the post-
lexical phonology; but if we adopt such an approach, we may need to
account for various *non*-occurrences of nasal assimilation at phrase level.
Kiparsky suggests, for example, that the reason the labial *m* does not
assimilate to a coronal at phrase level in Catalan (we find [som dos] 'we
are two', for example, with no assimilation of the *m*) is that nasal
assimilation is ordered before the rule that fills in the point of articulation
of *d*; hence there is no point of articulation that *can* spread to the *m*. *m*
does not associate to a following velar across word boundary, either, but
under the analysis in question this would be for a different reason, not
because of the extrinsic counterfeeding order just mentioned. In this case,
the structure *m#k* would be as in (11), to which nasal assimilation (8)
will not apply, Kiparsky suggests, 'because the configuration [+high,
+labial] is banned by a marking condition both lexically and postlexical-
ly'. Though we have seen a suggestion here that a rule is blocked because
its output violates a condition, this is not yet structure preservation, since
the condition is not one that can be (or at least, has been) motivated as
part of the lexical phonology of Catalan.

(11)

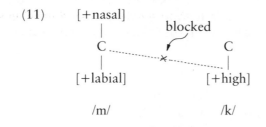

Kiparsky suggests that filter (9) can be appealed to account for the last
remaining example of non-application of nasal assimilation at the phrase
level, that which does not occur when ŋ is followed by a palatal, such as
λ. Here Kiparsky suggests that the reason such assimilation fails to take
place is quite different. On this analysis, if lexical filter (9) did not exist,
then at the point in the phrase-level phonology when nasal assimilation
was about to apply, we would find the structure illustrated in (12).
Although nothing within this account would block rule (9) from applying, the suggestion is made that the post-lexical, phrase-level rules are

(12)

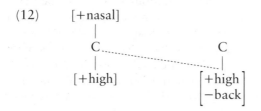

extrinsically ordered in such a way that nasal assimilation precedes (and is counterfed by) the rule that deletes a word-final velar. That is, any word that appears to end in a velar nasal when pronounced in isolation (such as [tiŋ] 'I have', or [baŋ] 'bank') must actually end in a stop (/k/ or /g/) through to the final level of the lexical phonology by structure preservation, and hence at least part way into the post-lexical phonology. If we assume that the rule that finally gets rid of it follows nasal assimilation, then the velar stop can be viewed as a phantom segment intervening between the nasal that is almost, but not quite, at the end of one word, and the consonant at the beginning of the next.

When all is said and done, then, it is reasonably clear that this particular version of structure preservation does not do a great deal of work that could not be done better another way. In chapter 3, we investigated how restrictions on point of articulation should be treated, and concluded that striking and basic patterns could be understood in terms of the ways in which languages can license a point of articulation autosegment. In a quite a few languages, the coda can never license a point-of-articulation; in Catalan, the coda can license a point of articulation, but the restriction appears to be that a sonorant position (either onset or coda) can never license a velar point of articulation.[17] The rhyme, like the onset, can license only one point-of-articulation autosegment, and thus a sequence of a nasal and a consonant with distinct points of articulation will not be permitted.

This restriction, since it derives from licensing, holds at the word level. Thus (13a) is ill-formed there, since one of the point-of-articulation autosegments would not be licensed; (13b) is well-formed.

We suggest that the crucially operative principles at work in Catalan are the following: (i) a rule of nasal assimilation that provides a point of articulation only to nasals that are unspecified for a point of articulation, formulated much as in rule (8) above, though applying in a fashion discussed below; (ii) a rule that specifies that adjacent consonants with identical points of articulation *share* a point-of-articulation autosegment;[18] (iii) post-lexical specification of non-contrastive features. All three of these points are already present, though in slightly different form, in the account Kiparsky offers.

The filter in (9), however, must be replaced by conditions on licensing in a coda. Quite generally, licensing considerations at word level will block any nasal that is specified for a point of articulation if there is another consonant specified for point of articulation in the same coda, since only one point-of-articulation specification may appear licensed by any given licenser. All other things being equal, a nasal that is alone in its coda will take on any point of articulation that the coda licenses, in Catalan just as in English, via rule (8).

(13)   (a)

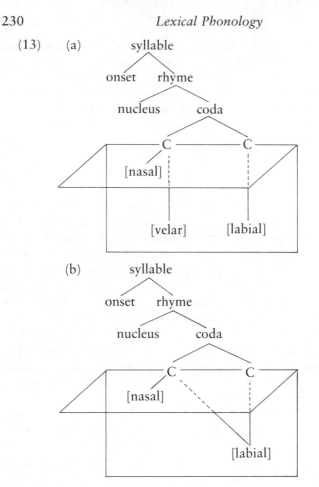

In Catalan, as in English, there is no underlying segment ŋ. That is to say, the structure in (14a) is possible (where the broken line associating [velar] with the nasal position is not present underlyingly, and is filled in only later), though that in (14b) is not. As we have seen, and as (14) illustrates again, the notion of licensing explicates how segments that are not allowed as underlying segments may arise by assimilation – even within the lexical phonology.

The use of (9) to block nasal assimilation via a change-inhibiting view of structure preservation involved explanations of why (8) did not apply to the *m*, the *ñ*, and the *ŋ* that were produced through the lexical application of nasal assimilation. Kiparsky suggests that the proper conception of rule application is one in which an assimilation rule, of the sort we have seen in (8), will apply equally to underspecified segments and fully specified segments, being blocked only by the sorts of conditions as in (9).

(14)   (a)

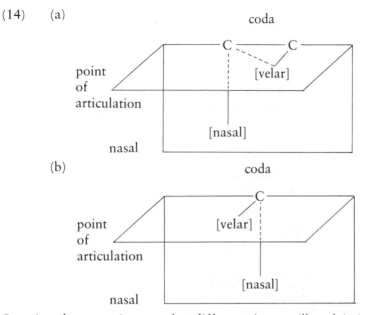

(b)

Our view, however, is somewhat different. As we will explain in more detail below, we suggest that a large range of phonological rules are best understood when formulated so as to apply just in case their application serves to create a well-formed representation out of one that was ill-formed.[19] If we distinguish here simply between an underlying representation, a level representing essentially the output of the lexical phonology (the word level), and the phrase level, we have a picture as in (15), with phonotactics of the sort in (16) defined at the latter two levels of representation, the word level and the phrase level. The establishment of phonotactics as in (16) makes it possible for the phonotactics to then trigger the application of such a rule as in (8). (16) makes explicit certain properties of the skeleton/point-of-articulation tier chart, the chart on the horizontal plane in (14). This phonotactic indicates that all [+consonantal] segments on the skeleton are freely associating segments in the point-of-articulation chart, and that at the phonetic level they must associate with a point-of-articulation autosegment. Put simply, (16) says that all consonants must be specified for point of articulation; rule (8) helps nasals that are in violation of that phonotactic to come into line with it.

(15)   Underlying representation
        ‖ ← rule (8) may apply
        Word level: phonotactic in (16) is applicable
        ‖ ← rule (8) may apply
        Phrase level: phonotactic in (16) is applicable

(16)   Word-level and phrase-level phonotactic
         Skeleton/nasal chart
             Freely-associating segments: {+consonantal, ∅}
             Minimum/maximum association: skeletal tier: (1,1)

Finally, we assume that, when a word-final *m* (a labial nasal) is
followed by a word-initial labial consonant, as in the second example of
(10a), the two consecutive, identical point-of-articulation autosegments
merge to form a single autosegment, as illustrated in (17b). When the
non-contrastive feature specifications are filled in, marking the continuant as a labio-dental, this information regarding specific point of
articulation is shared by both consonants, the nasal and the continuant.[20]

(17)   (a) Sequence of *m–f* across word boundary

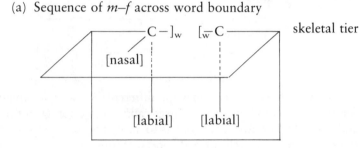

(b) Merger of two adjacent, identical consonants

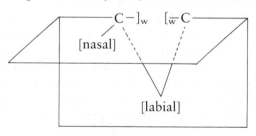

(c) Post-lexical specification of labio-dental

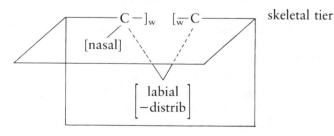

It is worth pointing out that there is a close relationship between underspecification and the conception of structure preservation. In a framework in which segments are fully specified, if any single feature is changed, then the chances are good that the result will not be a permissible underlying segment; phonological systems are rarely so symmetric. For example, if, when voiced, an *s* becomes not *z* but *r*, then all the other features other than just voicing that distinguish an *r* from a *z* (e.g. [sonorant]) will have to be changed as well, if structure preservation is to be maintained. On the other hand, if only a small number of distinctive features are specified, then rules that take away feature specifications will always (or almost always) be structure-preserving (since even the totally unspecified segment is going to become something, either a *t* or a glottal stop, or whatever, as the language chooses). Rules that add features will also tend more frequently to be structure-preserving, especially if they are applying to a highly underspecified segment already.

Consider the case of Klingenheben's Law in Hausa, for example, according to which a *p* or *k* in coda position becomes a round glide *w*.[21] If *p* and *k* are underlyingly specified as [-continuant] and [-voice], then these features will have to be modified in the process; if the features are underlyingly unspecified, and filled in only post-lexically, then the deletion of the point-of-articulation features, and their replacement by the feature [+round] (assuming that that is the correct statement of the change) is all that needs to be said, as in (18). Note that the change here involves actual replacement of the features on the left.[22]

(18)   [−coronal] → [+round]

Consider the more complex case of Kuman, spoken in Papua New Guinea (Lynch 1983). If we look closer at this system, we find reason to conclude that, in the contrast between a plain *l* and a pre-velarized *gl*, the latter is, surprisingly, the unmarked lateral in the language, and with a circumspect use of underspecification, the alternation between *gl* and *t* can be analyzed as a change of a single feature, [voice].

(19)   p t k
         b d g
               s
         m n
               l gl
         w y

The segment transcribed as *gl* deserves special attention. It is a velarized liquid, arguably a single segment, since it may occur in in syllable rhyme where no clusters otherwise appear. An underlying t, when in syllable onset position, is realized on the surface as [r] except word-initially, where it is realized as [t]; a *t* in coda position is realized as a [t] when an *n* immediately follows, and as an [r] otherwise.

There is a phonological contrast between *l* and *gl*, but there are relatively few *l*s at all in the language. Some are created by rule, from a merger of *gl* and *i*; others occur in borrowings. Lynch suggests that at an earlier stage of the language there was only one liquid, which presumably changed (perhaps in all positions except before *i*) to *gl*. Subsequently, in a relatively small number of words, a contrast has arisen between *gl* and *l*; the dominant majority of liquids are of the velarized form. As we noted, Lynch suggests that, synchronically, some *l*s are created by a fusion of *gl* and *i*. Observe the imperative paradigms in (20) for the stems *yu* 'bring', *pr* 'hear', and *yagl* 'plant'. The singular, dual, and plural suffixes are *o*, *iro*, and *io*, and Lynch suggests that *gl*+*i* generally becomes surface [l].

(20)

	bring	hear	plant
singular	yuo	pro	yaglo
dual	yuiro	priro	yaltro/yagltro
plural	yuio	prio	yalo

Let us assume that there is presently in Kuman a lexical contrast between the velarized *gl* and the plain *l*, and that an unmarked liquid will be specified as [+prevelarized] post-lexically. An *l* that does not surface as [gl] is lexically specified as [-prevelarized]; that is, that feature *is* lexically contrastive, but the unmarked value is positive, and is relevant only to the liquids.

There are two rules in Kuman that devoice the *gl*, making it a derived *t*. In the case of the output of rule (21a), a quite transparent rule, this surfaces as a [t] (see (22)); in the case of (21b), a much more opaque but still plausible rule, its surfaces as an [r], as *t* will do, as mentioned above (see (22)).

(21)   (a) gl → t / — n
        (b) gl → t / — V gl

The following data illustrate both rule (21b) and a rule deleting *gl* before *b*, as well as several other processes that we will not focus upon: several epenthesis processes, including that of *u* between a *b* and a stop; and voicing of the *k* in the indicative suffix *ka* in an environment that is not entirely clear – after voiced consonants, and apparently after vowels,

(22)   (a) stems with final *gl* with possessive suffixes ('my leg', etc.)

	kagl 'leg'	*yobugl* 'bone'	*mabugl* 'forehead'	*siragl* 'thing'
1 sg.	kat-na	yobut-na	mabut-na	sirat-na
2 sg.	kat-n	yobut-n	mabut-n	sirat-n
3 sg.	kagl-e	yobugl-o	mabugl-o	siragl-mo
non-sg.	kat-no	yobut-no	mabut-no	sirat-no

(b) stems with final *t*

	bit 'head'	*piut* 'chest'	*kobt* 'navel'
1 sg.	bit-na	piut-na	kobut-na
2 sg.	bit-n	piut-n	kobut-n
3 sg.	br-e	piur-ie	kobr-ie
non-sg.	bit-no	piut-no	kobut-no

but before epenthesis. The first-person singular subject marker is *i* with vowel-final stems, such as *yu* 'bring'. There is a thematic *n* in the future conjugations of vowel-final stems. The third-person singular *w* also metathesizes to the right, as we see in (23). In these data, we see several examples of *gl* becoming *t* before *n*, by rule (21a); we also see the stem final *gl* of *yagl* becoming *t* (which surfaces as [r] in onset position) before the future morpheme *-agl*, as when *yagl-agl-ka* surfaces as [yaratnga].

(23)   (a) Singular subject markers

	1st	2nd	3rd
aorist	ø/i	n	w
future	ø	n	b

(b)

		yu 'bring'	*pr* 'hear'	*yagl* 'plant'
Aorist	1st	yuiga	prika	yaglka
	2nd	yunga	pitnga	yatnga
	3rd	yugwa	prukwa	yaglkwa
Future	1st	yunaglka	praglka	yaraglka
	2nd	yunatnga	pratnga	yaratnga
	3rd	yunabuka	prabuka	yarabuka

The question we may now return to is just what rule (21a) really looks like. The change from the phonetic segment *gl* to *t* seems like it comprises a goodly number of featural changes: *gl* is velarized, while *t* is not; *gl* is voiced, while *t* is not; *gl* is a sonorant, while *t* is not. However, if we specify only the marked values of the distinctive features that specify *gl*, we can simply describe it as [+consonantal, +sonorant]. It is, in the context of the consonant system in (19), the unmarked sonorant, just as *t* is, in that context, the unmarked obstruent: unmarked both for point of articulation and for all other secondary markings, such as nasality and voicing. (Recall that *gl* is taken to be unmarked for velarization, while *l* is specifically marked as [−prevelarized].) Thus the change from *gl* to *t* is minimal: it is the change from sonorant to obstruent. The 'structure-preserving' character of the change followed, more or less automatically, from the underspecification approach, since, at the point in the derivation where the change takes place, the phonological properties of the *gl* which would have to have been eliminated in order to make a *t* out of a *gl* are simply not specified.

Regardless of whether or not rules may be blocked in their application by the principles of structure preservation, other examples do support the conclusion that the output of lexical phonological rules will normally negotiate in order to produce an output that is consistent with the word-level phonotactics of the language. Let us consider two kinds of examples that illustrate a this point.

The first is illustrated by the discussion surrounding example (25) in chapter 1, where it was pointed out that a language (Sukuma, in the discussion there) may have a restriction on the number of association lines associated with a given vowel position, for example. In a language where the maximum is one, if a rule should reassign a tone to the vowel in question, the rule is not blocked from applying by structure preservation or anything of the sort (as Kiparsky's view would predict); as we saw in several tonal examples in chapter 1, the association line added by rule is preserved, and the association line that had previously been present is eliminated in order to maintain the constraint on permissible structures.[23]

Consider another example of a similar sort, this time one involving elements that are less prosodic in character. Shaw (1980) reports a rule of vowel coalescence in Dakota, where the underlying inventory of vowels consists of the canonical five oral vowel system {i, e, u, o, a} and the canonical three nasal vowel system {į, ų, ą}. When a nasalized /ą/ is followed by a front vowel, the result is a high front nasal vowel, and when it is followed by an /o/ (no examples of /u/ are given), a high back nasal vowel is formed. (I simplify the matter of boundaries, which is irrelevant to the point at hand.)

As Shaw points out, this process is remarkably similar to another rule that she motivates, simply deleting an oral /a/ in the same context. In that case, the mid vowels that remain behind, so to speak, do not need to be raised (e.g. /ka + epča/ > [kepča]). But there are no nasal mid vowels in the inventory of the language; so when the /a/ is lost, and its nasality is

(24) (a) ą + i > į

  cʰą + i + čoγa > [čʰįčoγa]

  (b) ą + e > į

  ptą + ehą > [ptįhą]

  (c) ą + o > ų

  xʔą + o + tʔa > [xʔųtʔa]

preserved (an instance of what we called 'stability' in chapter 1), the result is a nasal mid vowel. But there are no nasal mid vowels in the inventory of underlying or word-level vowels in the language, and so it is not surprising that the result that would independently be expected – a nasal mid vowel – is modified immediately to form a nasal high vowel, which is a possible word-level vowel of the language. If, in line with the discussion of vowel features presented in chapter 6, we take mid vowels to be specified for the feature [low] and high vowels not to be, then the result described here can be viewed as quite similar to the tonal case sketched above. Dakota has vowels that are specified [+round] and [+ low], i.e. /o/, and also those that are [−round] and [+low], i.e. /e/. It also has vowels that are specified as [−round] and [+nasal] /į/; but it has no vowel that is [−round] and [+low] and [+nasal], i.e. a front, mid, nasal vowel. When [+nasal] is associated to a vowel that is [−round] and [+ low], the combination is not allowed, and one of the previously associated elements (in this case, the feature [+low]) is removed, allowing the resulting combination ([−round] and [+nasal]) to remain.[24]

5.1.4 *Strata*

In addition to dividing the rules of phonology into the two major classes of lexical and post-lexical rules, lexical phonology allows for the lexicon to be divided into what are called *strata* (or, interchangeably, *levels* or *layers*), as we had already seen in the basic architecture given in (3) above. This division affects three major and distinct points. Through the formal use of strata, lexical phonology makes claims about (i) the reanalysis of what once were called phonological boundaries; (ii) the ordering of morphological elements, i.e. affixes; and (iii) the cycle in phonology. We will return to the notion of the cycle in section 5.2 below, and so will not discuss it here, except in passing and to define the basic organization of strata.

  Strata are small compartments in which affixation processes and phonological rules come packaged together. They are linearly arranged, so that the first stratum has as its potential input (or domain on which to operate) the monomorphemic roots of the language. Each such root may undergo affixation of one of the stratum 1 affixes, at which point it will have the opportunity to pass through all the stratum 1 phonological rules, some of which it may chance to trigger.

Now, clearly, the idea that morphological affixation simply 'happens' to a form as it passes through the stratum, as if by chance, is not a very appealing metaphor; but since this is more a theory of the interaction of morphology and phonology than of morphology *per se*, we shall have to bear with it. There certainly is no very sensible way to think of the affixation of various derivational suffixes as being triggered, as it were, by some cloud of meaning that is hanging over the stem waiting to be 'realized' by some affixation process. We cannot attach a meaning to a morphological root, and pass it through a morphological flow chart, expecting it to pick up just those suffixes that allow the expression of that meaning – certainly not in the case of lexical meaning expressed by derivational morphology. In any event, the point is simply to acknowledge that this is not a good way of thinking about derivational suffixation as far as its connection to meaning is concerned, but it will have to do for our expository purposes.

Strata themselves may be either cyclic or non-cyclic, though the former has often been assumed to be the normal case. In a cyclic stratum, as in (25), as each affix is in turn added to the base by morphological processes, the entire set of rules of that layer will have an opportunity to apply. In a non-cyclic layer, the phonological rules of the layer will not apply until all the affixes of the layer have been attached.

As a form passes through a stratum, it is bracketed in a way that shows its history within that stratum (see (26)). These brackets are not labeled,

(25)   Internal structure of a stratum

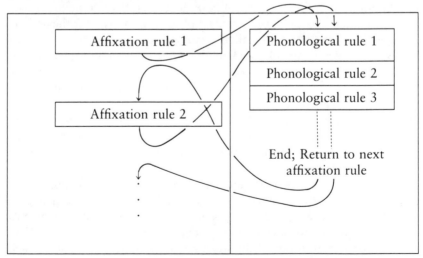

(26)   [[[instrument] al] ity]

except perhaps insofar as a left bracket differs from a right bracket. Phonological rules within a stratum can make reference to brackets and bracketing. (But frequently they will not need to when it might have been thought necessary, because the Strict Cycle Condition will guarantee that most lexical rules apply only across morpheme boundaries.)

At the end of each stratum, all the internal bracketings are dropped, so that rules of a given layer can never make reference to any internal structure that was created on an earlier stratum. To use traditional terminology, if in a given language the stem is created by the first stratum, and the word is created by the second stratum, then the morphology and phonology of the second stratum can make no reference to any morphological boundaries strictly inside the stem. Likewise, the post-lexical phonology can make no reference to any word-internal boundaries. This restriction is called the *Bracketing Erasure Principle* in the literature.

This leads to an important position within lexical phonology: phonological representations do not contain labeled boundaries, such as the + and # of Harris (1951) or Chomsky and Halle (1968). Instead, there is a nesting of domains defined entirely by the morphology, from the root outwards, as in (27), for example, and the rules of the phonology will be

(27)   [prefix [[root] suffix]]

able to look at larger and larger domains, starting with the smallest. The functions served by boundaries in earlier theories are translated into other functions, in other ways. (And of course, the translation is not utterly perfect, in the sense that it is not the case that anything that can be done the one way can be done the other: if this were so, why should it matter which way we did it?)

Let us first classify the principal functions of boundaries in phonological rules. Using the boundary symbols of classical generative phonology, we may list four. (i) Certain rules apply only across morpheme boundaries, and we can express that by writing $X \rightarrow Y / - +Z$. (ii) Certain rules apply only across word boundaries, and we can express this by writing $X \rightarrow Y / - \#\# Z$. (iii) Certain rules apply only at word boundary (typically, word-finally). (iv) Certain rules cannot apply across a word boundary. This last function can include two kinds of cases: one where the rule applies strictly inside words, but not into material that would be introduced with the # boundary, and the other where the rule strictly refuses to apply outside of the phonological word.

These various boundary-oriented phonological effects are treated in different ways in lexical phonology. If we take the morphemes introduced with a + boundary to be introduced on the first stratum, and those introduced with a # on the second, then rules that must apply across a + boundary become lexical rules of the first stratum, and the rule's failure to apply to stratum 1 segments that are not separated by a + boundary becomes the responsibility of the Strict Cycle Condition, discussed above. Rules that apply only across true word boundaries have to have those boundaries explicitly stated; but they will be, necessarily, post-lexical rules, and there is a bracketing in the phonological string that indicates true word bracketing. Thus we could write a rule whose structural description is as in (28), as we have already seen in KiHunde; if applying post-lexically, this means that the forms are separated by word-level bracketings.

(28)   V]$_w$ CV
           | |
           H   H

On the third point, rules that apply only at word boundaries can be treated in more than one way. They can be post-lexical, with a word-level bracket indicated, just as in (28). However, they can also be rules of the last stratum of the lexical phonology. If the rule in some way involves a feature that is not lexically distinctive, then it must necessarily be post-lexical; however, if it does not, then it may be either post-lexical or lexical.

Finally, a rule that cannot apply across a # boundary (in the older terminology) may be reinterpreted in one of two ways. If it is a rule that applies to stem material, though not across a #, then it may be a stratum 1 phonological rule, as with the rule deleting a schwa before vowel in English. This rule deletes the schwa in *buddha+ism*, but not across a #, as in *Indiana#ism*. On the other hand, the rule may be a stratum 2 rule, if it applies more broadly inside a word, but not outside the phonological word more generally.

One point that on occasion is not clearly made in the literature is that the development of strata has been to some extent a way of formalizing an increasing dependence of phonological rules on particular morphemes without making the point explicitly, and this can be suspiciously, even dangerously, misleading. An extreme case may make that clear. If there were a grammar with as many strata as there were morphemes, then (all other things being equal) whatever phonological rules the affixation of a particular morpheme required could be assigned to the stratum in question. So if, for example, there is a strong past-tense suffix -*t* in English which triggers shortening of vowels (*keep/kept*, perhaps *say/said*, and so on), and we call 'stratum 17' the stratum that contains just that affixation process, then the shortening rule would be made a phonological rule of stratum 17, and would apply only to forms derived in that stratum. In this extreme case, phonological rules would be directly linked to particular morphological processes with no explicit and formal indication of the fact.[25]

Lexical phonology embodies the hypothesis that the morphemes that trigger particular phonological processes form a discrete and identifiable set, and that the affixation processes corresponding to them can be ordered together as an uninterrupted series of rules.

The bulk of classical generative phonology is concerned with how morphemes are modified when juxtaposed, and we have already seen, during our discussion of the Elsewhere Condition above, that lexical phonology is designed in order to integrate the proposal that a lexical rule may restrict itself to applying only in a derived environment, which is to say that a rule will refrain from applying in a context where all the conditions for the rule's application are found strictly within a single morpheme (or, more accurately, where all the conditions for the rule's application were already found within that single morpheme in its underlying form).

Interesting and intricate arguments have been made for and against this Strict Cycle Condition. In any event, one of the central principles of lexical phonology has been this limitation on lexical rules to a kind of application that can change a feature specification only when it is explicitly the addition of morphological material that has satisfied the rule's structural description. But this general principle also follows, it should be clear, from a rather different interpretation of the significance of many lexical rules, in particular, the interpretation according to which these rules are explicitly linked to morphological processes.[26]

Let us take a brief look at the structure of the Bantu verb from the point of view of a theory of lexical phonology. The first set of questions involves dividing the phonology into the lexical and the post-lexical phonology. Post-lexical rules in a Bantu language such as KiRundi include the rule that affects adjacent vowels across word boundaries, reducing them to a single, short vowel with the quality of the vowel on the right, a rule whose effects were noted in chapter 1, in connection with example (46) there. Within the lexical phonology, it is necessary to consider whether the phonology or the morphology motivates the division of the lexicon into two or more strata. Bantu languages support a distinction between the processes that build a stem out of a root (or 'radical'), on the one hand, and the processes that build an inflected word out of a stem. These two aspects are described within a lexical phonology with two distinct strata, one for each series of steps.

The first stratum consists of the suffixation of derivational suffixes of the form V(C) (called 'extensions', in the Bantu literature) to a radical that is typically of the form CV(V)C. This series of affixations, with each step the formal expression of the morphosyntactic features associated with the suffix in question, leads to a verbal stem with the structure shown in (29). The domain thus defined is also the crucial domain for the assignment of tense-specific tonal patterns in most Bantu languages; in KiRundi, this includes a L–H (Low–High) melody used in subordinate

(29)

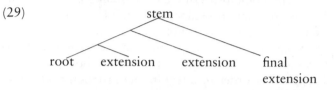

and negative clauses. In addition, when two vowels are juxtaposed within this domain, rather than being affected as they would be in the post-lexical component, they obey a different principle. The result of juxtaposing two vowels is a long vowel here, and if the first is the low vowel *a* and the second is a high vowel (i.e. *u* or *i*), then the quality of the composite vowel is a mid vowel otherwise like the second vowel; thus *a+i* becomes *e*, and *a+u* becomes *o*. For example, the root *ha*, meaning 'to give', plus the applicative suffix *ir*, forms *heer*.[27]

The verb, in turn, is formed by prefixing inflectional elements on a second stratum. When vowels are juxtaposed on this second stratum, a distinct rule is invoked which again creates a long vowel, but one whose quality is fully determined by the vowel on the right of the input string. Thus a sequence *a+i* creates *i:* as its output, as in the sequence *n+a+i:+som+er+a* [niisomera] 'I read for myself', precisely as in Luganda, a closely related language that we looked at in some detail in chapter 2. The morphological structure of the output of this second stratum will look like (30). By indicating no structure below the node marked 'stem' – i.e. the output of the first stratum – I intend to emphasize the fact that bracketing erasure has made the internal structure of that sequence no longer linguistically visible. Thus a layered picture of the KiRundi verb might look like (31).

(30)

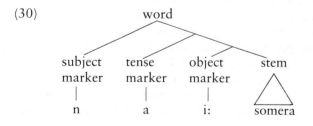

(31)   radical

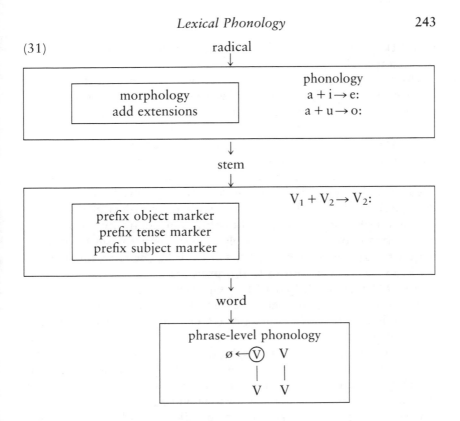

5.1.5 *Underspecification theory*

Underspecification theory involves several notions which have appeared
in generative and non-generative theory, and which can in principle
be accepted or rejected independently of the other ideas of lexical
phonology, but which fit comfortably with the central ideas of the
theory.[28,29] I have already summarized the two core ideas of underspecification theory with the following principles. (i) First, *eliminate redundant features from the lexical phonology*: features that are not distinctive
in a subpart of the the inventory of underlying segments must not be
expressed with segments in that subpart – they are ruled out by what we
have called feature filters. (ii) Second, *eliminate 'unmarked' feature
specification from underlying forms*: in any given phonological context,
each remaining (i.e. non-redundant) feature has an expected, or unmarked, value and a less expected, or marked, value; only the latter may
be explicitly present in underlying forms. These two principles differ
considerably, and represent two different types of underspecification
theory. The line between them is on occasion a hard one to find, but if we

step back slightly, we should be able to get a clear grasp of the difference between them.[30]

The first principle is in effect a set of restrictions on feature co-occurrence. We saw in the case of Digo, the Bantu language discussed in section 1.6, that there was a Low tone on all voiced obstruents on the surface. This generalization is so strong and straightforward that we can draw the conclusion that this Low tone is not in any way constrastive: it is totally predictable. The 'eliminate redundant features' principle would then force the conclusion (which we adopted anyway in the analysis of Digo) that the Low tone is not present underlyingly. In a model that distinguishes between a lexical phonology and a post-lexical phonology, it would furthermore be predicted that this non-contrastive Low tone is not inserted until the post-lexical phonology. Similarly, since voicing is not contrastive among the sonorants in English, sonorants could not be marked for voicing according to this principle.

It must be acknowledged that this principle (which seems in many ways just like phonological good sense turned into an explicit principle) is often difficult to apply in practice because one not infrequently finds oneself in a situation where two distinctions (or features) are redundant in a given description, but it is hard to see which one is logically dependent (and thus predictable, and thus to be eliminated from the description in the lexical phonology), and which is logically prior (and thus to be maintained in the lexical phonology). For example, if a language had a vowel system with just {i, e, u, o}, the front/back contrast and the round/unround contrast would be difficult to untangle: which one is contrastive, and which predictable? Is a vowel in such a language round *because* it is back, or is it back because it is round? Typically, one must look deeper into the system to determine the right way to analyze it.

Many cases present no difficulty at all. Voicing, for example, is rarely distinctive among the sonorant segments of a language (the vowels, glides, nasals, and liquids), and it is generally distinctive among the obstruents, or a significant subset of the obstruents – as in English, for example. Among the sonorants in English, then, voicing is non-contrastive, and by the 'eliminate redundant features' principle it would not be specified in the lexical phonology. It follows, then, that no rule of lexical phonology in English can refer to the voicing of a sonorant in English, either in the structural change or in the structural description of a rule; an obstruent could not assimilate in voicing to a sonorant within the lexical phonology precisely because the sonorants are not voiced within the lexical phonology: they are redundantly voiced later, within the post-lexical phonology. Generalizations of this sort may be stated in terms of the filter given in (2) above, eliminating as ill-formed any structure within the lexical phonology which is both [+sonorant] and [+voiced] – or [−voiced], for that matter. The rule that fills in the feature [+voiced] for the sonorants in English must be a post-lexical rule, since no structure within the lexical phonology would allow such a rule to do its job, given the filter in (2). This situation will contrast with what we find for the second kind of underspecification, to which we turn now.

The second core idea of underspecification theory goes one large step further in reducing the amount of information stated in the deepest representation. It proceeds along the following line of reasoning. Consider a feature such as voicing which has been restricted by our first principle from co-occurring with any [+sonorant] segment in a language such as English. This leaves only the [−sonorant] segments, the obstruents, for the feature voicing to co-occur with. A [-sonorant] segment can be thus be either [+voice] or [−voice]. But therein too lies a redundancy; for the obstruent in English *must* be the one or the other – it *must* be either [+voice] or [−voice]. The second principle of underspecification theory says that we must eliminate this redundancy from the underlying form as well, and one of the two feature values ([+voice] or [−voice]) must be eliminated from the underlying forms, and instead be assigned by rule. This rule will be – and must be – a lexical rule, however; we will call it a *lexical default rule*. The main reason it must be a lexical rule is that, most simply stated, it will be written just to assign the default value of the feature (say, [−voice], in this case). This assignment must not apply, of course, to segments that are already (e.g. underlyingly) marked as [+voiced] – that was the whole point of this default rule, which allowed us to conceive of the +/−voice contrast as being underlyingly privative. As we have seen, the Elsewhere Condition will give us this result, if we take this rule to be a lexical rule, for the Strict Cycle Condition says that a lexical rule will not *change* a feature value in a non-derived context. Thus we see, even within the theory itself, there is a deep and fundamental distinction between the two kinds of underspecification.

There is another, more traditional, vocabulary that can be conveniently used to express this second principle. It can be viewed as an attempt to view all feature oppositions as being underlyingly *privative*, in Trubetzkoy's (1967) terms, which is to say, involving an opposition between a positive something, on the one hand, and nothing, on the other. Trubetzkoy distinguished between such an opposition and what he called an *equipollent* opposition, in which both feature values play an equal role in the phonology. The second principle of underspecification theory, the 'eliminate unmarked feature specifications' principle, can be restated thusly: all features are underlyingly privative.

It remains an open question precisely to what extent this second position is correct, whether in its strongest version or in some weaker version, such as that there is a strong tendency to use features privatively in the lexical phonology. The issue is a complex one, interacting with virtually every other theoretical issue current today, and, as I have indicated, the matter remains unsettled. The position adopted in this book is that, except for major class features, there is a strong tendency for features to be privative underlyingly; but under certain circumstances, when a language can reduce two privative features to one equipollent feature, the language will opt for the use of a single equipollent feature. On this point, see further discussion in section 6.3.1.

There is a second way in which the lexical default rules may be evaluated from the perspective of lexical phonology. We mentioned earlier that within lexical phonology, there is no special set of phonological redundancy rules apart from other rules; rather, all lexical phonological rules will function sometimes as lexical default rules, spelling out explicitly what is an unmarked 'expected' phonological sequence or structure in a language, and at other times as 'true' phonological rules, actually *changing* phonological features or structure.

A lexical default rule such as (32), which says that obstruents will be voiceless unless otherwise specified, looks especially like a default rule and not very much like a rule that will apply across morpheme boundaries, but only because the structural description of the rule is so small. Another example, though, is considered by Kiparsky (1982a), who suggests that rule (33) of trisyllabic shortening (cf. Chomsky and Halle 1968) expresses a generalization about morphologically simple forms.

(32) $[-\text{sonorant}] \rightarrow [-\text{voice}]$

(33)   Trisyllabic shortening
        (a) $V \rightarrow [-\text{long}] / \underline{\quad} C_o \begin{bmatrix} V \\ -\text{stress} \end{bmatrix} C_o V$

        (b) Long vowel   Short vowel

             divine   divinity
             serene   serenity
             opaque   opacity
             omen   ominous
             declare   declarative
             derive   derivative

Trisyllabic shortening, understood as a generalization across non-derived lexical forms in the language, suggests that it is much more common for a vowel to be short if followed by an unstressed vowel, if that unstressed vowel itself is not word-final. *Canada* fits this description; *stevedore* or *nightingale* does not. If we count relevant entries in a list of monomorphemic English words, we will find, Kiparsky suggests (and I believe he is correct), that the majority will fit this pattern. Thus, short vowels, like the first one in *Canada*, may underlyingly be unspecified for length; this literal 'unmarkedness' is interpreted as a statement regarding inherent complexity of any given underlying form.

Any phonological generalization, like this one concerning the distribution of vowel length, which becomes a redundancy rule of the language[31] is thus a rule of the lexical phonology, and will by the same token come to apply to morphologically derived items in a new way. Now they may not simply specify an underlyingly unspecified feature: they may change an existing feature. Thus a long vowel, marked [+long] underlyingly, will become short ([−long]) when the suffixation of a morpheme places it in the appropriate environment for trisyllabic shortening, as when *divine* is suffixed to form *divinity* – the second vowel of the word becomes short.

We may summarize the general trend in the following way. For any given feature, the language 'prefers' one feature value in a given context, and it is the function of the lexical rules to spell out which this preferred feature value is. This preference will show up both in terms of statistical predominance in monomorphemic words, and in the changes that occur when affixes are attached. The prediction is, then, that the alternations that are produced when affixes are attached always make the resultant word 'simpler' or 'less marked' from the phonological point of view of the language – they never produce a more marked segment. That certainly is an interesting claim, and it is one worth discussing further; for, while it makes correct predictions in a good number of cases, one cannot say that the analysis of English given within the framework of lexical phonology has looked at the point closely. It is certainly not obvious that the presence of /s/ in front of /i/ is more natural and less costly in the underlying representation of an English word, as rule (1), velar softening, proposes. *King* is not obviously more unwieldy than *sing*, though that is ultimately the position of lexical phonology. But it should be clear now that ultimately the claim of lexical phonology, and what puts it at odds with almost every traditional view of morphophonemics in the broadest sense is this: lexical phonology takes entirely seriously the idea that the principles that create systematic phonological changes in the sound shape of a base and an affix when the two are juxtaposed are *no different in kind* from the principles that determine the markedness or complexity for monomorphemic structures.[32] In the case of velar softening, for example, this seems unlikely. This unlikeliness is increased, it seems to me, by the fact that the vowel or vowels that trigger the rule are vowels which, though we may casually write them as *i*, mirroring the orthography, are typically schwa-alike in quality. In fact, the *locus classicus* on the matter is Harris (1951: 221), who observes that:

all morphemes which have members ending in /k/ when not before *ity*, have members ending in /s/ instead when before *ity*: *opaque/opacity*; {*ic*} in *electric-electricity*. . . . In such cases, it is possible to say that all morphemes which occur before *ity* will in that position have members differing in certain phonemes from the other members of the respective morpheme. . . . This statement has now become a statement about *-ity* rather than about *electric*, *sane*, etc., since the alternation does not occur before other morphemes which can be considered phonemically similar to *ity* (e.g. we have no alternation before *al*, *er*, which also begin with /ə/: *electric-al*, *saner*).

It is by no means obvious that the governing factor in the *k/s* alternation of 'electric'/'electricity' is the high vowel quality of the following vowel in close juncture. We will return to this question below.

Let us summarize our discussion in (34).

(34)   (a) Absolute constraints on lexical representations
           1. They hold throughout the lexical phonology, from start to finish.
           2. They eliminate the possibility of using either value of a given feature.
           3. They define what is a **possible** and what is an **impossible** phonological representation in a language.
           4. They are stated as static filters.
           5. They express the 'eliminate redundant features' claims of underspecification theory.
        (b) Markedness statements about underlying forms
           1. They gradually fill in unspecified values throughout the lexical derivation, operating as ordered rules; before their operation, the unmarked value of their feature must be unspecified; after their operation, the unmarked value is specified.
           2. That is, they turn a privative opposition into an equipollent opposition.
           3. They define what is a 'better' (less marked) representation, and what is 'worse' (more marked), though they do not define what is 'good' ('possible') or 'bad' ('impossible').
           4. They are no more and no less than the lexical rules of the phonology; hence they may also serve to change

feature specifications if they chance upon a derived representation.

5. They express the 'eliminate unmarked feature specifications' part of underspecification theory.

5.2   CYCLIC DERIVATIONS IN ENGLISH

5.2.1 The cycle

The cycle is one of those notions behind which lies a very solid and reasonable conceptual core, but which has been used, often thoughtlessly, in such a fashion as to make well-minded citizens highly suspicious of its functioning in good society. We have already seen its formal side; we have seen how strata can be organized in a cyclic fashion, so that phonological rules have a chance to apply after each bout of affixation. Let us turn from that to the other, more practical, side of the notion.

Every language has processes for making new words, typically by affixing prefixes and suffixes, and if the base to which the affixal material has already undergone the phonological modifications necessary to make a well-formed word out of it, there will be a kind of *benign pattern of cyclicity*, in that the same principles that might have been necessary to make the base into a word will now have to come into play in order to make the combined structure a well-formed word; cf. (35).

(35)   Morpheme in its underlying representation
$\quad$ | ←————Phonological rules (e.g. stress)
$\quad$ [word-1]
$\quad$ | Affixation process
$\quad$ [word-1]   affix
$\quad$ | ←———— Phonological rules (same as above)
$\quad$ [[word-1] affix] $_{word-2}$

The cycle played an important role in the formal system of Chomsky and Halle's *Sound Pattern of English* (1968), but it was Brame (1974) who first put his finger on a crucial point: that the *word* is the unit that functions recursively, and that allows for the benign cyclicity that is illustrated in (35). This notion was taken up by Aronoff (1976), and served as the basis for what he referred to as a *word-based theory* of morphology, a point that was then crucial to the development of Strauss (1979) and Kiparsky (1982a).

Harris (1982) provides an excellent and precise illustration of the

conceptual core of the notion of a *word*-based approach. He observes
that in Spanish, the root *desdeñ-* 'disdain' is not a word, and therefore is
not subject to the word-level restriction that forbids word-final palatal
nasals /ñ/ in Spanish. *desdeñ* is a morpheme; words, not morphemes, are
the targets of such constraints as are embodied in rules such as (36).[33]
The root *desdeñ* appears in the verb *desdeñar* and its related inflected
forms, including the second-person singular subjunctive *desdeñes*, which
derives from a stem *desdeñ+a* (including the thematic vowel *a*) and an
inflectional suffix *-es*. The verbal derivation may perhaps be best analyzed
in two cycles; that is, it may be that the stem to which inflectional
material (as in KiRundi, above) is added is best analyzed as a word, in the
relevant sense. Be that as it may, such a stem still includes the thematic
vowel *a*, and therefore the palatal nasal is not in word-final position, and
hence is not subject to rule (36). On the other hand, the noun *desden*
'disdain' (and the plural formed from it, *desdenes*' is derived from the *root*
without the thematic vowel, and hence rule (36) applies to the underlying
form /desdeñ/ which is trying to become a *word*, forming the surface
form *desden*.

(36)   ñ → n / —] $_{\text{word}}$

We have, then, the result of *benign cyclicity*: the theoretical result of
claiming that (at least some) morphology is word-based, which is to say
that it is constructed out of already formed words. Other notions of
cyclicity would arise from a claim that rules applied cyclically to domains
that were not independently motivatable as words. We shall not explore
this apparently unnecessary notion here.

When correctly understood, then, the notion of cyclic derivations
derives from the idea that certain morphological processes that *produce*
words may themselves take as their input certain objects that have
already been turned into well-formed words. Certain generalizations that
involve word-level units may then hold both of the larger unit and the
smaller unit, but ultimately this should be no more surprising or
controversial than the proposition that main clauses may contain subordinate clauses.

As we shall see in some detail below, English contains many highly
productive morphological processes that very clearly – one is tempted to
say, ostentatiously – mark this cyclic character, with very distinctive
indications that a word is contained within a word. Compounding is just
one obvious example of this, but (as we shall discuss below) so is a
certain kind of productive word formation based on the suffix *-ism*, as in
Indianaism [ɪndiænəɪzm] 'a way of speaking peculiar to people from
Indiana'. The larger word is clearly derived from the internal word by
suffixation: [[Indiana]ism].

Where a good deal of uncertainty has remained concerns those aspects of word formation in English where there is good reason to believe that two words are related, but the boundary (or 'juncture') between the base and the suffix is not clearly marked phonologically. For example, it certainly seems *reasonable* to believe that the words *secrecy* and *presidency* are derived from the words *secret* and *president*, but at first blush one could hardly say that the case for such a derivation is transparent. The point is that, after all, even if *presidency* is formed from *president*, we need evidence that the base form *president* is being treated as a word, and is thus undergoing phonological rules as a word, before the affixation of the suffix *y*. Put another way, what is needed is a reason to treat *presidency* differently from *fraternal*, for though most of us would be willing to agree that *fraternal* is derived by the affixation of *-al* to *fratern-*, there certainly is no evidence that the base *fratern-* is analyzed and treated phonologically as a word or anything else *prior to* the affixation.

There are grounds for believing, however, that certain kinds of affixation in English are productive word-based processes which produce words that have no obvious word-type juncture inside them. For example, the suffix *-ic* can be productively added to many classes of words (e.g. *capitalist/capitalistic*), including even some monomorphemic proper names; I encountered *Agamemnonic* recently in a novel. Some of the word-level phonological effects that the base word would be expected to undergo have been either undone or undercut by the processes of *-ic* affixation, clearly. For example, the *m* of *orgasmic* is not syllabic, though it is in the base form *orgasm*, which is clearly the result of the syllabification process mentioned in chapter 3 in reference to words like *meter*. Perhaps similarly, the stress structure of the base words *Agamemnon* is modified in the nonce-formation *Agamemnonic*, and the stress form is modified even more in the case of other *-ic* suffixations, such as *metallic* or *atomic*, where syllables that otherwise would have no stress at all are now stressed. Similarly, segmental material can be lost, in formations like *tantra/tantric*, in order to avoid certain vowel sequences that are not found word-internally in English.

This kind of word formation (which, looking ahead, we may call *close-juncture* formation) seems to do its best to hide the independent wordhood of the base – covering up, so to speak, or hiding the right-hand boundary of the word that serves as the base of the affixation. In this kind of word-formation, the right-hand part of the word is modified along with the suffixation – modified, interestingly enough, not just in any way, but by and large in a way that makes the word look more like a non-derived word, phonologically speaking. But what would support a cyclic approach would be evidence over in the left-hand side of the word that supports a view that the word was processed first *as a word* before the affix was attached. In addition, as a highly related question, we may consider the case of whether, when two of these close-juncture suffixes are added successively, there is evidence that each stage is treated phonologically as a word, or whether we wait until both suffixes are added before applying the word-level rules and constraints. We return to this question with regard to English below, when we have looked at a few processes in more detail. We will see then that there is positive evidence in support of the cyclic view.

5.2.2   The vowel system

In this section we will look at English stress and vowel quality. Some aspects of the stress patterns of English words are quite uncontroversial once a few grounds rules have been made explicit. Other aspects of the problem require a deeper look at the complex morphophonemic alternations that arise when derived words are formed. One area where a simplification of these alternations can be achieved involves the sub-area of vowel alternations, and to understand that we must discuss the analysis of the English vowel shift and vowel reduction as proposed in *The Sound Pattern of English* (Chomsky and Halle 1968).

We must first distinguish between *main stress* (or equivalently, *primary stress* or *1 stress*) and *non-main stress* (or *subsidiary*, or *secondary/tertiary stress*). All lexical items of a major grammatical category (noun, adjective, non-auxiliary verb) have a syllable that bears main stress. Native judgments are sharp and reliable concerning which syllable bears the primary stress; the only shakiness concerns a handful of words where the primary stress may appear on either of two syllables. These words are typically trisyllabic, with the main stress falling either on the first or the last syllable, as in *cigarette* or *magazine*. Primary stress can be identified by the high pitch associated with it and the low pitch found immediately following it.

Most words of more than one syllable also have syllables bearing a stress that is not primary. There has raged for decades a controversy as to whether there are distinctions among the stresses of non-primary stressed syllables. Some say that all non-primary stressed syllables bear the same degree of stress ('secondary stress'); others, following the Trager and Smith (1951) tradition, assign several distinct levels of stress. Virtually all of the work in metrical phonology (as well as in classical generative phonology) has followed the second assumption, though evidence in its favor is remarkably slim. The issue necessarily involves the treatment of long words, as a moment's thought makes clear, and judgments are extremely subtle. For example, it has been observed that there are two different possible pronunciations of the word *Ticonderoga*. In both, the main stress falls on the penultimate syllable, and in both the third and fifth syllables are unstressed. In both, the first and second syllables are stressed; but the two pronunciations differ with respect to which of the first two syllables has higher stress. In the Smith–Trager tradition, these two pronunciations are represented

3 4 0 1 0   4 3 0 1 0
Ticonderoga and *Ticonderoga*,

where '1' marks primary stress '3' a non-primary stress, and '4' a non-primary stress lighter than '3'. It is not entirely clear what status should be given to this observation. The difference between these levels of 4-stress and 3-stress in such words is clearly not contrastive, in the sense of representing possible lexical or morphemic contrasts. Some speakers apparently report preferring one pronunciation; others report free variation. One analysis (Kiparksy 1979) bases an argument for a certain theoretical position on the fact that unanalyzed words, such as *Ticonderoga*, have two possible pronunciations (those just indicated), whereas superficially similar words that are derived from other, smaller words have only one possible pronunciation (for example, *sensationality*, where the first syllable may never be perceived as more prominent than the second; cf. also *categorization*, based on *category*, or *iconoclastic*, *anticipation*, or *superiority*).

Fortunately, most of the issues we will be concerned with do not involve the question as to whether there is more than one level of non-primary stress in English, since the very nature of the facts themselves is unclear. What is most important is whether a syllable is stressed or not, for once it has been determined which syllables are stressed, it is generally easy to predict mechanically which syllable will be assigned the primary stress (Schane 1979b). Holding aside some special cases,[34] the general principle is this: the rightmost stressed syllable that is not in the final syllable will bear the main stress. For example, the first and third syllables are stressed in both *telephone* and *telephonic*, but in the first case, main stress falls on the first syllable because the last syllable is not a possible candidate for bearing primary stress. Once a syllable is added, as in *telephonic*, the third syllable can bear the main stress, because it is the rightmost stress and it is not in the final syllable. This operation of main-stress assignment can hardly be a clear example of a cyclic operation, of course, since the choice of main stress must await all suffixal syllables (or, more accurately, all suffixal syllables of a certain large class). Better to apply the operation just once, after all the relevant syllables are in place.

The distinction between a stressed syllable (which means, here and elsewhere, a syllable that has either primary stress or non-primary stress) and an unstressed syllable is, generally speaking, not difficult to make. It has generally been assumed that any syllable with a reduced vowel, or schwa, is unstressed; while this has on occasion been questioned (Schane 1979a), I shall maintain this assumption as well. Similarly, the diphthongs of English appear only in stressed syllables.

Thus, the first syllable of *atomic* is unstressed, because it is a schwa, though we can see that it is underlyingly the vowel [æ], as the form *atom*, with stress on the first syllable, brings out. The main (and only) stress in *divine* is on the second syllable, and there we find a diphthong [ay].

However, there do remain a good number of cases where there is some uncertainty as to whether or not a lax vowel is stressed, as, for example, in the second syllable of the word *indignation*.[35] In general, the literature has appealed in these difficult cases to theoretically neutral observers, usually the pronouncing dictionary of Kenyon and Knott (1944), but this is not the most satisfactory arrangement imaginable. Appealing to authority, no matter whose dictionary, is only a stopgap measure.

As we noted above, all of the work done within the framework of lexical phonology has assumed the theory of English phonology proposed in Chomsky and Halle's (1968) *Sound Pattern of English* (SPE) concerning the treatment of the vowel system, and the problematic long vowels (or diphthongs). At a superficial level (roughly, a systematic phonetic level), American English has a vowel system like that in (37), which is my own; inasmuch as I am from New York, the details concerning the low vowels differ from those of many other speakers of what might otherwise be considered standard American English. (Whether [a] is short remains controversial.)

(37)   (a) Short vowels
             [ɪ] kit   [ʌ] putt   [ʊ] put
             [ɛ] pet
             [æ] cat   [a] cot   [ɔ] caught
        (b) Long vowels
             [iy] key   [uw] boot
             [ey] pay   [ow] go   [ɔy] toy
             [ay] tie   [æw] cow

Morphophonemic alternations relate pairs of vowels – generally, pairs consisting of a long vowel and a short vowel – that are phonetically quite different, for a historical reason. The long vowels of English underwent a systematic change called the Great English Vowel Shift. For example, what five hundred years ago was a long front mid vowel (e:) was raised, to become a long front high vowel. This rule was a late rule in the phonological system at the time, however, and it applied only to long vowels, so an underlying /e:/ could escape this raising if the addition of a suffix to the morpheme containing a long vowel caused the vowel to shorten. For example, the second vowel of *serene* /sere:n/ was underlyingly long, and so the pronunciation [sere:n] shifted to the more modern [seri:n] (ignoring here the offglide). But the derivation of the word *serenity* involved affixation of the suffix *-ity*, and this suffixation in turn occasioned the shortening of the preceding vowel, producing the intermediate form /seren+ity/. Here the second vowel has shorted, and so will fail to undergo the late rule of vowel shift (e: → i:). We will thus find, in the grammar of this stage of English, alternations between short [e] and long [i:]. And this is still found in modern-day English, as illustrated by the alternations in (38), modified from a table in Halle

(38)   Alternations involving vowel shift
        (a) ay ~ I   divine/divinity
                     crucify/crucifixion
                     satire/satiric
                     Christ/Christmas/christian
                     five/fifth/fifteen (but cf. nine/ninth, and eight/
                     eighth)
                     wide/width
                     Palestine/Palestinian
        (b) iy ~ ɛ   serene/serenity
                     intervene/intervention
                     hygiene/hygienic
                     deep/depth, heal/health, steal/stealth
                     plead/pled, bleed/bled, flee/fled, feel/felt
                     mean/meant, meet/met, keep/kept
        (c) ey ~ æ   sane/sanity
                     volcano/volcanic
                     marginal/marginalia
        (d) æw ~ ʌ   profound/profundity
                     pronounce/pronunciation (and other words
                     with *-nounce*, like *denounce*)
                     south/southern
                     abound/abundant
                     flower/flourish
                     tower/turret
        (e) ow ~ a   verbose/verbosity
                     telephone/telephonic
                     cone/conic
                     harmonious/harmonic
        (f) uw ~ ʌ   reduce/reduction

(1977). It is the position of *The Sound Pattern of English* (a position, as noted above, that is maintained by lexical phonology) that this is an accurate synchronic picture of English today as well.

The alternation among the pairs of front vowels in (37a–c) is reasonably regular and productive, though the same can hardly be said for the back vowels (see especially McCawley 1986). As I indicated above, the *SPE* analysis posits a regular phonological rule that recapitulates the historical change. Thus, the front mid vowel [e] may be long or short, in the lexical phonology. If it is short it is also lax, and surfaces as [ɛ]; if it is long, then it undergoes the vowel shift rule, and is raised to [i:]. Eventually all long front vowels get a *y*- offglide, by a late post-lexical rule. Finally, it is worth bearing in mind that, within the logic of the system, a long vowel that undergoes vowel shift may either be long underlyingly, never being shortened during the derivation, or be short underlyingly, and become lengthened during the derivation (e.g. *marginal, margin-a:l-ia*).

The point of this discussion is to see how the *SPE* description encourages us to try to account for the phonological differences between many pairs of derivationally related words in a purely phonological way. The vowel quality differences noted in (38) can be abstracted away from if we can provide a reasonably small number of phonological rules that shorten or lengthen the vowels in question, leaving it for a much later rule to effect the vowel quality changes.

But derivationally related forms in English differ not just in vowel quality, but also, quite frequently, in their stress patterns (e.g. *compete/competition, atom/atomic*). Lexical phonology, following a number of workers in this area,[36] has defended the position that there exist phonological rules that shorten and lengthen vowels, and assign metrical structure after such length-affecting rules; further length-affecting rules will also apply after metrical structure has been established. The stress pattern of a morphologically derived English word, then, is claimed to be predictable according to the regular patterns established for monomorphemic words, except that some shortening and lengthening rules apply before the stress rules apply, and others apply also after the stress rules. We will explore this by first presenting a brief overview of the principles of stress assignment for monomorphemic words in English.

5.2.3   English stress rules

We have looked at the basic operation of the English stress rule in our discussion of metrical phonology. Most work in lexical phonology is in agreement on the following main points of English stress.

The rule that assigns the rightmost stress to a word is the quantity-sensitive rule that we discussed in chapter 3 which assigns a foot – i.e. a stress – to the right-hand end of the word, skipping over extrametrical material and one light syllable, if there is one. However, a final syllable which is extrametrical but contains a long vowel will nonetheless be marked as stressed, i.e. will form a foot. This is possible primarily in the case of nouns, whose final syllable is extrametrical. Nonetheless, a final syllable with a tensed vowel will find that syllable stressed. In additional, certain adjectival suffixes may have this property of attracting stress, such as *-oid* and *-ory*.[37]

Reviewing, then, from chapter 3, the stress pattern of the sorts of words in (39) will be predictable. If the final syllable contains a long vowel, as in (39d), that final syllable is stressed. Otherwise, stress falls on either the penultimate or the antepenultimate, depending on the weight of the penultimate. If the penultimate is heavy, as in (39b) or (39c), it is stressed; otherwise, as in (39a), the antepenult is stressed.[38] A syllable, of course, can be heavy either by virtue of having a diphthong, or by virtue of being closed, as in the penultimate syllables of (39b) and (39c), respectively.

(39) (a) America (b) aroma   (c) veranda   (d) Naverone
          cinema   balalaika   agenda   magazine
          asparagus   hiatus   consensus   antidote
          metropolis   horizon   synopsis
          javelin   corona   utensil

These principles have been called the Main English Stress Rule; they are followed by a related rule or set of rules that gives rise to something close to a pattern of alternating stress earlier in the word. The precise nature of these rules is crucial for the formulation of the arguments concerning the cyclic nature of English stress assignment, as is the precise formulation of the several rules of destressing that are necessary, as we shall see.

Hayes (1982) argues that the principles of stress assignment involved here are as might be sketched in (40). He argues that the rule of stress retraction, which he calls Strong Retraction, is quantity-insensitive,

(40) Stress retraction

$$\acute{\sigma}\ \sigma\ \acute{\sigma}\ \sigma\ \acute{\sigma}\ \sigma\ \sigma\ ]$$ by stress retraction (quantity-insensitive)

          Main English
          Stress Rule
          (quantity-sensitive)

unlike the Main English Stress Rule. The arguments for this position are moderately complex, and reviewing all the arguments would require a book in itself; nonetheless, this assumption is crucial to one of the most often-cited arguments for cyclicity, which is essentially as follows. The words *compensation, condensation*, and *compurgation*[39] have essentially identical surface syllable structures. However, only the third of these is stressed in a non-cyclic fashion, and the lack of stress on the second syllable, despite its status as a closed (and thus heavy) syllable, shows that the pattern of stress retraction leftward across the word will skip over a heavy syllable as it constructs metrical feet, as in (40); this is illustrated in (41). Thus retraction is not quantity-sensitive.

(41)   x   x
        xx   xx   xx   x
        com pur ga   tion

But the stress pattern in *condensation*, it is suggested, has distinct stress on the second syllable, unlike both *compurgation* and *compensation*. This is the result of the stress (Row 1 grid mark) that appears on the second syllable of the base form, *condense*, arguably; no other factor could account for this distinct stress pattern.

There are two important destressing rules to bear in mind. Both may be viewed profitably as stress-clash-reducing principles. The first Hayes calls 'prestress destressing'; mnemonically, we might refer to it as the 'banana/bandanna' rule, because it is the rule responsible for the deletion of stress on the initial syllable of *banana*, which is originally assigned a stress pattern just like that of *bandanna*, as we see in (42). Prestress destressing (44), however, removes the stress from a (degenerate) monosyllabic foot which immediately precedes another foot, and which consists of a single, light syllable, thus removing the stress from the first syllable of *banana*, as in (43).[40] This rule applies only when the syllable that immediately follows is the main stress of the word as a whole, giving rise to differences in the stress on the first syllable in pairs such as *department/departmental*, or *relax/relaxation*. In both cases the second syllable is stressed, but only in the first of each does it bear the main stress of the word, and only there is the first syllable unstressed.

Following the *SPE* analysis, this rule is often conflated with the process that shortens and destresses long vowels in such forms as *explanation*

(42)   x   x
               x x   x x
               x x x   xx x   x
        (a) banana   (b) bandanna

(43)
$$x$$
$$x$$
$$x \quad x \quad x$$
banana

(44)   Prestress destressing

Condition: F_2 is main stress of word

(from *explain*) and *invitation* (from *invite*). This process of shortening does take place even when the stressed vowel does not bear the main word stress; for example, any verb ending in *-ate* will find that *-ate* shortened, and destressed, before the suffix *-ory*, as in *deprecate/ deprecatory, congratulate/congratulatory*.

The second rule of destressing applies rightward, deleting a stress foot on an open, light syllable immediately following a stressed syllable. The effect of this rule is particularly noticeable in the apparent alternations it gives rise to in a suffix like *-ory*, which has a full stressed vowel in words like *deprecatory, promissory* or *equivocatory*, where the preceding vowel is unstressed, but loses both length and stress in words like *advisory* and *illusory*, where the immediately preceding syllable is stressed.[41]

5.2.4   Strata in English

We have now completed a quick survey of the basic principles of English stress assignment, and we can begin to approach some of the thornier problems that arise in dealing with the question of the extent to which English derivation can be treated as cyclic phonology.

(1)   A great deal is known about English morphology, and yet at the same time there is considerable controversy about how to interpret what is known. In this section I shall explain what the main dimensions are along which investigators have found differences in the affixation processes in English, and shall indicate several of the ways that have been suggested for integrating these observed differences into theoretically coherent programs, of which lexical phonology is one.

Let us start with a simple example or two. There are, it appears, two kinds of ways that suffixes in English can be found attached to their *base*. In the first, the base is an existing word, with a meaning, a stress pattern, and a syllabification that it would have standing alone; and when the suffix is attached, it leaves that base alone, phonologically. This is most clearly seen in cases where the juncture between the base and the suffix forms a sequence that cannot be found within monomorphemic words. I have already mentioned a few examples of this sort. While we cannot have geminates word-internally, we find these in words like *coolly*, *cleanness*, *tailless*. We cannot have non-high vowels followed by another vowel word-internally, but we find this in words like *Indianaism* or *Bermudaize*. The same point holds for prefixes as well, yet we find geminates with the prefix *un-*: *unnatural*, for example. Following traditional terminology, we may refer to this as *affixation with open juncture*. Not all affixes ever participate in this kind of juncture, as we shall see. It is a fact – and not a logical necessity – that, in all cases of affixation with open juncture, the base is an independently existing word, with a stress pattern that remains unchanged when affixed, and a meaning that is composed to form the meaning of the whole word.

Many cases of affixation exist, of course, where the base to which the affix is attached either does not exist as a free standing word (e.g. *paternal*, *plagiar-ize*, *inocul-ate*), or has undergone some segmental modification (e.g. *buddh[]-ism*, where a schwa has vanished, or *jeopard[]-ize*, where a *y* of some sort has vanished, or *syllab-ic*, where an *l* has vanished, or *libid[in]-ous*, where an *o* has vanished and an *in* has taken its place). Despite certain complications which we shall discuss below, it can be said that, in all of this second kind of affixation, the base plus the suffix together satisfy the phonotactics of monomorphemic English words, and that the global stress pattern of such words also satisfies the rules of English monomorphemic words. For want of a better descriptive term, we will call this *close juncture affixation*.

This distinction between types of affixation has been described and categorized in different ways. The most familiar view attributes the difference to a difference of the *suffix*, and labels the two types of affixation we have described as affixations of, respectively, *stress-neutral* and *stress-affecting* suffixes; or *stratum 2* and *stratum 1* suffixes; or *#* suffixes and *+ suffixes*. From the examples we have looked at so far, it is not obvious, of course, that the difference in the kind of juncture is the responsibility of the particular suffix that was chosen – it may, after all, have been the base that determined the kind of juncture that occurred. Since it has been taken for so long to be the suffix that is responsible for the type of junction, however, we should consider more carefully the pros and cons of this position. One argument that has been given for ascribing the junction type to the suffix is that it has been observed that the same base can appear sometimes in close juncture with one suffix, and in open juncture with another:

Close juncture	Open juncture
curiosity	curiously
deceptive	deceiving
obligatory	obliging

Thus, goes the first argument, if the base were the object responsible for the kind of juncture we find in a suffixed form, no base would allow itself to be found in suffixed forms with different kinds of juncture. Therefore, it must be the suffix that determines the junction type.

The second argument for handing the junctural responsibility over to the suffixes derives from trying to identify minimal pairs among morphemes, where one always comes with close juncture, the other always with open juncture. If juncture type goes hand in hand with the particular meaning of the suffix, then surely it would follow that the suffix is formally responsible for the junction type. For example, there is a suffix *-ism* that marks characteristic speech forms, and which comes with open juncture, and a suffix *-ism* that indicates a philosophy, in a broad sense, with close juncture. This gives us a number of close and actual minimal pairs; cf. (45).

(45)

Close juncture	Open juncture
cathóli[s]ism	cátholi[k]ism
Buddhism	?Buddha-ism
communism	??commune-ism
	Indiana-ism
	Indian-ism (from *Indian*, not from *Indiana*)

There is certainly something to this generalization, but most of what is right about it has to do with new formations that we might make up, not with existing words. If we make up a word with the speech-mannerism sense, we will, in all likelihood, employ a suffixation process with open juncture (*Turkism, Yankeeism*); but the other thing we might well do is attach *-ism* to a base ending in *-ic*, whereupon the *ic* will become *i[s]*, phonologically: *gallicism, italicism, slavicism, anglicism, sinicism* (or *sinocism?*), and so forth. Which of these already exist and which have just been invented I am not quite sure, and that is the point. It is certainly not clear, to say the least, that this second group is an instance of suffixation with open (#) juncture. And there do exist a good number of suffixed *-ism* words that have close juncture but the mannerisms meaning, rather than the philosophy meaning, of which one is perhaps *mannerism*, depending on whether the base, *manner*, has the appropriate meaning (e.g. *archaism*, *hebraism*, perhaps *rhotacism*).

Thus, our generalization about the speech-forms sense of *-ism* always taking open juncture is not terribly strong; and, going the other way, *cannibalism* (although it may, irrelevantly, have the speech-form sense!) generally has the philosophy sense, but it has the stress pattern of the word *cannibal* with *-ism* attached as an open juncture – otherwise we would expect to get stress on the second syllable, as in *calamity*.

The point of this extended discussion is to indicate that the *prima facie* evidence in favor of ascribing *to the suffix* the determining role in deciding whether we get open or close juncture in a particular base–suffix combination may be a bit hasty. After all, the first part of the argument as sketched so far is that there are bases that occur with both open and close juncture in different words. But it is not hard to find – and we have already seen – cases where what looks for all the world like the same suffix is sometimes attaching in close juncture, and sometimes in open juncture. We have seen such cases with the speech-manner *-ism*; the same point can be seen with the open juncture *-ize* in *Bermuda-ize* and the close juncture in *notar[]ize, synchron[]ize*, or *Catholicize*. In the first two forms, a word-final /y/ is elided, a sign of close juncture, and in the third, the stress pattern has been modified drastically in the base. And perhaps it need not be said, but we should also be aware that the mere fact that certain suffixes (*-ity*, for example, as in *sanity, divinity*, or *electricity*) will not attach to certain bases (*tallity, ?fabulosity*) is no more a fact about the *suffix* than it is about the *base*; that is, just as one can generalize across the various stems that *-ity* will not attach to, one can generalize over the various suffixes that *tall* will not attach to (*tallity, *tallous, *tallic, *tallible*, and so forth).

(2) *Historical interlude* In order to discuss current approaches, it is necessary to sketch a certain number of generalizations that have been noted in the literature, and which serve as the basis for most of the models currently under discussion.

Siegel (1974) followed Chomsky and Halle (1968) in assigning to each suffix a boundary, thereby claiming that the juncture that was found was grammatically the result of the choice of suffix. Some suffixes came with a + boundary, leading to close juncture, in general (though she did not use that term), and others came with a # boundary; she referred to these as class I and class II suffixes, respectively, and gave the examples shown in (46).

Siegel made the following observations. (i) Class II suffixes attach, with only a handful of exceptions,[42] to independently existing words. Class I suffixes attach either to words or to stems, i.e. bound morphemes. (ii)

(46)

Class I	Class II
-ation	-ness
-able	-less
-y (nominalizing)	-ly
-al	-al (nominalizing)
-ity	-y (adjective forming)
-ate	-ful
-ify	-ment
-ic	

Class I suffixes will occasion a shift in stress from the pattern found on the independently existing base word, whereas class II suffixes do not. (iii) Class I suffixes can follow each other (e.g. *histor-ic-al, illumin-at-ion, in-determin-ate/in-determin-ac-y*), and class II suffixes can follow both class I suffixes (*fratern-al-ly, transform-ate-ion-less*) and class II suffixes (*weight-less-ness*). Class I suffixes can never, however, follow a class II suffix (**weight-less-ity, *fatal-ism-al*) (though I will disagree with this point below). (iv) Certain class II suffixes place conditions on the stress pattern that independently exists on their base word; class I suffixes never do. (Siegel discusses the *-al* nominalizing suffix,[43] the *-(e)teria* suffix, and the *-ful* suffix).

Siegel united these observations in the hypothesis that the morphological process of suffixation should be divided into two layers, with the stress rules applying after all class I suffixation but before all class II suffixation, as indicated schematically in (47). This proposal was quite influential, and led in an almost direct path to the construction of the model of lexical phonology. To arrive at the conception of Kiparsky (1982a,b), the notion was needed in addition that the stress rules operate cyclically, after each of the class I suffixes is added,[44] and that class I suffixes are simply the first-stratum suffixes. The class II suffixes could

(47) Roots

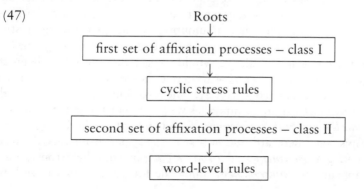

now be added on a later – perhaps the second – stratum. Any stratum 2 process would leave unaffected the stress pattern of the derived word.[45]

Inherent in the model proposed by Kiparsky (1982a,b) is the idea that close juncture is what is produced by forms going through the stratum 1 rules; a form that has managed to get through the roster of stratum 1 rules will satisfy the word-internal phonotactics of English. Suffixes affixed in the second stratum are the sources of open juncture, for they are not subject to the stratum 1 rules that would be responsible for such affairs as the deletion of the schwa in *Buddhism*. Thus juncture is translated into strata, so to speak; word-level phonotactics (which is to say, close juncture) becomes a matter of stratum 1 rule effects.

Determining which stratum a given suffix is in, though, can be harder than it may seem at first. This is apparent just from comparing the several lengthy studies that have looked into this hypothesis (Siegel 1974; Allen 1978; Aronoff 1976; Selkirk 1982b); their classification of this basic point for various suffixes is by no means uniform. Selkirk is, for her part, explicit about the point that some suffixes are in both classes, but she suggests that 'the vast majority' of English affixes are clearly in one class or the other.

We should be careful in evaluating the result of being faced with suffixes that individually belong to both classes. On the one hand, if it is true that individual suffixes do, in fact, come with different kinds of juncture, then we need a model that can recognize that, and treat it adequately, and not require that each suffix be assigned to one kind of juncture or affixation. On the other hand, assigning a suffix to both classes without independent justification can, under certain circumstances, be just a sign that the model is in trouble, and is making wrong predictions. Consider an example of the second sort.

The class I/class II model in (47), and its descendants, make the strict prediction that class I suffixes never appear to the right of class II suffixes. Now, the suffix *-al* is a clear case of a class I suffix, since it easily attaches to non-words (*patern-al*), and changes the stress pattern of its base (*parent-al*). The suffix *-ment*, however, has to be a class II suffix; as Siegel (1977) points out, only that assumption would give the right stress pattern for *abolishment*; for even if (in more recent terminology) the final syllable were extrametrical, we would expect the stress to fall on the penultimate. Only if we let *abolish* derive its stress on the first stratum can the form be derived correctly. The problem is, though, that the sequence *ment-al* is quite common, as we see in words like *governmental, ornamental, elemental, supplemental,* and so forth. Selkirk suggests that this shows that there are two suffixes *-ment*, one from class I, which appears in *govern+ment* and *orna+ment*, and another from class II which appears in *employ#ment*. Only the former can appear with the class I suffix *-al* following it. This, of course, is merely recognizing the problem, not solving it.[46] We shall offer a solution to it below.

(3) In section (1) we reviewed the various characteristics of English word formation that motivate distinguishing between word formation with open juncture and that with close juncture. In section (2) we considered the various approaches that have been proposed to incorporate certain further hypotheses regarding these kinds of junctures, all of them following upon Siegel's perspective (what Selkirk calls the *Affix Ordering Generalization*: close juncture is always closer to the root than any open juncture), including most importantly the 'stratification' of morphology in lexical phonology. In this section, we will review the various arguments that have been given subsequently which cast serious doubt on the Affix Ordering Generalization and its descendants.[47] It is important to bear in mind, however, that rejection of this hypothesis is independent of the question of cyclicity, which we return to in the next section, where we will provide an analysis of a class of data in English that is simultaneously an argument *for* cyclicity and *against* the Affix Ordering Generalization, in that an open juncture suffix precedes a close juncture suffix, both of which apply cyclically.

The arguments against the Affix Ordering Generalization, and thus the division of affixes into strata, include (i) those based on prefix/suffix incompatibilities; (ii) those based on inverted orders among the suffixes, with stratum 2 suffixes preceding stratum 1 suffixes; and (iii) problems regarding the placement of compounds within a stratal account. I shall present an example of the second kind in detail in the next section, and leave the third kind to interested readers.[48] The arguments based on prefix/suffix incompatibilities are of considerable interest, and I will indicate their general form here.

Referring to a number of striking observations in Williams (1981), Strauss (1982b) observes that the Affix Ordering Generalization has problems when it encounters words like *ungrammaticality*, *reorganization*, and even forms like *South American*, under certain assumptions about compounding. In each case, the suffix is a stratum 1 suffix, but there is good reason to believe that the base to which it is attached has undergone stratum 2 prefixation (*un-grammatical*, *re-organize*), or even compounding, (*South America*) *before* the affix is attached. This is sketched graphically in (48).

In cases (48a,b), the prefixes have the familiar properties of layer 2 affixes (they attach to existing words, they are thoroughly productive, they allow segment sequences at their juncture that are not found morpheme internally), but the argument that the correct hierarchical structure is as given in (48) is quite strong. In case (48a), *un-* attaches

(48)   (a)

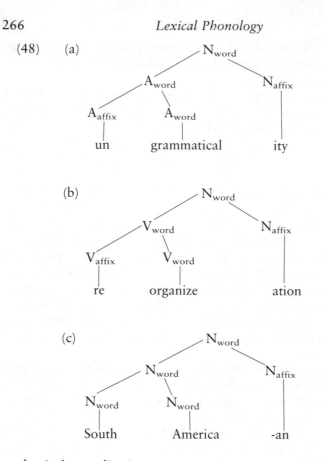

productively to adjectives, not to nouns; *ungrammatical* exists, but *un-* does not productively attach to nouns. *Re-* similarly attaches productively to verbs, not to nouns, and of course in case (48c), the adjectival form *South American* is based on the compound *South America*.[49]

Strauss characterizes these 'paradoxes' as involving prefixes and suffixes, and it certainly does seem to be correct that it is difficult or impossible to assign to morphemes that flank a stem a relative *order* that is consistent with what we know about the rest of the language.[50] In the next section I will suggest further reasons for not incorporating level ordering into our account of morphology.

5.2.5   The cycle in English

A number of arguments have been given for a cyclic account of English stress placement. As I indicated above, many of these rest on elusive data, but I will offer the following argument in favor of a word-based cyclic account of English stress. As noted above, the notion of benign cyclicity can be reduced to the less striking statement that words are formed from other words, and that word-level rules can therefore have applied to subparts of words as well as to the whole word itself. But a cyclic account leads to some rather surprising results, as well.

We have seen that the metrical grid assigned to a given word forms a chart, the bottom row of which associates to the skeletal tier in ways that we have explored in preceding chapters. Halle and Vergnaud (1987) have proposed that the notion of cyclicity in stress assignment be understood in terms of autosegmental charts as well. They suggest that each cycle produces a distinct metrical grid, associated to the skeleton, and that there are limited ways in which information can pass from the grid corresponding to an earlier cycle to the grid of the later cycle.[51] They suggest that in English, a word-level stress (that is, the main stress of a word, a grid mark on the third row) is copied over to the next cycle, though other (secondary) stresses are not copied.[52] This predicts a derivation as in (49) for the pairs of words *condense*, *condensation*, in which the second syllable should be stressed in both forms.

(49)　　(a)　　　x
　　　　　　x　x
　　　　　　xx　xx
　　　　　condense

(b)

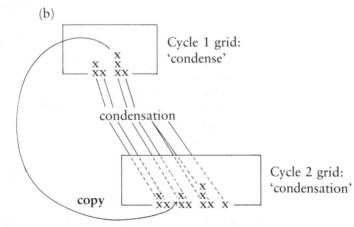

The strongest argument for a word-based cyclic approach to English stress would be one that (i) involves a restriction on morphology that accounts for combinations of morphemes of a sort that have never been heard, but which sound totally unacceptable, and (ii) follows naturally from, and only from, an account with more than one grid chart simultaneously associated with a word. The argument I will provide, in fact, is based on the behavior of words with *three* simultaneous grid charts, making the case even stronger.

Consider first the set of data given in (50), first discussed in Strauss (1983), who points out that in (50a), there are a number of words formed with the suffix *-ist* that do not allow for acceptable suffixed forms with *-ic*, while in (50b), the forms are fine. In parts (c) and (d), we find examples of trisyllabic *-ist* words which allow *-ic* suffixation, and in (e), trisyllabic forms that do not allow *-ic* suffixation.

(50) (a) sexist   *sexistic   (b) sadist   sadistic
           faddist   *faddistic   fascist   fascistic
           rightist   *rightistic   linguist linguistic
           leftist   *leftistic   deist   deistic
           racist   *racistic   theist   theistic
           rapist   *rapistic   jurist   juristic
           putschist   *putschistic   sophist   sophistic

      (c) fatalist   fatalistic   (d) masochist masochistic
           regalist   regalistic   plagiarist plagiaristic
           humorist   humoristic   populist   populistic
           socialist   socialistic   atheist   atheistic
           humanist   humanistic   aphorist   aphoristic
           realist   realistic   hedonist   hedonistic
           communist   communistic   anarchist anarchistic

            (e) cartoonist *cartoonistic
                 escapist   *escapistic
                 falangist   *falangistic
                 alarmist   *alarmistic
                 defeatist   *defeatistic
                 adventist   *adventistic
                 conformist *conformistic
                 extremist   *extremistic
                 reservist   *reservistic
                 careerist   *careeristic

Strauss proposes that the generalization is that '*-ic* may attach to an X+*ist* base provided the final syllable of X is not primary stressed if X is a lexical item.' Thus an example in (50a) (e.g. *rightistic*) is bad because *right* is a lexical item with final stress; *rightist* is formed from it; and therefore we cannot add on *-ic*. Likewise, we cannot form, *cartoonistic* from *cartoonist*, because it has been built from an existing word, *cartoon*, with final stress. *Sadist*, however, is not synchronically built from an existing word (surely not from *de Sade*, synchronically) and thus

Strauss's restriction does not apply, allowing *sadistic*, just as *fatalistic* is allowed, because although *fatalist* is built from an existing word, *fatal*, that word does not have final stress.

This does seem, admittedly, like magic. The generalization is too good to be true – almost literally, for, although the correct predictions are being made, it seems impossible that one's own judgments could be driven by Strauss's generalization. How, after all, could we have learned to put such a affix- and language-particular restriction on the *-ic* suffixation rule? Surely we must look deeper.

Let us step back a moment and listen to the impossible word *alarmistic*. What makes the word impossible is not too hard to determine: it is that we cannot figure out how to stress it, because it feels like we want to give the second syllable a word stress, and also the third syllable, and we simply cannot figure how to do both at the same time, that is, with a single articulation – so we give up, and say it is unacceptable.

The problem, then, is clearly one of stress-clash, but how, and why? Let us review a few things about stress-clash in English. First of all, some stress-clashes are fine. There are many bisyllabic words where both are stressed (e.g., *nýlòn, Révlòn, Ràngóon*) and polysyllabic words with adjacent stresses (*Ìllíní, Tìcònderóga*, etc.). Monomorphemic words put no major constraints on the pattern of adjacent stresses.

Furthermore, there are some kinds of suffixation that look like they will lead to a stress-clash which is then resolved one way or the other with no great difficulty – not every potential clash leads to the phonological breakdown felt in *alarmistic*. A word like *admonish*, for example, with penultimate stress, has a stress pattern just like that of *alarmist*; but because its stress is in an open syllable, it shortens and destresses when the *-ion* suffix is added, as in *admonition*, which has (or can have) an unstressed second syllable. A word like *abnormal*, again with stress on the second syllable, does not have to lose that stress when the suffix *-ity* is added, since it is in a closed syllable, but the stress on the third syllable is clearly stronger (as can be the stress on the first syllable) than that of the second syllable in *abnormality*. Both of these cases involve close juncture, and neither seems to be troubled by stress-clash – in one case because the stress is deleted, in the other because it is somehow sufficiently subordinated.

There *are* productive morphological processes that clearly are directly more sensitive to stress-clash, however, such as *-ize* suffixation. We have already observed that the suffix *-ize* can be found with either close juncture or open juncture: the cases included *catholicize/notarize* and *Bermudaize*, respectively. The task of determining which kind of juncture we have here is not that easy, however. On any of the accounts of verbal stress assignment discussed in this chapter and chapter 4, the correct stress pattern can be obtained whether the suffix *-ize* is added on stratum 1, with cyclic stress assignment, or on stratum 2, even if we assume no application of the Main English Stress Rule (if we allow a rule to stress word-final long vowels in the second-stratum phonology).[53] To see why, consider the case of a word like *standardize* or *cannibalize*. If stress is assigned to *standard* and *cannibal* on the first cycle, and then if *-ize* is attached on a second stratum 1 cycle, stress will be assigned to the final syllable (*-ize*) because it is heavy, and nothing further will happen. Stress retraction, discussed above (see (40)), does not apply when there are no 'unfooted' syllables, i.e. no syllables that have not yet been gathered into feet.[54]

In short, a monosyllabic verbal suffix (like *-ize*) is going to turn out not to affect the stress pattern of the base to which it is attached on stratum 1, just because of the way the English rules are set up, and because stress retraction obeys the Strict Cycle Condition, and thus does not *change* the metrical structure that it finds, but instead only applies to fill structure in. On the other hand, if *-ize* is a stratum 2 suffix, then all the more so it will not affect the stress pattern of the base to which it is attached, just by the way we have set things up: the Main English Stress Rule does not apply on stratum 2.

So if we want to determine in a particular case whether we have open or close juncture with a particular *-ize* verb, and if we recognize that the decision may have to be made on a case-by-case basis, we can only conclude that stress will not help us in this task.

I suggest that, in cases of indeterminacy, the default assumption to make is that we have open juncture – that is, from the point of view of stratal ordering, a stratum 2 juncture. The judgment is a delicate one, but it is based in part on the following peculiarity.

The suffix *-ize* is highly productive, but it has some phonological limitations. Consider the forms and judgments in (51). The fact that we can *autumnize* an heating system, for example, but not *fallize* it, suggests two things. First, it affirms our decision to treat this as open juncture, since the /n/ of *autumnal* does not appear in this form; that is, we have a true word inside *[[autumn]ize]*. Second, it suggests that there is a phonological, not a semantic or pragmatic, reason why we do not have *fallize*. The generalization is a simple one, to be sure; *-ize* does not attach to a word with final stress, which includes all monosyllables. But should this be stated as a fact about *-ize*, as we have put it, or is it part of a larger generalization? In fact, it seems that this is part of a larger generalization that prohibits stress clash over an open suffix juncture.

We suggest that there is a prohibition in English against adjacent stresses across open juncture when the material on the right is suffixal (52). We label

(51) (a) winterize (b) alphabetize (c) *Montrealize
          summerize   radicalize   *New Yorkize
          autumnize   departmentalize   Bostonize
          *fallize   *?cartoonize   ?Chicagoize
          *springize   journalize
                           ?*magazineize
                           ?*reviewize
                           *bookize
                           publicize
                           legalize

the *morphological* bracketing with its corresponding *phonological* juncture type, open (#) or close (+). (Note that the prohibited clash involves successive syllables, not moras.)

(52) Prohibited: *   *   foot
                   *   *   syllable
              $\sigma]_{\#} \; \sigma]$

Such clashes are not prohibited, however, as long as they do not occur across an open juncture (which is written with a word-labelled bracket in filter (52)). As we have observed, stress-clashes word-internally do not offend the phonological sensibilities of the English language, nor are such clashes across a close juncture impossible, as *abnormality* illustrates.

With filter (52) in mind, we can return to the account of Strauss's generalization involving *alarmistic*. The productive, word-based formation with *-ist* is again one with open juncture, just as is the case with *-ize*. That is the crucial point, for when we add the next suffix, *-ic*, stress will fall on *-ist*, yielding a stress-clash across open juncture. This is illustrated in (53).

As we observed, this account violates the Affix Ordering Generalization; class I suffixes follow class 2 suffixes, and in general I believe that is correct, and not theoretically ruled out. As indicated above, when the literature has faced this observation, the most frequent response to the perceived problem has been to say that a given morpheme can play the role of either a class I or a class II suffix. But as noted above, in reference to Selkirk's treatment of the problem of why *ment+al* will not attach to free-standing verbs, that is a recognition of the problem, not a solution.

We can now return to the problem now of why we find the pattern in (54), and can immediately see the reason why the forms in the third column of (54b) are bad. They are bad for the same reason that *alarmistic* is bad: they require a stress-clash across an open juncture.

In summary, then, we have here an argument against the Affix Ordering Generalization, and thus against a stratal approach to English

(53)

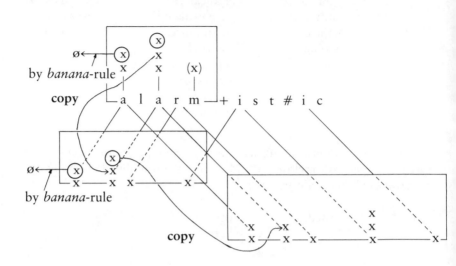

(54)   (a) develop   development   developmental

        (b) employ   employment   *employmental
            recruit   recruitment   *recruitmental
            govern†   government   *governmental

        (c)   ornament   ornamental
                           government   governmental
                           supplement   supplemental

```
                    x           Row 2
                x   x           Row 1
                x   x   x       Row 0
        (d)     [ [employ] ment ]
                        #                   Second cycle

                        x           Row 2
            x   x   x           Row 1
            x   x   x   (x)     Row 0
        [ [ employ] ment ] al ]
                #       +                   Third cycle
```

†In the linguistic sense; e.g., a verb 'governs' an object.

morphology and to lexical phonology.[55] On the other hand, it is a positive argument for a cyclic and word-based approach to English stress assignment. What is crucial is the kind of juncture that is found between a base and a suffix; the default case is open juncture, since English adheres to a word-based morphology.[56] Such a juncture does not cause restructuring of the metrical grid. However, open juncture does just that, while preserving earlier word main stress, as Halle and Vergnaud have elucidated.

In this short study of a few morphological processes in English, we have focused on open juncture operations. In the case of words built with close juncture, corresponding to stratum 1, or class I, formations, the case must be built with considerable care, and we will not look much further into the details in this book. A certain amount of the discussion (e.g. Kiparsky 1982a: 35–45) might lead one to believe that accepting a cyclic account of these words necessarily meant accepting accounts of words like *hypocrisy*, in which the first syllable is underlying long, and later shortened by rule, or *presidency*, which is formed by the suffixation of a *y* on stratum 1.

The fact is that the phonological effects of close juncture suffixes are quite varied, and are difficult to phonologize. Nonetheless, lexical phonology's core idea does make a contribution to our understanding here, for there is a strong generalization lurking behind these analyses: the vowel length and stress modifications that are occasioned on the final syllable of a word by the suffixation of class I suffixes are changes that simplify the word, in the sense of making it look more like a mono-morphemic word. Lexical phonology's premise – that the lexical phono-logical rules are one and the same with the set of rules defining natural underlying forms – states this direction of change correctly. The changes induced with suffixation are strong tendencies; a vowel in English tends to be short when followed by an unstressed vowel in non-final position, and we call the tendency in this direction 'trisyllabic shortening' (rule (33) above). When stems shift in this direction under affixation, we see this rule applying in a structure-changing fashion, though it may have exceptions, both scattered (such as *obesity*) and systematic (such as *exploitative*, since the diphthong *oy* will never shorten: it has no shortened form).[57] This is an important result which any version of a lexical phonology must maintain in its theoretical core; and, along with lexical phonology's contribution to our understanding of the importance of underspecification in the deeper part of the phonology, it forms the basis of a major contribution to phonological theory.

6
Further Issues

6.1 INTRODUCTION

In this final chapter, we shall discuss briefly several remaining areas of current interest. First, we shall consider the relation of feature analysis to autosegmental structure, and look at recent proposals for feature trees in phonology. Second, we shall briefly consider the nature of some vowel systems and the treatment of vowel harmony within an autosegmental framework. Third, we shall examine the Obligatory Contour Principle and the Morpheme Tier Hypothesis, two proposals governing the organization of feature specifications on autosegmental tiers. Finally, we shall consider some proposals concerning the nature of phonological rule application and their relation to phonotactic conditions.

6.2 FEATURES

6.2.1 *Introduction*

What are features? The term has been used to cover a number of related notions, and closely related terms (such as *components*) have been used in similar ways. The term *feature* covers two notions which are logically distinct, but which have considerable overlap in actual practice.

First, 'feature' refers to a notion that organizes a *classificatory* scheme; it provides a way of establishing what the 'natural classes' in phonological statements will be. This use has been most clearly described in, e.g., Halle (1962). The idea is by now a familiar one: statements regarding distribution and phonological processes typically involve not a single segment, but larger and smaller groups of segments, which we call *natural classes*. The sense in which these classes are 'natural' is that they recur across the generalizations of a single language, and across the various human languages of the world. Features are used to define and, to some degree, predict what possible natural classes are. Each feature F defines two sets of segments, those that are +F and those that are −F, and the claim of classical generative phonology has been that the natural classes of human languages are defined by the various intersections of these sets.[1] For example, the feature [voice] defines the set of segments that are [+voice] and the set of segments that are [−voice], and the feature [sonorant] similarly defines two sets, those that are [+sonorant] and those that are [−sonorant]. The intersection of two or more of these, such as the set of segments that are [−sonorant, −voice], is a natural class, and such sets can be found undergoing phonological rules as a group. This conception of features is often called *classificatory*.

Second, features may be viewed as a way of specifying the several and simultaneous characteristics that comprise what is, from the point of view of the flow of time, a single articulatory or acoustic event. This latter conception of features (or 'components') is most clearly developed in the post-Bloomfieldian phonology[2] of the 1940s and 1950s, especially in work of Harris (1944), Hockett (1947, 1955) and Bloch (1948), and it has recently re-emerged in discussions of autosegmental phonology (Sagey 1986, Halle 1988, *inter alia*), as well as in Anderson (1974) in a slightly different context. We will refer to this as the *componential* notion of the feature.

By and large, the post-Bloomfieldian tradition was steeped in positivism, the view that scientific discourse and practice has as its goal the classification and organization of particular experiences (rather than, for example, methodically speculating about the internal workings of a physical or biological device which we will never actually be able to peer into). Scientific knowledge, on one version of this empiricist view, is pyramidal in shape, and rests on a broad base of observations and experiences accessible to all interested scientists; in this case, those observations and experiences are particular linguistic utterances in space and time. The true foundations of an empiricist phonology, then, will be the principles that govern how descriptions of linguistic utterances are consistently classified and described, and one view of features fits naturally into this perspective.

The process of classifying and encoding particular linguistic utterances was traditionally viewed as a problem of making 'vertical cuts', and sometimes 'horizontal cuts' as well − slicing the continuously divisible flow of time into chunks, which could be viewed as more or less homogeneous throughout. As a number of linguists observed, if we record the linguistic act in question from the point of view of the articulatory apparatus, then it makes considerable sense − both common sense and linguistic sense − to focus separately on individual aspects of the speech event, to make horizontal cuts for each such aspect. Thus the sequence of actions in time for each subact might be viewed as forming a stream in time, and this stream would be sliced vertically into segments. If it should turn out that there was a reasonably simple relationship between the slicing, or segmentation, for each articulator whereby the cuts would more or less line up appropriately in time, like the playing of a well trained orchestra, then we could think of the chunks of the smaller-scale actions as the features, or components, of the complete unit, the total action of the articulatory apparatus. In (1), I have reproduced Hockett's (1955: 134) tiered account of a Nootka utterance, in a passage immediately followed by the quotation that appears in the Introduction to the present volume.

(1)   q' a· q' a n a ƛ' a ʔ i· ḥ

	q'	a·	q'	a	n	a	ƛ'	a	ʔ	i·	ḥ
Position	bd		bd		ap		lt				
Spirant/glottal	gl		gl				gl		gl		
Spirantal release	−		−				+				+
Nasal					+						
Pharyngeal constriction									+	(+)	+
Height		lo		lo		lo		lo		hi	
Round/front										fr	
Shortness		−									−

(bd = back dorsal; ap = apical; lt = lateral)

Hockett observed, as well, that the horizontal slicing induced in (1) is not the only one possible; it is imposed not by the data, but by our analytical process and choice. The features that arise in this fashion roughly correspond to the features familiar in most of classical generative phonology, though the point-of-articulation feature in (1) is not binary. However, another account is possible, in which each row corresponds to a separate articulator. Such an arrangement was avoided (for better or worse) in the representation in (1) because in Nootka, as Hockett observes, oral articulators function almost exclusively one at a time. An alternative tiered account includes a tier for each of the following: the lower lip; the apex of the tongue; the blade of the tongue; the tongue as a whole; the front part of the dorsum; the back part of the dorsum; the velic; the pharynx; and the glottis. Hockett then arrives at the account given in (2) of the same Nootka word as in (1), where *k* stands for 'closure', *kl* for what we might call 'lateral closure', *c* for 'constriction', *o* for 'open', and *v* for 'voicing'.

This componential notion of the feature takes its inspiration from an exploration of articulatory phonetics, and not from acoustic phonetics, which provides no such natural way of slicing spectrograms horizontally.

(2)

	q' a·	q'	a	n	a	λ'	a	ʔ	i·	ḥ
Lips										
Tongue	a·		a		a		a		i·	
Tip				k						
Blade							kl			
Dorsum/front										
Dorsum/back		k		k						
Velic						o				
Pharynx									c		c
Glottis		k v k v k v k v k v									

But at least two componential views are possible, as suggested in (1) and (2): we may refer to them as the stream-of-information approach, and the independent-articulator approach, respectively. The stream-of-information approach is less oriented to articulatory reality; one dimension (on this view) is point of articulation, a feature whose value (labial, alveolar, velar, etc.) can be realized phonetically by any of quite a few articulators. The independent-articulator approach overtly defines the dimensions of analysis as what each of the independent articulators is actually doing. This may seem a minor point, but in actual cases the difference between the two as regards the choice of phonological features can be significant. A recent proposal (Halle 1988) synthesizing current work steers a middle ground between the two, offering a system (3) of eighteen features, organized into groupings whose significance we will return to in the next section.[3]

Certainly there is a close kindredness of spirit between the componential view of segmentation and autosegmental phonology. From the point of view of the phonologists who have developed and applied it, though, autosegmental phonology does not derive its multi-tiered structure from a decision as to how best to translate a fine-grained description of an articulatory event into one consisting of the discrete units called segments, autosegments, or components.[4] No doubt the structure of the articulators, and the neurological network that governs their behavior, serves as the starting point in the development of the phonological system (it is no coincidence that most features correspond to independent articulators); but the anatomic system proposes, while the phonology disposes.

The statement that the segment is a 'simultaneous actualization of a set of attributes' (Halle 1964) emphasizes the componential view of the segment, but it should be clear that not all characteristics that are features in the *classificatory* sense are *ipso facto* features in the componential sense, and the ways in which the two can differ are several, of

(3)

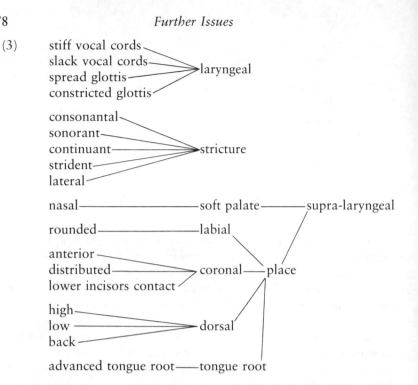

               stiff vocal cords
               slack vocal cords
               spread glottis   laryngeal
               constricted glottis

               consonantal
               sonorant
               continuant   stricture
               strident
               lateral

               nasal————————soft palate————supra-laryngeal

               rounded————————labial

               anterior
               distributed————————coronal——place
               lower incisors contact

               high
               low   dorsal
               back

               advanced tongue root——tongue root

which we shall mention only a few. First, a classificatory feature may have a purely temporal realization; for example, one may establish a feature [±long] (though we have seen empirical reasons not to); such a feature is not componential. Second, along a similar line, the stress of a vowel may be analyzed as a feature (as it was in the *SPE* tradition); but, as was emphasized in early metrical work, there is little or no simple phonetic *manifestation* of such a classificatory feature. Once again, such a feature manifests itself, in part, in a more global set of temporal properties. Third, a consistent phonological difference may have no specific phonetic basis that can be impressed into servitude. The classic example is the feature that separates the final segment of *wife* and *knife* from *cliff* and *dove*; if the last two are voiceless and voiced, respectively (i.e. /f/ and /v/), then what is the final segment of *wife*, a segment that undergoes a rule voicing it when followed by a voiced segment within the same word (cf. the plural forms *wi[vz]*, but *cli[fs]*)? Some feature must distinguish it from both *f* and *v*. In a purely classificatory scheme, a new feature could be set up, and much debate ensued as to just how far removed from the componential sense classificatory features should be allowed to be.[5] Virtually all linguists agree that little divergence between the two should be permitted, but disagreement still arises as to how little is too much.[6]

In the discussion in the literature to date, relatively little work has gone into the differences in feature systems that might arise from the division of phonology into lexical and post-lexical branches; the two components naturally lean toward classificatory and componential views of features, respectively. As we noted in the preceding chapter, much work on lexical phonology has proceeded on the assumption that all features are gradually changed from privative to equipollent[7] during the lexical phonology, and that a number of (equipollent) features are unavailable for each given language during its lexical phonology. Relatively little concern has been expressed in recent work as to whether the differences in the sets and the organization of features may vary in the two components of the grammar.[8]

6.2.2 Two models of feature organization

In this section, we will sketch two models that are currently being considered for the organization of features.[9] Most of the processes that have appeared to be relevant to the subject have been post-lexical, so one may interpret these discussions as being aimed primarily at providing a model of the post-lexical phonology. Discussions in the literature for the most part have not addressed the question as to whether a particular proposal is intended to be interpreted as holding in the lexical or the post-lexical phonology, presumably on the unspoken assumption that, all other things being equal, one would not want to posit two distinct feature structures, one for the lexical phonology and one for the post-lexical. The assumption has also generally been made that there is a fixed set of phonological features available to spoken languages, and whatever hierarchical structure is imposed is done to a fixed, universal format, with no variation across languages. Finally, the assumption has generally been made implicitly that (in a sense that still requires a certain amount of clarification) all features are fully specified, where 'full specification' means that there are no features left unspecified in a language-particular fashion to be interpreted by a phonetic component outside of phonology.[10]

Both models propose that all features are placed on separate tiers, implying that assimilation of any feature is possible. But the theories differ with regard to their treatment of assimilations involving more than one feature. The first model, developed by primarily Mohanan (1983), Clements (1985b), and Sagey (1986), involves crucially the use of so-called *class nodes*. These are segments on a tier of their own which serve to organize the grouping of the individual features. A class node on a *point-of-articulation* (or *place*) *tier* would be associated with the feature-autosegments that determine point of articulation, and it itself might in turn be associated with a higher class node on yet another tier (in (3), this is the 'supra-laryngeal node'), one that gathered together all of the autosegmentalized features of the segment to its left in (3).) *All* of the segment's specifications would be associated to a *root* node, and that segment would, in turn, be associated to the skeletal position; for purposes of simplicity, we have conflated the skeletal and root tier in (4)-(5), but we return to this on pp. 292–4). When the point of articulation of one segment associates leftward, for example, onto a preceding segment, it is the class-node autosegment that reassociates, on this view. All this is exemplified in the sketch of the word *spin* in (4), assuming a set of features as in (3). In (4a), I indicate only the distinctive feature specifications; in a framework that did not use underspecification, full specification of each feature would be required, and the representation would be quite difficult to place on a piece of paper. In (4b), I give an example of what one vertical 'slice' of that representation would look like, for the segment *s*, the first segment in *spin*. Each of the four segments in (4a) would be equally spelled out for each feature, on such a view.

One characteristic of this model that may render it less transparent is that the notion of 'tier' becomes more abstract, and it plays more than one role. Class nodes define specific tiers; the class node for 'place', for example, appears on a tier all to itself. But it has no features specific to it: it serves only as a geometrical way-station for the passage of information

(4)   (a) the word *spin*

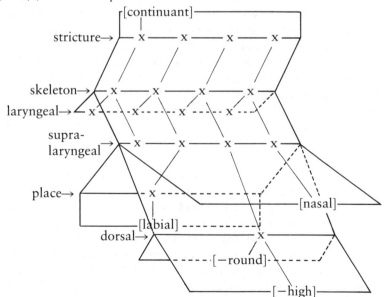

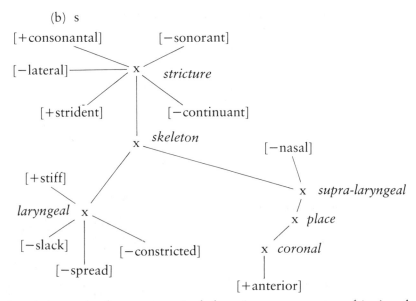

(b) s

up and down the feature tree. And there is an asymmetry of 'up' and 'down' as well, for feature information only flows upward, and never downward. Nothing comparable to this is found in the other autosegmental models that we have studied so far.

Looking at a slightly more specific example, we might write an assimilation by a nasal of the point of articulation of a following consonant as in (5).

The prime alternative to the class-node model is one that retains the *spiral-notebook* (or *rollodex*) model of features proposed in the mid-1970s by Morris Halle, which provides each feature with a separate autosegmental tier, associating directly to the skeletal tier, as in (6), where I have simplified matters slightly by assuming that multiple features may appear on the uppermost point-of-articulation (P of A) tier; the example chosen is somewhere more specified that (4a) and less than (4b), to illustrate most clearly its geometric properties. (6a) presents only some of the features overtly, and (6b) shows a side view of the same structure, showing how all the features associate directly with the skeletal tier.

Before going further into these models, let us look at a few simple examples that illustrate the ways in which familiar features act autosegmentally, and can be treated autosegmentally.

6.2.3 KiRundi

In this section we will review evidence that consonants are composed of

(5)   Assimilation of a nasal's point of articulation

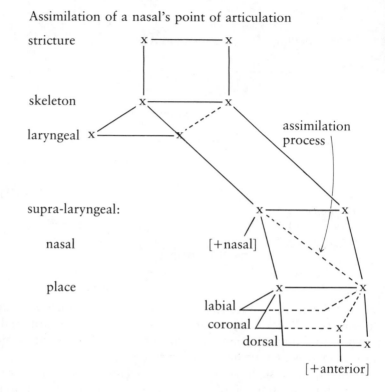

separate subsections corresponding to material on separate autosegmental tiers, of which the most striking is point of articulation, a notion that
we have encountered quite a few times in the discussions of Spanish,
Catalan, Selayarese, English, and several other languages. Most of the
phenomena that we observe in this section concern rules of assimilation,
and it is natural to hypothesize that all rules of assimilation must be
treated autosegmentally — that is, that all rules of assimilation must be
analyzed as the spreading of an autosegment over a larger domain.[11]

As already noted (chapter 1), KiRundi is a Bantu language, and as in
all Bantu languages, a nasal must be homorganic with a following voiced
consonant, as illustrated in (7a). Underlyingly, there is a contrast among
the nasals between three of the four points of articulation, as can be seen
in the nasals in onset position in (7b); there is no underlying velar nasal.
In this respect it is much like the situation in Catalan that we considered
in chapter 5.

The contrast among the nasals is lost, however, before a voiced
consonant; there we find homorganic sequences as in (7a) only. On the
surface, though, the sequence of nasal+voiceless consonant presents a
different pattern. Here, we find all four surface nasals (*m, n, ñ, ŋ*)

(6)   (a) Spiral-notebook model

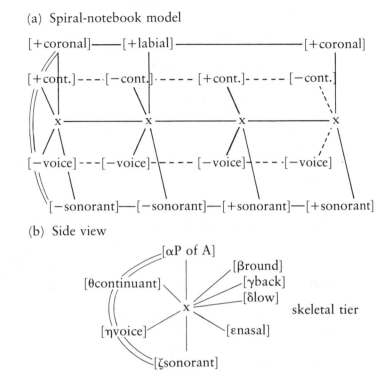

(b) Side view

contrasting, but we do not find the nasal followed by a voiceless stop; where we might expect that, we find instead an *h*. It is quite obvious what is happening here, doubly so in the light of alternations as in (8). Clearly, in traditional segmental terms this would be described in two steps. A nasal is always homorganic to a following consonant, and a voiceless consonant following a nasal loses its oral point of articulation, leaving only its aspirate character behind, what we transcribe as an *h* in syllable onset position.

If we establish a separate autosegmental tier for point of articulation,

(7)   Kirundi

(a) Nasals homorganic to following voiced consonant
ku-m-bona   'to see me'
i-n-dobo   'bucket'
umu-gaŋga   'doctor'

(b) ku-nanira   'to be hard for'
ku-mera   'to grow'
ku-ñwa   'to drink'

(8)   (a) ku-temera   'to cut for someone'
            ku-n-hemera   'to cut for me'
        (b) gu-korera   'to work for'
            ku-ŋ-horera   'to work for me'

then we can represent the phonetic form of a nasal +homorganic voiced consonant as in (9), and a nasal+homorganic voiceless consonant as in (10). We may posit a rule that assigns a laryngeal point-of-articulation to any consonant that is bereft of a point of articulation specification, changing (10(ii)) to (iii) (i.e., 'laryngeal' becomes the post-lexical default specification for point of articulation); we return to this assumption below.

(9) Nasal+voiced consonant: surface

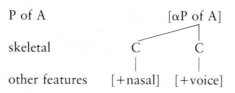

(10) Nasal+*h*: surface

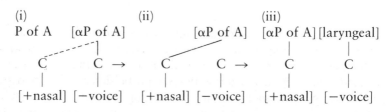

It follows, then, that if the surface sequence of nasal+*h* derives from a deeper representation in which the nasal is followed by a voiceless consonant with a real point of articulation, then we must have two rules at work here. One spreads, or assimilates, the point-of-articulation autosegment from the obstruent leftward to the nasal; the second dissociates the point-of-articulation autosegment from the voiceless consonant, so that it becomes, so to speak, an *h*.

How do we formulate the rule that assimilates the point of articulation of the nasal to that of the following consonant? This question is easy to answer, in light of our autosegmental formalism: it is as in (11) (a rule that we have already seen; cf. chapter 5, rule (8), for Catalan). The rule that deletes the point of articulation of the voiceless consonant is given in (12).

(11)   [+nasal]

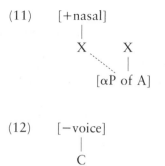

(12)   [−voice]
        |
        C
        |
        ([αP of A])→ø

We have seen so far, then, two of the phonological characteristics of autosegments in the behavior of point of articulation: (i) the spreading of the autosegment – a many-to-one association – and (ii) the deletion of the autosegment, with the material to which it is associated staying behind.

The analysis suggested for KiRundi in the preceding section holds equally with few changes for Spanish. Here too we find a lack of contrast in the point of articulation of nasals before consonants, and in general a pattern of homorganicity in that position.[12] This holds both within words and across word boundaries; see (13). Consonants in the onset do not lose their point of articulation in Spanish like the voiceless consonants in KiRundi, but Spanish does show one further development. In many Caribbean dialects, nasals show no contrast in point of articulation when in coda position, but manifest this by having a consistent velar articulation instead of being homorganic to a following consonant. In still others, as Harris (1969: 15–16) observes, a contour nasal is created. Harris notes that 'many Cubans pronounce *enfermo* as [eɱ̍fermo], where the first nasal, presumably a systematic phoneme *n*, is realized with no alveolar contact at all, but rather with a labio-dental articulation superimposed on a dorso-velar articulation.'

(13)   Indefinite article *un* preceding consonants in Spanish (after Harris 1969)

        u[m] beso   'a kiss'
        u[ɱ] foco   'a focus'
        u[n] dedo   'a finger'
        u[ŋ] gato   'a cat'

Spanish does not line up with KiRundi, however, in affecting a voiceless consonant in the onset of its syllable, whether a nasal precedes or not. However, many Western Hemisphere dialects, as well as a few continental ones, do possess a process by which an *s* in coda position loses its oral gesture, and is typically identified as a phonetic *h*; this process is referred to as *aspiration* in the literature. A prevocalic *s* (i.e. an onset *s*) is not aspirated; thus the *s* in *eso* 'that' is not aspirated, but the *s* in *frasco* 'bottle' is aspirated.

The KiRundi and Spanish examples, along with early work in this area by Thráinsson (1978) on Icelandic, point to a consistent pattern according to which consonants weaken to *h*, and autosegmental representations have attempted to integrate the traditional notion according to which this weakening is the loss of any gesture-specification in the articulatory tract above the larynx. There is a sense, then, that we should like to capture in which the laryngeal *h* is truly unspecified for its oral point of articulation, though in a somewhat different sense from the way the term 'unspecified' has been used up to now. In the lexical phonology, all underspecified consonants that we have seen have been realized as alveolar consonants; now, in the post-lexical phonology, we find that, when a segment loses its point-of-articulation specification, it is realized as a glottal segment. Why this difference? One simple answer would be that there is a rule P that specifies obstruents as alveolar if unspecified for point of articulation. Any rule deleting a point-of-articulation specification *after* rule P has its chance to apply will create an *h*; any before, an alveolar. If rule P is a post-lexical rule, this will have the desired results. This conception is certainly too simplistic to serve as an ultimate solution to the observed difference in the two types of 'unspecification', but it serves as an adequate way to summarize our observations.

6.2.4   Toba Batak

Hayes (1986b) offers an account of several assimilation and weakening processes in Toba Batak that is rich in consequences for the theory of placement of features on separate tiers, and for underspecification theory, as well as for the theory of licensing and the Conjunctivity Condition (referred to as the 'Linking Constraint' in Hayes (1986a)).

Syllables in Toba Batak are maximally of the form CVC, with a restricted range of consonants appearing in the coda. Of the consonants in the phonemic inventory (see (14)), only the three nasals, *l*, *r*, and the four non-low voiceless obstruents appear in the coda before various optional sandhi rules apply. The onset may be host to any of the fourteen consonants; cf. (14). If we attempt to analyze these segments into their component features, we may arrive at the system in (15), should we follow Hayes, who takes all features to be equipollent at this post-lexical level.

(14)

	Bilabial	Alveolar	Palato-alveolar	Velar	Glottal
	p	t		k	
	b	d		g	
			j		
		s			(h)
	m	n		ŋ	
		r			
		l			

(15)

	p	t	k	b	d	g	j	s	h	m	n	ŋ	r	l	ʔ
Anterior	+	+	−	+	+	−	−	+	−	+	+	−	+	+	−
Coronal	−	+	−	−	+	−	+	+	−	−	+	−	+	+	−
Continuant	−	−	−	−	−	−	−	+	+	−	−	−	−	−	−
Strident	−	−	−	−	−	−	−	+	−	−	−	−	−	−	−
Sonorant	−	−	−	−	−	−	−	−	−	+	+	+	+	+	−
Nasal	−	−	−	−	−	−	−	−	−	+	+	+	−	−	−
Voice	−	−	−	+	+	+	+	−	−	+	+	+	+	+	−
High	−	−	+	−	−	+	+	+	−	−	−	+	−	−	−
Glottis:															
Spread	−	−	−	−	−	−	−	−	+	−	−	−	−	−	−
Constricted	−	−	−	−	−	−	−	−	−	−	−	−	−	−	+

Hayes's chart (16) specifies the possible changes that may occur to sequences of consonants appearing across syllable boundary, whether within the same word or across word boundary. To determine the surface form of a C_1C_2 sequence, we find the first consonant (the one in the coda position) by reading down the side, and the second by reading across.[13] There are four major processes at work here, and Hayes

(16)

		C_2													
		p	t	k	h	s	b	d	j	g	m	n	ŋ	r	l
C_1	p	ʔp	ʔt	ʔk	pp	ʔs	ʔb	ʔd	ʔj	ʔg	ʔm	ʔn	ʔŋ	ʔr	ʔl
	t	ʔp	ʔt	ʔk	tt	ʔs	ʔb	ʔd	ʔj	ʔg	ʔm	ʔn	ʔŋ	ʔr	ʔl
	k	ʔp	ʔt	ʔk	kk	ʔs	ʔb	ʔd	ʔj	ʔg	ʔm	ʔn	ʔŋ	ʔr	ʔl
	s	sp	st	sk	ss	ss	sb	sd	sj	sg	sm	sn	sŋ	sr	sl
	m	pp	pt	pk	pp	ps	bb	md	mj	mg	mm	mn	mŋ	mr	ml
	n	pp	tt	kk	kk	ss	bb	dd	jj	gg	mm	nn	ŋŋ	rr	ll
	ŋ	kp	kt	kk	kk	ks	ŋb	ŋd	ŋj	ŋg	ŋm	ŋn	ŋŋ	ŋr	ŋl
	r	rp	rt	rk	rh	rs	rb	rd	rj	rg	rm	rn	rŋ	rr	ll
	l	lp	lt	lk	lh	ls	lb	ld	lj	lg	lm	ln	lŋ	lr	ll

formulates them as shown in (17)–(20). *n*-assimilation, written with only two tiers (a skeletal tier, and a tier for all other features), instructs us that a segment following an *n* will be associated to the *n*'s skeletal position. In rules (18)–(20), Hayes assumes that the features are split onto three tiers:

(17)   *n*-assimilation

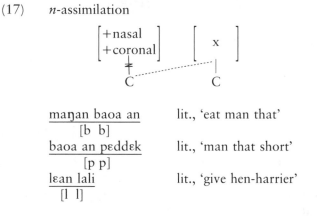

maŋan baoa an   lit., 'eat man that'
  [b b]

baoa an pɛddɛk   lit., 'man that short'
  [p p]

lɛan lali   lit., 'give hen-harrier'
  [l l]

a skeletal tier, a *central* tier for the point-of-articulation features and manner features (continuant, sonorant, etc.), and a *peripheral* tier, for the nasal and laryngeal features. Denasalization (18) shifts a nasal to its corresponding voiceless stop when a voiceless consonant follows. *h*-assimilation (19) spreads a voiceless obstruent from a coda position to a following onset position when the onset is filled only by an *h*. In the second example in (19), the word-final *m* is first denasalized by (18) before (19) applies. Finally, a rule of *glottal formation* (20) applies, which converts all obstruent stops in coda position to glottal stops.

Hayes observes that an autosegmental account of the assimilation processes in (17), (18), and (19) predicts that structures that have undergone such assimilations will no longer be eligible for (20), glottal weakening, on the basis, he suggests, of the Conjunctivity Condition. This prediction is correct. *tt* created from *th*, for example, does not then undergo glottal formation (and thereby produce ʔ*t*). If we analyzed the data from a purely segmental and linear point of view, this result would require some special ordering statement; viewed as autosegmental re-structuring, the result is expected.[14] Similarly, if denasalization involves the spreading of [−voice] on the peripheral tier, then a linked structure is created, and glottal formation will not apply to any *kp* structure, for example, *if* it has been derived from an underlying *ŋp* structure, though of course the rule does apply to a non-derived *kp* structure. Finally, *n*-assimilation will create geminates such as *tt* derived from a deeper *nt*; these geminates are not subject to glottal formation, and no surface ʔ*t* results from the structure, again as expected.[15]

(18)   Denasalization

[+nasal]   [−voice]   peripheral tier

$$C \qquad C$$

nan̠inum tuak	lit., 'drink palm wine'
[p t]	
manaŋ pulpen	lit., 'or pen'
[k p]	

m t > p t

[+nasal]   [−voice]

$$C \qquad\qquad C$$

$$\begin{bmatrix} -\text{coronal} \\ +\text{anterior} \\ -\text{continuant} \end{bmatrix} \qquad \begin{bmatrix} +\text{coronal} \\ +\text{anterior} \end{bmatrix}$$

6.2.5 Feature hierarchies and class tiers

The conclusion that the point of articulation of a consonant acts as a unit in many languages – in particular, as an autosegment on a separate tier – raises as many questions as it answers. For example, (i) do we interpret 'point of articulation' now as a single feature, on a single autosegmental tier? Or as more than one feature, but still on a single tier? (ii) If we interpret it as several features, each on their own tiers, how do we express the fact that these feature specifications act so consistently as a single unit, a bundle assimilating as a group? (iii) If we take that analytic route, we will then also ask: do other subsets of features have such a property?

In this section we will look at the feature-hierarchy approach of the sort sketched in (3), or the earlier proposal of Clements (1985b) in (21), an approach that establishes a fixed set of features and an organization of them on separate tiers. This organization, in turn, defines which sets of features may assimilate together as a single group, with point of articulation being the prototypical example of a class node. These are well presented in diagram (22), from Clements (1985b). This feature-hierarchy model allows for rules that assimilate individual features, or a set of features found under specific class nodes, or all features of a given

(19)   *h*-assimilation

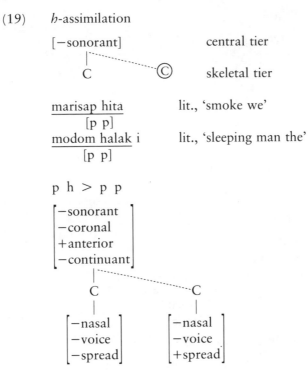

segment, i.e. those found under the root node. By limiting assimilation rules to only adding a single association line, such constraints are naturally built into the model, and certain strong predictions are made regarding what is a possible rule.

Of course, much depends on our assumptions regarding the appropriate set of features. The familiar features [anterior] and [coronal] would be odd candidates for this model, since they assimilate only in special sorts of ways. The feature [coronal] never spreads onto non-coronal segments, for example; there is no language, to my knowledge, that assimilates labials to alveolars, and velars to alveopalatals; yet this is what would happen if there were a rule assimilating just the feature [coronal] (i.e. leaving the feature [anterior] unchanged). Similarly, no rule of assimilation exists to my knowledge assimilating just the feature [anterior], and leaving [coronal] untouched. If such a rule did exist, it would change labials to velars (and vice versa), and alveolars to alveo-palatals (and vice versa). Only the latter is found – rules changing *s* into *š*, or the reverse, for example – and such rules are found in abundance.[16] That is, the feature [anterior], distinguishing two types of coronal segments, assimilates or spreads *among* [+coronal] segments, but not among [−coronal]

(20)   Glottal formation

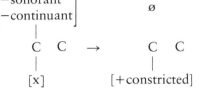

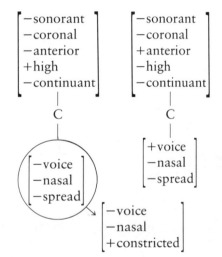

halak Batak	lit., 'person Batak'
[ʔ b]	
halak Korɛa	lit., 'person Korea'
[ʔ k]	

k b > ʔ b

segments. Some way of indicating this dependence is necessary, and a feature representation as in (21) does not quite do that. More generally, any serious argument for setting up two features, F and G, under a class node should include an argument that both F and G act as individual features, which is to say, that each feature can participate in a natural assimilation process on its own. This is not always possible to do.

Other questions about the independence of the features proposed under a given class node can arise in other ways. Clements (1985b) puts forward an argument for the structure offered in (21) illustrating the autosegmental coherence of the laryngeal features responsible for aspiration and glottalization. He provides clear evidence of the stability (and

(21)   Feature nodes   Class nodes

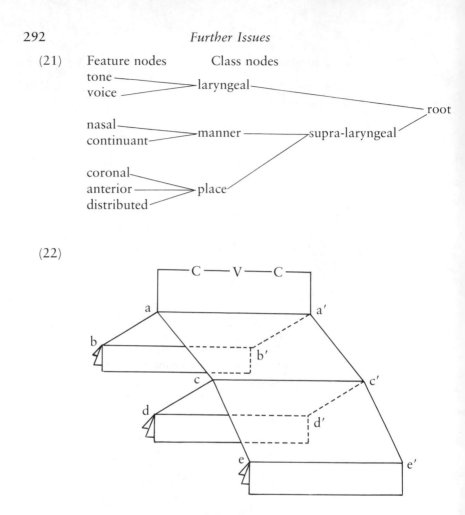

aa′ = root tier, bb′ = laryngeal tier, cc′ = supralaryngeal tier,
dd′ = manner tier, ee′ = place tier

thus the autosegmental status) of the laryngeal features of [spread glottis]
and [constricted glottis], which characterize voiceless sonorants and *h*,
and glottalized sonorants, respectively, in Klamath. Segmentally viewed,
the alternations given in (23) are found. This set of alternations reduces
to two closely related processes involving the reassociation of the oral
gesture that comprises the three versions of *l* (the plain, the glottalized
l' and the voiceless l̥). Any sequence of anterior, coronal sonorant, when
followed by an /l/, will undergo the rule in (24).

Clements further assumes, for purposes of simplicity, that the l which
is neither glottalized nor voiceless is not associated to any segment on the

(23)   nl → ll
        nl̥ → lh
        nl̥' → l?
        ll → lh
        ll̥' → l?

(24)   Skeletal tier

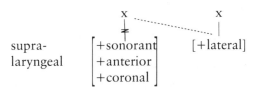

laryngeal tier, in accord with underspecification theory.[17] Under this assumption, the *l* geminated by rule (24) will be simplified by rule (25) in just the right cases. However, the argument for the existence of the laryngeal class node here rests heavily on the assumption that the features

(25)   Degemination
        laryngeal   x
                                         |
        skeleton   x   x
                                  ╱   ╪
        supra-laryngeal   [+lateral]

for aspiration and for glottalization are distinct, and that there is not a single laryngeal feature, which we might call [glottalic width], which takes on the feature [−glottalic width] to form glottalized consonants, [+glottalic width] to form voiceless sonorants, and no marking for 'normal' sonorants. If we have such a binary feature, which may take on a third unmarked value, then the argument for a laryngeal class node is considerably weakened. Similarly, the argument for a laryngeal class node (in Klamath or elsewhere) would be strengthened if it were shown that the feature(s) governing glottalization and voicing formed a true natural class in an autosegmental rule along with tonal features, but such arguments have not been forthcoming.

In the example from Klamath above, I simplified matters by not explicitly taking into account the presence of the root-node tier, referring in the representations here to associations directly to the skeletal tier. In this hierarchical account, however, it is crucial that the skeletal positions associate directly to a root-node tier, not to other, lower, class nodes, because we would not be able to account for the very simple and natural cases of total assimilation with the addition of a single association line, an important goal to the project defined in Clements (1985b). The assimilation of *nl* to *ll*, for example, would more properly be represented in this framework as in (26).

(26)   *nl* to *ll* with root tier

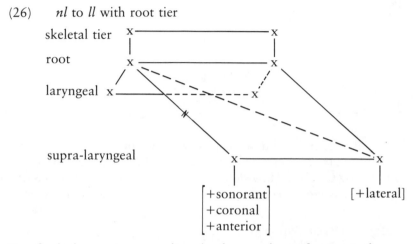

$$\begin{bmatrix} +\text{sonorant} \\ +\text{coronal} \\ +\text{anterior} \end{bmatrix} \qquad [+\text{lateral}]$$

One final observation regarding the degree of specification in feature hierarchies. Much depends upon one's assumptions regarding the degree of featural specification that is required and appropriate at various levels of phonological representation. The geometrical picture offered in (26) assumes more or less full specification of all features at the level of representation we are concerned with, and much work has implicitly or explicitly assumed that all features are represented and specified at a phonetic level. Many of the traditional arguments in classical generative phonology for highly specified phonetic representations go by the boards within the more modern context of autosegmental phonology. Consider the following typical example.

Many languages display the pattern that we have already observed for English, Catalan, and Spanish: there are both bilabial and labio-dental consonants, but there is no contrast as such between these two points of articulation, since the continuants are labio-dental and the stops are bilabials. However, in Spanish and Catalan, a nasal that assimilates to a following consonant in point of articulation will agree with that consonant down to this non-contrastive difference, and a nasal preceding a bilabial will be bilabial, just as a nasal in front of a labio-dental will be labio-dental. If we write this assimilation process as a segmental rule, then there will have to be a feature available in the grammar of Spanish or Catalan whose value can be 'transmitted' to the preceding nasal. If, however, the process of nasal assimilation is one that spreads the consonant's point-of-articulation autosegment leftward onto the nasal, then it does *not* follow that there must be a feature to distinguish the labio-dental position from the bilabial. Nonsegmental rules of phonetics may clarify the nature of the gestures available in the language, and define the articulators available for stop and fricative production – this is determined on the basis of the contrastive points of articulation, and the manner of articulation. But once the labial position is determined (labio-dental vs. bilabial), that determination is spread over both the nasal and the following consonant.

There is thus a close connection between the degree of over- or underspecification in a phonological representation, on the one hand, and the extent to which a hierarchical organization of features is motivated on the other. The more features there are, and the more specified they are, the more we stand in need of an explicit organization of them in our phonological representation.

6.2.6 *Feature organization*

As noted above, an alternative geometrical model for features is that given in (6), called variously the 'spiral-notebook model', the 'rollodex model', and the 'bottlebrush model'.[18] On this view, there is something much closer to the traditional segment as a 'bundle of features', rather than as a hierarchically organized structure of features. Instead of viewing features-with-values as the elements of an unordered set, as in the classical generative model, we take features to be autosegments, each on their own separate tier, forming charts with the skeletal tier in each case. Viewed end-on, we arrive at a picture as in (27), in a system with eight features, with the skeletal tier in the center, and all other tiers facing it.

As Hayes (1988) notes, features that naturally assimilate as a unit may be identified as forming a constituent in a fashion consistent with the

(27)

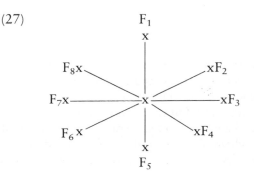

geometry of (27) by establishing a constituent structure on the tiers, rather than by establishing additional class-node tiers to do the structuring, as in the hierarchical model discussed in the previous section. For example, if features F_1 and F_2 in (27) are the features [low] and [round] which define the vowel system of a language, and if these features typically assimilate together in the language, we would naturally like to develop a way of expressing this connection between the features, and a way of expressing the rule of assimilation; cf. (28).

(28)

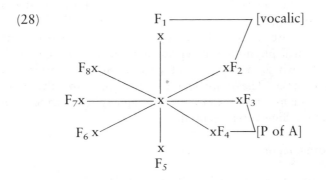

One way to express such a rule would be as follows. We recognize that there is some property – a feature, in effect, though not an autosegment – which is necessary to indicate the class of tiers to which the nucleus of a syllable associates. This property is shared by the tiers that define vowel quality; let us call this *vocalic*; this term therefore specifies the set of tiers with autosegments that freely associate to syllable nuclei (F_1 and F_2, in the example at hand). We may then write an assimilation rule as in (29), where the tier(s) contributing the autosegment(s) that spread is defined indirectly; (29) thus abbreviates two spreading rules, one for the tier F_1 and the other for tier F_2.

(29)   Assimilation rule
          'vocalic'   x
                          |
          skeleton   x   x

In effect, we have transferred the generalizations across features from the geometry of tiers to properties of tiers, and certain other possibilities can be envisaged. The significance of this point is not so much in the particular proposal sketched in (29), but rather in the clarification of the kind of alternative that may be offered to the hierarchical feature model.

An alternative may be sought in order to avoid the following 'diphthongization paradox', observed by Steriade. Perhaps the most important single claim that distinguishes the feature-hierarchy model and the rollodex model is the constraint offered by the feature-hierarchy model that all rules of assimilation can be expressed by the addition of a single association line. If some common assimilations require more than one association line, then there is no particular need to organize features into class nodes; the class nodes serve the purpose of making wholesale association of separate features possible at a low geometrical cost (i.e. by adding only one association line). This constraint leads directly to the postulation of a root tier, distinct from the skeletal tier; for otherwise it would not be possible to express total assimilation with the addition of a single association line and still maintain that each feature is on a separate tier. (Total assimilation is the case where a segment completely assimilates, in every feature, to a neighboring segment, as with *n*-assimilation in Toba Batak in (17).) Such a total assimilation is illustrated in a hierarchical scheme as in (30). Thus, total assimilations will always create a structure in which one root-tier position is associated to two skeletal-tier positions.

(30)   Geminates

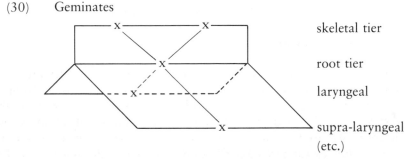

However, there are a number of cases in which structures as in (30) occur (either underlyingly or as the result of a rule) in which *one* of the halves of structure undergoes a change, the creation of a diphthong from a long vowel being a typical example. Other cases include one discussed by Clements (1985b), originally analyzed by Thráinsson (1978), whereby Icelandic long aspirated tense stops (pp^h, tt^h, kk^h) become pre-aspirated stops (hp, ht, hk). If such geminates are represented with a single root node, as in (31a), this process cannot be represented; only if the geminate is represented as in (31b) can the process be naturally represented, as illustrated in (31c).

In short, if the unity and identity of a geminate is to be represented as the double association of a single node – in this case, the root node – then we have no natural way to specify any change that could take place internal to one half or the other of that long segment. This suggests that, indeed, a representation such as (31b) is correct for Icelandic (as

Clements does propose), from which we may safely infer that not all geminates are formed as in (30) with a single root node. But now the root node is doing no work for us − nothing the skeletal tier itself could not do. This, in turn, weakens to a considerable degree the prima facie attractiveness of the feature-hierarchy-cum-root-tier model.

In sum, current work is actively pursuing a number of alternative approaches to the issue of feature geometry. Of all the issues that heavily influence the ultimate decision in this matter, without a doubt the most important remains the question of the degree of specification appropriate for post-lexical phonology. Intimately tied up with this is the question of the universality of features, and the extent to which features may be only binary. To the extent that features may be multivalent, taking on several values (as, for example, Hockett's feature of 'position' (i.e. point of articulation) in (1)), several arguments for hierarchical structure become significantly less compelling. Much work remains to be done in this area.

6.3   VOWEL SYSTEMS AND VOWEL HARMONY

6.3.1   *Vowel systems*

We turn now to briefly consider appropriate autosegmental representation of vowel systems.[19] Much of the interest of this area comes from its interaction with treatments of vowel harmony, which we turn to in the next section. The issue of redundancy and underspecification is also closely related to the choice of vowel features. In recent years, most of the work within lexical phonology[20] has been based on the assumption that the core features of vowel space are those given in (32), where the feature specification of the canonical five vowel system is presented.

There is a thoroughgoing redundancy in such a system that permeates all representations and rules: a vowel cannot be specified as both [+low] and [+high], and, as we have observed many times, redundancy in features is an aspect of the representation that underspecification theory aims to eliminate. It has often been observed, in perhaps too offhand a way, that the restriction against [+high, +low] segments, while incorporated into phonology, has its origins in a simple phonetic fact: the tongue cannot be both high and low at the same time, just as any physical object cannot be in two places at the same time.

A more appropriate response to the matter might just as well be to rethink the matter of these features, for the dimensions that we use to analyze vowel space phonologically are not simply present in the data, passively open to inspection: to the contrary, the traditional observation

(31)

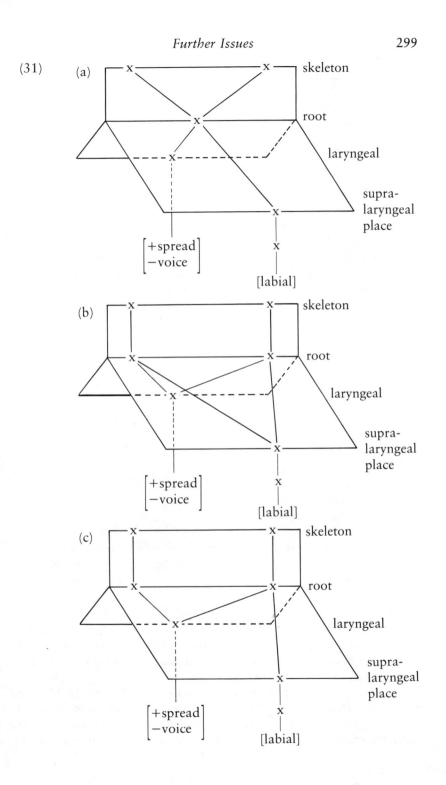

(32)

	a	e	i	o	u
Back	+	−	−	+	+
Round	−	−	−	+	+
High	−	−	+	−	+
Low	+	−	−	−	−

that the lax vowel [ɪ] is lower than the tense vowel [i] but higher than the tense vowel [e] is a phonetic fact that is lost (so to speak) in the translation into phonological terms, a translation whereby the lax [ɪ] is just as *high* as [i], but is marked as [−tense]. Transferring this issue to the five-vowel system in (32), we may ask whether there is *phonological* reason to believe that (33a) is more correct than (33b) — that is, whether *a* is different from the other vowels with respect to a feature of height. Is there reason to believe that *a* is lower than *e* and *o*? If we take (33b) to be correct, our feature specifications would minimally change from (32) to (34).

(33)　　(a)　i　u
　　　　　　　e　o
　　　　　　　　a

　　　　(b)　i　u
　　　　　　　e　ao

(34)

	a	e	i	o	u
Back	+	−	−	+	+
Round	−	−	−	+	+
High	−	−	+	−	+

We have, so to speak, 'phonologized out' a large redundancy in the feature values given in (32). But further reduction is conceivable, with interesting and suggestive linguistic consequences. The shift from four distinctive features in (32) to three in (34) makes sense in that three binary features can characterize $2^3 = 8$ distinct segments: why would we need more than that just to characterize five vowels? A further reduction to two features may seem to be impossible if we want to characterize the distinctions among five vowels. But the possibility is worth exploring, in the following way.

Instead of considering the features [back], [round], and [high], let us reverse the values of one of the features and rewrite (34) as in (35), using the label [low] to represent [non-high]. Just as our discussion of the internal composition of consonants from an autosegmental point of view helped us rethink our conception of consonantal features, let us approach the representation of this canonical five-vowel system from an auto-segmental point of view. What would the tiers be, in such a scheme?

(35)

	a	e	i	o	u
Back	+	−	−	+	+
Round	−	−	−	+	+
Low	+	+	−	+	−

Let us consider what the vowel system would look like if we had three separate tiers, one for each of the features in (35). Let us further assume, for the moment, that each feature is represented privatively, so that at the present level of representation only one feature value is overtly repre-sented. A lack of representation indicates the equivalent of the other, non-marked, value for the feature. The features are [+round], [+low], and [−back] (in short, the features of rounding, aperture, and palatality; see Donegan 1978). In such a system, we would expect, given all possible associations, to find an eight-vowel system, as in (36), which would represent the vowel system in (37a), as in Turkish, or, if the case with no associations is left aside (the high, back, unrounded vowel), the seven-vowel system in (37b), as in Khalkha Mongolian. Here I have presented a situation where all features are taken to be privative; that is, they have only one value that functions at this point in the derivation.

That is fine, to be sure, but it does not get us any closer to reaching a natural representation of the five-vowel system that we have been concerned with. What is inadequate about the representation in (36),

(36)

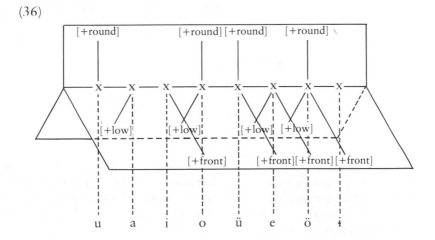

(37)   (a)   i ü   ɨ u
              e ö   a o
        (b)   i ü   u
              e ö   a o

where the features [round] and [front] are on separate tiers, is precisely the freedom the representation gives to those two features. [round] and [front] do *not* combine freely in the canonical five-vowel system: rather, the one is essentially predictable from the other except in the case of the vowel *a*. We propose, then, the representation in (38), which expresses directly an intuition that was only covertly expressed in the traditional chart in (32), with four 'distinctive' features for vowels. The notion expressed in (38) is that *a* does not minimally contrast with *o* with respect to height, nor with *e* with respect to fronting. (38) expresses the idea that the vowel *a* steps out of the system of front/back and round/non-round contrasts that the vowels {i, e, o, u} participate in. This is expressed autosegmentally by using an equipollent feature [round], with front/backness being nondistinctive and fully predictable from rounding, but not requiring that all vocalic positions be associated with one value or the other. Front/backness will be predicted by the general post-lexical rule (39): [back] is not a distinctive feature of the system all.[21] In short, *a* is neither round nor non-round, and thus neither front nor back.

(38)

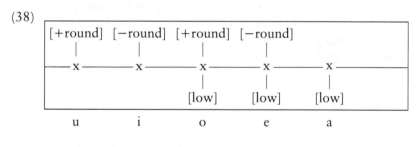

(39)   Default [back]-specification

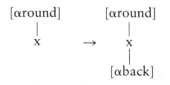

This system for representing the canonical five-vowel system has an immediate advantage over the familiar one in (32). In the present system, there is an immediate account for one of the most basic and widespread facts about the canonical five-vowel system, the fact that the merger of the vowels *i* and *a* forms the vowel *e*, while that of the vowels *u* and *a* is *o*.

This recurring pattern, seen, for example, in the Kirundi example in chapter 5, is perhaps the most common vowel merger pattern found in languages, but our traditional feature account, as in (32), offers no explanation for it. On the present account, it is a matter of merger of skeletal positions, as in (40).

(40)   *a+i* to *e*

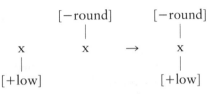

What is surprising about this system, if anything is, is the way autosegmental phonology allows a natural niche for something like a three-way contrast when a binary feature is involved. Within the tonal realm, this very natural distinction can often be seen, as in the case of Sukuma, discussed in chapter 1, where vowels could be associated with a High autosegment, a Low autosegment, or no autosegment. We can see that the same situation arises in the case of other underlyingly equipollent features, such as [round] in the canonical five-vowel system.[22]

On the present treatment, then – which does not rule out the traditional account in (32) *per se*, though it suggests an alternative possiblity – there is a formal naturalness to the process, often observed, of neutralization in unstressed position to the extent that, from a larger five-, seven-, or ten- vowel system, only the three cardinal vowels {i, u, a} may appear in unstressed position. On the account in (32), these vowels do not form a natural class;[23] on the reanalysis in (38), they are the vowels with a single association of vowel quality to a skeletal position.

Furthermore, we can specify a sense in which the equipollent feature [round] and the privative feature [low] may be said to generate three natural vowel systems, and other less natural vowel systems. If we look at the vowels in (38), there is one more that might be considered: the vowel with a skeletal position and no associations. We may call such a vowel – one with no vowel quality associations – the *schwa* of the system. The vowel system that allows any number of associations, from 0 to 2, of these features is the six-vowel system, {u, i, o, e, a, ə}; this range of association we will refer to as (0, 2), and such a six-vowel system is *complete*, in the sense that all combinations are found. The five-vowel system of (38) is a (1, 2) system, allowing either one or two vocalic associations per skeletal position; and the three-vowel (sub-)system consisting of {i, u, a} is the (1, 1) system, with no more and no less than one association per vowel position on the skeleton. The notion of *completeness* for a vowel system is an important one, one which we take to be a strong desideratum of an analysis of a vowel system.[24]

6.3.2   Vowel harmony

Vowel harmony is a term used to describe a restriction on the set of vowels possible within a given phonological domain, typically the word. We may offer the following definition: a vowel harmony system is one in which the vowels of a language are divided into two (or more) (possibly overlapping) subsets, with the condition that all vowels in a given word (or *domain*, more generally) must come from a single such subset. Such a definition does not focus on the character of the restriction, though, and in most cases of vowel harmony the restriction is relatively transparent or natural from a phonological point of view. In such cases, we find that all the vowels in the domain share a particular phonological feature that is distinctive for vowels, such as [back], [tense], or [round]. More to the point, vowel harmony systems are best understood in general as cases where vowel features act strikingly autosegmentally, spreading over a domain that is greater than a single segment. Put slightly differently, a vowel harmony system is what arises when a vocalic feature starts to lose its strict one-to-one association with the skeletal tier, and begins to behave more like tone.

A well-known example of vowel harmony is found in Turkish, where the examples in (41) (from Clements and Sezer 1982, from which I draw heavily here) illustrate the pattern of agreement of vowels in a word. Based on the behavior of vowels in the suffixes, we might arrive at the following statement, the traditional one: all vowels in the word agree with respect to backness, and a high vowel, such as in the genitive suffix, will be round if it follows a round vowel.

Vowel harmony in Turkish consists, we see, of two distinct spreading

(41)   Turkish

Gloss	Nom. sg.	Gen. sg.	Nom. pl.	Gen.pl.
rope	ip	ip-in	ip-ler	ip-ler-in
girl	kɨz	kɨz-ɨn	kɨz-lar	kɨz-lar-ɨn
face	yüz	yüz-ün	yüz-ler	yüz-ler-in
stamp	pul	pul-un	pul-lar	pul-lar-ɨn
hand	el	el-in	el-ler	el-ler-in
stalk	sap	sap-ɨn	sap-lar	sap-lar-ɨn
village	köy	köy-ün	köy-ler	köy-ler-in
end	son	son-un	son-lar	son-lar-ɨn

processes of vocalic features: one involving the feature [back], and the other involving the feature [round]. [round] spreads under more restricted conditions, in that only the high vowels, and not the low vowels, act as 'receptors' to such a spreading feature, and the feature will not 'jump over' non-low vowels to spread the feature [round], as we see from a form like *sonlarin*.

Should this system be represented as in (36), with three privative vowel features? Clements and Sezer suggest instead representing it with three equipollent features ([±back], [±round], and [±high]), as in (42). For consistency's sake, I change their [αhigh] to [−αlow].

(42)

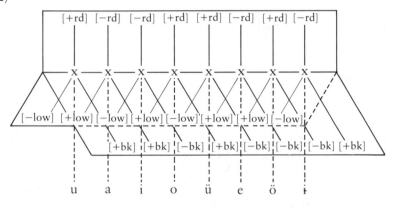

The process of back/front harmony would work as in (43a) (*el-ler*), where the feature [back] spreads to a suffix whose vowel is itself specified only for the feature [low]. Rounding harmony spreads the feature [round] rightward, but only onto an adjacent [−low] segment, as in (43b) (*pul-un*). Rounding harmony could be written in a familiar notation as in (43c) (though Clements and Sezer indicate it somewhat differently).

However, while such generalizations hold for suffixal vowels in general, Clements and Sezer argue that within the lexical stem these generalizations no longer hold true for the modern language. The stem itself is not governed by these harmony principles, we may say, though the affixal material is. But it is not the case that *any* vowel can appear in any position in the stem; the generalization, they suggest, is that in polysyllabic stems, any of the vowels from the set {a, e, i, o, u} may co-occur; in fact, these are the only vowels that can occur underlyingly in the suffixes as well, once we abstract away from the harmony processes.

This suggests that the naturalness of the canonical five-vowel system that we discussed in the previous section is indeed one that arises from its phonological character, not from (or not simply from) its phonetic

(43)　(a)

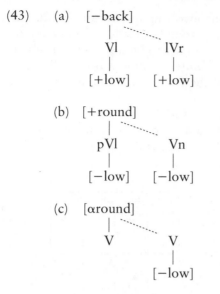

(b)　[+round]
　　　　　|　．．．．．
　　　　pVl　　　Vn
　　　　　|　　　　|
　　　　[−low]　[−low]

(c)　[αround]
　　　　　|　．．．．．
　　　　V　　　　V
　　　　　　　　　|
　　　　　　　　[−low]

properties. Clements and Sezer (1982: 228) argue that there is a morpheme structure condition to the effect that 'the vowels /ü, ö, ɨ/ do not occur disharmonically in VC$_0$V sequences'. That is, instead of saying that the principles of vowel harmony apply within the stem, Clements and Sezer suggest that there is free choice among the vowels within the stem, except that the three vowels of the system that do *not* belong to the canonical five-vowel system may not freely appear; they appear only if they are 'harmonic', i.e. if they could be derived by a vowel harmony rule from a simpler form.

Clements and Sezer's account of Turkish suggests the following reanalysis, focusing on the one hand on the close connection between the presence of the canonical five-vowel system and on the other on the redundancy of the features [±round] and [±back], as suggested in rule (39) (default [back] specification) in the canonical five-vowel system.[25] I suggest that words with vowels chosen entirely from the system {i, e, a, o, u} do not contain a specification for the feature [back] underlyingly, but rather are represented as in (38). Since the feature [back] is not present at this level, one cannot speak of vowels violating or respecting back/front harmony; all combinations of vowels are permitted within a stem, as Clements and Sezer illustrate in (44).

The three vowels of Turkish that may appear in a stem that are not of this system are {ö, ü, ɨ}. In words containing these vowels, the feature [back] must also be present in the lexical representation of the stem, as in (45). However, as Clements and Sezer inform us, such words do not permit violation of backness harmony. Put another way, when the

(44)   Clements and Sezer's canonical nonharmonic stems

       (a) a, i: va:li   'governor'   izmarit 'sea-bream'
       (b) a, e: hareket 'movement'   hesap 'bank account'
       (c) o, i: orkinos 'tunny fish'   sifon   'toilet flush'
       (d) o, e: rozet   'collar pin'   metot   'method'
       (e) u, i: zigurat 'ziggurat'   muzip   'mischievous'
       (f) u, e: su:ret   'copy'   mebus   'member of
                                                   parliament'

       (g) underlying form of *hareket*

$$
\begin{array}{ccccccc}
 & [-\text{round}] & & [-\text{round}] & & & \\
 & | & & | & & & \\
h & V & r & V & k & V & t \\
 & | & & | & & | & \\
 & [\text{low}] & & [\text{low}] & & [\text{low}] &
\end{array}
$$

(45)   köprü – ler – e   'to the bridges'

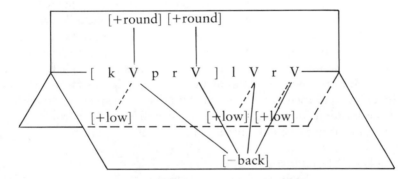

feature [back] is present, it *must* spread across a word, as indicated in
(45). In short, when the feature is not necessary to represent the vowels of
the stem, as in (44), it is redundant, and is not used. The default
specification for rounding, (39), is put into effect, and all [−round]
vowels are marked as [−back], while all others are marked as [+back]
(including the low vowel *a*), giving us the representation in (46), where
we have the appearance (and, indeed, the reality) of backness violation.
This arises, however, out of the fact that no backness specification was
present underlyingly.

    Let us summarize so far. Apparent violations of harmony within a
stem that contain only the vowels {a, e, i, o, u} are marked for the
features [round] and [low] underlyingly, but become fully specified for

(46)   Derived form of *hareket*

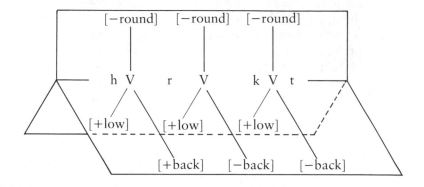

the features [back], [round], and [low] by the default rule, summarized in
(47). Stems that contain a specification for the feature [back] will have
that feature value spread over the entire word, as in (45). This specification may be present only once in a stem, and simplicity considerations
suggest that this is permissible *only* on the first vowel. This will give rise
to the appearance of vowels outside of the canonical {a, e, i, o, u},
though there is no reason to say that this spreading must be present in the
underlying form. Rather, we shall specify that at the word-level representation – the inflectional stem to which suffixes are attached – all three
vowel features must be equipollently specified, and as far as the feature
[back] is concerned, there are two ways that this can be accomplished. If
a specification for the feature is present underlyingly, it will spread, by
rule (48); if not, the default rule in (47a) will take effect.

(47)   Default specification
         (a) back: [−round] → [−back]
              (otherwise, [+back])
         (b) vowel unmarked for low → [−low]
         (c) vowel unmarked for round → [−round]

(48)   Spread [back] to the right
              [αback]
              | ↘
              V

One more thing needs to be said about rounding harmony (43c).
There is one respect in which the canonical nonharmonic stems of (44)
differ from the more familiar stems as in (45). In the former, the feature
[±round] could appear contrastively on any vowel, while in the latter –

in stems where the feature [±back] is marked – the feature [±round] can occur only on a vowel that is also marked [+low]. Elsewhere, among the high vowels, rounding is nondistinctive, and is specified by the 'round-ness harmony' rule (43c).

In sum, the Turkish vowel harmony system illustrates one way in which vowel features act autosegmentally, producing the effect that is known traditionally as 'vowel harmony' by spreading. In addition, underspecification theories lead to natural accounts of apparent viola-tions of harmony, as when a feature is filled in by a default rule, and is thus not subject to any autosegmental spreading that would create a harmonic span. Finally, we see from within the vocalic features some of the kinds of reasons for taking certain features to be equipollent and others to be privative, and also for permitting this parameter to be different at different levels of the representation (underlying and word level, in this case).[26]

6.4 THE OBLIGATORY CONTOUR PRINCIPLE AND THE MORPHEME TIER HYPOTHESIS

Three recent papers (McCarthy 1986, Yip 1988, and Odden 1988) have focused attention on a principle known as the Obligatory Contour Principle – hereinafter, the OCP. First formulated as such in Goldsmith (1979) and drawing on insights of Leben (1973), the OCP is a principle (or rather, a family of closely related principles) that prohibits consecutive or adjacent identical segments. Leben had observed that, in more than one African tonal system, there appeared to be an effect in operation whereby, if the morphology produces a concatenation of two adjacent, identical tones, the two fuse into a single tone before the tones are 'mapped onto' their corresponding vowels. In Tiv, for example, follow-ing earlier work by Arnott (1964), Leben suggests that the pattern for the imperative verbal form is 'BHL', meaning the 'base', or underlying, tone of the radical, followed by H and L. If the radical is underlyingly High, then this sequence is 'HHL', and Leben suggests that, before this sequence is mapped onto a string of syllables, such an HHL sequence will be simplified to HL, as in (49).

In Goldsmith (1979), where autosegmental phonology was first prop-osed and explored, the possibility was raised that this could be a general property of autosegmental systems. The issue in its earliest form focused on two matters. First, there are the potential ambiguities (or uncertain-ties) of representation in autosegmental phonology *vis-à-vis* segmental

(49)   Syllables: ti re [basic tone=H]
            Imperative   B H L
              Fill in B   H H L
                OCP   H L
            Mapping   ti   re
                              H   L

phonology: given a bisyllabic word with two high-toned vowels, how can we determine whether the proper representation is as in (50a) or (50b)? Second, if we focus on languages in which tones and vowels are mapped onto one another in a straightforward one-to-one fashion as discussed in chapter 1, can we make the strong claim that no such language will have trisyllabic words with a HHL pattern, as in (51)?

(50)   (a)   CV   CV   (b)   CV   CV
                  | | \   /
                  H   H   H

(51)   CV   CV   CV
          | | |
          H   H   L

Since there are languages with words that *seem* like they have a HHL tone pattern – English, for example, in the neutral pronunciation of a word such as *linguistics*, or any word with the same stress pattern – the question was posed as to whether we could immediately draw the conclusion that the language possessed some kind of accent system from the mere presence of a word possessed of a HHL pattern (or, equally, LLH, or any other violation of the OCP). An accent system would allow for the association of a distinguished ('accented') tone with the primary-accented syllable, wherever it might occur in the string of syllables, as in (52).

(52)

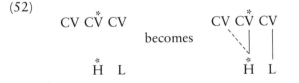

In Goldsmith (1979), it is argued that the OCP is *not* operative actively in the phonology, in the sense that adjacent identical segments are not automatically and universally reduced to one, on the basis of a small number of languages in which there was no independent evidence of an accent system, and in which there were found to be adjacent same-toned vowels which were apparently *not* associated with the same tone; see (53).

(53)   Etung (Edmundson and Bendor-Samuel 1966)
        e se be   'sand'
        | | |
        H H   L

More importantly, perhaps, it was argued there that there are good and general reasons to expect that the OCP will appear to operate as a design strategy in the phonology of natural languages – not because the principle is overtly present, but because it follows from basic considerations of how phonology is learned. The segments in our underlying phonological representations do not, after all, come from nowhere, and we must bear in mind that they actually come from the phonetic representations presented to us during the acquisition stage. Details aside, it is obvious that underlying representations of morphemes (at any given stage of language acquisition) will match surface forms, except insofar as underlying forms may leave out redundant information, and insofar as they must differ from surface forms to account for perceived allomorphic variation. In short, underlying representations match surface forms as much as possible; but this is not a principle either inside a grammar or, for that matter, in a repository of Universal Grammar: it is a general property of how a system learns, when its inner representations are set up to correspond to outer form, as a child must do when acquiring a language.

What does this have to do with the OCP? When a language acquirer approaches the phonetic signal, he or she may break it down into various channels of information (as indicated in (1) and (2) in this chapter). In the case of (50a,b), the tonal part of the phonetic signal is a period of high pitch, and nothing else – which, when represented with phonological segments, is represented as (50b). In the absence of any reason to analyze the form differently, then, the underlying form will be like the phonetic form, and we will see the effects of the OCP on the underlying representation of morphemes – not as an absolute, inviolable principle, but rather as a strong tendency. This interpretation has as its consequence that any clear cases where two successive, identical tones from *separate* morphemes merge into a single segment during the derivation must be cases of language-particular rules of merger. We will refer to this interpreation of the OCP as the 'naturalness' interpretation, alluding to Postal's (1968) 'naturalness principle' in phonology.[27]

Our awareness of the significance of the OCP has been heightened by work by McCarthy (especially 1979a, 1981, 1982). McCarthy argued that, given his autosegmental account of Arabic morphology (which we studied in chapter 1), the joint assumption of the OCP and left-to-right association of consonants to skeletal positions has as its consequence that we may find stems such as *samam* in Arabic, as in (54a), but never forms like *sasam*; there would be no way to derive such forms, except from underlying *ssm* consonantal roots, which in turn would be ruled out by the OCP. (Forms like *samam*, of course, would derive from *sm*, not *smm*, which McCarthy argues is correct.) The 'naturalness' interpretation of the OCP does not, strictly speaking, rule *out* the possibility of an underlying root such as *ssm*, but McCarthy observed that phonological theory may indeed prefer a stronger version of the OCP, one that will unconditionally rule out such a possibility; cf. (55). This suggestion is based on the generalization made by Greenberg (1960) that in Arabic adjacent consonants in the root may not be homorganic. As McCarthy observes, much (though by no means *all*) of Greenberg's generalization will be predicted by the stronger interpretation of the OCP as a strict constraint on underlying representations of individual morphemes.

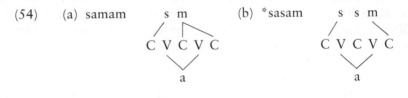

(54)   (a) samam   (b) *sasam

(55)   **OCP-1:** There can be no adjacent identical segments on the melody tier in underlying representation of morphemes.

It should be clear that one consequence of the generalization in (55) is that all tautomorphemic (i.e. morpheme-internal) geminate consonants must be 'true geminates', as mentioned in chapter 2 (56a). Accidentally identical consonants across morpheme boundary will *not* be true geminates; they will be only apparent geminates, at least, given what we have said so far; more remains to be said.

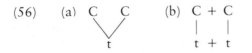

(56)   (a)   (b)

McCarthy (1986) proposes a version of the OCP in (57), one that is somewhat different from the OCP-1 in (55) above. A number of serious questions arise in connection with the deceptively simple word 'pro-

(57)   **Ocp-2:** At the melodic level (i.e. on non-skeletal tiers), adjacent identical elements are prohibited.

hibited' (to which we return in connection with our discussion of Yip 1988), such as what the consequences are taken to be of a rule 'attempting' to apply and thereby creating a violation. But McCarthy notes that there is a close connection between his use of the OCP and his analysis of Arabic, in which vowel and consonants are represented on separate autosegmental tiers. He is at pains to show that, while there are clear reasons to interpret multiple copies of a single *root* consonant in Arabic as multiple associations of a single consonant on a separate tier (58a), this effect disappears when we face two consonants that are phonologically identical but which come from separate morphemes, as in (58b). McCarthy suggests that there is clear evidence that the two *m*s of (58a) are simply two realizations or associations of the same autoseg- ment *s*, while the two *t*s of (58b) reflect two distinct autosegments *t*. In this way, the morphological origin of a segment may have consequences as far as the autosegmental geometry is concerned. If all consonants were on the same tier underlyingly (if the underlying representation were as in (58c), then at the deepest level, only OCP-1 (55) would hold – not OCP-2.

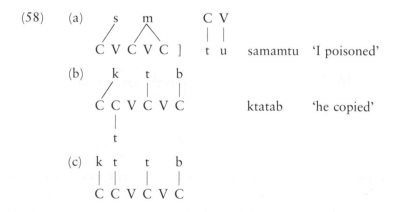

An alternative view, and the one that McCarthy prefers, is to adopt version OCP-2, and to do as I have indicated in (58a,b): to place separate morphemes onto separate melodic tiers at the deepest level at which the morphemes are joined together, the underlying representation of the phonological derivation.

This proposal is known in the literature as the *Morpheme Tier Hypothesis*, although, like the OCP, it is a family of closely related variant hypotheses, all of which aim at assigning separate tier status to separate morphemes.[28] One immediate consequence for McCarthy's analysis is that the root consonants of the Arabic stem will be placed on a separate tier from those of the grammatical infix, as in (58b). (See the discussion in section 2.3.2 as well.)

McCarthy (1986, and elsewhere) also notes that conflicting demands are placed on the tier organization when we look further at the phonologies of various Semitic languages; for, while language-game and other morphologically oriented processes point toward a separation of root and grammatical consonantisms, purely phonological processes suggest a rather different picture. For example, in Tiberian Hebrew, there is a process of spirantization of post-vocalic (non-pharyngealized) oral stops; *b* becomes β, for example, in post-vocalic position. Geminate stops do not undergo this process, and if we analyze this 'inalterability' property, as Steriade (1982) suggests, in terms of autosegmental association (cf. the discussion of the Conjunctivity Condition in chapter 1, and of inalterability in chapter 2), then the spirantization of a post-vocalic *b* is blocked when that *b* is multiply associated. But in (59) spirantization is blocked only for the surface geminate; the *b* that is multiply associated to non-adjacent consonant positions does indeed undergo spirantization.

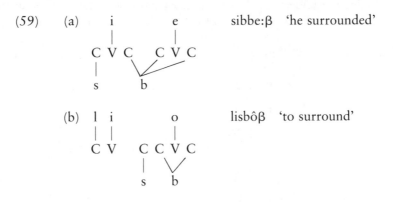

(59)   (a)   i   e   sibbe:β 'he surrounded'

(b)   l i   o   lisbôβ 'to surround'

McCarthy cites a suggestion by Younes (1983) regarding what McCarthy calls *tier conflation*. He suggests that there is a universal process that reshapes underlying structures, which have been molded tierwise in accordance with the Morpheme Tier Hypothesis, into structures in which the tier–morpheme connection is erased, and in which vowels and consonants now appear concatenated on a single tier. Tier conflation, however it is made precise, would be understood to have an effect whereby (59) is modified into (60).[29]

(60)   (a) C V C   C   V C   (b) C V C C V C
             | | \/   / | | | | | | |
             s i   b   e b   l i s b ô b

The general principle is this, then, McCarthy suggests: before tier conflation, phonological segments are organized morphologically, in accordance with the Morpheme Tier Hypothesis; after tier conflation, the only autosegmental effects are the 'local' ones that we have considered up to now, involving geminate consonants and long vowels.

It is not too hard to see that, although the OCP-2 and the Morpheme Tier Hypothesis are logically independent, there is nonetheless a close connection between them. If the segments of separate morphemes are on separate tiers, then only tautomorphemic segments stand as a test to the OCP, and adjacent identical consonants from separate morphemes simply will not be relevant to determining the truth or falsity of the OCP (e.g. as in *cool-ly*). While the strongest evidence proposed for the OCP may be with respect to underlying forms, this may simply be because the morpheme–tier structure makes other effects of the OCP-2 less visible.

McCarthy suggests that the OCP-2 should be understood not only as a condition on possible underlying forms (as in OCP-1), but also as part of the algorithm involved in rule application – in the sense that, if a rule's structural description is met but its output would contain a violation of the OCP, the rule will fail to apply, and the derivation will continue as before.

This suggestion makes the prediction, for example, that rules of vowel deletion will automatically be constrained so as not to apply to vowels flanked on either side by identical consonants. Tonkawa provides an example of a language with a vowel-deletion rule subject to such a constraint, as illustrated in (61). A version of the rule is given in (61a), and its effects are illustrated in (61b). (See Kenstowicz and Kisseberth 1979 for further discussion.) In (61c), we see that, when the consonants on either side of the consonant that is subject to deletion are identical, the vowel does not delete.

On McCarthy's account, then, the OCP is not violated in underlying morphemic representations. It certainly is not violated in the deep phonological representations, because separate morphemes are kept on separate tiers; and at tier conflation, identical segments that are brought together are fused by convention, i.e. by an active, dynamic version of the OCP – a rule (or rather, a convention) that fuses any two adjacent identical segments precisely at the point of tier conflation (but cf. n. 30).

Odden (1988) undertakes a reanalysis of McCarthy's range of observations, and points out a number of problematic features, several of which I shall mention here.

1   There are simple empirical counter-examples to OCP-1 in its strict form. Odden offers Chukchi (citing Krause 1980) and Hua (Haiman 1980) as languages with rules of schwa-insertion that break up clusters of consonants, even when these consonants are identical. Presumably, if

(61)   (a) V → ø / VC — CV

(b) /picena/ 'cut'

he Xes it	*progressive*	*he Xes them*	*progressive*
picnoʔ	picnanoʔ	wepcenoʔ	wepcenanoʔ

		he Xes me	
		kepcenoʔ	kepcenanoʔ

/notoxo/ 'hoe'

notxoʔ	notxonoʔ	wentoxoʔ	wentoxonoʔ
		kentoxoʔ	kentoxonoʔ

(c) /hewawa/   'die'
     hewawoʔ   'he is dead'

     /ham̓am̓a/   'be burning'
     ham̓am̓oʔ   'he is burning'

adjacent consonants are identical and the OCP-1 holds, then integrity would not allow this schwa-insertion. For example, in Chukchee there is a rule inserting schwa between two word-final consonants when the penultimate consonant is not glottalized: cf. (62). The final example in (62) illustrates the behavior of an underlying stem /ekke/, where the sequence of *kk* does not display the expected behavior of a geminate.

(62)

Abs. sg.	Abs. plural	Gloss
miməl	miml-ət	water
wiwər	wiwri-t	board
ekək	ekke-t	son

2   The original motivation for taking the OCP as an absolute restriction on underlying forms rather than a matter of simplicity and tendency was the Greenberg generalization cited above regarding the strict prohibition against consecutive homorganic consonants in the Arabic root. But the Greenberg generalization is larger than the OCP; it rules out sequences of homorganic consonants even when they are not identical. Thus the OCP, if it is to do the necessary work, must be informed (so to speak) to focus on just one sub-tier, the point-of-articulation sub-tier. But that is not motivated by OCP-1, and implementing such a proposal takes us far beyond the original spirit of the principle.

3   No examples have ever been found where consonant deletion is blocked when that would create sequences of identical vowels. And

counter-examples are attested; Odden cites the case of Estonian, and the consonant-weakening processes in several Eastern Bantu languages that have produced sequences of identical vowels as their output. One may sense a reflection of the same problem here as in the previous problem; many OCP effects do revolve around point-of-articulation specifications, which of course vowels do not possess. In any event, once again, to the extent that the OCP is proposed as a general theoretical property of the geometry, the asymmetry of vowels and consonants in this respect is disturbing.

4   Odden reports several cases where vowel deletion applies regardless of whether it creates geminates. For example, he reports that in Hindi (citing Bhatia and Kenstowicz 1972) there is a schwa syncope rule that applies regardless of whether the flanking consonants are identical (e.g. *kaanən+i* > *kaann+i* 'garden') or not (*daanəw+i* > *daanwi* 'demon'). He suggests that this rule is 'phonological' enough to distinguish between stem vowels, where it applies, and vowels to the right of the stem, and he concludes that any attempt to characterize as 'merely phonetic' those rules that fall outside the constraining effect of the OCP is not justified at this point.

5   There are phrase-level (post-lexical) rules of vowel deletion which apply only when their output *creates* geminate consonants. The fact that the rules may apply at phrase level, and between words, confirms the notion that the two consonantal autosegments on either side of the deleting vowel are distinct, and are not the multiple association of a single consonantal autosegment. Thus, for example, in Koya (Taylor 1969), there is a phrase-level rule that deletes word-final vowels when the consonants on either side are identical. Thus, *na:ki ka:va:li* 'to me it is necessary' surfaces as *na:kka:va:li*, and *a:ru ru:pa:yku* as *a:rru:pa:yku* '6 rupees'. This is illustrated in (63).

(63)

Odden offers a number of additional counter-arguments, leaving little doubt that in its strongest form McCarthy's proposal is not tenable. Odden's conclusion is that, to the extent that there are OCP effects active in phonology, these are language-particular, and rule-particular, effects. There are language-particular rules that achieve the fusion of two adjacent, identical segments, rules that have been informally dubbed 'OCP effects' in the literature; but they are not different in *kind* from other rules.[30]

Yip (1988) also approaches McCarthy's suggestions, but from a perspective considerably different from Odden's. While Yip's position is fundamentally more sympathetic to McCarthy's argument, it leads to a proposal that is itself far more radical that McCarthy's, a proposal that ultimately leads us to the heart of the final section of this chapter and the discussion of harmonic rule application.

Yip suggests that the OCP, as in (57) (OCP-2), is a well-formedness condition on representations, and that there is a class of rules that is triggered to apply to a given representation just in case it violates the OCP. She suggests that these rules are of a special type; they are rules with no structural description, applying when and only when they are needed to repair violations of the OCP. More tentatively, Yip also suggests that there is a late point at which an active merger of any two identical adjacent autosegments, following, perhaps, McCarthy's account (see note 30). However, Yip is at pains, as we shall see, to show that there can be representations in the phonology of a language *after* tier conflation (which is to say, in the 'normal' part of the phonology, where vowels and consonants are properly intercalated) where the OCP is violated; her point is that there may be various strategies at hand which undo OCP violations that are present – epenthesis, metathesis, deletion, and so forth. On Yip's account, merger of adjacent identical segments might just as well be yet another language-particular strategy for avoiding OCP violations, although she does not choose that particular approach, leaving fusion as the automatic and final solution to the OCP's demands.

Thus, the following example, which is offered by Odden (1988) as a counter-example to McCarthy's position, may be interpreted as a clear case working as Yip would have it. In Lenakel (Lynch 1978), a schwa is inserted between identical consonants, as when underlying *i-ak-ken* 'I eat' becomes *yagəgen*. On Yip's view, this would be the result of a rule written with no context, which therefore 'knows' that its application is governed by the principle that it should apply just in case its application resolves a violation of the OCP, thus separating two adjacent, identical consonantal segments.

On the whole, there is clearly something right about each of the papers cited in this section. I believe that McCarthy is correct in drawing our attention to the importance of the OCP as a principle expressing well-formedness of representations at several levels. Odden (1988) correctly informs us that the extremely strong claims offered in McCarthy (1986) cannot be accepted at face value, but Yip (1988) suggests a radically different perspective from McCarthy's, and from most familiar generative accounts. It is very much in line with various ideas regarding rule application that have come up several times in the course of this book.

6.5   HARMONIC RULE APPLICATION AND AUTOMATIC SPREADING

The final topic that we shall consider is one of the most far-reaching, and we cannot do it full justice in just a few pages. On a number of occasions during the course of the preceding five chapters, we have alluded to the notion that certain processes must be understood as applying just in case they encounter a violation of a well-formedness condition (i.e. a phonotactic) which will be removed by the application of the rule. The rule, in short, constitutes a particular 'repair strategy' as far as that phonotactic is concerned, and it acts only in that capacity.

This notion has a special place in the development of autosegmental theory, where in early years it was associated with the question as to whether there is 'automatic spreading' in tone languages. Let us review how this question, and its treatment, arose in the development of the theory.

In the earliest work on autosegmental phonology (Goldsmith 1979), a principle known simply as the 'Well-formedness Condition (WFC)', was suggested, and much later work generally assumed the validity of the condition. The WFC consisted of the statement in (64), and an algorithm (65) that utilizes that condition. I have added to (64) the phrase 'phonotactic', for reasons which we shall see below.

(64)   **Well-formedness Condition (-Phonotactic)**
   1. All vowels are associated with at least one tone.
   2. All tones are associated with at least one vowel.
   3. Association lines do not cross.

(65)   **Implementation of WFC-phonotactic**
   Apply the operation in (66) in a minimal fashion so as to maximally satisfy the WFC-phonotactic in (64).

(66)   Repair operation

   V
   ⋮
   T

The WFC itself, in (64), describes a state of affairs that may or may not be met in a given representation; the representations in (67) illustrate cases violating each of the first two clauses. According to this theory, violations of the WFC trigger the implementation of the algorithm (taken in those works to be universal) given in (65).

(67)   (a) CV CV CV   (b) CV

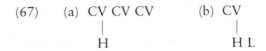

Taken altogether, this meant that the grammar would add the minimum number of association lines (in ways that would not violate the WFC itself) but always in such a way as to maximally satisfy the WFC. This would have the effect of changing the forms in (67) into the corresponding forms in (68); the rule in (66), we might conveniently say, acted like a particular kind of repair strategy for the WFC-phonotactic.

(68)   (a) CV CV CV   (b) CV

Later work[31] emphatically showed that languages could have surface forms that were in some cases massively in violation of the WFC. That observation was not in itself too surprising, for the original formulation had clearly left open the possibility of such cases (to allow, most importantly, for floating tones underlyingly and floating tones on the surface, in the latter case to act as downstep triggers). What was surprising was that cases like Sukuma (see chapter 1) could exist, where, as in (69), High tones could show no tendency at all to spread.

(69)   CV CV CV CV CV CV CV
                      |
                      H

This observation was widely taken to show an inadequacy in the WFC itself. However, the assumptions of early autosegmental phonology that led to the automatic spreading in question here were three in number, as we have seen: the WFC-phonotactic (64), the 'instruction' or 'rule' in (66), and the universal algorithm (65) instructing how to apply the 'rule' in a minimal fashion to maximally satisfy the WFC. If any one of these failed to be universal, then the spreading effect would no longer be universal.

Now, the notion of rule that was adopted by the early works in autosegmental phonology was in all important respects that of traditional generative phonology. A rule was, in this light, a language-particular statement, and it would relate two adjacent representations in a derivation just in case the deeper of the two representations satisfied the particular structural description of the rule. In fact, the static picture of derivations in which rules relate adjacent stages in the derivation is sometimes less effective as a metaphor than the more common active metaphor according to which rules actually come along and modify representations, since, when a representation satisfies the structural description of a rule, it must 'undergo' the rule, which is to say there must be another stage in the derivation corresponding to the 'output' of the rule.

With this much borne in mind, it should be clear that the tripartite nature of the Well-formedness Condition with its implementation algorithm simply did not fit into the picture of phonological derivations of classical generative phonology. If accepted, it had to be viewed as something overlain upon the true phonological rules, a universal mechanism that stood outside the set of phonological rules that constitute the phonological grammar of the language. More than for any other reason, this was because phonological rules in the classical generative picture were not conceived of as applying or not applying in a fashion dependent on whether or not their output achieved a specifiable output structure. But that was precisely what governed the implementation of the association line additions demanded by the Well-formedness Condition.

Contemporaneous with the proposal of autosegmental phonology, Sommerstein (1974) suggested that a wide range of generative phonological rules (though how wide he was silent about) could best be analyzed into two parts: a set of changes that operated upon a representation – we may refer to this as the conditional rule; and a set of surface phonotactic conditions linked to one or more (conditional) rules in the following fashion.[32] A conditional rule will apply if and only if its input violates one of its phonotactic conditions and its output satisfies that condition. His arguments on the point are quite straightforward, and address traditional segmental problems of Latin phonology. Sommerstein observes, for example, that a rule of final coronal obstruent deletion can be written in a complex fashion, if we choose to do so; but positive statements on possible word-final clusters are simpler to state, and allow us the following possibility: we can express our rule of final coronal deletion with no 'environment' in the rule, other than to say that it applies word-finally, as long as we specify that the rule is one that applies if and only if its input violates a phonotactic condition and its output satisfies the condition.

A more intricate example given by Sommerstein concerns the process of fricative deletion in Latin, which applies if any of five independently motivated phonotactics are violated. By indicating that the rule applies if and only if it repairs a violation of such a phonotactic, a single, simple rule can be formulated, even though in some cases its effect is to resolve a violation of a voicing-agreement constraint, in others a violation of an obstruent-resonant cluster constraint, in still others a violation of a constraint against obstruent-glide clusters, and so on. In short, to write separate rules where each specifies the particular *way* in which a phonotactic can be violated – and to call that, then, the 'structural description' of the rule, as if it were that *particular* sequence that caused the rule to apply, rather than the representation's failure to satisfy the phonotactic – is to miss a string of important generalizations.

Although the connection was not remarked upon at the time, Sommerstein's conception of language-particular rule application and the procedure for implementing repairs of the WFC-phonotactic were fundamentally the same. And Sommerstein's work has by no means gone unnoticed. Singh (1987), for example, explicitly argues in favor of adopting a strong version of Sommerstein's view, emphasizing once again the importance of phonotactics, and the insights gained in trading off rule complexity against phonotactic specifications.[33]

This suggests the following reconstruction of the organization of phonology.[34] A phonological level will be defined as a set of phonotactics placed on representations. The *word-level* (W-level) in a particular language, for example, will consist of a set of phonotactics, or well-formedness conditions, that apply to phonological representations in that language. A general theory of word-level phonotactics will constrain the technical language in which such phonotactics can be specified, and the work discussed in this book suggests the following hypothesis: language-particular word-level phonotactics consist entirely of syllable structure-conditions, including autosegmental licensing specifications and autosegmental restrictions on the minimum/maximum number of associations. Other word-level phonotactics are universal. We return to some cases of this sort below.

Along with a set of (universal and language-particular) phonotactics for the W-level, each language will contain a set of rules that operate as repair strategies, applying just in case their output eliminates the violation of a phonotactic in their input. There is no guarantee that all violations will, in fact, be resolved by the time all the rules have done their work; in fact, it seems quite clear that it will *never* be the case that all such W-level phonotactics are perfectly resolved. Rather, the W-level phonology attempts to achieve a maximal satisfaction of its constraints, subject to the resources it has for fixing problematic violations.[35]

We may understand the word-level, then, as a series of representations $\{W_1, \ldots, W_n\}$, where the last one satisfies the W-level phonotactics as well as the language can manage, and the first is supplied by the morphology in a way that we shall return to momentarily. If we think of well-formedness – or its opposite, ill-formedness – as a matter of degree, then the path that the representation takes as it moves, so to speak, from W_1 to W_n may be conveniently thought of as a downhill path towards a 'local minimum' of ill-formedness, where the rules of the language define what an allowable path is. The W-level representation of a given form is then the entire sequence of representations $\{W_1, \ldots, W_n\}$, and we may refer to the 'repair strategy' rules that apply internally to that level as '(W, W)' rules, in the sense that their input and output are both parts of the W-level representation. Schematically, this may be represented as in (70).

$$(70) \qquad \begin{bmatrix} W_1 \\ \vdots \\ W_n \end{bmatrix} \leftarrow (W, W) \text{ rules}$$

We hypothesize that there are two more levels relevant to the phonology: one essentially morphological in character (therefore, an *M-level*), and one of systematic phonetics (a *P-level*). As with the W-level, these other levels consist of a sequence of representations aimed at achieving maximal well-formedness in accordance with level-specific tactics. We may furthermore take there to be one further set of rules aligning the levels: one set of (M, W) rules aligning the M-level with the W-level, and one aligning the W-level with the P-level. We then arrive at the diagram in (71), which we shall refer to as a *harmonic phonology*.[36] P_n serves as the representation of systematic phonetics, and as the interface with the phonetic component. M_1 is the representation that interfaces with the morphosyntax.

Current work suggests that, within a level, rules apply in the manner generally referred to as 'free reapplication', subject, unsurprisingly, to the Elsewhere Condition, in the sense that, when a language has two competing repair strategies for a phonotactic violation within a given level, it chooses the one that is more specific for the task at hand. Inter-level rules (M, W) and (W, P) operate in non-interactive ways, i.e. simultaneously. Typical examples of various processes are sketched in (72).

I will conclude by reviewing several significant advantages to this conception of rule application within phonology. The issue that is involved is a broad, difficult, and important one, and, while it goes beyond the bounds of the present book, I will spell out some of the important differences that have come to light in distinguishing between traditional and harmonic modes of rule application.

(71)   Harmonic phonology

$$\begin{bmatrix} M_1 \\ \vdots \\ M_n \end{bmatrix} \leftarrow (M, M)\ \text{rules}$$ Intralevel rules
: free reapplication
· of unordered rules

$\leftarrow (M, W)\ \text{rules}$

$$\begin{bmatrix} W_1 \\ \vdots \\ W_n \end{bmatrix} \leftarrow (W, W)\ \text{rules}$$ Intralevel rules
‖ simultaneous
‖ single application
‖ of a set of rules

$\leftarrow (W, P)\ \text{rules}$

$$\begin{bmatrix} P_1 \\ \vdots \\ P_n \end{bmatrix} \leftarrow (P, P)\ \text{rules}$$

(72)

Type of rule	Example
(a) (M, M)	Melody spreading before tier conflation
(b) (M, W)	Tier conflation
(c) (W, W)	Syllabification; epenthesis
(d) (W, P)	Default feature specification
(e) (P, P)	Flap formation in English

I will sketch eight areas where this approach shows a solid, coherent advantage over other approaches. These are intended as illustrative, not exhaustive, cases, as indicated above. If the suggestions considered here are correct, then the general principle of harmonic application governs all essentially phonological rule application.

(1) We often arrive at a considerable simplification of individual rules, as noted in part by Sommerstein, Singh, and Paradis, among others, when we do the following three things: (i) remove the structural description from the rule itself; (ii) invert it, specifying not what is *dis*allowed, but rather what tactics must positively be met; and (iii) note that the positive conditions determining whether a rule will apply involve reference to the output of the rule, not the input – though, of course, an element in the input of the rule may be deleted in order that the output satisfy a condition.

Many languages have rules of epenthesis and of cluster simplification (i.e. consonant deletion) whose target structure is the well-formed syllable of the sort we have discussed.[37] Wiltshire (1988), for example, discusses the syllable structure of IṛuLa, a Dravidian language, on the basis of materials in Diffloth (1968). She analyzes the phonotactics as deriving from a W-level coda capable of licensing only the feature [nasal] and vowel quality features – apparently only the feature [±round]. As in Selayarese and several other languages we considered in chapter 3, geminate consonants are permitted intervocalically, as are nasal-stop clusters. Vowels may be contrastively long or short regardless of whether the coda is associated with a consonant or not. There is considerable modification of the phonological form between the underlying representation – our M_1 – and the surface form, but virtually all of the complexity derives from various strategies pursued by IṛuLa to achieve well-formed syllable structure, as determined by the coda licensing condition. An (M, W) rule applies between coronal-final verb roots and the past-tense suffix *t*, creating a geminate, as in (73).[38]

As the reader will notice, other processes come into play when there are consonants that cannot be licensed. The strategy of deletion is used for word-final sonorants, but only for them. Elsewhere, as we see in (73d), epenthesis of U, a short, centralized vowel, applies in order to create a licensing environment – the syllable node – for that consonant. Of course, where the gemination-formation process of (73b) applies, the epenthesis rule does not need to apply to create a well-formed position for the first consonant; no epenthesis occurs after the stem-final consonant that spreads rightward above – the property of 'geminate integrity' that we have discussed. We return to this point below. Wiltshire suggests a third rule, which may be operative in the (W, W) component, a rule deleting the first of three consonants, as koḷ-nd-eṉ > koṇde, again aiming at W-level well-formedness.

(2) Yip's interpretation of the OCP as a motivator for a certain class of phonological rules is automatically derived. We differ from her account only in that we take all intra-level rules (i.e. (M, M) rules, (W, W) rules, and (P, P) rules) to have the character that they apply just in case they improve the well-formedness of their input, and we take the OCP to be only one of several such tactics that may hold of levels. We furthermore interpret Odden's impressive scholarship as establishing that the OCP is a tactic that must be specified in a language-particular way for each of the three levels of the phonological grammar.

(3) As suggested in note 16 of chapter 2, the principle of rule application in harmonic phononology – that rules apply only if their application improves the well-formedness of a representation along a certain 'dimension' – when combined with the theory of autosegmental licensing

(73)   (a) Underlying form: peṭ +t+t
             Surface: [peṭ ṭ UdU]   'give birth+past+3rd person'
ṭ is an alveolar stop; voicing is non-distinctive word-medially.

        (b) Rule

```
        C -------------------- C
        |                      |
   ⎡coronal ⎤          ( [coronal] )
   ⎣alveolar⎦                      ↘ ø
```

        (c) Rule: insert U

        (d) Schematic derivation

```
        C    V       C            C           C
        |    |       |            |           |
        p    e   ⎡coronal ⎤   [coronal]   [coronal]
                 ⎣alveolar⎦
```

```
W₁   C    V       C          C           C
     |    |       |         ╱             |
     p    e   ⎡coronal ⎤              [coronal]
              ⎣alveolar⎦
```

```
                σ                        σ                  σ
              ╱ ╲                      ╱ ╲                ╱ ╲
             O   R                    O   R              O   R
             |  N ╲ C                 |   N              |   N
             |  |    |                |   |              |   |
W₂   C   V       C          C         V              C          V
     |   |       |        ╱           |              |          |
     p   e                          U            [coronal]      U
              ⎡coronal ⎤
              ⎣alveolar⎦
```

proposed in chapter 3 serves to account automatically for the most compelling examples of geminate integrity and inalterability. With regard to inalterability, the clearest examples are all of the general character that a coda-weakening process fails to apply to geminates. Klingenheben's Law in Hausa, readers will recall, is a typical example of this sort, according to which obstruents in coda position become sonorants. This shift is entirely conditioned by licensing considerations. Hausa does not license point of articulation in its coda, a W-level phonotactic; however, the coda may associate with a point of articulation autosegment just in case that autosegment is also associated with an onset position, which licenses it. Thus, it follows that geminate obstruents do not violate the W-level phonotactic, and Klingenheben's Law will not apply – will not be even be *tempted* to apply, so to speak. Precisely parallel considerations arose in the case of Toba Batak earlier in this chapter; see note 15.

(4) We may capture significant 'soft' cross-linguistic universals which formerly eluded formal capture. One of the most striking of these arose several times in chapter 3, in connection with the natural relationship between heavy syllables and prosodic prominence. Heavy syllables are syllables with a coda that licenses association with a second Row 0 grid mark, as in (74a); a prosodically prominent, or stressed, syllable, is one with a Row 1 grid mark, as in (74b). The two are distinct, but nonetheless there is a clear connection between them. We may express this as a universal W-level[39] phonotactic, which specifies that syllable–grid associations are well-formed in those cases where the syllable is heavy if and only if the syllable is stressed.[40] This leads to four relations of inequality with regard to weight and prominence, as shown in (75).

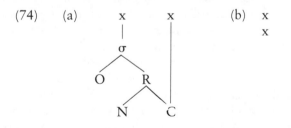

Each of these relative statements of well-formedness can serve as triggers for simple rules of grid or syllable adjustment. Case (a) is, of course, just the principle that governs the rule of quantity-sensitivity (QS), discussed in chapter 4. Case (b) arose several times in our discussions in chapter 3, in connection with Selayarese, with the Scandanavian languages, and with Zoque. In each case, a rule added a mora to a

(75)   (a) x   is better-formed than   o
            x x   x x

A stressed heavy syllable is better-formed than an unstressed heavy syllable.

(b) x   is better-formed than   x
    x x   x

A stressed heavy syllable is better-formed than a stressed light syllable.

(c) o   is better-formed than   o
    x   x x

An unstressed light syllable is better-formed than an unstressed heavy syllable.

(d) o   is better-formed than   x
    x   x

An unstressed light syllable is better-formed than a stressed light syllable.

stressed syllable, just in case the syllable *needed* that mora in order to be heavy – in other words, the language would lengthen a vowel in a stressed open syllable. But not all languages do such things, and that is an aspect that the treatment provided by harmony phonology deals with especially well. A language such as the three mentioned above may take an especially simple route to make its W-level structures better-formed. The rule will be simply: add a coda position – and it will apply only in the right cases, those where it improves the well-formedness of certain syllables with respect to (75b). Other languages may contain rules that are somewhat more complex. Chamorro (Chung 1983), for example, has a rule that lengthens a stressed vowel in an open syllable when there is a stressed, closed syllable preceding in the word – as Chung notes, a harmony principle of a rather abstract sort. From our point of view, the important conclusion from the Chamorro case is that the kinds of phonological resources the language has available – its (W, W) rules – are typically, but not always, simple; what they share cross-linguistically is their common direction of improvement, as specified by principles like those given in (75).

Case (75c) represents the motivation for all languages that shorten vowels in unstressed position. This is a common process, though often not recognized for what it is. A particularly interesting example of this is given by Selkirk (1986) for the Bantu language Chimwiini. Finally, case (75d) represents all cases where light syllables are destressed, a not uncommon process at word-periphery, where it does not wreak havoc with the permissible foot structure of a language.

What is important to see in all these cases is that to specify the precise environment for each rule is sometimes formally difficult and always unnecessary insofar as it simply recapitulates the universal tactic. Rule (61) of chapter 3, for example, in effect adds a mora to a stressed syllable in case the syllable is monomoraic, but geometrical representations are notoriously poor ways of representing what something is *not*. As we have noted on several occasions, our autosegmental and metrical forms of representations and of rules are not well suited for expressing a *lack* of associations. From the point of view of harmonic phonology and its conception of rule application, this is as it should be, because those rules whose function is to add association lines or metrical structure when it is not yet there are always rules aiming at satisfying a 'completeness' or a 'saturation' of a representation, or some other related kind of phonotactic, such as that in (75).

A similar perspective is offered in Goldsmith (1987c, 1990), with respect to the interaction of tone assignment and metrical structure.

(5) This naturally brings us back to a consideration of the original 'Well-formedness Condition' of autosegmental phonology, in (64). We may now re-ask the question: first, is there a WFC in autosegmental phonology? and second, is spreading of the sort that it induces universal? The answer is that the Well-formedness Condition in (64) is just one of many W-level or P-level phonotactics that can be stated in terms of the (minimum, maximum) notation discussed in chapter 1. In particular, (64) says that, on the skeleton-tone chart, the skeleton is specified for a (1, x) value, and the tone tier is likewise specified for a (1, x) value (where 'x' means not specified). Is this universal? At this point, the answer is uncertain. It may be that in all cases where less than the minimum association is provided there simply is no rule available in the language that would allow the representation to become well-formed in this respect. In short, it may well be universal. The implementation procedure (65), we suggest, *is* universal with respect to (M, M) rules, (W, W) rules, and (P, P) rules. However, rule (66) itself is not universal: it is a language-particular rule.

(6) On a related point, in our discussion of Kiparsky's analysis of Catalan, we noted that a proper phonological account of point-of-articulation assimilation for nasals needed to be specified as a rule that applied only to nasals that were not already specified for a point of articulation, as sketched in (15) and (16) of chapter 5. The present notion of harmonic application provides just that notion. The phonotactic in (16) there required that all consonants be specified for a point of

articulation. The autosegmental spreading rule of assimilation would accomplish that end, if relevant; otherwise, a context-free default specification would assign a point of articulation.

(7) The naturalness of compensatory lengthening when an empty coda position is produced can be captured in the same way as the other cross-linguistic 'soft' constraints that we have discussed, from the point of view of harmonic application. Readers will recall that the generalization we wish to capture is as follows. Syllable and coda structure is established on the basis of segmental material that may later undergo deletion. If such a deletion process leaves a coda position unassociated with any melodic material (consonantal or vocalic features), then there is a strong (but soft) universal tendency for an element, on either the left (a vowel) or the right (a consonant), to reassociate to that coda position. The phonotactic may be as simple as this: that a licenser must license at least one melodic (vocalic, consonantal) autosegment at the W-level and one at the P-level.

(8) Finally, the distinction used here – between M-level, the level at which segmentally represented morphemes are represented, and W-level – motivates those uses of the Morpheme Tier Hypothesis that can be empirically motivated. The M-level representation is essentially devoid of phonological motivation; its representations may violate every conceivable phonotactic, every conceivable phonologically oriented constraint of the language. Its sole function is as a repository of the minimal information necessary to capture the sound characteristics of the morpheme. It is a structure that incorporates the morphemes that provide the realization of the morphosyntactic information. The W-level, on the other hand, is the level at which such phonological information is restructured in order to maximally satisfy the language-particular organization principles which we call syllable and autosegmental phonotactics, of which licensing is an important, though not a unique, member. The W-level representation thus expresses the form the language squeezes its morphemes into in order to satisfy the alternating rhythm of consonants and vowels, of properly licensed coda and syllable material, of tonal association, and so on. The phonological rules of the language are its ways of manipulating the phonological substance present at the deeper M-level, and they express the options open to the language with regard to how much the language can 'deform' the underlying representation in order to maximally satisfy the multitude of competing demands of well-formedness at the W-level.

Thus, it seems reasonable that the morphological procedures responsible for construcing an M-level representation may produce a 'pseudo-phonologized' representation in which morphemes are placed on separate tiers. The process of forming a W-level representation, then, requires what McCarthy calls tier conflation, which is one particular technique for restructuring an M-level representation into one that satisfies the universal and language-particular demands of W-level.

6.6   CONCLUSION

A theory of phonology is built of three parts: it is a theory of the nature of phonological representations; it is an inventory of levels of representation, and a characterization of each level; and it is a theory of phonological rules, the statements that relate representations on each level.

This book is aimed primarily at the first part, the nature of phonological representations. We have explored the nature of autosegmental representations, metrical grids, and syllable structure. We have offered autosegmental licensing as a characteristic that determines the essential properties of syllable structure.

At the same time, we have had to develop a certain number of ideas concerning levels of representation, and we have emphasized the importance of W-level structure, that structure over which licensing conditions serve as the primary phonotactic, or well-formedness condition. We have explored lexical phonology as one explicit account of several levels within generative thought, and have tried to separate some of the more useful from the less useful ideas in that area.

With respect to the notion of rules, throughout most of this book we have retained the traditional generative conception, according to which rules come with a structural description and apply if that description is met. As indicated briefly in the last two chapters, and especially in the preceding section, I believe that this notion stands in need of serious revision, although, as we have seen, ongoing research in phonological theory has been able to enunciate a powerful conception of phonological representations, independent of any further changes in the theory of rules. Now, however, with this new theory in hand, we may proceed to a novel and even more compelling picture of the nature of phonology, in which rules interact with phonotactic conditions on a small number of levels to develop representations at each level satisfying the conditions stated there. This picture has much in common with current work in a number of other areas of linguistic theory.

In phonology, the model we arrive at is one that looks much more like a model of chemistry than the models of classical generative phonology, in which the phonological grammar resembled nothing more than a computer program. In the model that is emerging currently, representations have a complex geometric structure, but relatively few degrees of freedom in the changes they may undergo. Rules define possible changes in the structure of the phonological material, and in each and every case, the changes are motivated by an attempt to achieve a greater satisfaction of well-formedness conditions. This bears a striking similarity to the notion that chemical systems tend toward a lower energy level, consistent with the physical properties that they have. The application of this kind of model has been urged elsewhere in cognitive studies by Smolensky (1986), for example, and the convergence of work in phonology with that in other areas of cognitive science offers great hope for continued advances of the sort that we have seen in phonology in the last fifteen years.

Notes

Chapter 1   *Autosegmental Representation*

1   Thirty years ago, to use the term *mental* in a linguistic analysis would be risking grave opprobrium; today it is more a shibboleth of good intent. I do not mean, of course, that such segments are accessible to introspection, nor that they are meaningful. I personally believe that, as our understanding of the principles of the organization of lower-level neural functions increases, it should influence the range of hypotheses we take seriously in developing our phonological theory; but that is a position quite independent of the theories presented in this book.

2   Autosegmental theory was first proposed in Goldsmith (1976a, 1979, 1981b), where the notions of tiers, association lines, and autosegments are introduced. Earlier work on tone in generative phonology that attempted to incorporate the insights of Firthian scholars such as Carnochan, Robins, and Bendor-Samuel included Leben (1971) and Williams (1976). The earliest work on autosegmental vowel harmony is due to Clements (1976, 1977); on nasal harmony, to Goldsmith (1976a, 1979).

3   This section is based on Clements and Ford (1979) and Clements (1984).

4   See Goldsmith (1979), Haraguchi (1977), Clements and Ford (1979), and Goldsmith (1984b).

5   The theory of autosegmental licensing introduced in chapter 3 below suggests, however, that in the lexical phonology (a notion we have not yet introduced) only one tone can associate with a vowel. The suggestion in the following paragraph is based on Halle and Vergnaud (1982).

6   This material is based on Pike (1948), though Pike has returned to the analysis of Mixtecan in a number of places; see Pike (1972, *passim*).

7   See Hollenbach (1984) for a study along these lines.

8   The tonal system of Kirundi is described in more detail in Goldsmith and Sabimana (1985).

9   The examples come from my work with Father Joest Mnemba. See also various other works on Chichewa tone, including Peterson (1987) and Mtenje (1986, 1987).

10 This section is based on Kisseberth (1984).

11 This section is based on my own work with a speaker of KiHunde, Mutima Sinamenye; see Goldsmith (1986). I am grateful to Alicja Gorecka for several insightful suggestions.

12 The term *sandhi* refers to processes applying across word boundaries (strictly, *external sandhi*).

13   This point is developed in Schein and Steriade (1986), and Hayes (1986a), who calls it the Linking Condition. They do not exclude from its effects rules that only add or delete association lines, but a number of examples suggest that such rules are not subject to the kind of constraint we are discussing here.

14   This notion is close to, and a generalization of, the notion Clements has defined as a *P-bearing unit*; see e.g. Clements and Sezer (1982), Clements (1981).

15   This notation lacks a certain mathematical rigor that may concern some readers – though it really should not. The use of the '{   }' notation suggests that by this notation I mean to at least allude to true set notation, and readers may well wonder whether the pairs of bundles of features are themselves sets – in which case (90) is itself a set with two elements, each of which are sets, better represented as in (i). Other possibilities, too, could be imagined, but I think it is clear that for our purposes here the precise formalization is of no interest, and I will continue to (as Bourbaki would say) abuse the notation when our purposes are suited by it.

(i)   {{[+syllabic],[+High tone]},
        {[+voice,−sonorant],[−High tone]}}

Chapter 2   The Skeletal Tier

1   The proposal was first made in McCarthy (1979a, 1981), and much work in this area has been done since. Among the most notable references are Clements and Keyser (1983), McCarthy (1982), and some excellent papers in, among other places, Aronoff and Oehrle (1984) and Wetzels and Sezer (1985).

2   Cf. Kenstowicz and Pyle (1973).

3   With the introduction of syllable structure in the next chapter, we will be free to reinterpret these distinctions as structural, corresponding to location within the syllable. The C-position is the onset, where only non-syllabic material can be found; the V-position is the nucleus, where only syllabic material can be found; and the X-position is the coda, whether either is possible.

4   This section is based on Tucker (1962) and Clements (1985a).

5   See McCarthy (1979a), Harris (1980).

6   Recall (n. 3) that, as we proceed further with our discussion of syllable structure, we will adopt the position that in purely phonological systems, at least, all skeletal positions will be what we have called here 'x'. Onsets by their nature correspond to present 'c's, nuclear positions to 'v's, and codas may be either, except in specified circumstances.

7   A number of accounts of empty C-positions have been proposed. On French, see Clements and Keyser (1983), and Stemberger (1985); see also the critique in Dresher (1985).

8   See, for example, Archangeli (1983) on Yokuts.

9 Another example can be found in Alutiiq, a Yup'ik language of Alaska, as Jeffrey Leer has pointed out in recent unpublished work. While sequences of vowels may appear underlyingly, and contribute to making a syllable prosodically heavy (and thus stressed), such diphthongal sequences are only as long as single vowel on the surface when they appear in a closed syllable. Thus, the diphthong in the first syllable of *kuiget* 'rivers' is as long as a long vowel, while the same diphthong in *kuignet* 'from rivers' is only as long as a short vowel.

10 The evidence in Spanish involves late, post-lexical, representations (in the terms of lexical phonology – see ch. 5), rather than lexical representations.

11 Clements (1987), looking at a related process of 'intrusive stop formation' in English, involved in the creation of post-lexical stops between sonorants and stops, as in *warmpth* or *prince* [nts], suggests that the features [continuant] and [Point of Articulation] form a common tier (what we will see below in ch. 6 is called a 'class tier'). This is motivated in English by the fact that both the feature values for Point of Articulation and continuant assimilate, so to speak, in the same direction. In Spanish, interestingly, the directions of assimilation of each feature are opposite.

12 Straight (1976); Steinberg (1987).

13 See Ingria (1980); Leben (1980); and also Kenstowicz and Pyle (1973). See also Guerssel (1977, 1978); Hayes (1968a); Schein and Steriade (1986).

14 Steriade (1982), who presents a rather different account of why geminates show the resistances discussed here (inalterability and integrity), suggests that her account predicts that an infixal vowel should be able to break up a geminate, though a phonological rule of epenthesis should not. This is based on a version of the Morpheme Tier Hypothesis (on which, see ch. 6), motivating the notion that the infixal vowel appears on a separate tier. Steriade cites a case from Saib (1976), in which the Ntifa and Zayan dialects of Tamazight Berber appear to allow such breakups, as in the derivation of /ettefẓaẓ/ 'to chew' from the zero form /feẓẓ/. This type of derivation permits geminates to be 'split'; purely phonological epenthesis does not.

15 Schein (1981), Kenstowicz (1982), Schein and Steriade (1986).

16 A large proportion of the examples of inalterability, as with the examples of integrity, are consistent with another interpretation, which we will sketch here in a footnote, looking ahead to notions introduced later in this book. This involves cases where the phonological rule in question – either modifying skeletal structure or modifying phonemic tier content – is triggered by a failure of the structure to satisfy word-level phonotactics. The theoretical account of word-level phonotactics will be dealt with in more detail in ch. 3 and 5, in connection with autosegmental licensing; but, simply put, all features of a segment must be *licensed* by the syllable structure that they are found in – either by the syllable node or by the coda node. We find that the coda positions of most languages do not license anywhere near as much phonological material as their onsets do. Geminates, however, are associated with both a coda position and an onset position, so, while they get their licensing from their onset position, they then give rise to the presence of segmental material in the coda that would otherwise not have a

chance of appearing there. In ch. 6, we will suggest that a broad range of phonological rules applies just in case their application serves to remove a word-level phonotactic violation, of just the sort sketched above. The rules discussed in the literature under the rubric of inalterability and integrity typically have this property: when they apply to non-geminates, it is in order to achieve compliance with a word-level phonotactic. Geminates, however, do not violate the phonotactic precisely because of licensing considerations. Thus, the rule in question *need* not apply, and hence does not. An example of this is Klingenheben's Law in Hausa, discussed below in ch. 3, which weakens obstruents to (certain non-nasal) sonorants (*w*, *r̥*) in Hausa, a rule whose *raison d'être* is the inability of the coda in Hausa to license the [point of articulation] features. However, a [point of articulation] feature may *associate* with a coda, just as long as it is also associated with an onset, for it is the onset that licenses it. Hence geminate obstruents do not violate the licensing restriction, and Klingenheben's Law need not apply – and hence does not.

17 There are other relevant aspects of Sierra Miwok not explored here. See also, e.g., Smith (1985), and the parallel problems in discussed in Archangeli (1983).

18 See Kenstowicz and Pyle (1973).

19 This treatment of geminate consonants is influenced by Sauzet (1985).

20 The issue is complex, and some aspects of it are discussed in Steriade (1986), though the method of inducing vowel copying across consonants on a single-chart analysis appears to me to be a far more serious problem than Steriade acknowledges; the issue remains to be resolved whether reduplicative copying is a mechanism separate from autosegmental spreading.

Çhapter 3　Syllable Structure

1 Among the important and instructive papers on the issues in the classical generative period, Anderson (1969) and especially Fudge (1969) should be noted. Fudge's article is often cited, but perhaps less often read, which is certainly a pity; it contains a number of basic points which took a good deal of time to be recognized by other phonologists. Anderson's paper, and the paper by Kohler to which it is a response, amply illustrate how the passion that attaches to the significance of the syllable for phonological theory antedates *The Sound Pattern of English*. Another, much earlier, paper (which is, again, often cited, but required a rediscovery to have its final theoretical impact) is Pike and Pike (1947), which discusses the internal structure of the syllable. See also Hockett (1955), as well as Haugen (1956a), from which is drawn the epigraph to this chapter.

2 Haugen (1956a) says that the 'only reference to syllabification in Harris's searching analysis of linguistic method is one which eliminates it in favor of juncture' (pp. 213–14). Perhaps; but the spirit in Harris is willing, even if the words do not come through.

3 Further restrictions apply to word-initial and word-final positions, as well as to clusters within a syllable.

4 Readers may recognize that some of the Semitic languages have been analyzed as having an underlying structure along these lines.

5 The issue has been raised in recent work on American Sign Language (ASL), for example, as to what the syllable is in ASL. (See Wilbur 1987 for a number of references on this subject.) That there is something that should be called a syllable in ASL is far from clear to me, for the reason alluded to in the text: one crucial fact about spoken language, without which the notion of the syllable may make no sense, is the pattern of alternation at the lowest physical level. (In the case of spoken language, it is essentially alternation of consonant and vowel.) The only nominees for this possibility are Movement and Hold (cf., e.g., Liddell and Johnson 1985), but there is far less prima facie evidence of such alternation at the surface in ASL than is found in spoken language when considering the C/V patterns. It may be, however, that there is a prosodic unit in ASL, distinct from the morpheme and the word, which serves as the formal domain of a single set of co-occurrence statements. In the sense explicated by licensing (see below), this may be the syllable in ASL.

6 If we were to try to express the phrase structure of the system, we would have to use some kind of unrestricted right-branching structure, perhaps setting up an 'S-phrase', with three expansions as in (i). One could write

(i) $\text{O-phrase} \rightarrow \text{O} + \begin{Bmatrix} \text{V-phrase} \\ \text{S-phrase} \end{Bmatrix}$ $\text{V-phrase} \rightarrow \text{V} + \begin{Bmatrix} \text{O-phrase} \\ \text{S-phrase} \end{Bmatrix}$

$\text{S-phrase} \rightarrow \text{S} + \begin{Bmatrix} \text{V-phrase} \\ \text{O-phrase} \end{Bmatrix}$

pages on why this would be an inadequate formalization of the system; I leave the exercise to readers.

7 Hockett (1955) is dubious about assigning clear structural status to 'interludes', the span of consonantal material in between successive nuclei. Haugen (1956a) takes specific issue with him on this, arguing that all such interludes must be understood as being composed of a coda followed by an onset.

8 See Hale (1973).

9 The idea that the syllable is a unit of hierarchical constituent structure is by no means shared by the important writings on the syllable in phonological theory. The major alternative is the approach that is described in Zellig Harris's *Structural Linguistics* (1951), in which there are not syllables *per se*, but rather syllable boundaries – as Harris would put it, a kind of juncture or zero phoneme. Syllables would then roughly correspond to the material that is found between successive syllable boundaries. Such a view differs from the view discussed here in several ways, of which the most important is the lack of internal structure to the syllable. Harris's boundary account also eliminates the possibility of defining non-syllabified material, a possibility discus-

sed below in the text, and of ambisyllabic segments, that is, segments simultaneously associated with two adjacent syllables. Kahn (1980) and Clements and Keyser (1983) offer theories of syllables that do not use syllable boundaries, but in which syllables have no internal structure as such.

10 See Pike and Pike (1947); Fudge (1969); Cairns and Feinstein (1982); Lapointe and Feinstein (1982); Anderson (1984).

11 See Steriade (1982), van der Hulst (1984), Clements (1988).

12 See, e.g., Kenstowicz and Kisseberth (1979). Hockett (1973) lists all the work on the language published to that point, and reviews it critically.

13 There seems to be no doubt that the nucleus is an obligatory component of the syllable, and that no language takes the coda to be an obligatory component of the syllable. However, there is reason to believe that the onset may be obligatory in some languages; this point is discussed, for example, in Mutaka and Hyman (1987), in the context of Kinande (Bantu) syllable structure.

14 This kind of approach is found, for example, in Kahn (1980), Steriade (1982), Clements and Keyser (1983), and Archangeli (1988), though Kahn and Clements–Keyser impose no onset/rhyme structure.

15 This approach is first mentioned in Halle (1978); see also Lowenstamm (1979), Selkirk (1981), Piggott and Singh (1985), Kaye and Lowenstamm (1984) and ter Mors (1988), and Ito (1988).

16 See Broselow (1980) for an interesting exploration of the differences of two Arabic dialects (Cairene and Iraqi) with respect to the placement of the epenthetic vowel. The difference between dialects with respect to where an epenthetic vowel is placed to break up an unsyllabifiable sequence of three consonants ($C_1C_2C_3$) may be analyzed in a less derivational fashion. When the vowel is placed between C_1 and C_2, the epenthetic vowel will surface in a heavy syllable; when it is placed between C_2 and C_3, it surfaces in a light syllable. The former appears to be the more common situation, but in any event, the two contrasting modes of epenthesis can be described without recourse to a derivational model as such.

17 See Singh (1987) for a discussion of this in a related context.

18 For reasons that are no doubt no more than historical, it has often been tempting to think that syllabification is only a 'late', quite superficial, phenomenon, from which it may be inferred that rules that are conditioned by morphological category, for example, would never be bled by rules sensitive to syllable structure (i.e. would never apply crucially after such syllable rules, in a particular way). However, such an assumption would be incorrect; it is not difficult to find examples in which word-level syllabification (cf. ch. 5), and word-level rules conditioned by syllabification, must take priority over (i.e. precede) other rules which are morphologically conditioned.

19 The question naturally arises whether such licensing considerations do not suggest that a more appropriate constituent structure for the syllable might not be one in which the syllable was divided first into a 'body' (to use Paul Smolensky's apt suggestion) and a coda, with the body then further divided

into an onset and a nucleus. A large range of both linguistic and psycholing-uist evidence points to the existence of a strongly bound rhyme constituent, however; see Fudge (1969) and especially Fudge (1987) for a review of some of this literature. The phonological interaction between the nucleus and the coda may be more pervasive than that between the onset and the nucleus, and psycholinguistic evidence suggests that the rhyme is taken as a perceptual and articulatory unit. Nonetheless, the issue remains open.

20 See Fujimura (1976, 1979), and Hirst (1985). See also the recent discussion in Fujimura (in press).

21 The prevalence of this pattern was first pointed out, to my knowledge, by Prince (1984). Ito (1988) provides a quite different account of the general-ization.

22 That parameter, it should be clear, is precisely what has up till now been taken to be responsible for whether the language was *quantity-sensitive* or not. We see that this distinction – whether the language is quantity-sensitive or not – falls together with the general phenomenon of coda weakening, from the point of view of autosegmental licensing.

23 Other general kinds of argumentation can be provided for this approach as well, including the arguments in the literature for dividing up the function-ing of the processes that link the onset to the nucleus, on the one hand, from the processes that establish the coda, a point that Steriade has argued (1982).

24 And perhaps certain vowels, too: the status of word-final long vowels is unclear in many Arabic dialects.

25 As noted above, this point was inspired by an observation at the end of Prince (1984).

26 This is clearly true over a much wider range of languages than just English, but whether it is universally true or not remains to be determined. In Dakota, for example (Carter 1974), there is a restricted set of consonants that can appear in clusters, but these clusters can appear word-initially. The underlying consonantal inventory is {p, t, c, k, s, š, x, l, n, m, w, ʔ}, and both *p* and *k* can precede any consonant (avoiding geminate clusters, and following Hollow in taking /pk/ to be the source of [tk]). However, while words can end with a single consonant, word-medial clusters consisting of three consonants are not allowed, though we would expect that if syllables could in general start with any of the observed clusters. Thus, if word-initial syllables in Dakota do indeed license two distinctive points of articulation, it would still appear that the second licensing effect is due to the word-initial position. I am endebted to Willem de Reuse for directing me to this material.

27 Exception: the *th* of *seventh* and of *width*; on this, see below.

28 Thereby providing an argument that the two *a*s in *saha* are distinct autosegments.

29 There is a generalization that might well be worth capturing to the effect that vowel positions are created by rule (either by being in a stressed open syllable or by appendix conversion) are filled by spreading vowels, con-

straints permitting, while underlying specified empty coda positions are filled by consonants. This is no doubt related to the fact that there is no vowel length contrast.

30 See Borgstrom (1937, 1940); Clements (1986); and Bosch (1988), who discusses the case in the terms described in the text.

31 Clements and Keyser (1983) similarly breaks down the analysis of possible English syllable into positive and negative statements which must be simultaneously met by the segments in question, though crucially differing from Fudge in utilizing no syllable-internal structure. Fudge (1987) addresses Clements and Keyser's skepticism regarding the status of the rhyme.

32 Admittedly, this leaves the word *sphinx* improperly licensed.

33 Including Wang (1968), Zimmer (1969), Hyman (1973, 1975), and Sagey (1986).

34 Unless the *s* is a separate morpheme, a point to which we return (*legs*).

35 One could claim these forms were underlying monosyllabic, I supposed, but at the W-level, which is what is relevant for our purposes, the constraint certainly appears to be violated. The trisyllabic pronunciation of *mountaineer* might be taken to support the underlying bisyllabicity of *mountain*, though the form of the juncture, and the nature of the derivation, would have to be settled before the argument could be considered decisive; see ch. 5. (Other words like *mountain* include *lightning, poultry, soldier, moisture, vintner,* and *dangerous*.)

36 An alternative which we will not pursue here would be to tighten word-internal coda feature distribution by means of the brace notation of (40), requiring *all* features in the coda to appear in the same segment – thus allowing no clusters in the coda.

37 Some speakers say *height-th*. This innovation is entirely in line with the analysis proposed here, for this word-final sequence (*t-th*) is possible not for just any English words, but only when the *-th* is one of the two morphemes mentioned in the text.

38 Again, this fits very naturally into the general notion of what it means for a syllable to allow certain combinations of distinctive features. The notion that the suffixes *-th* license their own material allows us to express the traditional notion that this material wears its morphemic allegiance on its sleeve, so to speak: one knows it comes from a separate morpheme just by looking at its phonological makeup. The case is a bit unusual, in that the same morpheme provides both the segmental material and the licenser, which is not the usual case. In French, for example, the subjunctive and third-person plural verbal suffixes are morphological licensers, which license the appearance of otherwise unassociable consonants in second and third conjugation verbs; the feminine marker is likewise a licenser for a subset of nouns and adjectives of the lexicon.

39 In the dialect being described here, my own.

40 The cases in which this identity might be questioned are cases in which we find, in a single heavy syllable, two vowel qualities in which neither can be accurately described as a glide with respect to the other; I am not aware of any clear cases of this sort. We take it, then, that the element(s) associated

with the head position of the rhyme is (are) the syllabic element(s).

41 See, e.g., Kaye and Lowenstamm (1984), and Levin (1985), which I have not had an opportunity to see. See also, for the development of a notion of a timing tier that does not assign a special position to onset material (all elements that correspond to the same mora associate to a single unit on the timing tier), Hyman (1985), Hayes (1987).

42 Cf. also Trubetzkoy (1967: 196–200). Within a framework that is extremely close to the present, see the discussion in Hockett (1947, 266–7). More recently, the matter has been taken up in Selkirk (1982a: 343) and Kaye and Lowenstamm (1984: 130), to mention just two other places.

43 Looking ahead to ch. 5, this point brings out a difference between the notions being employed here and those proposed by Kiparsky's (1982a, b) model of lexical phonology. On his account, the difference between suffixes like *-al*, which rescue the /n/ of *hymn* from deletion, on the one hand, and those processes, like compounding (cf. *hymn-almanac*, *hymn-outliner*, where the /n/ is deleted), which do not, on the other, involves stratal ordering: the *n* will have been deleted by the end of the lexical phonology. The word-level phonotactics of English, however, apply to structures that have completed (so to speak) all their stratum 1 activities.

44 The material ter Mors presents suggests that length may not be phonologic-ally lost if it is morphologically contrastive, in the sense that consonantal lengthening can itself constitute a morpheme, and such lengthening is perhaps not subject to deletion for purely phonological reasons.

45 This interesting article is explicitly quite tentative in its formulations, presenting two good arguments for syllabification within a generative treatment, and ending with the modest remark, 'These questions may indicate to you that I have only scratched the surface of a huge research field and that the real digging is yet to be done.' Vennemann (1986) presents a different view of the field, one that is not quite accurate. He correctly points out that Chomsky and Halle (1968) do not employ the notion of the syllable, which had been developed by a number of phonologists; in this, as we have noted, they were influenced by both Harris and Jakobson, though of course Jakobson and Halle (1956) do present the syllable as a significant element within their system. Vennemann also suggests that his 1972 paper established the importance of the syllable in lexical and phrase-level phonology, but was in part responsible for setting syllable phonology on a misguided path, by encouraging concern for questions involving the specific character of universal and language-particular syllabification rules, the properties of these rules, their interaction with other rules, etc., questions that Vennemann now takes to be wrongly posed (1986: 24–5). A review of the literature in this period suggests that the very tentative steps taken by Vennemann and Hooper were influential in the resurgence of concern for the syllable, as the literature cited in this chapter bears witness to, but that lack of concern for formal questions was the primary cause of the failure of large numbers of phonologists to be converted to their specific program. It is perhaps worth noting, though, that some of the earlier efforts in generative terms to incorporate the notion of the syllable were ungracious in failing to

give any serious credit to Hooper's work; see, e.g., Lowenstamm (1981: 576–8), though Lowenstamm was hardly unique in this respect.   ˙

46   Readers may recall that the languages in question are quite closely related.

47   This is the dialect of KiHunde that I studied with Mutima Sinamenye, discussed above in ch. 1.

48   The notion of rules applying at the phrase-level – 'post-lexically' – is an important notion which we will discuss at length in ch. 5.

49   For more on the internal stem structure of the Bantu verb, see ch. 5.

50   This is, of course, reminiscent of the difference mentioned above between Norwegian and Swedish, on the one hand, and Icelandic, on the other, and of the copied vowel of Selayarese that cannot go on any further.

51   Thus, the notion of autosegmental licensing can perform here the function of defining what Freely Associating Segments are, in the terminology of ch. 1.

Chapter 4   Metrical Structure

1   See Liberman and Prince (1977), and also Liberman (1979), the theoretical source of the former. Hayes (1980), circulated for several years by the Indiana University Linguistics Club, presented a clear general framework of arboreal metrical phonology, and was very influential in the development of a general metrical theory; its perspective pervades the first five sections of this chapter. Later work in metrical theory, especially that emphasizing grids, has been heavily influenced by Prince (1983); see below for this and other references.

2   The terms *left-dominant* and *right-dominant* are also sometimes used, but in Hayes (1980), a somewhat different technical sense is assigned to these terms.

3   The thoughtful reader who is less than satisfied with the temporal metaphor in this notion of iterative rule application may prefer to consider the parameter to determine, instead, whether the degenerate foot created in an odd-numbered domain is on the left edge or the right edge. In an even-numbered domain, 'direction' is irrelevant.

4   In order to maintain the tight fit between metrical prominence and geometrical structure, one can resort to extensive measures that are ultimately not worth the effort. In order to account for a system such as in Yup'ik, in which long vowels are heavy but VC rhymes are not, one can insist that long vowels constitute a branching nucleus, while VC rhymes have only one segment, the V, in the nucleus and another segment, the C, in the coda. See Anderson (1984) for a sympathetic discussion of this maneuver.

5   (20a) is cited in Halle (1987), a good overview of the tree/grid controversy. It is, incidentally, quite difficult to find convincing examples of unbounded quantity-insensitive foot structures; they are historically unstable. In the introduction to Clements and Goldsmith (1984), we argue that it was this instability, combined with the ongoing process of increasing word length,

that led to the rise of the Bantu accentual system. See also Goldsmith (1987b) on this point.

6 Though it has been suggested that, in a very small set of cases, there may be languages where there is a bounded metrical structure gathering groups of two (but no more) of adjacent metrical feet into units that are smaller than the word. If this is correct, then the bounded/unbounded parameter might be necessary above the foot level as well.

7 Recent work on Bantu tone systems has led to a similar conclusion. There we find evidence of accentual systems whose surface effects are all mediated through the tonal system, in that tones are reassociated towards positions that are more heavily accented. The metrically prominent positions themselves, however, have no greater loudness or duration. See Goldsmith (1987b, 1987c); Goldsmith and Sabimana (1985).

8 As with other languages of similar antiquity, there is uncertainty and scholarly disagreement as to the historically accurate description of the pronunciation of Classical Arabic (there are several distinct traditions recognized), and even, in the final analysis, of the precise meaning of such a question. While there is no doubt that an interplay between the stress principles at work in the modern colloquial dialect of a given Arabic speaker and the stress (s)he assigns to classical vocabulary, there are discussions in the literature which indicate some clear and systematic divergences which would allow us to set up at least some notion of a stress pattern of Classical Arabic with properties much like those described; see McCarthy (1979: 460–1).

9 However, Stuart (1957) reports that, 'in polysyllabic words, the accent falls on the first long vowel or diphthong, or if these be lacking, on the second syllabic vowel other than short /i/.' Odden cites Poppe (1951) as his source; Hayes gives Streeter (1963).

10 The existence of the last foot in (26a) and the first in (27a) will be questioned momentarily.

11 The development in this section is largely based on Prince (1983).

12 We will not pursue the intricacies of phrase-level stress in English in detail. A good introduction to the extant literature on this subject can be found in Hogg and McCully (1987), which, despite the name, overlaps hardly at all with the present book in content.

13 This can be treated as a separate issue, though, by maintaining grid representation, and marking constituency by means of bracketing grid marks on a given row. See, for example, Halle (1987), Hammond (1987), and references there.

14 This may be too simple, and it certainly reflects a prejudice inherent in the arboreal account to the effect that primary stresses are chosen from among the secondary stresses, which are independently assigned. But in a good number of languages, primary or word-level, stress is assigned first, and secondary stress is assigned on the basis of the position of the word-level stress that is already assigned.

15 Prince (1983) has raised the question of whether the bottom row need be bimoraic in all cases of quantity-sensitive systems. For present purposes, we assume the answer is yes, but cf. p. 271.

16 Sources: (i) Wright (1971), McCarthy (1979) and references there; (ii) McCarthy (1980); (iii) Kenstowicz (1980). See also Prince (1980), Welden (1980).

17 See McCarthy (1979: 451–2), on Classical and Cairene, and McCarthy (1980: 96, fn 5), on Damascene. The former source suggests that final CVVs are stressed in Cairene and unstressed in Classical Arabic. Kenstowicz (1980) is clear on the point that final CVV syllables are stressed in Cairene.

18 Examples from Hayes (1982).

19 It is important here to focus here on the presence of stress, not the presence of main (word) stress. We return to the treatment of word stress in English in section 5.2.3, where we will see that the location of main stress in English is predictable once the (secondary) stresses have been placed, roughly speaking – the guiding principle being that the rightmost stressed syllable that is *not* word-final receives the word stress.

20 I modify the form of his suggestions to suit the version of metrical theory we are employing here.

21 This accounts leaves open why long vowels in final syllables are unambiguously treated as heavy, surprisingly. However, as we noted in Chapter 3, the second half of the long vowel (or diphthong) in English is normally in complementary distribution with the non-coronal obstruent in coda position; hence when both appear, the offglide of the vowel must be in an appendix position.

22 In this respect, then, English differs from Arabic, where the appendix does associate with a grid position.

23 For example, on phrase-level stress, readers may look at the lengthy exposition in Hogg and McCully (1987) and the references given there, including Hayes (1983), (1984), and Selkirk (1984). With regard to the relation between the foot and segmental processes, one may see, for example, the papers by Leer in Krauss (1985), and the extended discussion in Nespor and Vogel (1986).

Chapter 5   Lexical Phonology

1 An early discussion of this is in Strauss (1982a), a revision of Strauss (1979). More influential have been the papers by Kiparsky (1982a,b), which develop a set of approaches to a broad class of traditional phonological problems, and Mohanan (1982, 1986). Pesetsky (1979) and Siegel (1974) were also extremely influential in the development of this approach.

2 Cyclicity of this sort is a hallmark of classical generative work, and was developed further in Aronoff (1976), under the influence of Brame (1972a, 1974).

3 Readers skeptical about one or both of these rules are invited to wait for a discussion of these points below. The formulation given of velar softening in (1) is more for expository convenience than out of conviction with regard to the phological environment.

4 Readers may fairly be warned that this is a somewhat unorthodox reading of

the literature on lexical phonology, but one that I shall attempt to justify in the course of this chapter. A more orthodox lexical phonological view of the matter would hold either that there are no lexical rules of the first sort mentioned above, or, more likely, that such rules are theoretically insignificant or irrelevant. The issues involved here are (i) the degree to which the rules are automatic (i.e. are not governed by particular morphemes), and (ii) the degree to which the rules are transparent (in Kiparsky's sense) and interpretable as aiming at satisfaction of a phonotactic. We return to this at the very end of the chapter; see n. 57.

5 Certainly one could ask whether such post-lexical rules are necessary in all cases. That is, one should look for language-specific evidence that features filled in by such default rules really are motivated in the phonology of the language. The alternative is to leave the matter in the hands of a phonetic theory that does not utilize phonological representations, but we will not explore this question here.

6 Wonderly (1951); see also Kenstowicz and Kisseberth (1979: 35ff.).

7 One view (see Kiparsky 1982a) takes feature filters to be special cases of the rules such as in (4a) which specify the unmarked value of a lexically contrastive feature, but as I have indicated, we will consider an alternative view in section 5.1.5 below.

8 In fact, the main difference between traditional structuralism and lexical phonology as regards what information must go in the lexical phonology as distinctive, and what must go in the post-lexical phonology, derives from the difference between the 'hearer's perspective', the fundamental point of view of structuralist phonology ('phonemics takes the point of view of the hearer,' says Wells 1947), and the speaker's (or, perhaps better, the knower's) point of view in generative phonology. See the remarks on the notion of 'segment' from the structural and generative points of view at the beginning of ch. 1.

9 This notion is also discussed in the recent literature in Anderson (1969, 1975) (see further references there), and Koutsoudas, Sanders, and Noll (1974).

10 In Goldsmith (1984a), I argue that the notion of precedence in application must be kept distinct from that of linear rule ordering, on the basis of a complex set of data in Tonga; a similar situation is found in Sukuma (Goldsmith 1985a).

11 Pulleyblank (1986a: 221ff., 235–6, fn. 20, and elsewhere) notes similar doubts about this interpretation of structure-preservation, and calls the reader's attention to similar points made in Mohanan and Mohanan (1984).

12 I have changed the relation of the tiers slightly from Kiparsky's formulation for clarity of exposition, but in a way that does not affect the validity of the argument one way or the other.

13 These heterorganic clusters *would* be evaluated as slightly more marked than the homorganic sequences, since the former would have their nasal point of articulation left unspecified underlyingly. But as we shall see when we discuss underspecification theory in more detail below, this difference would be the equivalent of the difference between, for example, *nightingale*, with its long first vowel, and *Canada*, with its short first vowel – hardly the

difference between impermissible and permissible sequences.

14 Kiparsky suggests just that, in prose (1985: 100): '[w]hen not assimilated, unspecified nasals ... are assigned the unmarked feature values... If we block these default values from being assigned lexically, the Elsewhere Condition will guarantee that they will not be assigned in the postlexical phonology until after Nasal assimilation has applied there.' If we take the filter in question to act like other lexical phonological rules, and enter into an Elsewhere relationship with the rule of nasal assimilation, then the filter will not block the assimilation rule, as needed; but in that case the filter will not *block* anything, because a lexical phonological rule is always overriden by the Elsewhere Condition, and a specific lexical entry 'overrides', in that sense, a lexical rule. If such feature filters do not participate in the Elsewhere relationship to lexical phonological rules like nasal assimilation, then the filter will block assimilation within the lexicon, which would undo the whole analysis. Of the two choices, the latter appears to be Kiparsky's theoretical position; cf. Kiparsky (1985: 98) where he says that feature filters should block the application of assimilatory rules, in accordance with the change-inhibiting interpretation. We may consider a third logical possibility, and suggest that feature filters enter into an Elsewhere relationship with lexical phonological *rules* but not with lexical entries – saying, in effect, that lexical entries may *not* violate the feature filters, but lexical phonological rules can create structures that do. This position requires abandoning one of the most important aspects of the interpretation of lexical phonology under discussion here, the notion that lexical entries and lexical phonological rules are the same kind of theoretical object, in the relevent respect. The correct solution to the present case, I will suggest shortly, is that no negative feature filter is required for most of the work, and the one that is required derives from the notion of autosegment licensing.

15 Kiparsky suggests that the principles of underspecification theory should surely not be taken to mean ruling out the possibility of specifically referring to the unmarked value. We believe that this *is* an important characteristic of an underspecification model of phonology, and that such references to unmarked values should in fact be ruled out. However, segmental positions that are unspecified for a particular feature (i.e. with respect to a particular autosegmental chart) may undergo assimilatory rules that other segments do not undergo in order to satisfy well-formedness conditions (phonotactics), such as that all consonants must be associated with a point of articulation at the phonetic level.

16 Put another way, the nasal segment that is still unmarked for point of articulation by the end of the phonology surfaces as an alveolar.

17 There may be further restrictions on point of articulation in the coda; this analysis is consistent with or without further conditions.

18 See the discussion of the Obligatory Contour Principle in ch. 6.

19 This conception of rule application is somewhat orthogonal to the subject of this book, which is the nature of representations rather than of rules or phonological levels. However, the conception of rule application in lexical phonology as Kiparsky has proposed it incorporates the traditional *SPE*

conception of rule application, which is precisely what is at issue here. For more discussion, see pp. 322ff.

20 This follows Kiparsky's analysis as well.

21 See Schuh (1972), and Newman and Salim (1981), though our analysis differs from theirs considerably. Within the present context, the synchronic and historical motivation for Klingenheben's Law is clear: the coda does not license a point of articulation. Hausa differs from most languages with this restriction in that it turns neither to epenthesis nor to cluster simplification for a resolution, but to glide formation.

22 No structural description need be specified if we follow the proposal mentioned just above (and discussed further in section 6.5) that word-level rules apply if and only if their application reduces the set of violations of phonotactic conditions.

23 This point is made forcefully in Halle and Vergnaud (1982). The fact that the specific rule of Sukuma mentioned also applies post-lexically may make the example less than an ideal illustrative example. See Pulleyblank (1986a: 221–3) for a parallel discussion.

24 Other recent work has applied a version of structure preservation that does not inhibit changes, but subjects the output of rules to higher-level procedures to insure structure preservation. Hayes (1986b), for example, develops a 'convention' for the feature [sonorant] whereby a segment that becomes [+nasal] by rule also becomes [+sonorant], and a non-continuant that loses its [+nasal] specification also becomes [−sonorant].

25 At least one suggestion has been made, in principle, that would indirectly put constraints on such a move; but the constraints are so indirect, and require such considerable analysis in order to put the constraints into effect, that in actual practice the braking effect of the constraint would be seen less rather than more frequently. The suggestion comes from Mohanan's work (1982), and involves the proposal that, if a rule is present in more than one stratum, then the sequence of strata that the rule is found in must form a continuous span in the phonology.

26 Thus once again, we see that lexical phonology is structured in such a way as to permit the maximal *phonologization* possible of processes affecting phonological segments, as opposed to any morphologization. To put the matter in a way suggested to me by B. Darden, the Strict Cycle Condition began as the Alternation Condition of Kiparsky (1968), which said something quite unobjectionable – that neutralizing sound changes effected strictly morpheme-internally are no longer synchronically active, having become part of the underlying form. Kiparsky (1982a) and later work on lexical phonology takes this not as a result of how languages are learned, but rather as a fact about the formalism of rule application, and interprets it as a formal device that would *explain*, in some sense, why a proposed rule should fail to apply morpheme-internally. To the extent that such an account is available to explain non-applications, to be sure, more freedom of movement to propose phonological rules applying at morpheme boundary is available to the linguist.

27 There is another process that lowers a suffixal *i* to *e*, and one might therefore

wonder whether this form *heer* derives from an intermediate *ha+er*. However, the rule lowering *i* applies after radicals with a mid vowel *e* or *o*, not after radicals with a low vowel *a*. Thus a radical of the form *CaC* takes the applied suffix *-ir-*, not *-er-*.

28 There is a useful discussion of the notions dealt with here in Steriade (1987), which unfortunately contains a large number of arguments that are vitiated by a change in the vowel features that are adopted for dealing with vowel systems; see ch. 6 below, and Goldsmith (1987a). To my knowledge, the first suggestion of underspecification theory as it has come to be known within the generative context is in Ringen (1988, [1975]), in the context of the treatment of vowel harmony. Clements (1988) also presents a clear discussion of the issues. As this book goes to press, a collection of papers on the subject has appeared (*Phonology*, vol. 5, n. 2, 1988), with a useful introduction by Archangeli (1988b).

29 They also are interpreted very naturally, as Pulleyblank (1983, 1986a) was the first to emphasize, within the framework of autosegmental phonology. We have used these notions quite a few times already, especially in attempting to license only specified (contrastive) features.

30 There is another important difference between these two types of restriction countenanced by underspecification theory. Feature specifications that are ruled out by the first ('eliminate redundant features') principle are ruled out throughout the lexical phonology; sonorants in English, that is to say, are not voiced at any point in the lexical phonology. Such constraints are thus part of the 'structure' that is 'preserved' during the lexical phonology. The rules that fill in the unmarked value of an opposition are lexical rules, and hence are not conceived of as *changing* a structure, or, put another way, are not thought of as creating a structure that is preserved throughout the lexical phonology.

31 And of course therein lies a difficult question: how are such generalizations collected by the language learner? Does he/she rely crucially on alternations noticed when a word takes on a suffix, and finds its vowel shortened, or is that just evidential icing on the cake? The question remains a knotty one.

32 See, for example, Dressler (1985) for a thorough review of the positions in the literature on the relations among the various rules of morphophonemics, in the broadest sense.

33 We would prefer a different formulation of this constraint, as careful readers will observe. Bearing in mind our discussion of the Catalan nasals above and the fact that syllabification is imposed on the word-level representation in Spanish, we would say that in Spanish no point of articulation specification may be present on a coda that is specified as nasal.

34 To wit, all words with main stress on the final syllable, such as *boutique* or *Peking*. Of course, if the only stressed syllable in a word is the final syllable, it will receive the main stress, but this is hardly an exception to anything (e.g. *balloon*, *remark*). Other questions arise with words such as *legislature*, which we cannot go into here.

35 An important case that is difficult for some speakers to judge involves the pair *compensation/condensation*, which Chomsky and Halle (1968) offer as a pair in which the second syllable is unstressed in the first word but stressed

in the second, as their theory predicts, based on their derivations from *compensate* and *condense*, respectively. Halle and Vergnaud (1987) mention three other examples, where a secondary stress is perceived on the second vowel, suggesting earlier derivation, including e*/ec*tricity, in*/es*tation. Judgments here are too delicate for this linguist's ear.

36 Including notably Liberman and Prince (1977) and Hayes (1982), among many others.

37 Hayes suggests that assigning stress to such final syllables by means of a process distinct from the main English stress rule is supported by the prediction that in such cases the *next* stress, scanning leftward, will be assigned in a quantity-sensitive way (so-called 'weak retraction'). On Hayes's account, no other stress assignment rule is quantity-sensitive, for the rhythmic assignment of stresses to alternating syllables leftward across a word will be done in a quantity-insensitive fashion.

38 A good range of simple words like *vanilla* exist with stress on the penultimate where the principle suggested here predicts antepenultimate stress. These accounts have only limited things to say about such words. A large proportion of them have a stressed [æ] and end in schwa, as in *Alabama*, but as *vanilla* shows, not all of them have these properties. All of the examples in (57b, d, e) of ch. 4 above similarly illustrate aspects of non-predictable English stress patterns.

39 A medieval form of refereeing.

40 The same rule appears to apply in an extended way to certain heavy syllables when they form Latinate prefixes (e.g. *con-taminate*, where the prefix has a reduced vowel because the following syllable is stressed, contrasting with *con-sternation*, where the prefix has a full vowel).

41 This rule and trisyllabic shortening share a common feature that our present analysis does not capture, unfortunately. There are generalizations about *derived* stress feet in English that we have not considered; see Selkirk (1980) for some remarks that can be interpreted along these lines. She offers an account that includes feet with two unstressed syllables following a stress syllable (as in *Canada*, for example). While such feet have no systematic place as such in the analysis discussed in the text above, there do appear to be significant properties about such derived feet whose recognition would allow us to simplify the formulation of the destressing rules. For example, such derived feet do not normally contain more than three moras. Thus, none of the syllables in such ternary feet can be heavy, either by reason of containing a long vowel or by reason of containing a closed syllable. This generalization stands behind trisyllabic shortening, to be sure. (A small class of exceptions exists to this generalization, such as the much-discussed *obesity*, with a long stressed vowel, or the proper name *Sepulveda*, with main stress on the second syllable.)

42 She lists five: *gruesome, hapless, feckless, winsome*, and *fulsome*.

43 The nominalizing suffix *-al* attaches only to bases that independently have final stress, as in *arriv-al, renew-al* (cf. *arrive, renew*), but not *perjural (cf. *perjure*, with initial stress).

44 A suggestion along these lines was made by Pesetsky (1979) for Russian, and by Strauss (1982b) for English, on the basis of some material we will reconsider below.

45 This division even suggests a natural difference in the phonological behavior of the two kinds of 'zero derivation' in English, the word-category change that can take place with no overt affixation, as in pairs like *contŕast* (v) / *cóntrast* (n). In cases such as this one, where the two forms are either apparently of the same degree of 'basicness' in the language, or in cases where the noun appears to be derived from the verb, we find that the noun displays the stress pattern appropriate for nouns, and the verb displays the stress pattern appropriate for verbs. On the other hand, when a verb is clearly created from a noun, it retains the stress pattern of the base noun (e.g. *to pattern*, as in 'the adjectives pattern with the nouns phonologically'; as we have already seen, a verb ending with two consonants would normally receive final stress, which is not the case here).

46 Selkirk (1982b: 104) cites Siegel (1977) as having drawn the same conclusion regarding the behavior of *-ment*. As I read Siegel, she proposes that the *ment* of *government* is neither class I nor class II, but rather that there is a boundary symbol (#) inserted with all class II suffixes which can also irregularly appear in a few underlying forms. We may distinguish three kinds of morphophonological theories: the boundary-driven type, as in Chomsky and Halle, and Siegel; the rule-block driven type, as in lexical phonology; and the domain-labeling type, adumbrated in Selkirk and discussed further below.

47 An excellent discussion of this can be found in Aronoff and Sridhar (1983). I have also benefited from reading Badecker (1988).

48 See Aronoff and Sridhar (1983), Mohanan (1986), and references there.

49 Williams (1981) proposes an account according to which the correct structure is the one predicted by the Affix Ordering Generalization (i.e. [un[[grammatical]ity]]]), and he suggests that structures of the form [x[y[z]]] will be recognized by the grammar as being 'related' to other structures of the form [x[y]]. If correct, this proposal would have the amusing property of relating non-constituents in compounds as well, such as *union suit* and *union suit-tailor* (since the latter has the form [union [suit [tailor]]]. The former is a kind of garment; the latter a progressive worker. One can construct other examples of this sort, such as *maternity suit* and *maternity suit-case*.

50 Pesetsky (1985) discusses these problems from a different perspective, though my remarks in this section and the next indicate why I am not in sympathy with his particular solution to the 'paradox'.

51 An interesting precursor of this approach is seen in Chung (1983), who is concerned with choosing between transderivational constraints and cyclic accounts in the face of phonological processes in Chamorro that optionally take 'earlier cycles" stress specification into account.

52 Halle and Vergnaud actually achieve this through a mechanism of *conflation* of the second and third row, essentially the same as what we referred to as suppression of secondary stresses. This leaves a grid mark on the second row only on the syllable with the main (word) stress, which is then copied.

53 We are using stratal terminology here, to be sure, though in the final analysis we will not conclude that it is appropriate to account for the present data.

54 This formulation of the restriction is tree-oriented in its statement. A less constituent-oriented formulation would be that the right-to-left perfect grid (quantity-insensitive) application that constitutes stress retraction applies only to stretches of unstressed syllables, which is the way Perfect Grid always works; in addition, there is no forward clash ovrride, again the unmarked case. Kiparsky (1982a) offers one example of a case where stress retraction does not work this way: the case of *solidify*, where he suggests that the 'unfooted' *i* of the suffix -*ify* is enough to trigger stress retraction. It is equally reasonable to suppose that this is a case of close juncture, precisely as Kiparsky proposes for such 'irregular' forms as *democratize*, where stress retraction does indeed appear to have overriden the stress pattern of the base.

55 The same point is made on independent grounds in Fabb (1985).

56 See the typological remarks in Booij and Rubach (1987).

57 The skeptic who was trying to establish a case against treating trisyllabic shortening as a phonological process might proceed suffix by suffix, looking a bit more closely to see whether alternations (like the one cited by Kiparsky 1982a, *omen/ominous*) holds up across the range of words in the English lexicon. A glance through a backwards-alphabetized dictionary, such as *Walker's Rhyming Dictionary*, suggests that there is no large class of words formed with an -*ous* suffix attached to an independently existing word base. Some exist, to be sure, such as *humorous*, related to *humor*, or *scandalous*, or *perilous*. Others, like *ominous*, the example mentioned by Kiparsky, are rather distantly related to the word that looks like it might serve (or might once have served) as a base, since calling a sky ominous is not to call it an omen. Still others look like they are formed with an -*ous* suffix but have no plausible base; the pattern *felicitous/felicity* is not matched by *jealous/jelly*.

A glance, then, at the eight or nine hundred -*ous* suffixes in English turns up only one clear case where the adjectival form has a short vowel, but the related base has a long vowel: *libido/libidinous*, but the short vowel [I] found in the derived form is not the expected vowel (we would expect ɛ]) – nor, of course, is the *in* expected. A good number exist that violate the shortening prediction, such as *cretinous, mountainous, libellous, poisonous, sonorous* (for some speakers, such as myself), *scrupulous, numerous, gratuitous, odorous,* or *cumulous*. It may not be accidental that most of these examples involve long round vowels, which may simply not fall under the generalization expressed by trisyllabic shortening; but be that as it may, the -*ous* forms cannot be said to provide positive suport for the existence of trisyllabic shortening as a rule in English. What the examples do suggest, however, is that the direction of change that is induced in the stem by the juxtaposition of affixes is in the direction of what would be found in nonderived forms.

Chapter 6 Further Issues

1 Or rather, the intersection of these intersecting sets with the set of segments in the language at hand. On a related point, one interpretation of a theory of

privative feature values is that each feature F defines only *one* set of segments; natural classes would then consist of the intersections of the various sets thus defined.

2   I use the term 'post-Bloomfieldian' to describe the set of views on phonological theory outlined in various ways in the now classic reader Joos (1957). (See Hymes and Fought 1981 for an excellent discussion of the term and the trend.)

3   Several of these features deserve some mention, because they are not very familiar. Voiceless obstruents are [+stiff vocal cords]; voiced obstruents are [+slack vocal cords]. Aspirated obstruents are [+spread glottis], as is *h*; glottalized obstruents are [+constricted glottis], as is ˀ.

4   At least one statement appears in the literature that adopts such a view (Sagey 1988), though that note misconstrues the basis of a theory of phonology, in my opinion. Sagey discusses a model of autosegmental phonetics – i.e. a model for the description of articulatory events in time – rather than a theory of phonology. In addition, she attempts to show that properties of an autosegmental model of phonology (or, as I suggest, phonetics) may derive from 'extralinguistic knowledge' (p. 109). Again, this seems to me to be mistaken in principle, not in detail. If we take the term 'knowledge' in a strictly cognitive and reflective sense, then such knowledge is irrelevant to the structure of phonological representations; if we take it in some other sense (though what sense that might be is difficult to imagine), a sense that would extend to the phonetic events that take place in time spans measuring no more than 10–100 milliseconds, then the axiomatization of our common sense notion of time (p. 110) is certainly false – in a wide range of areas, subjective events at the micro-level do not organize themselves in a fashion that respects our common-sense view of time; deriving phonetic principles from an *a priori* axiomatization of time in such a case does not show that the principles derive from some external knowledge in that case (even leaving aside, as I have said, the problematic notion of 'knowledge' that is involved).

5   See, for example, Kiparsky (1968).

6   Another case in which a classificatory feature has seemed appropriate – though it is not matched, it would seem, by a phonetic manifestation in any direct way – are the features of juncture, such as the featural difference between a '+' boundary and a '#' boundary, in the *SPE* analysis.

We not infrequently find segments that are identical (for our practical purposes) in two or more different languages, but whose phonological behavior is distinct in an unexpected way. Both *b* and *d* have sonorant-like properties in several West African languages, while *v* and *w* are also segments that may act like a sonorant in one language, an obstruent in another. A common way to deal with this problem is by changing the specification of this segment for the feature [sonorant], but that is just a way of saying that a phonological use of a feature may diverge from a fixed and constant phonetic realization.

7   Readers will recall that a feature is used as a *privative* feature if only one value of that feature is permitted in a representation, and it is used as an

equipollent feature if two values (+ and −) are permitted in the representation.

8 This question is raised, though not answered, in the interesting discussion in Hockett (1961: esp. 41). Fudge (1967) considers an interesting, but currently unpopular, view. On the general subject of the difference between 'phonetic features' and 'phonological features', see Vennemann and Ladefoged (1973), and the apposite remarks of Hayes (1986b: 477).

9 A number of useful papers will appear in van der Hulst and Smith (to appear), of which I have seen only Dikken and van der Hulst (1988).

10 This remark may deserve some further elaboration. Some aspects of the sound signal go unrepresented in the phonological and phonetic representations. Aspects that are universal and difficult to represent at these levels are prime candidates for characteristics to be left out of such representations, such as the effect of vowel height on fundamental frequency or on duration. In this way, then, phonetic representations unabashedly underrepresent the speech signal, but that is not problematic. The question becomes thornier with respect to characteristics of a speech signal that may be language-particular, and yet which we do not need to represent explicitly in a phonological representation at any level, as far as we can see. An example of this sort might be voicing of vowels in English. To my knowledge, there is no evidence, or reason to believe, that vowels in English are marked for voicing, though cross-linguistically this feature may well be contrastive for vowels. In short, underspecification theories of the sort we considered in ch. 5 drive *out* a good deal of the featural specification in underlying representations; our question now is to determine precisely what 'overspecification' theory (so to speak) requires that such feature specification should be put back in, and at what point. As should be apparent, I believe that considerable caution is in order with respect to a strong 'full specification' or 'overspecification' position, as of the sort mentioned in the text above. I have been influenced here by unpublished work by Osamu Fujimura on these issues from a phonetician's point of view; cf. Keating (1988), which appeared shortly before this book went to press.

11 Cf. Goldsmith (1981), Halle and Vergnaud (1980).

12 Complications arise in the palatal member of the series, because the palatal consonants to which the nasal assimilates are laminal, rather than apical, and the assimilating *n* remains apical; see Harris (1969: 9–13). For a phonological account of this general area, see Carreira (1988). Harris (1984) discusses the general problem of nasal assimilation in Spanish from an autosegmental point of view in much greater detail than I do here.

13 There are three optional alternative forms given by Hayes: the *ph*, *th*, *kh* sequences can be optionally *ʔh*; the *ts* can be *ss*, and the *ms* can be *ss*. I have changed two apparent errors: Hayes give the *st* combination as *sp*, and the *kl* combination as *ʔr*.

14 This is an excellent example of the more general proposition that geometrized autosegmental and metrical analyses tend to require far less extrinsic ordering, all other things being equal, than purely segmental analyses.

15 While Hayes has undoubtedly presented an elegant and insightful account of Toba Batak, certain questions do remain regarding the degree of 'overspeci-

fication' of the representation he employs. That is, the kinds of generalization that we observed in chs 3 and 5 regarding weakenings of consonants in coda positions arise here in Toba Batak, and such processes can be described only in the context of an underspecification theory. Assimilation processes, such as those by which coda consonants assimilate to onset positions for point of articulation, are motivated and guided by licensing restrictions that block a coda position from licensing a point of articulation. The formation in Toba Batak of a glottal stop in coda positions that are not otherwise geminated (on Hayes's account, protected therefore by the Conjunctivity Condition) is highly reminiscent of the effects that we observed in ch. 3, if we assume that in Toba Batak there is a phrase-level syllable representation at which certain licensing conditions are imposed. Such conditions would have to permit in coda position a glottal stop (an obstruent unspecified for point of articulation), but to rule out a voiceless stop specified for point of articulation, a condition very similar to what we saw in a number of languages in ch. 3. However, that cannot be *quite* right for the case at hand, because an independent point of articulation *is* permitted in coda position just so long as the consonant is nasal (i.e. *m*, *n*, and *ŋ* appear contrastively in the coda). Licensing does not provide an account of why point of articulation may not be licensed except in the presence of a nasal autosegment in the coda. However, there is an alternative possibility worth considering. We assume that, despite the fact that these rules apply post-lexically, they apply to representations that satisfy underspecification criteria; as we have just observed, this is a necessary condition for using a licensing approach. Nothing prevents us, however, from assuming as well that the value of the feature [nasal] that is operative in Toba Batak is [−nasal]. On this account, a segment *un*specified for this feature is nasal, and oral obstruents must be explicitly marked as [−nasal]. Three factors suggest that this is indeed correct. First, this interprets an *n* as the totally unspecified consonant, and the rule of *n*-assimilation (17) becomes formally more natural, as it is interpreted as the assimilation of the total unspecified consonant to its right-hand consonantal neighbor. Second, the rule of denasalization (18) clearly demonstrates that the feature [−nasal] is present and can spread autosegmentally; its doubly-linked character in the output representations of (18) is what serves to block the application of (20), glottal formation. Denasalization (18) will be simplified further by eliminating the change whereby a [+nasal] autosegment is deleted, since there will be no such autosegment present. The modified form of the rule will be as in (i). Third,

(i) Denasalization (reformulated)

$$[-\text{voice}] \qquad \text{Peripheral tier}$$

the rule of glottal formation (20) now is revealed as a coda restriction blocking the simultaneous licensing of a [−nasal] and point of articulation on a coda consonant. If we assume the following feature specification in (ii), then we may identify the coda in Toba Batak as licensing a maximum of *one* of the following distinctive features at the phrase level in question (not including major class features, as before). Segments specified with no more than one feature are: *m, n, ŋ, s, l, r,* ʔ. The other segments, the oral stops, are combinations of point of articulation and [−nasal]. (We have little information about the liquids *l* and *r* on which to base their featural analysis.)

(ii)

	p	t	k	b	d	g	s	h	m	n	ŋ	r	l	ʔ
P of A	lab.	cor.	vel.	lab.	cor.	vel.	alv.		lab.	cor.	vel.			
Nasal	−	−	−	−	−	−	−							−
Rhotic												+		
Lateral													+	
Voice				+	+	+								

16 See Cook (1987) and Poser (1982), for two examples.

17 It is, unfortunately, not clear whether this process is taken to apply in the lexical phonology or in the post-lexical phonology, a point bearing on the suggestion in n.15. If the creation of geminate *l*s creates a form that is not present in underived forms, then the well-known version of lexical phonology discussed in ch. 5 would predict that the rule is post-lexical, since structure preservation would prevent a rule from creating a type of structure within the lexical phonology that was not found in underived forms. If this is the case, then this represents a case of underspecification in post-lexical phonology as well.

18 This section is heavily influenced by Hayes (1988), who attributes the discussion on the 'diphthongization paradox' to Steriade (forthcoming), which I have not seen. I have modified Hayes's notation a bit, substituting a geometric model for an algebraic formalism.

19 This section is based on Goldsmith (1985b, 1987a); for more details, see these references.

20 Most notably, the papers by Kiparsky (1982a, 1982b, 1985), Pulleyblank (1986a, 1986b). On the other hand, several studies have considered more substantive revisions of vowel representations, including Goldsmith (1985b), Rennison (1985), a number of papers by van der Hulst and Smith (cf. 1985), and papers by Schane (1984), and Kaye, Lowenstamm, and Vergnaud (1985), among others.

21 Given the symmetry of [round] and [front], we could in principle choose to call the feature [front] and make rounding predictable post-lexically, in the simple five-vowel system.

22 There has been considerable discussion in the literature as to how one might allow underspecification of one sort or another without allowing anything that smacked of a three-way formal distinction for features. Put another way, the discussion has addressed the question, if binary features cannot be used in a ternary fashion, what are the consequences for formal phonology? As the discussion in this chapter suggests, this seems to me to be premature; binary features, used in an equipollent fashion, *can* give rise to distinctions that are in effect three-way.

23 One can establish ordered default rules in such a way as to make these vowels arise out of the fewest underlyingly marked feature specifications. That is hardly the point; one can *make* any set of vowels be the least marked. The task is to establish a representational system in which the correct result has a natural basis.

24 It is similar to the familiar notion of *symmetry*, to be sure, but formalized in a slightly different fashion.

25 This analysis is very similar in spirit to the accounts given in Goldsmith (1985b), where I argue that both Hungarian and Finnish should be viewed synchronically as having a canonical five-vowel system, with one equipollent feature, [round], and one privative feature, [low]. In Hungarian and Finnish, the privative feature [back] may be present as well in the lexical entry. See also Goldsmith (1987a), and Ringen (1988b).

26 See Clements and Sezer (1982) for further discussion of Turkish, and the important matter of its interaction with consonantal specification.

27 This proposal was first made in Goldsmith (1979, ch. 4). It is aptly discussed by Singler (1980) and Odden (1986) (both excellent studies of this principle), but is not correctly represented in McCarthy (1986: 253–4), at least as I read it; McCarthy cites only Odden's (1986) paper (not yet published).

28 Pulleyblank (1988) offers several appealing arguments for the Morpheme Tier Hypothesis.

29 McCarthy actually suggests that (60b) will maintain the prefixal material *li* on a separate tier from the stem material *sbob*, for reasons that need not concern us here concerning the ordering of processes.

30 McCarthy's (1986) position regarding fusion is guarded, it appears. As Odden notes, he suggests that the function of the OCP 'is not that sporadically assumed in the tonal literature ... [that of] a process that fuses adjacent identical tones into a single one' (208); 'I reject the fusion interpretation of the OCP' (222). Yip (1988) interprets McCarthy as including OCP fusion effects as part of the tier conflation process, though McCarthy actually offers this at the end of his paper as a notion 'in the realm of speculation' (257); through the substantive part of the paper, he is clearly at pains to avoid any such suggestion.

31 See Liberman (1979), Halle and Vergnaud (1982), Haraguchi (1977), and most forcefully Pulleyblank (1986a).

32 Sommerstein (1977) offers a broader discussion of the issue, though in less detail, and suggests (73) that his conception is 'to some degree under the influence of' stratificational grammar, as articulated, for example, in Lamb (1966).

33 Paradis (1988) more recently, following up on Singh (1987), has extended and developed some of these ideas. I have also profited from Bosch (1988) and Wiltshire (1988), who explore these issues with respect to Scottish and IṛuLa respectively.

34 There are more than a few parallels to central considerations of stratificational phonology, it may be noted; see Sommerstein (1977). Of course, even lexical phonology is considerably more stratificational than classical generative phonology.

35 This type of notion of a 'soft' – a violatable – well-formedness condition is extremely important to the approach being suggested here, and in outlook is at odds with the classical generative approach. Nonetheless, it has clear antecedents in the literature that we have mentioned. For example, this is precisely the claim of the 'Well-formedness Condition' of Goldsmith (1979) discussed above; it is noted in Liberman and Prince (1977: 311), who distinguish between situations that produce 'pressure for change', and language-particular specifications of when and how permission is granted to change a representation. Yip (1988) also observes this point, though she takes it to be the case that one 'repair strategy' (for the OCP, in the case at hand) will always be available, though no evidence is presented for this.

36 One especially obvious aspect that is overlooked in this representation is the characterization of cyclic morphology, as discussed in the last section of ch. 5. For purposes of clarity, I will leave the diagram as it is, recognizing that additional complexity is required. The term 'harmonic' alludes to work by Smolensky (1986), to which we will briefly return below.

37 The pervasiveness of this process and its linkage to well-formed syllabification was the basis of a large part of Kisseberth's influential notions concerning 'conspiracies' (Kisseberth 1970).

38 I simplify Wiltshire's presentation in (71b); she argues for a coplanar representation of the various coronal points of articulation, along the lines suggested in Archangeli (1985).

39 There is some evidence that this should hold of the P-level in some languages.

40 Clearly there is more to be said about how such well-formedness conditions should be properly stated, but this question takes us well beyond the bounds of this chapter.

Bibliography

The following entries are listed by date of publication, which in some cases is several years later than the date of initial circulation, either in the underground or by the Indiana University Linguistics Club. When a dissertation appeared at an earlier date than the date of publication, this year is indicated in the bibliographic reference.

BLS   Berkeley Linguistics Society
IJAL   *International Journal of American Linguistics*
JL   *Journal of Linguistics*
LA   *Linguistic Analysis*
Lg   *Language*
IULC   Indiana University Linguistics Club
LI   *Linguistic Inquiry*
LSA   Linguistics Society of America
NLLT   *Natural Language and Linguistic Theory*

Allen, Margaret (1978). *Morphological Investigations*. PhD dissertation, University of Connecticut.

Anderson, John (1979). Syllabic or non-syllabic phonology? *JL* 5:136–42.

Anderson, Stephen R. (1969). *West Scandinavian Vowel Systems and the Ordering of Phonological Rules*. PhD dissertation, MIT.

Anderson, Stephen R. (1974). *The Organization of Phonology*. New York: Academic Press.

Anderson, Stephen R. (1975). On the interaction of phonological rules of various types. *JL* 11:39–62.

Anderson, Stephen R. (1976). Nasal consonants and the internal structure of segments. *Language* 52: 326–44.

Anderson, Stephen R. (1982). Shwa in French, or How to get something for nothing. *Language* 58: 534–73.

Anderson, Stephen R. (1984). A Metrical Interpretation of Some Traditional Claims about Quantity and Stress. In Aronoff and Oehrle (1984).

Anderson, Stephen R. (1985). *Phonology in the Twentieth Century*. University of Chicago Press.

Aoun, J. (1979). Indexing and Constituency, Part I. Unpublished paper, MIT.

Archangeli, Diana (1983). The root CV–template as a property of the affix: evidence from Yawalmani. *NLLT* 1 (3): 347–84.

Archangeli, Diana (1985). Yokuts harmony: evidence for coplanar representation in nonlinear phonology. *LI* 16: 335–72.

Archangeli, Diana (1988a). *Underspecification in Yawelmani Phonology and Morphology*. PhD dissertation, MIT, 1984. New York: Garland Press.

Archangeli, Diana (1988b). Aspects of underspecification theory. *Phonology* 5: 183–207.

Arnott, D. W. (1964). Downstep in the Tiv verbal system. *African Language Studies* 5: 34–51.

Aronoff, Mark (1976). *Word-formation in Generative Grammar*. Linguistic Inquiry Monograph Series, no. 1. Cambridge, Mass.: MIT Press.

Aronoff, Mark and Oehrle, Richard (eds) (1984). *Language Sound Structure: studies in phonology presented to Morris Halle by his teacher and students*. Cambridge, Mass.: MIT Press.

Aronoff, Mark and Sridhar, S. N. (1983). Morphological Levels in English and Kannada; or, Atarizing Reagan. In *Papers from the Parasession on the Interplay of Phonology, Morphology, and Syntax*, ed. John Richardson, Mitchell Marks, and Amy Chukerman. Chicago Linguistic Society.

Aschman, Herman P. (1946). Totonaco phonemes. *IJAL* 12: 34–43.

Badecker, William (1988). Affix Raising and the Level Ordering Hypothesis. Unpublished paper, Johns Hopkins University.

Bargery, G. P. (1934). *A Hausa–English Dictionary and English–Hausa Vocabulary*. Oxford University Press.

Bell, Alan and Hooper, Joan eds. (1978). *Syllables and Segments*. Amsterdam: North-Holland.

Bender, Byron (1968). Marshallese phonology. *Oceanic Linguistics* 8: 16–35.

Bhatia, T. and Kenstowicz, M. (1972). Nasalization in Hindi: a reconsideration. *Papers in Linguistics* 5: 202–12.

Birk, D. B. W. (1975). The phonology of MalakMalak. In *Papers in Australian Linguistics*, no. 8, ed. M. C. Sharpe, L. Jagst, and D. B. W. Birk. Pacific Linguistics Series A, no. 39.

Birk, D. B. W. (1976). *The MalakMalak Language, Daly River (Western Arnhem Land)*. Pacific Linguistics Series B, no. 45. Canberra: Australia National University.

Bloch, Bernard (1948). A set of postulates for phonemic analysis. *Lg* 24: 3–46.

Bloch, Bernard and Trager, George (1942). *Outlines of Linguistic Analysis*. Baltimore: LSA Special Publication.

Bloomfield, Leonard (1933). *Language*. New York: Henry Holt; reprinted, University of Chicago Press, 1984.

Booij, Geert and Rubach, Jerzy (1987). Postcyclic versus postlexical rules in lexical phonology. *LI* 18: 1–44.

Borgstrom, C. Hj. (1937). The Dialect of Barra in the Outer Hebrides. *Norsk Tidsskrift for Sprogvidenskap* 8: 71–242.

Borgstrom, C. Hj. (1940). *A Linguistic Survey of the Gaelic Dialects of Scotland*. Vol. 1: *The Dialects of the Outer Hebrides*. Norsk Tidsskrift for Sprogvidenskap, Suppl. Bind 1, Oslo.

Bosch, Anna (1988). VC Syllable Structure in Scottish Gaelic: some implications for syllable theory. Unpublished paper, University of Chicago.

Bosch, Anna, Need, Barbara and Schiller, Eric (eds) (1987). *23rd Annual Regional Meeting of the Chicago Linguistics Society. Part Two: Parasession on Autosegmental and Metrical Phonology.* Chicago Linguistics Society.

Brame, Michael (1972a). The Segmental Cycle. In Brame (1972b).

Brame, Michael (ed.) (1972b). *Contributions to Generative Phonology.* Austin: University of Texas Press.

Brame, Michael (1974). The cycle in phonology: stress in Palestinian, Maltese, and Spanish. *LI 5:* 39–60.

Broadbent, S. M. (1964). *The Sierra Miwok Language.* Berkeley and Los Angeles: University of California Press.

Broselow, Ellen (1980). Syllable structure in two Arabic dialects. *Studies in the Linguistic Sciences* 10: 13–24.

Cairns, C. and Feinstein, Mark (1982). Markedness and the theory of syllable structure. *LI* 13: 193–226.

Callaghan, C. (1965). *Lake Miwok Dictionary.* University of California Publications in Linguistics, vol. 34.

Carlson, Robert (1985). A Sketch of Supyire Tone. Unpublished paper.

Carreira, Maria (1988). The Structure of Palatal Consonants in Spanish. *Papers from the 24th Annual Regional Meeting of the Chicago Linguistic Society,* Vol. 1, ed. Lynn MacLeod, Gary Larson, and Diane Brentari. Chicago Linguistic Society.

Carter, Richard T. Jr (1974). *Teton Dakota Phonology.* University of Manitoba Anthropology Papers, no. 10.

Chomsky, Noam and Halle, Morris (1968). *The Sound Pattern of English.* New York: Harper and Row.

Chung, Sandra (1983). Transderivational relationships in Chamorro phonology. *Language* 59: 35–66.

Clements, George N. (1976). *Vowel Harmony in Nonlinear Generative Phonology.* Distributed by the IULC, 1980.

Clements, George N. (1977). The Autosegmental Treatment of Vowel Harmony. In W. U. Dressler and I. E. Pfeiffer (eds), *Phonologica 1976.* Innsbrucker Beitrage zur Sprachwissenschaft, vol. 19.

Clements, George N. (1981). Akan Vowel Harmony: a nonlinear analysis. In G. N. Clements (ed.), *Harvard Studies in Phonology,* vol. 2. Distributed by IULC.

Clements, George N. (1984). Principles of Tone Assignment in Kikuyu. In Clements and Goldsmith (1984).

Clements, George N. (1985a). Compensatory Lengthening and Consonant Gemination in Luganda. In Wetzels and Sezer (1985).

Clements, George N. (1985b). The geometry of phonological features. *Phonology Yearbook* 2: 223–52.

Clements, George N. (1986). Syllabification and Epenthesis in the Barra Dialect of Gaelic. In *The Phonological Representation of Suprasegmentals,* ed. by Koen Bogers, Harry van der Hulst, and Maarten Mous. Dordrecht: Foris Publications.

Clements, George N. (1987). Phonological Feature Representation and the Description of Intrusive Stops. In Bosch et al. (1987).

Clements, George N. (1988). Towards a Substantive Theory of Features Specification. In *Proceedings of the 18th Annual Meeting of the North East Linguistics Society.* Amherst, Mass.: Graduate Linguistic Student Association.

Clements, George N. and Ford, Kevin (1979). Kikuyu tone shift and its synchronic consequences. *LI* 10: 179–210.

Clements, George N. and Goldsmith, John (eds) (1984). *Autosegmental Studies in Bantu Tone.* Dordrecht: Foris Publications.

Clements, George N. and Keyser, S. J. (1983). *CV Phonology.* LI Monograph Series, no. 9. Cambridge, Mass.: MIT Press.

Clements, George N. and Sezer, Engin (1982). Vowel and Consonant Disharmony in Turkish. In van der Hulst and Smith (1982, Part II).

Cook, Eung-Do (1987). An Autosegmental Analysis of Chilcotin Flattening. In Bosch et al. (1987).

Crowley, Terry (1982). *The Paamese Language of Vanuatu.* Pacific Linguistics Series B, no. 87. Canberra: Australian National University.

Diffloth, Gérard (1968). *The IruLa Language, A Close Relative of Tamil.* PhD dissertation, UCLA.

Dikken, M. den and Hulst, Harry van der (1988). Segmental Hiearchicture (preliminary version). To appear in *Features, Segmental Structure and Harmony Processes*, ed. H. van der Hulst and Norval Smith. Dordrecht: Foris Publications.

Dinnsen, Daniel (ed.) (1979). *Current Approaches to Phonological Theory.* Bloomington: Indiana University Press.

Donegan, Patricia (1978). *On the Natural Phonology of Vowels.* PhD dissertation, Ohio State University.

Douglas, Wilfrid H. (1981). Watjarri. In *Handbook of Australian Languages*, vol. 2, ed. R. M. W. Dixon and Barry J. Blake. Canberra: Australian National University Press.

Dresher, B. Elan (1985). Constraints on empty positions in tiered phonology. *Cahiers Linguistiques d'Ottawa* 14: 1–52.

Dressler, Wolfgang U. (1985). *Morphonology: the dynamics of derivation.* Ann Arbor, Mich.: Karoma.

Dressler, Wolfgang U., Luschützky, Hans C., Pfeiffer, Oskar E. and Rennison, John R. (eds) (1987). *Phonologica 1984.* Cambridge University Press.

Durand, Jacques (ed.) (1986). *Dependency and Non-Linear Phonology.* London: Croom Helm.

Edmundson, T. and Bendor-Samuel, J. T. (1966). Tone pattern of Etung. *Journal of African Languages* 5: 1–6.

Elbert, Samuel H. and Pukui, Mary Kawena (1979). *Hawaiian Grammar.* Honolulu: University Press of Hawaii.

Fabb, Nigel (1985). The Relation Between Phonology and Morphology: a new approach. Unpublished paper, University of Strathclyde.

Frajzyngier, Zygmunt (1980). The vowel system of Pero. *Studies in African Linguistics* 11: 39–74.

Freeland, L. (1951). *Language of the Sierra Miwok.* Indiana University Publications in Anthropology and Linguistics.

Fudge, E. C. (1967). The nature of phonological primes. *JL* 3: 1–26.

Fudge, E. C. (1969). Syllables. *JL* 5: 253–86.

Fudge, E. C. (1987). Branching structure within the syllable. *JL* 23: 359–377.

Fujimura, O. (1976). Syllables as Concatenated Demisyllables and Affixes. Presented to the 91st meeting of the Acoustical Society of America, April 1976, Washington DC.

Fujimura, Osamu (1979). English syllables as core and affixes. *Zeitschrift für Phonetik, Sprachwissenschaft und Kommunikationsforschung* 32: 471–76.

Fujimura, Osamu (in press). Demisyllables as Sets of Features: Comments on Clements's paper. In J. Kingston and M. E. Beckman (eds), *Papers in Laboratory Phonology I: Between the Grammar and the Physics of Speech.* Cambridge University Press.

Fujimura, Osamu and Lovins, Julie (1978). Syllables as Concatenative Phonetic Units. In Bell and Hooper (1978).

Goldsmith, John (1976a). An overview of autosegmental phonology. *Linguistic Analysis* 2: 23–68.

Goldsmith, John (1976b). Tone Melodies and the Autosegment. In R. K. Herbert (ed.), *Proceedings of the Sixth Conference on African Linguistics*, Ohio State University Working Papers in Linguistics, no. 20: 135–47.

Goldsmith, John (1979). *Autosegmental Phonology.* PhD dissertation, MIT, 1976. Distributed by IULC. New York: Garland Press.

Goldsmith, John. (1981a). Subsegmentals in Spanish Phonology. In *Linguistic Symposium on Romance Languages*, vol. 9, ed. by William W. Cressey and Donna Jo Napoli. Washington: Georgetown University Press.

Goldsmith, John (1981b). English as a Tone Language. In D. Goyvaerts (ed.), *Phonology in the 1980's.* Ghent: Story-Scientia. Circulated in 1974.

Goldsmith, John (1984a). Tone and Accent in Tonga. In Clements and Goldsmith (1984).

Goldsmith, John (1984b). Meeussen's Rule. In Aronoff and Oehrle (1984).

Goldsmith, John (1985a). On tone in Sukuma. In Goyvaerts (1985).

Goldsmith, John (1985b). Vowel harmony in Khalkha Mongolian, Yaka, Finnish and Hungarian. *Phonology Yearbook* 2: 251–74.

Goldsmith, John (1986). Tone in KiHunde. *Wiener Linguistische Gazette*, vol. 5. Institut für Sprachwissenschaft, University of Vienna.

Goldsmith, John (1987a). Vowel Systems. In Bosch et al. (1987).

Goldsmith, John (1987b). The Rise of Rhythmic Structure in Bantu. In Dressler et al. (1987).

Goldsmith, John (1987c). Tone and Accent and Getting the Two Together. *Proceedings of the Thirteenth Annual Meeting of the Berkeley Linguistics Society*, ed. Jon Aske, Natasha Beery, Laura Michaelis, and Hana Filip. Berkeley: BLS.

Goldsmith, John (1990). Tone and Accent in Llogoori. In *The Joy of Syntax: papers in honor of James McCawley*, ed. Diane Brentari, Gary Larson, and Lynn MacLeod. University of Chicago Press.

Goldsmith, John and Sabimana, Firmard (1985). The KiRundi Verb. Unpublished paper, University of Chicago.

Goyvaerts, Didier (ed.) (1985). *African Linguistics.* Amsterdam: John Benjamins.

Greenberg, Joseph (1960). The patterning of root morphemes in Semitic. *Word* 6: 162–81.

Guerssel, Mohammed (1977). Constraints on phonological rules. *LA* 3: 267–305.
Guerssel, Mohammed (1978). A condition on assimilation rules. *LA* 4: 225–54.
Guerssel, Mohammed (1986). Glides in Berber and syllabicity. *LI* 17: 1–12.
Haas, Mary R. (1977). Tonal accent in Creek. In *Studies in Stress and Accent*, ed. Larry M. Hyman. Southern California Occasional Papers in Linguistics, no. 4.
Haiman, J. (1980). *Hua: a Papuan language of the Eastern Highlands of New Guinea*. Studies in Language Companion Series, no. 5. Amsterdam: John Benjamins.
Hale, Kenneth (1973). Deep-surface canonical disparities in relation to analysis and change: an Australian example. *Current Trends in Linguistics* 11: 401–58.
Halle, Morris (1962). Phonology in generative grammar. *Word* 18: 54–72.
Halle, Morris (1964). On the Bases of Phonology. In *The Structure of Language: Readings in the Philosophy of Language*, ed. Jerry A. Fodor and Jerrold J. Katz. Englewood Cliffs; NJ: Prentice-Hall.
Halle, Morris (1977). Tenseness, vowel shift, and the phonology of the back vowels in modern English. *LI* 8: 611–25.
Halle, Morris (1978). Metrical Structure in Phonology. Unpublished paper, MIT.
Halle, Morris (1987). Grids and Tress in Metrical Phonology. In Dressler et al. (1987).
Halle, Morris (1988). Features. In *Encyclopedia of Linguistics*. Oxford University Press.
Halle, Morris and Vergnaud, Jean-Roger (1978). Metrical Structure in Phonology. Unpublished paper, MIT.
Halle, Morris and Vergnaud, J.-R. (1980). Three-dimensional phonology. *Journal of Linguistic Research* 1: 83–105.
Halle, Morris and Vergnaud, Jean-Roger (1982). On the Framework of Autosegmental Phonology. In van der Hulst and Smith (1982, Part I).
Halle, Morris and Vergnaud, Jean-Roger (1987). Stress and the cycle. *LI* 18: 45–84.
Halle, Morris and Vergnaud, Jean-Roger (1988). *An Essay on Stress*. Cambridge, Mass.: MIT Press.
Hammond, Michael (1987). Accent, Constituency, and Lollipops. In Bosch et al. (1987).
Hammond, Michael (1988). *Constraining Metrical Theory: a modular theory of rhythm and destressing*. PhD dissertation, UCLA, 1984. New York: Garland Press.
Hamp, Eric (1955). Componential restatement of syllable structure in Trique. *IJAL* 20: 206–9.
Haraguchi, Shosuke (1977). *The Tone Pattern of Japanese: an autosegmental theory of tonology*. Tokyo: Kaitakusha.
Harris, James (1969). *Spanish Phonology*. Cambridge, Mass.: MIT Press.
Harris, James W. (1980). Nonconcatenative morphology and Spanish plurals. *Journal of Linguistic Research* 1: 15–31.
Harris, James W. (1982). *Spanish Syllable Structure and Stress: a nonlinear analysis*. Linguistic Inquiry Monograph, no. 8. Cambridge, Mass.: MIT Press.
Harris, James W. (1984). Autosegmental Phonology, Lexical Phonology and Spanish Nasals. In Aronoff and Oehrle (1984).
Harris, Zellig (1944). Simultaneous components in phonology. *Lg.* 20: 181–205.

Harris, Zellig (1951). *Methods in Structural Linguistics*. University of Chicago Press.

Haugen, Einar (1956a). The Syllable in Linguistic Description. In *For Roman Jakobson*, ed. M. Halle, H.G. Lunt, H. MacLean, and C.H. Van Schooneveld. The Hague: Mouton.

Haugen, Einar (1956b). Syllabification in Kutenai. *IJAL* 22: 196–201.

Hayes, Bruce (1980). *A Metrical Theory of Stress Rules*. PhD dissertation, MIT; circulated by the Indiana University Linguistics Club, 1981.

Hayes, Bruce (1982). Extrametricality and English stress. *LI* 13: 227–76.

Hayes, Bruce (1983). A grid-based theory of English meter. *LI* 14: 357–94.

Hayes, Bruce (1984). The phonology of rhythm in English. *LI* 15: 33–74.

Hayes, Bruce (1986a). Inalterability in CV phonology. *Language* 62: 321–51.

Hayes, Bruce (1986b). Assimilation as spreading in Toba Batak. *LI* 17: 467–99.

Hayes, Bruce (1987). Compensatory Lengthening in Moraic Phonology. Unpublished paper, UCLA.

Hayes, Bruce (1988). Diphthonization and Coindexing. Unpublished paper, UCLA.

Hirst, Daniel (1985). Linearisation and the Single Segment Hypothesis. In *Grammatical Representation*, ed. J. Guéron, H. Obenauer, and J.-Y. Pollock. Dordrecht: Foris Publications.

Hockett, Charles (1947). Componential analysis of Sierra Popoluca. *IJAL* 13: 259–67.

Hockett, Charles (1955). *A Manual of Phonology*. *IJAL* 21(4), Part 1. Memoir 11.

Hockett, Charles (1961). Linguistic elements and their relations. *Language* 37: 29–53.

Hockett, Charles (1973). Yokuts as testing-ground for linguistic methods. *IJAL* 39: 63–79.

Hogg, Richard and McCully, C. B. (1987). *Metrical Phonology: a coursebook*. Cambridge University Press.

Hoijer, H. (1946). Tonkawa. In *Linguistic Structures of Native America*. New York: Viking Fund Publications in Anthropology.

Hollenbach, Barbara (1984). *The Phonology and Morphology of Tone and Laryngeals in Copala Trique*. PhD dissertation, University of Arizona.

Hooper, Joan B. (1972). The syllable in linguistic theory. *Language* 48: 525–40.

Hulst, Harry van der (1984). *Syllable Structure and Stress in Dutch*. Dordrecht: Foris Publications.

Hulst, Harry van der and Smith, Norval (1982). *The Structure of Phonological Representations*, Parts I and II. Dordrecht: Foris Publications.

Hulst, Harry van der and Smith, Norval (1985). Vowel features and umlaut in Djingili, Nyangumarda, and Warlpiri. *Phonology Yearbook* 2: 277–303.

Hyman, Larry M. (1973). The feature [grave] in phonological theory. *Journal of Phonetics* 1: 329–37.

Hyman, Larry M. (1975). *Phonology: theory and analysis*. New York: Holt, Rinehart and Winston.

Hyman, Larry M. (1985). *A Theory of Phonological Weight*. Dordrecht: Foris Publications.

Hymes, Del and Fought, John (1981). *American Structuralism*. The Hague: Mouton.

Ingemann, Frances and Sebeok, Thomas (1961). *An Eastern Cheremis Manual*. Bloomington: Indiana University.

Ingria, Robert (1980). Compensatory lengthening as a metrical phenomenon. *LI* 11: 465–95.

Itkonen, E. (1966). *Kieli ja sen tutkimus*. Helsinki: WSOY.

Ito, Junko (1988). *Syllable Theory in Prosodic Phonology*. PhD dissertation, University of Massachusetts, 1986. New York: Garland Press.

Jakobson, Roman, and Halle, Morris (1956). *Fundamentals of Language*. Vol. 1: Janua Linguarum. The Hague: Mouton.

Joos, Martin (1957). *Readings in Linguistics*. University of Chicago Press.

Kahn, Daniel (1980). *Syllable-based Generalizations in English Phonology*. PhD dissertation, MIT, 1976. New York: Garland Press.

Kaye, Jonathan D. and Lowenstamm, Jean (1984). De la syllabicité. In *Forme sonore du language: structure des représentations en phonologie*, ed. François Dell, Daniel Hirst, Jean-Roger Vergnaud. Paris: Hermann.

Kaye, Jonathan D., Lowenstamm, Jean and Vergnaud, Jean-Roger (1985). The internal structure of phonological elements: a theory of charm and government. *Phonology Yearbook* 2: 305–28.

Keating, Patricia A. (1988). Underspecification in phonetics. *Phonology* 5: 275–92.

Kenstowicz, Michael (1970). On the notation of vowel length in Lithuanian. *Papers in Linguistics* 3: 73–113.

Kenstowicz, Michael (1980). Notes on Cairene Arabic syncope. *Studies in the Linguistic Sciences* 10(2): 39–54.

Kenstowicz, Michael (1982). Gemination and spirantization in Tigrinya. *Studies in the Linguistic Sciences* 12(1): 103–22.

Kenstowicz, Michael and Kisseberth, Charles (1979). *Generative Phonology*. New York: Academic Press.

Kenstowicz, Michael and Pyle, Charles (1973). On the phonological integrity of geminate clusters. In Michael Kenstowicz and Charles Kisseberth (eds), *Issues in Phonological Theory*. The Hague: Mouton.

Kenyon, J. S. and Knott, T. A. (1944). *A Pronouncing Dictionary of American English*. Springfield, Mass.: Merriam.

Key, Harold and Key, Mary (1953). The phonemes of Sierra Nahuatl. *IJAL* 19: 53–56.

Kiparsky, Paul (1968). How Abstract is Phonology? Reprinted as Abstractness, Opacity, and Global Rules, 1973. In *Three Dimensions of Linguistic Theory*, ed. O. Fujimura. Tokyo: TEC.

Kiparksy, Paul (1973). Elsewhere in Phonology. In *A Festschrift for Morris Halle*. Stephen Anderson and Paul Kiparsky. New York: Holt Rinehart and Winston.

Kiparsky, Paul (1979). Metrical structure assignment is cyclic. *LI* 10: 421–41.

Kiparsky, Paul (1982a). Lexical Morphology and Phonology. In I.-S. Yang (ed.), *Linguistics in the Morning Calm*. Seoul: Hanshin.

Kiparsky, Paul (1982b). From Cyclic Phonology to Lexical Phonology. In van der Hulst and Smith (1982, Part I).

Kiparsky, Paul (1985). Some Consequences of Lexical Phonology. *Phonology Yearbook*, vol. 2.

Kisseberth, Charles (1970). Vowel Elision in Tonkawa and Derivational Constraints. In J. M. Sadock and A. L. Vanek (eds), *Studies Presented to Robert B. Lees by his Students*. Champain: Linguistic Research Inc.

Kisseberth, Charles (1984). Digo Tonology. In Clements and Goldsmith (1984).

Knudson, Lyle M. (1975). A Natural Phonology and Morphophonemics of Chimalapa Zoque. *Papers in Linguistics* 8: 283–346.

Koutsoudas, Andreas, Sanders, Gerald, and Noll, Craig (1974). The application of phonological rules. *Language* 50: 1–28.

Krause, S. (1980). *Topics in Chukchee Phonology and Morphology*. PhD dissertation, University of Illinois.

Krauss, Michael (ed) (1985). *Yupik Eskimo Prosodic Systems: Descriptive and Comparative Studies*. Alasaka Native Language Center Research Papers, no. 7.

Krupa, Viktor (1966). *Morpheme and Word in Maori*. The Hague: Mouton.

Lamb, Sydney (1966). Prolegomena to a theory of phonology. *Language* 42: 536–73.

Lapointe, Steven G. and Feinstein, Mark H. (1982). The Role of Vowel Deletion and Epenthesis in the Assignment of Syllable Structure. In van der Hulst and Smith (1982, Part II).

Leben, William (1971). Suprasegmental and segmental representation of tone. *Studies in African Linguistics*, Supplement 2: 183–200.

Leben, William (1973). *Suprasegmental Phonology*. PhD dissertation, MIT.

Leben, William (1977). Estonian Quantity. Unpublished paper, MIT.

Leben, William (1980). A metrical analysis of length. *LI* 11: 497–509.

Lerdahl, Fred and Jackendoff, Ray (1983). *A Generative Theory of Tonal Music*. Cambridge: MIT Press.

Levin, Juliette (1985). *A Metrical Theory of Syllabicity*. PhD dissertation, MIT.

Liberman, Mark (1979). *The Intonational system of English*. PhD dissertation, MIT, 1975. New York: Garland Press.

Liberman, Mark and Prince, Alan (1977). On stress and linguistic rhythm. *LI* 8: 249–336.

Liddell, Scott and Johnson, Robert (1985). The Phonological Base. Unpublished paper, Gallaudet University.

Longacre, Robert (1952). Five phonemic pitch levels in Trique. *Acta Linguistica* 7: 62–82.

Longacre, Robert (1955). Rejoinder to Hamp's 'Componential Restatement of Syllable Structure in Trique'. *IJAL* 21: 189–94.

Lowenstamm, Jean (1979). *Topics in Prosodic Phonology*. PhD dissertation, University of Massachusetts.

Lowenstamm, Jean (1981). On the maximal cluster approach to syllable structure. *LI* 12: 575–604.

Lozano, M. Carmen (1978). *Stop and Spirant Alternations in Spanish Phonology*. PhD dissertation, Indiana University. Distributed by the Indiana University Linguistics Club.

Lynch, John (1978). *A Grammar of Lenakel*, Pacific Linguistics Series B, no. 55. Canberra: Australian National University.

Lynch, John (1983). On the Kuman 'liquids'. *Language and Linguistics in Melanesia* 14: 98–112.

Marlett, Stephen and Stemberger, Joseph (1983). Empty consonants in Seri. *LI* 14: 617–39.

Mascaró, Joan (1976). *Catalan Phonology and the Phonological Cycle*. PhD dissertation, MIT.

McArthur, H. and McArthur, L. (1956). Aguacatec (Mayan) phonemes in the stress group. *IJAL* 22: 72–6.

McCarthy, John (1976). kt. *Proceedings of the Seventh Annual Meeting of the North Eastern Linguistic Society*, ed. Judy Anne Kegl, David Nash, and Annie Zaenen. Cambridge, Mass.: Harvard University.

McCarthy, John (1979a). *Formal Problems in Semitic Phonology and Morphology*. PhD dissertation, MIT. Distributed by IULC.

McCarthy, John (1979b). On stress and syllabification. *LI* 10: 443–66.

McCarthy, John (1980). A note on the accentuation of Damascene Arabic. *Studies in the Linguistic Sciences* 10: 77–98.

McCarthy, John (1981). A prosodic theory of nonconcatenative morphology. *LI* 12: 373–418.

McCarthy, John (1982). Prosodic templates, morphemic templates, and morphemic tiers. In van der Hulst and Smith (1982, Part I).

McCarthy, John (1986). OCP effects: gemination and antigemination. *LI* 17: 207–63.

McCarthy, John (to appear). Feature geometry and dependency: a review. Articulatory organization – from phonology to speech signals. *Phonetica*, special issue.

McCawley, James (1986). Today the world, tomorrow phonology. *Phonology Yearbook* 3: 27–45.

Michelson, Karin (1985). Ghost R's in Onondaga: an autosegmental analysis of *R-stems. In Wetzels and Sezer (1985).

Minor, Eugene E. (1956). Witoto vowel clusters. *IJAL* 22: 131–37.

Mithun, Marianne and Basri, Hasan (1986). The phonology of Selayarese. *Oceanic Linguistics* 25: 210–54.

Mohanan, K. P. (1982). *The Theory of Lexical Phonology*. PhD dissertation, MIT.

Mohanan, K. P. (1983). The Structure of the Melody. Unpublished paper, MIT.

Mohanan, K. P. (1986). *The Theory of Lexical Phonology*. Dordrecht: D. Reidel.

Mohanan, K. P. and Mohanan, T. (1984). Lexical phonology of the consonant system in Malayalam. *LI* 15: 575–602.

Mtenje, Alfred Dailex (1986). *Issues in the Nonlinear Phonology of Chichewa*. PhD dissertation, University College London.

Mtenje, Al (1987). Tone shift principles in the Chichewa verb: a case for a tone language. *Lingua* 72: 169–209.

Mutaka, Ngessimo and Hyman, Larry M. (1987). Syllables and Morpheme Integrity in Kinande Reduplication. Unpublished paper, University of Southern California.

Myers, Scott (1987). Vowel shortening in English. *NLLT* 5: 485–518.

368   Bibliography

Nespor, Marina, and Vogel, Irene (1986). *Prosodic Phonology*. Dordrecht: Foris
    Publications.
Newman, Paul (1972). Syllable weight as a phonological variable. *Studies in
    African Linguistics* 3: 301–23.
Newman, Paul (1986a). Contour Tones as Phonemic Primes in Grebo. In *The
    Phonological Representation of Suprasegmentals*, ed. Koen Bogers, Harry van
    der Hulst, and Maarten Mous. Dordrecht: Foris Publications.
Newman, Paul (1986b). Tone and affixation in Hausa. *Studies in African
    Linguistics* 17: 249–67.
Newman, Paul and Salim, Bello Ahmad (1981). Hausa diphthongs. *Lingua* 55:
    101–21.
Nida, Eugene A. (1949). *Morphology: the descriptive analysis of words*. Ann
    Arbor: The University of Michigan Press.
Odden, David (1979). Principles of stress assignment: a crosslinguistic view.
    Studies in the Linguistic Sciences 9 (1): 157–76.
Odden, David (1986). On the obligatory contour principle. *Language* 62: 353–
    83.
Odden, David (1988). Anti-antigemination and the OCP. *LI* 19: 451–75.
Paradis, Carole (1988). On constraints and repair strategies. *Linguistic
    Review* 6(1): 71–97.
Payne, David L. (1981). *The Phonology and Morphology of Axininca Campa*.
    Dallas: Summer Institute of Linguistics.
Pesetsky, David (1979). Russian Morphology and Lexical Theory. Unpublished
    paper, MIT.
Pesetzky, David (1985). Morphology and logical form. *LI* 16: 193–246.
Peterson, Karen (1987). Accent in the Chichewa Verb. In Bosch et al. (1987).
Phelps, Elaine (1975). Iteration and disjunctive domains in phonology. *LA* 1:
    137–72.
Piggott, Glynn and Singh, Rajendra (1985). The phonology of epenthetic
    segments. *Canadian Journal of Linguistics* 30: 415–51.
Pike, Evelyn (1956). Tonally differentiated allomorphs of Soyaltepec Mazatec.
    IJAL 22, 57–71.
Pike, Kenneth (1948). *Tone Languages: a technique for determining the number
    and type of pitch contrasts in a language, with studies in tonemic substitution
    and fusion*. University of Michigan Publications in Linguistics, no. 4. Ann
    Arbor: University of Michigan Press.
Pike, Kenneth (1952). Operational phonemics in reference to linguistic relativity.
    Journal of the Acoustical Society of America 24: 618–25; reprinted in Pike
    (1972).
Pike, Kenneth (1972). *Kenneth L. Pike: Selected Writings*, ed. Ruth M. Brend.
    The Hague: Mouton.
Pike, Kenneth and Pike, Eunice Victoria (1947). Immediate constituents of
    Mazateco syllables. *IJAL* 13: 78–91.
Plank, Frans (1984). Romance disagreements: phonology interfering with syntax.
    JL 20: 329–49.
Poppe, N. (1951). *Khalkha-Mongolische Grammatik*. Wiesbaden: Otto Harras-
    sowitz.

Poser, William (1982). Phonological Representations and Action-at-a-Distance. In van der Hulst and Smith (1982, Part II).

Postal, Paul (1968). *Aspects of Phonological Theory*. New York: Harper and Row.

Prince, Alan S. (1980). A metrical theory for Estonian quantity. *LI* 11: 511–62.

Prince, Alan S. (1983). Relating to the Grid. *LI* 14: 19–100.

Prince, Alan S. (1984). Phonology with Tiers. In Aronoff and Oehrle (1984).

Pukui, Mary K. and Elbert, Samuel (1971). *Hawaiian Dictionary: Hawaiian–English, English–Hawaiian*. Honolulu: University of Hawaii Press.

Pulleyblank, Douglas (1986a). *Tone in Lexical Phonology*. Dordrecht: D. Reidel.

Pulleyblank, Douglas (1986b). Underspecification and low vowel harmony in Okpe. *Studies in African Linguistics* 17: 119–53.

Pulleyblank, Douglas (1988). Tone and the Morphemic Tier Hypothesis. In *Theoretical Morphology*, ed. Michael Hammond and Michael Noonan. New York: Academic Press.

Rand, Earl (1968). The structural phonology of Alabaman, a Muskogean language. *IJAL* 34: 94–103.

Rennison, John (1985). Tridirectional Vowel Features and Vowel Harmony. Unpublished paper, University of Vienna.

Rice, Keren (1987). Metrical Structure in a Tone Language: The Root in Slave (Athapaskan). In Bosch et al. (1987).

Richardson, Irvine (1959). *The Role of Tone in the Structure of Sukuma*. University of London School of African and Oriental Studies.

Ringen, Catherine O. (1988a). *Vowel Harmony: Theoretical Implications*. PhD dissertation, Indiana University, 1975. New York: Garland Press.

Ringen, Catherine O. (1988b). Transparency in Hungarian vowel harmony. *Phonology* 5: 327–42.

Rischel, Jørgen (1974). *Topics in West Greenlandic Phonology*. Copenhagen: Akademisk Forlag.

Rood, David (1975). The implications of Wichita phonology. *Language* 51: 315–37.

Ross, John Robert (1972). A Reanalysis of English Word Stress (Part I). In Brame (1972b).

Sabimana, Firmard (1986). *The Relational Structure of the Kirundi verb*. PhD dissertation, Indiana University.

Sagey, Elizabeth (1986). *The Representation of Features and Relations in Nonlinear Phonology*. PhD dissertation, MIT.

Sagey, Elizabeth (1988). On the ill-formedness of crossing association lines. *LI* 19: 109–118.

Saib, J. (1976). *A Phonological Study of the Tamazight Berber Dialect of Ayt Ndhir*. PhD dissertation, UCLA.

Sauzet, Patrick (1985). Remarques sur la représentation des géminées. Paper presented at the Colloquium on 'Phonologie Plurilinéaire' at the University of Lyon.

Schane, Sanford (1975). Noncyclic English Word Stress. In D. Goyvaerts and G. Pullum (eds), *Essays on the Sound Pattern of English*. Ghent: Story-Scientia.

Schane, Sanford (1979a). The rhythmic nature of English word accentuation. *Lg* 55: 559–602.

Schane, Sanford (1979b). Rhythm, accent, and stress in English words. *LI* 10: 483–502.

Schane, Sanford (1984). The fundamentals of particle phonology. *Phonology Yearbook* 1: 129–55.

Schein, Barry (1981). Spirantization in Tigrinya. In *Theoretical Issues in the Grammar of Semitic Languages*, ed, Hagit Borer and Youssef Aoun. MIT Working Papers in Linguistics Vol. 3.

Schein, Barry and Steriade, Donca (1986). On geminates. *LI* 17: 691–744.

Schuh, Russell (1972). Rule inversion in Chadic. *Studies in African Linguistics* 3: 379–97.

Selkirk, Elisabeth (1980). The role of prosodic categories in English word stress. *LI* 11: 563–605.

Selkirk, Elisabeth (1981). Epenthesis and Degenerate Syllables in Cairene Arabic. In *Theoretical Issues in the Grammar of Semitic Languages*, ed. Hagit Borer and Youssef Aoun. MIT Working Papers in Linguistics, vol. 3.

Selkirk, Elisabeth O. (1982a). The syllable. In van der Hulst and Smith (1982, Part II).

Selkirk, Elizabeth O. (1982b). *The Syntax of Words*. Linguistic Inquiry Monograph Series, no. 7. Cambridge, Mass.: MIT Press.

Selkirk, Elizabeth O. (1984). *Phonology and Syntax: the relation between sound and structure*. Cambridge, Mass.: MIT Press.

Selkirk, Elizabeth O. (1986). On derived domains in sentence phonology. *Phonology Yearbook* 3: 371–405.

Sezer, Engin (1985). An Autosegmental Analysis of Compensatory Lengthening in Turkish. In Wetzels and Sezer (1985).

Shaw, Patricia A. (1980). *Theoretical Issues in Dakota Phonology and Morphology*. PhD dissertation, University of Toronto, 1976. New York: Garland Press.

Shih, Chi-lin (1985). From Tonal to Accentual: Fuzhou Tone Sandhi Revisited. *Proceedings of the Eleventh Annual Meeting of the Berkeley Linguistics Society*, ed. M. Niepokuj, Mary VanClay, Vassiliki Nikiforidou, and Deborah Feder. Berkeley Linguistics Society.

Siegel, Dorothy (1974). *Topics in English Morphology*. PhD dissertation, MIT.

Siegel, Dorothy (1977). The Adjacency Condition and the Theory of Morphology. Unpublished paper.

Singh, Rajendra (1987). Well-formedness Conditions and Phonological Theory. In Dressler et al. (1987).

Singler, John (1980). The status of lexical associations and the obligatory contour principle in the analysis of tone languages. *BLS* 6: 442–56.

Smith, Norval (1985). Spreading, Reduplication, and the Default Option in Miwok Nonconcatenative Morphology. In *Advances in Non-Linear Phonology*, ed. H. van der Hulst and N. Smith. Dordrecht: Foris Publications.

Smolensky, Paul (1986). Information Processing in Dynamical Systems: foundations of harmony theory. In *Parallel Distributed Processing: Explorations in the Microstructure of Cognition*, Part 1, ed. David Rumelhart, James McClelland, and the PDP Research Group. Cambridge, Mass.: MIT Press.

Sommerstein, Alan H. (1974). On phonotactically motivated rules. *JL* 10: 71–94.
Sommerstein, Alan H. (1977). *Modern Phonology*. London: Edward Arnold.
Stanley, Richard (1967). Redundancy rules in phonology. *Language* 43: 393–436.
Steinberg, Elisa (1987). Topics in Yucatec Mayan Phonology and Morphology. Unpublished paper, University of Chicago.
Stemberger, Joseph Paul (1985). CV phonology and French consonants: a concrete approach. *JL* 21: 453–7.
Steriade, Donca (1982). *Greek Prosodies and the Nature of Syllabification*. PhD dissertation, MIT.
Steriade, Donca (1986). Yokuts and the vowel plane. *LI* 17: 129–46.
Steriade, Donca (1987). Redundant Values. In Bosch et al. (1987).
Steriade, Donca (forthcoming). On Class Nodes. In *Segment Structure*, ed. Bruce Hayes. Orlando: Academic Press.
Straight, H. S. (1976). *Yucatec Maya Pedolectology: a segmental approach*. PhD dissertation, University of Chicago.
Strauss, Steven L. (1979). *Some Principles of Word Structure in English and German*. PhD dissertation, City University of New York.
Strauss, Steven L. (1982a). *Lexicalist Phonology of English and German*. Dordrecht: Foris Publications.
Strauss, Steven L. (1982b). On 'relatedness' and related paradoxes. *LI* 13: 695–700.
Strauss, Steven L. (1983). Stress assignment as morphological adjustment in English. *LA* 11(4): 419–27.
Streeter, J. C. (1963). *Khalkha Structure*. Bloomington: Indiana University Press.
Stuart, Don Graham (1957). The phonology of the word in modern standard Mongolian. *Word* 13: 65–99.
Tauli, V. (1954). The origin of the quantitative system in Estonian. *Journal de la société finno-ougrienne* 57: 1–19.
Taylor, S. (1969). *Koya: an outline grammar, gommu dialect*. University of California Publications in Linguistics, no. 54.
ter Mors, Christine (1988). Sierra Miwok Phonology Riddles. In *University of Chicago Working Papers in Linguistics*, no. 4, ed. Ann Farley et al. University of Chicago Press.
Thráinsson, H. (1978). On the phonology of Icelandic preaspiration. *Nordic Journal of Linguistics* 1: 3–54.
Trager, G. L. and Smith, H. A. Jr (1951). *An Outline of English Structure*. Studies in Linguistics, Occasional Papers, no. 3. Norman, Oklahoma: University of Oklahoma Press; reprinted by ACLS, Washington DC, 1956.
Trubetzkoy, N. S. (1967). *Principes de phonologie*, first published 1939. Paris: Klincksieck.
Tucker, A. N. (1962). The syllable in Luganda: a prosodic approach. *Journal of African Languages* 1: 122–66.
Vennemann, Theo (1972). On the theory of syllabic phonology. *Linguistische Berichte* 18: 1–18.
Vennemann, Theo (1986). *Neuere Entwicklungen in der Phonologie*. Berlin: Mouton de Gruyter.

Vennemann, Theo and Ladefoged, Peter (1973). Phonetic features and phonological features. *Lingua* 32: 61–74.

Walli-Sagey, Elisabeth (1985). On the Representation of Complex Segments and their Formation in Kinyarwanda. In Wetzels and Sezer (1985).

Wang, William (1968). Vowel features, paired variables, and the English vowel shift. *Language* 44: 695–708.

Welden, Ann (1980). Stress in Cairo Arabic. *Studies in the Linguistic Sciences* 10: 99–120.

Wells, Rulon (1947). Review of *The Intonation of American English. Language* 23: 255–73.

Wetzels, Leo and Sezer, Engin (eds) (1985). *Studies in Compensatory Lengthening*. Dordrecht: Foris Publications.

Wilbur, Ronnie B. (1987). *American Sign Language: Linguistic and Applied Dimensions*, 2nd ed. Boston: Little, Brown.

Willett, Elizabeth (1982). Reduplication and accent in southeastern Tepehuan. *IJAL* 48: 168–84.

Williams, Edwin (1976). Underlying tone in Margi and Igbo. *LI* 7: 463–84.

Williams, Edwin (1981). On the notions 'lexically related' and 'head of a word'. *LI* 12: 245–74.

Wiltshire, Caroline (1988). Syllable Structure in I̠ruLa: the role of one licensing condition in I̠ruLa phonology. Unpublished paper, University of Chicago.

Wonderly, W. (1951). Zoque I, II, II, IV. *IJAL* 17: 1–9, 105–23, 137–62, 235–51.

Wright, Martha (1983). A Metrical Approach to Tone Sandhi in Chinese Dialects. PhD dissertation, University of Massachusetts.

Wright, W. (1971). *A Grammar of the Arabic Language*. Cambridge University Press.

Yip, Moira (1980). *The Tonal Phonology of Chinese*. PhD dissertation, MIT.

Yip, Moira (1988). The obligatory contour principle and phonological rules: a loss of identity. *LI* 19: 65–100.

Younes, R. (1983). The Representation of Geminate Consonants. Unpublished paper, University of Texas.

Zimmer, Karl (1969). Psychological correlates of some Turkish morpheme structure conditions. *Language* 45: 309–21.

Index